JERUSALEM TIME LINE

Jerusalem is one of the most important cities on earth. Scripture calls it "the city of our God" (Ps. 48). Jerusalem has been—and still is—a focal point for Jews, Muslims, and Christians. The name Jerusalem means "city of peace," yet throughout history it has been one of the most fought-over cities of all time. It has been razed and rebuilt, abandoned and filled; wars have been fought over it, and yet pilgrims, even today, travel long, arduous journeys just to set foot in the holy city.

Jerusalem before King David:

- The earliest mention of Jerusalem is in Egyptian texts dating from the 20th or 19th century BC.

- According to archaeological finds, Jerusalem became a fortified city with a complex water system in the 18th century BC.

- The first mention of Jerusalem in the Bible is in Genesis 14:18 when Abraham encounters Melchizedek, the "king of Salem." (Salem is believed to be a shortened name for Jerusalem.)

- Also in Genesis, Abraham is tested by God and offers his son Isaac on Mt. Moriah (Gen. 22:2), a location later identified as the site where King Solomon built the temple in Jerusalem (2 Chron. 3:1).

- Abraham's descendents, the sons of Jacob (Israel), moved to Egypt because of a famine in Canaan. They remained there and increased in number until 400 years later when Moses led them out of Egypt (the Exodus).

- Moses' successor Joshua led the Israelites back to Canaan to possess the land God had promised to them. Although Joshua conquered the land, he was unable to drive out the Jebusites who controlled the city of Jerusalem (2 Sam. 5:6–10). It would be nearly four centuries later before a man named David would capture this formidable city and make it the capital of Israel.

Religion of Ruling Power:

| JEWISH |
| CHRISTIAN |
| MUSLIM |
| OTHER |

c. = approximately

10 years between vertical lines

Black indicates the present walls of Old City Jerusalem

Colored portion indicates the size of Jerusalem at that time

1000 BC

Reign of King David: brings ark of the cove Jebusite on Mt. Moria

JERUSALEM AT THE TIME OF JEBUSITES AND KING DAVID c. 1850 –971 BC

Population: 2,000

King David brings ark c

| BABYLON PERSIAN | HELLENISTIC PERIOD | HASMONEAN DYNASTY |

300 BC   200   100 BC

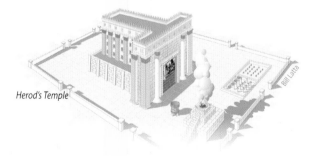

Herod's Temple

Bill Latta

Alexander the Great conquers Jerusalem and spreads Greek culture (Hellenization). 332

Death of Alexander. His kingdom is divided between his generals. 323

Ptolemy I of Egypt, one of Alexander's generals, controls Jerusalem; takes many Jews to Egypt. 320

Ptolemies lose Jerusalem to Seleucid Empire of Syria (founded by Seleucus, another of Alexander's generals). 198

Seleucid ruler Antiochus IV Epiphanes bans Sabbath-keeping, Jewish feasts, and possession of Scripture. He pillages and defiles temple by sacrificing a pig on the altar. 167

Maccabean Revolt: Judas Maccabeus, from a Jewish priestly family, leads a successful revolt against Seleucids. Establishes Hasmonean Dynasty. 167

First Hanukkah: Judas Maccabeus cleanses and rededicates the temple. 164

HASMONEAN c. 167–37 BC

Population: 30,000–35,000

Civil war between Jewish princes Aristobulus II and Hycranus II. 67

Roman emperor Pompey exploits the civil war, conquers Jerusalem and enters the temple. Pompey is later defeated by Julius Caesar. 63

Herod, governor of Galilee, conquers Judea (inclu Jerusalem) and becomes a vassal king for the Romans

King Herod begins reconstruction o to gain favor with Jews: doubles the si complex, fortifies city walls, builds Tower

Jesus born in Bethl an infant at th

Death of King Herod. His son Arche 3,000 Jewish nationalists at Passov

Jesus (age 12) makes pilgrimage to Jeru

Roman

Jesus arrested, trial in Jerusa outside Jerusalem's walls. He ris seen by many before

1200   1300   1400

ssacre thousands of
om of Jerusalem."
an church. 1099

◎ **Mamluk Muslims** gain control of Jerusalem and rule the city for over 250 years. 1250

◎ **The Ramban** (Nachmanides) moves to Jerusalem, prays at Western Wall, establishes Ramban Synagogue. 1267

es the headquarters of
lar. 1118

◎ **Black Death** (Plague) spreads to Jerusalem from Europe. 1348

rch built. 1138

◎ **Sultan Saladin from Egypt** recaptures Jerusalem for Muslims. St. Anne's church becomes a Muslim school. Christians banned from entering Church of the Holy Sepulchre. 1187

◎ **Third Crusade fails.** Truce permits Jerusalem to remain under Saladin's control provided Christian pilgrimages are allowed. Christians are permitted to enter the Church of the Holy Sepulchre. 1192

Saladin captures Jerusalem

◎ **Fourth Crusade launched** to retake Jerusalem. Crusaders from the West do not even make it to Jerusalem, instead sack Eastern Christian capital of Constantinople. 1202

◎ **Jerusalem razed** by Muslim rulers to prevent Crusaders from retaking the city. Jerusalem's inhabitants abandon the city. 1219

◎ **Agreement** between Muslim rulers and Frederick II of Germany transfers control of Jerusalem to Christians. 1229

Mamluk soldier

◎ **Invasions** by Muslim dynasties leave Jerusalem virtually deserted. 1244

1099

1950   2000

ted by ◎
. 1951

Excavation of Warren's Gate in Western Wall tunnel ◎ leads to Arab demonstrations causing authorities to close the dig and seal the entrance. 1981

◎ **U.N. declares** Israeli sovereignty over Jerusalem illegal. 1998

ock overlaid with ◎
becoming gold in
ance. 1956–1964

Israel annuls Waqf ownership of Western ◎ Wall declaring it state property. 1984

◎ **Israel forbids Waqf construction** in Solomon's Stables on Temple Mount. Waqf begins construction anyway and dumps tons of archaeologically rich debris in Kidron Valley. 1999

Kathleen Kenyon discovers ◎
ting to 1800 BC. 1961–1967

Jerusalem Underground, a Jewish ◎ terrorist group, is arrested and charged with numerous attacks on Arabs, including a plot to blow up Dome of the Rock. 1984

JERUSALEM TODAY

◎ **Second Intifada** (Al-Aqsa Intifada) declared by Yasser Arafat after Ariel Sharon's visit to Temple Mount. Riots and terrorist attacks occur throughout Palestine. Temple Mount is closed to all non-Muslims for the next 3 years. 2000

es first pope to visit Jerusalem. 1964 ◎

OLD CITY

Palestine Liberation Organization ◎
(PLO) founded in Jerusalem. 1964

First Intifada (uprising) by ◎ Palestinians against Israelis results in about 160 Israeli and 2,160 Palestinian deaths. 1987-1993

Population: 774,000

◎ **Barrier wall built** by Israel between Jerusalem and West Bank. 2002

Six-Day War: Israel captures ◎
Old City, reunifying all of
Jerusalem. Israel returns religious
administration of Temple Mount
to an Islamic Trust (Waqf). 1967

◎ **Temple Mount Sifting Project** established to salvage artifacts in debris that had been dumped in Kidron Valley in 1999. (Legal disputes over Israeli archaeologists' right to remove artifacts had delayed excavation of debris for several years.) 2004

◎
Arab riots after Temple Mount Faithful group announces plans to lay a cornerstone for the third Jewish temple; 17 rioters killed by Israeli police. 1990

Status Quo Agreement: Muslims retain ◎
religious sovereignty over Temple Mount, but
overall control maintained by Israel. 1976

◎ **Discovery of a building in City of David** believed to be part of the palace of either David or Solomon. 2005

b ◎
8

President Anwar Sadat of Egypt visits ◎
Jerusalem, the first head of state of an Arab nation
to do so since State of Israel established. 1977

◎
Israel-Jordan treaty resolves territory disputes between the two nations. 1994

v. ◎
8

◎ **Discovery** of a section **of wall in City of David** believed to be part of the first temple complex. 2010

Israel passes law declaring that all of **Jerusalem**— ◎
including Old City—**is its capital**.* 1980

◎
Palestinians riot in response to Israel opening an exit to Hasmonean tunnel near Western Wall. Riot results in about 70 Palestinians and 15 Israeli soldiers killed. 1996

1950 ◎

*Most countries still do not recognize Jerusalem as Israel's capital and instead have their embassies in Tel Aviv.

900   1000   1100

...magne signs treaty with Muslims permitting Christian ...lem, sparking an influx of Christian pilgrims. 797

Fatimid Muslims conquer Jerusalem. 969 ◎

Fatimids raze Church of the Holy Sepulchre, destroy synagogues. 1009 ◎

Fatimids change policy and enable Christian and ◎ Jewish structures to be rebuilt. 1020

Major earthquake destroys much of Jerusalem's architecture. 1033 ◎

Al-Aqsa Mosque rebuilt. 1034 ◎

Church of the Holy Sepulchre is restored. 1048 ◎

Great Schism divides Church between East and West. ◎ Jerusalem Christians join Eastern Orthodox Church. 1054

Seljuk Turks capture Jerusalem, massacre ◎ inhabitants, forbid Christian pilgrimages. 1073

Pope Urban II calls for Crusade to return ◎ Jerusalem to Christian control. 1095

Fatimids retake Jerusalem from Seljuks. 1098 ◎

◎ **Crusaders capture Jerusalem**, ... Jews and Muslims, establish "Kin... Dome of the Rock becomes a Chri...

◎ **Al-Aqsa Mosque** becom... Order of the Knights Ter...

◎ **St. Anne's C**...

Pope Urban II

Al-Aqsa Mosque on Temple Mount

...the Rock. c. 747

Crusaders siege Jerusalem i...

1800   1900

...ealthy British Jew, founds first Jewish settlement ◎ ...lem walls. He later renovates Western Wall. 1860

...Jerusalem reaches 15,000; First recorded Jewish ◎ majority (8,000) since second century AD. 1864

Hurva Synagogue rebuilt. 1864 ◎

...loration Fund established by British archaeologists ◎ ...ergymen to fund expeditions in the Holy Land. 1865

...es Warren conducts first archaeological excavations ◎ in Old City, discovers "Warren's Gate." 1867–1870

...Britain claims he located "the place of the skull" where Jesus ◎ ...became known as the Garden Tomb or Gordon's Calvary. 1883

...es he will restore ◎ ...ed at Acre. 1799

...l excavation in Jerusalem, ◎ ...s denied permission. 1818

...iblical locations, including Hezekiah's ◎ ...ount ("Robinson's Arch"). 1838–1852

...d European nations on the pretext of a dispute ◎ ...an religious sites in the Holy Land. 1853–1856

...ce Leopold II becomes first non-Muslim (since ◎ ...sades) allowed to tour Dome of the Rock. 1855

Britain captures Jerusalem from ◎ Ottomans in World War I. 1917

Mandate for Palestine gives Britain ◎ control over Palestine. 1920

Western Wall Uprising: Jewish and Arab riots ◎ begin in Jerusalem and spread throughout Palestine; 133 Jews and 116 Arabs killed. 1929

Britain, in response to the riots, **limits** ◎ **Jewish immigration**. 1930

World War II ends. Jewish survivors of concentration camps ◎ settle in Palestine despite Britain's attempts to stop them. 1945

King David Hotel (site of British headquarters) in Jerusalem ◎ bombed by Jewish terrorists, killing 91. 1946

United Nations (U.N.) plans to establish a Jewish State and Arab ◎ State with Jerusalem governed by the U.N. 1947

Population of Jerusalem exceeds 160,000. 1947 ◎

◎ **First Zionist Congress** chaired by Theodore Herzl sparks waves of Jewish immigration (*aliyah*). 1897

State of Israel declared after Mandate ends. War breaks out between Israel and neighboring Ar... nations. Estimated 500,000–750,000 Arab Palestinians flee or are expelled from Palestine. 194...

Arab-Israeli War ends with Israel controlling West Jerusalem, Jordan controlling Old Ci... Jordan prohibits Jews from praying at Western Wall for the next 19 years. 194...

Israel declares Jerusalem as their capital."

King Abdullah of Jordan assassi... Muslim extremists in Al-Aqsa Mosqu...

Lead roof of Dome of the ... aluminum and bronze allo... appea...

British archaeologist Dam... wall in City of David d...

Pope Paul VI becom...

900   **800**   **700**

...e captures Jerusalem (city of Jebus) from the Jebusites, ...ant to Jerusalem, purchases threshing floor of Araunah the ...in Jerusalem to be the site of the temple. c. 1011–971

King Josiah of Judah recovers Law of Moses, reforms the land, tear... down pagan altars. Levites return ark to the temple (last mention i... the Bible of the whereabouts of the ark, 2 Chron. 35:3). 64...

...eign of King Solomon: Jerusalem experiences a time of peace and prosperity. c. 971–931

First temple built on Mt. Moriah by King Solomon. 967–960

◉ **Death of Solomon.** His kingdom is divided into Northern Kingdom of Israel and Southern Kingdom of Judah (includes Jerusalem). 931

◉ **Egyptian Pharaoh Shishak** attacks Jerusalem and plunders the temple. 926

King Joash of Judah and priest Jehoiada repair the temple. 835 ◉

...y of David
...Mt. Zion

King Jehoash of Israel attacks Judah, tears down ◉ Jerusalem's walls, takes temple treasures to Samaria. 796

Northern Kingdom of Israel falls to Assyria. Refugees relocate ◉ to Judah and Jerusalem's population grows. 722

King Ahaz of Judah pays tribute to the King Tiglath-Pileser III of Assyria using ◉ temple furnishings and treasures; defiles the temple with a pagan altar. 720

Reign of King Hezekiah of Judah: He cleanses the temple; constructs a long tunnel under City of David ◉ to tap into a water source to prepare for an Assyrian siege (701 BC); pays tribute to King Sennacherib of Assyria with temple treasures; foolishly shows temple treasures to a Babylonian prince, an event Isaiah prophesied would lead to the destruction of Jerusalem (2 Kings 20:12–19). 716–687

King Manasseh of Judah, Hezekiah's son, reverses his ◉ father's reforms and places idols in the temple. 697

KING SOLOMON
c. 971–931 BC

KING HEZEKIAH
c. 716–687 BC

Population: 5,000

Population: 25,000

Nehemiah rebuil...

...the covenant to Jerusalem

AD 1   **AD 100**   **200**

KING HEROD AND TIME OF JESUS
c. 37 BC–AD 66

PRE-ROMAN DESTRUCTION
c. AD 66–70

◉ **Temple destroyed** by Roman General Titus. Titus crushes the revolt and massacres thousands in Jerusalem, plunders temple vessels. 70

◉ **Josephus writes** *Jewish War* and *Jewish Antiquities*. c. 75–94

◉ **Second Jewish Revolt (Bar Kokhba Rebellion):** Roman Emperor Hadrian ... revolt, rebuilds Jerusalem as a Roman city renaming it *Aelia Capitolina*, build... temple on Temple Mount, banishes Jews from the city, renames Judea *Pales...*

...ing ◉
...37

...Jerusalem ◉
...e of temple
...f David. 20

Population: 40,000

Population: 80,000

...hem, dedicated as ◉
...e temple. c. 6–4 BC

...us rules Judea, kills ◉
...er in Jerusalem. 4 BC

...alem at Passover. c. AD 7 ◉

...sus baptized, begins ministry. c. 26 ◉

...rocurator Pontius Pilate kills Jewish ◉
...zealots protesting at the temple. 28

...em, crucified at "the place of the skull" ◉
...s from the dead on the third day and is
...returning to heaven 40 days later. c. 30

◉ **On Pentecost**, Peter preaches in the temple and 3,000 are baptized. c. 30

◉ **Stephen, first Christian martyr**, is killed in Jerusalem. c. 32

◉ **Roman Emperor Caligula** declares himself a god. Jews refuse his order to set up his statue in the temple. 39

◉ **Jerusalem Council** concludes that Gentile Christians are not required to observe Jewish religious laws. c. 49

◉ **Paul arrested** in Jerusalem and taken to Rome. 57

◉ **James, brother of Jesus**, martyred in Jerusalem. 62

◉ **First Jewish Revolt** against Romans begins. Jerusalem Christians flee rather than join the revolt. 66

Roman destruction of the temple

BYZANTINE ERA

AD 600   700   800

◉ **Muhammad founds Islam** and unites tribes in Arabian Peninsula. 610–632

◉ **Sasanian Parthians** (Persians) defeat Byzantine Christians in Jerusalem, kill thousands, allow Jews to return to the city. 614

◉ **Christian mob** kills Jewish governor of Jerusalem. 617

◉ **Muhammad's Night Journey:** According to Islamic tradition, an angel takes Muhammad from Mecca to Jerusalem where Muhammad tethers his celestial horse to Western Wall and ascends to heaven from the holy rock (the large stone inside Dome of the Rock). c. 620

◉ **Byzantine Emperor Heraclius** defeats Persians. He enters Jerusalem through Golden Gate of Temple Mount carrying the "True Cross." 629

◉ **Caliph Omar**, a successor of Muhammad, sieges Jerusalem and forces its surrender. According to tradition, Omar clears the Temple Mount of debris. 637–638

◉ **Muslim Umayyad Dynasty** gains control of Jerusalem. 661

◉ **Dome of the Rock** built on Temple Mount. 688–691

◉ **Al-Aqsa Mosque** built on Temple Mount. c. 705–715

◉ **Earthquake** damages Al-Aqsa Mosque and Dome

◉ **Frankish Emperor Cha**
building projects in Jeru

Muhammad's Night Journe

BYZANTINE
c. AD 324–614

Population:
55,000–60,000

MAMLUK PERIOD   OTTOMAN EMI

1500   1600   1700

◉ **Jews in Spain** facing the Inquisition escape to Jerusalem. 1492

◉ **Ottoman Turks conquer Jerusalem** and rule the city for 400 years. 1516

◉ **Ottoman Sultan Suleiman "the Magnificent"** rebuilds walls of Jerusalem that had laid in ruins for three centuries, embellishes Dome of the Rock, designates Western Wall as the place for Jewish worship, rebuilds Tower of David by Jaffa Gate to include a mosque and minaret (still standing today). 1537–1541

◉ **Suleiman seals Golden Gate** on eastern side of Temple Mount through which, according to tradition, the Messiah will enter the temple. 1541

◉ **Population** of Jerusalem grows to 13,000 after Ottomans encourage resettlement. 1553

Hurva Synagogue built. Burned by Arabs two decades later. 1700 ◉

Sir Moses Montefiore, a
outside Old City Jerus

Population o

Palestine Ex
and

Sir Char

Charles Gordon o
was crucified. Site

Napoleon invades Palestine, announ
Jerusalem to Jews, but is defe

William John Bankes of Britain conducts first archaeologi
though he does so secretly at night because he

American Edward Robinson discovers many
tunnel and first-century arch on Temple M

Crimean War fought between Russia, Ottoman Empire,
over Russia's supposed right to act as guardian of Chris

Belgian pr
C

Sir Moses Montefiore

Sir Charles Warren

Sultan Suleiman rebuilds Jerusalem

Golden Gate of Temple Mount

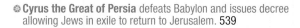

600   500   400

◉ **Jeremiah prophesies** that the Jews will return to Jerusalem after 70 years of exile (Jer. 25:11–12). c. 605

◉ **King Nebuchadnezzar of Babylon** invades Jerusalem and loots temple treasures. 605

◉ **Nebuchadnezzar returns**, takes more temple vessels to Babylon. Ezekiel taken into exile. 598–597

Babylonia invades Jerusalem and destroys temple

◉ **Judah falls to Babylon** upon Nebuchadnezzar's third invasion. Temple is destroyed, many Jews taken into exile in Babylon. 586

◉ **Ezekiel has a vision** of a magnificent new temple (Ezek. 40–48). c. 585–573

◉ **Cyrus the Great of Persia** defeats Babylon and issues decree allowing Jews in exile to return to Jerusalem. 539

Jerusalem's walls

NEHEMIAH, AFTER THE EXILE c. 444–432 BC

Population: 4,500

◉ **Zerubbabel and Joshua** the high priest lead Jews in exile back to Jerusalem. 539–538

◉ **Daniel**, in exile, receives the prophecy of the seventy "sevens" about Messiah's death in Jerusalem, destruction of the temple and its rebuilding and desecration (Dan. 9). c. 539–536

◉ **Temple rebuilt.** Those who remember the splendor of the first temple weep about this lesser second temple. 536–516

◉ **Ezra returns to Jerusalem** and exhorts the people to religious and moral reform. 457–456

◉ **Nehemiah governs Jerusalem** and rebuilds city walls. 444–432

300   400   500

◉ **Emperor Constantine** issues Edict of Milan legalizing Christianity across the empire. 313

ıts down the
s a pagan
ina. 132–135

◉ **Helena, Constantine's mother**, establishes basilica at Mt. of Olives, and according to tradition, finds a piece of the "True Cross" and the robe of Jesus. 323–333

Emperor Constantine

◉ **Church of the Holy Sepulchre** built by Constantine. 325–335

◉ **Julian "the Apostate,"** Constantine's nephew, allows Jews to return to Jerusalem and makes plans to rebuild the temple. 362

◉ **Earthquake** disrupts temple construction. 363

Church of the Holy Sepulchre

◉ **Julian is killed in battle.** Temple plans abandoned and Temple Mount becomes a site for dumping garbage. 363

◉ **Emperor Theodosius** officially declares Christianity the state religion. 380

◉ **Empress Eudocia** settles in Jerusalem and builds basilica in honor of the Christian martyr Stephen. 444

Emperor Justinian builds the New ◉ Church of St. Mary. 543

ROSE BOOK OF
BIBLE CHARTS
VOLUME 3

R🌹SE
PUBLISHING

Peabody, Massachusetts

Rose Book of Bible Charts Volume 3
© Copyright 2014 Bristol Works, Inc.
Rose Publishing, an imprint of Hendrickson Publishers Marketing, LLC
P.O. Box 3473
Peabody, Massachusetts 01961-3473 USA
All rights reserved
www.HendricksonRose.com
Register your Rose Publishing books at www.rose-publishing.com/register

Conditions of Use

Credits

Cover Design by Sergio Urquiza

All Scripture quotations, unless otherwise indicated, are taken from the Holy Bible, New International Version® NIV®. Copyright © 1973, 1978, 1984, 2011 by Biblica.™ Used by permission of Zondervan. All rights reserved worldwide.

Jerusalem Time Line © 2012 Bristol Works, Inc. Contributors: Megan Sauter, MA Biblical Archaeology; Cecil R. Price, ThM;
    Illustrations: Herod's Temple ©Bill Latta; Size of Jerusalem maps ©Ritmeyer Archaeological Design
Who I Am in Christ © 2010 Bristol Works, Inc. Authors: William Brent Ashby, BT; Benjamin Galan, MTS, ThM
What the Bible Says about Forgiveness © 2011 Bristol Works, Inc.
What the Bible Says about Money © 2009 Bristol Works, Inc. Author: Jessica Curiel, MA
What the Bible Says about Prayer © 2011 Bristol Works, Inc. Authors: Jessica Curiel, MA; William Brent Ashby, BT
Spiritual Gifts © 2011 Bristol Works, Inc. Author: Benjamin Galan, MTS, ThM
Spiritual Disciplines © 2009 Bristol Works, Inc. Authors: William Brent Ashby, BT; Benjamin Galan, MTS, ThM
One-Year Bible Reading Plan © 2009 Bristol Works, Inc.
24 Ways to Explain the Gospel © 2009 Bristol Works, Inc. Authors: William Brent Ashby, BT; Benjamin Galan, MTS, ThM
Life of Joseph © 2010 Bristol Works, Inc. Author: Benjamin Galan, MTS, ThM
Life of Moses © 2011 Bristol Works, Inc. Author: Benjamin Galan, MTS, ThM; Image credit: Stan Stein "The Tabernacle at Mt. Sinai"
Life of David © 2009 Bristol Works, Inc. Author: Benjamin Galan, MTS, ThM
Esther © 2009 Bristol Works, Inc. Author: Benjamin Galan, MTS, ThM
Ruth © 2013 Bristol Works, Inc. Author: Benjamin Galan, MTS, ThM
Psalms © 2013 Bristol Works, Inc. Author: Benjamin Galan, MTS, ThM
Proverbs © 2010 Bristol Works, Inc. Author: Benjamin Galan, MTS, ThM
Jonah © 2012 Bristol Works, Inc. Contributing author: Benjamin Galan, MTS, ThM
Gospels Side by Side © 2008 Bristol Works, Inc. Contributing authors: William Brent Ashby, BT; Benjamin Galan, MTS, ThM
Parables of Jesus © 2010 Bristol Works, Inc. Contributing authors: Benjamin Galan, MTS, ThM; Vincent Botticelli
Book of Acts © 2013 Bristol Works, Inc. Author: Benjamin Galan, MTS, ThM
Romans © 2013 Bristol Works, Inc. Author: Benjamin Galan, MTS, ThM
Book of James © 2011 Bristol Works, Inc. Author: Benjamin Galan, MTS, ThM
Understanding the Book of Revelation © 2009 Bristol Works, Inc. Contributing authors: William Brent Ashby, BT; Benjamin Galan, MTS, ThM
Baptism © 2008 Bristol Works, Inc. Contributing authors: William Brent Ashby, BT; Benjamin Galan, MTS, ThM
Lord's Supper © 2011 Bristol Works, Inc. Author: Benjamin Galan, MTS, ThM
What's So Great about Heaven © 2009 Bristol Works, Inc. Author: Benjamin Galan, MTS, ThM
Attributes of God © 2012 Bristol Works, Inc. Contributing authors: Shawn Vander Lugt, MA; Benjamin Galan, MTS, ThM
Creeds & Heresies: Then & Now © 2009 Bristol Works, Inc. Author: Benjamin Galan, MTS, ThM;
    Special thanks to Timothy Paul Jones, PhD and Paul Carden.

Many of these titles are available as individual pamphlets, e-books, wall charts, and ready-to-use PowerPoint® presentations.

Library of Congress Cataloging-in-Publication Data

Rose book of Bible charts.
    pages cm
"Volume 3."
Includes index.
ISBN 978-1-59636-869-9
1. Bible--Introductions. 2. Bible--Handbooks, manuals, etc. 3.
Bible--Charts, diagrams, etc. I. Rose Publishing (Torrance, Calif.)
BS475.3.R67 2014
220.022'3--dc23
                          2013031158

Printed through Asia Pacific Offset Ltd
Printed in China
April 2017, 4th printing

Contents

CHRISTIAN LIVING

who i am in CHRiST

because of what he has done

Because Jesus died, he can offer forgiveness. Because Jesus rose from the dead, he can give us life and victory. Forgiveness, life, and victory give us identity. We now live forgiven, abundant and victorious lives. Our lives are not perfect since we still experience pain and suffering. However, our hope is firm because it is based on Jesus' victory over death.

I am forgiven.

Eph. 1:6–8; Rom. 8:1, 38

All my sins are forgiven before God. God will not condemn me for:

- *Bad things I have done.*
- *Good things I have left undone.*
- *Evil things I have said.*
- *Wrong things I have thought.*

I am reconciled with God.

Rom. 5:10; 2 Cor. 5:18–19; Col. 1:21–22; Heb. 10:19–22

- *I have been reunited with God.*
- *The anger that was between us is gone.*
- *Because of Jesus, I now have free access to God.*

I am rescued.

Matt. 20:28; 1 Tim. 2:5–6

- *I have been rescued from a life-threatening situation.*
- *Jesus paid the ransom for my life with his own life.*
- *Sin no longer holds my life hostage.*

I am redeemed.

Eph. 1:13–14; Col. 1:14; Titus 2:14; Heb. 9:12; 1 Peter 1:18

- *I have had my life debt covered, and my future holds an inheritance from God.*
- *My life is no longer a worthless debt to sin.*
- *I now look forward to rich meaning and purpose in God's future plan for me.*

I am free.

John 8:32-36; Rom. 6:22–23; Gal. 4:7; 5:1

- *I have been set free.*
- *I am no longer a slave to sin.*

I am bought with a price and belong to God.

1 Cor. 6:19–20; 7:23

- *I have been paid for by God.*
- *God owns me.*
- *I no longer belong to myself.*
- *My old way of life no longer owns me.*

I am known by God.

Rom. 8:29; 2 Tim. 2:19

- *I have been known and cared about all along.*
- *God has been watching out for me from the beginning.*
- *God has cared for me from day one.*

I am chosen.

Rom. 8:30; Eph. 1:4; 1 Peter 2:9

- *I have been hand picked by God.*
- *My salvation was not accidental. God intended it for me.*
- *God called me out for salvation, even though I do not deserve it.*

I am justified before God.

Rom. 3:23–26, 5:1, 8:1, 30

- *God has declared me innocent because of Christ.*
- *Jesus has won my case by paying my penalty for me.*
- *I have been acquitted of all my crimes.*

I am accepted.

Rom. 15:7; Eph. 1:4-6; 1 Peter 2:10

- *I have been welcomed by God.*
- *I am no longer rejected.*
- *I am no longer an outsider.*

I am saved.

Rom. 5:8–10; 7:13–25; Eph. 2:1–10; Col. 1:13

I have been rescued:

- *From God's just anger.*
- *From sin.*
- *From myself.*
- *From death.*
- *From Satan and a sinful system.*

I am alive.

Rom. 6:11; 8:9–11; Eph. 2:4–5

- *I have received new life from God.*
- *My spirit has been brought to life and will never be dead again.*
- *My body will be made new after I die and I will live forever.*
- *I have new meaning and purpose and a new way of looking at life.*

I am loved.

Rom. 5:5; 8:39; 1 John 3:16; 4:19

- *God deeply loves me.*
- *I know this because he has given me his most precious gift—his Son, Jesus.*
- *I know that I am loved because God's Spirit of love is in my heart.*

I am taken care of.

John 6:37; Phil. 1:6; 4:19

- *I am secure in God's hands.*
- *I will not be abandoned; God will complete his work in me.*
- *God will supply all that I need.*

But how did we arrive here? Let's trace the story from the beginning…

who God created me to be

God created all things, visible and invisible. Because he is the creator, he is also the rightful owner of all things. In addition to being the rightful owner, God also rules over all of creation; his authority is final.

I am a creature.

Gen. 2:7

God made me.

- *Like a potter, God crafted me.*
- *God made me with skill and intention.*
- *I am complex and complicated.*
- *I have God's life-breath in me.*

I am like God.

Gen. 1:26–27

God made me more than just an animal.

- *I am made in God's image.*
- *I am made to relate to God and others in love.*

I am known.

Psalm 139; Jer. 1:5

God made me and knew me before I was born.

- *God made me.*
- *God knew me while I was still in the womb.*
- *God knows me better than I know myself.*

I am made to be God's caretaker of his creation.

Gen. 1:26–31; 2:15–17

God made me for caring responsibility.

- *I am made to help God in his ruling of creation.*
- *I am made to care for his earth.*

I am made to relate to his creation.

Gen. 2:19–24

God made me to relate to his entire creation.

- *I am made to love humans just as God loves me.*
- *I am made to love and enjoy God's creatures and nature.*

I am made for thankful, obedient worship to God.

Gen. 1:28–30; 2:16–17

God made me to glorify and enjoy him forever.

- *I am made to praise God by doing what he intended for me.*
- *I am made to enjoy myself as I enjoy God.*

image of God

In Genesis 1:27, the Bible says, "So God created man in his own image, in the image of God he created him; male and female he created them." What is the image of God? The Bible says that Jesus is the perfect image of God (see Col. 2:9 and Heb. 1:3). However, Christians have understood this concept in three different though complementary ways:

1. The qualities and attributes that distinguish humanity from the animals. Some of these qualities are: reason, will, personality, etc.

2. The ability to be in a relationship with God. This relationship constitutes the image of God in us.

3. The caring of God's creation is what demonstrates God's image in human beings.

It is possible that all three things are involved in what the image of God is. Humans are the image of God because they are able to relate to God, to each other, and to God's creation. In addition, humans represent God in this creation. When humans are reconciled with God, the abundant life that results allows the image of God to come through more clearly.

who i am on my own — when i ignored God and went my own way.

Although God made us to be his representatives in creation, humans rebelled and sinned against God. Because of sin, humanity is unable to relate to God, one another, and creation. Death, pain, and suffering entered the universe. Because of human disobedience, the whole creation was thrown into darkness and chaos. Our very existence was in danger. God's amazing grace and endless mercy allowed us to live. However, we live limited and twisted lives. This is also part of humanity's identity.

I was broken.
Rom. 3:10–18

Because of Jesus, I am…
Rom. 6:6; Gal. 2:20
- *I am crucified with Christ.*
- *Jesus' body was broken for me.*

I was living my life for myself.
Eph. 2:3

Because of Jesus, I am…
Rom. 6:4; Col. 2:12
- *I am buried with Christ to my old life.*
- *Jesus' burial buried my old selfish life.*

I was a sinner.
Rom. 3:23

Because of Jesus, I am…
Rom. 6:8; 1 Peter 2:24
- *I am dead with Christ to sin.*
- *Jesus' death was the death of my sin.*

I was a user and abuser of God's creation.
Rom. 1:21–25; 3:13–18; Eph. 2:2

Because of Jesus, I am…
Rom. 6:4; Col. 3:1
- *I am raised with Christ to a new life.*
- *Jesus' resurrection raised me to a new relationship with God and his world.*

I was not living by God's instructions.
Rom. 1:21–2:1

Because of Jesus, I am…
Rom. 13:8–10
- *I am fulfilling God's law in Christ.*
- *Jesus' love for me makes me want to live his law of love.*

God is the solution.

He chose for himself a people, those who would carry his name and be an example to all people. He gave us his word, in which he described his will for humanity and his creation. However, the ultimate solution is Jesus himself. Because he is both human and God, Jesus came to do what no other human could. His life, death, and resurrection created the bridge that allows us to be reconciled with God once again.

The cross is the climax of the biblical story. In the cross, all paths converge; all stories are given the possibility of a new direction. In the cross, God brings restoration, hope, and a new life for a creation groaning for redemption.

I was someone who worshiped my own way.
Rom. 1:25

Because of Jesus, I am…
Eph. 1:12–14
- *I am glorifying God in Christ.*
- *Jesus' glorious victory makes me want to give all glory to God.*

I was a mess.
Rom. 7

Because of Jesus, I am…
Phil. 1:6; Col. 2:9–10; Heb. 10:14
- *I am complete in Christ.*
- *Jesus' perfect work has made my life complete. One day, when Jesus returns, he will make it perfect.*

I was dead.
Eph. 2:1

Because of Jesus, I am…
Col. 2:13
- *I am alive with Christ.*
- *Jesus' new life flows through me now.*

I am…

We live in a culture of extremes. On the one hand, the culture around us emphasizes self-sufficiency and independence over the healthy emotional development of children. On the other, it attempts to bolster children's emotional health and self-worth by constant praise and a sense of entitlement. Both extremes have damaged children who grow up with a broken sense of self and lack of acceptance and love.

A realistic understanding of who we are gives us the chance for a healthy self-regard. The Bible gives us a correct understanding of who we are: people deeply flawed and sinful, deeply loved and redeemed by God, and equipped and empowered by the Holy Spirit to be and do as Christ would.

The Apostle Paul

The Apostle Paul is one of the great champions of the faith and worthy of imitation (1 Cor. 4:16). Paul candidly spoke about his past: a past full of pride and violence. He strongly contrasted the person he was, what he valued and what gave him meaning, with the person he became after his encounter with the risen Christ. His value, his goal and meaning for life were linked to Christ.

Paul before and after
Gal. 1:13–14; Phil. 3:4–6

before, I was...	now, I am...
• born a Jew	• an apostle of Christ
• a Roman citizen	• an apostle to the Gentiles
• circumcised on the eighth day	• a new person, all of my ancestry and ethnic background is worthless compared to the value of Christ
• of the tribe of Benjamin	
• a Pharisee	
• persecutor of the church	• a prisoner of Jesus
• zealous for the tradition of my ancestors	• a slave to everyone

I have been crucified with Christ and I no longer live, but Christ lives in me. The life I live in the body, I live by faith in the Son of God, who loved me and gave himself for me.

—Gal. 2:20

who i am and who i will be in CHRiST

The story of the Bible does not end on the cross. In fact, the cross opened new possibilities. The goal of the biblical story is not just the salvation of humanity through the gracious work of Jesus on the cross. God desires to redeem and restore all of his creation. The conclusion of this magnificent story is the creation of new heavens and new earth. All things will be made new! In that new creation, God will make things the way they should be.

I am a new creature.
2 Cor. 5:1–5, 16–19; Phil. 3:20-21

• I have had a total makeover of my mind and spirit and my new body is on order.

• My inner self has been recreated after a new model of human being—Jesus.

• My body will be made new after the pattern of Jesus' resurrected body.

I am born of God.
John 1:12–13; Rom. 8:29; 1 John 4:7

• I have been born into God's family.

• I am now a child of God after the likeness of Jesus.

• Jesus is the "firstborn" example from the dead of what I shall be in the resurrection.

I am adopted of God.
Rom. 8:15; Eph. 1:5; Heb. 2:10–12

• God has selected me to be his child.

• I am no longer an orphan.

• Jesus is my older brother.

• Because of him, I now share in the glory of being God's child.

I am a child of the promise.
Rom. 9:8; Gal. 4:23

• I am a child of Abraham, a promised child.

• I am a spiritual descendant of the father of faith.

• I am called to carry on this spiritual heritage in the world.

I am Jesus' friend.
John 15:15

• Jesus considers me his friend.

• I am a servant of Jesus Christ, yet he calls me friend.

I am a citizen of heaven.
Eph. 2:19; Phil. 3:20

• I belong with all those through history who have loved God.

• I am a member of God's heavenly kingdom.

• My true identity is with the people of God.

I am blessed with every spiritual blessing.

Eph. 1:3; 2:7

- *I have all that can be had of God's treasures.*
- *I have been given unfathomable riches in Christ.*
- *It will take the rest of eternity to unfold all these blessings.*

I am God's workmanship.

Eph. 2:10

- *I am a work of art.*
- *I have been made by the most creative Artist ever.*
- *I am a poem of God's love.*

I am a temple of the Holy Spirit.

1 Cor. 3:16; 6:19; 2 Cor. 6:16

- *I have God living in me.*
- *I am God's house.*
- *I have been made holy for God to live in me.*

I am a member of Christ's body.

Rom. 12:5; 1 Cor. 12:27

- *I am connected in a living way to Jesus.*
- *I am a part of a living organism bigger than myself.*
- *I have a purpose and function in that body.*

I am sealed.

2 Cor. 1:22; Eph. 1:13; 4:30

- *I have God's royal seal upon me.*
- *I have God's seal of ownership.*
- *I have God's guarantee of a quality product in me.*

I am made pure.

1 John 1:9, 3:3

- *I am made clean.*
- *Christ's life and death purify me.*
- *I am being made holy for God by his Spirit working in me.*

I am secure.

Rom. 8:28, 31–38

- *I know that God works things for my good in all circumstances.*
- *I am free from all condemnation.*
- *I know that nothing can separate me from the love of God.*

I am safe.

2 Cor. 1:21–22

I am safe because God has
- *Anointed me.*
- *Set his seal of ownership on me.*
- *Put his Spirit in my heart as a guarantee.*

I am victorious.

Rom. 8:37; 1 Cor. 15:57

- *I cannot be beaten.*
- *I cannot be stopped by death, thanks to Christ.*
- *I shall be a winner in the end because God is for me.*

I am going to live forever.

John 5:24; 6:47; 11:25-26; 17:3

- *I will live on with God.*
- *My spirit shall not die but go to be with God.*
- *Even if my body dies, I will live again and get a new body in the resurrection.*

I am in God's planned will as an heir of all creation.

Rom. 8:17, 32; Eph. 1:9–11

- *I am going to inherit the universe with Christ.*
- *I know this because God has given all authority and power to Jesus and I belong to him.*

Let the peace of Christ rule in your hearts, since as members of one body you were called to peace. And be thankful.
—Col. 3:15

the three R's— Reconciled, Ransomed, and Redeemed

Reconciled—to be reconciled means to be united again or to become friends again. Human sin and rebellion caused hostility between God and humanity. However, Jesus united us again in friendship with God by his death on the cross.

Ransomed—a ransom is a price that is paid for release; to be ransomed is to be freed at a cost. The Bible tells us that humanity was held hostage to sin, death and the Devil. Jesus' death was the ransom paid to free us from that slavery and reconcile us to God.

Redeemed—to redeem means to buy back again. Jesus' death paid the voucher, canceling the debt we owed.

a new mind

At the center of the good news about Christ is the transformation of individual lives. Paul tells us in Rom. 12:1–2 that this transformation involves the renewing of our minds. He goes on to say in Phil. 2:5–8 that this renewal is about having a new mind-set or attitude that Christ himself had. In other words, we are to identify with and take for ourselves Jesus' whole way of thinking and living.

who are we?

The Bible describes our encounter with God as a new birth (John 3:3). The apostle Paul extends this idea when he writes that we mature as Christians, and that we must, eventually, give up milk for solid food (Heb. 5:11–14). Just as children need to find their identities, we as spiritual children need to find our Christian identities as well.

Our identities begin with the recognition that we no longer belong to ourselves but to God. That is, we need to recognize that if Christ bought us at a high price, then we belong to him.

In the Scriptures, we learn who we are, where we came from, why we are here, and where we are going. When we read the stories of the Patriarchs in Genesis, we learn how God relates to us, imperfect people who long for him. When we read the Psalms, we learn a vocabulary of praise and petition. This vocabulary gives us words to praise God, to express our grief, and make our requests.

In the prophets, we learn what it means to be God's people in moments of difficulties and challenges, what it means to fail and receive God's grace and forgiveness. In the stories of the apostolic church, we see how the Holy Spirit guides and trains his church to carry on God's mission.

When we make ours the story of God's people, as told in the Bible and in the history of the church, our identity merges with that of God's people. In this process, we grow from infant believers to people mature in the faith. As we appropriate God's story with his people, we learn to teach others how to become part of this great story of salvation.

meaning of the word "Christian"

In Acts 11:25–26, Luke tells us that believers in Jesus were first called "Christians" at Antioch. The name obviously stuck, but what does it mean? *Christ* is the Greek term for the Hebrew *Messiah*, which means "anointed person." To be anointed in the Hebrew culture was to be set apart for some special service. It came to be associated in the prophetic writings of the Old Testament with God's promised savior of the line of king David— Jesus. The "ian" ending indicates belonging or membership. Christian means "one who belongs to Christ," or "one who is a part of Christ." Therefore, if a Christian is one who is connected to Christ, should it not be apparent in the way we act?

our identity—who we are, who I am—depends on the identity of God's people:

- I am a member of Christ's body;
- I am part of God's people;
- I am a child of God called to love him and his creation;
- I am a follower of Jesus because in him I am fully alive and willing to serve.

We are able to make this beautiful story ours only through the life, death, and resurrection of Christ. Through the Holy Spirit, we are renewed into the image of Jesus. By following his steps, we walk on the path of many believers before us, God's people, and we clear the path for those believers who are yet to come.

WHAT THE BIBLE SAYS ABOUT *Forgiveness*

Forgive us our sins, for we also forgive everyone who sins against us.—Luke 11:4a

With these familiar words in the Lord's Prayer, we are reminded that forgiveness should characterize our lives. But these few words, one might object, are a lot easier said than done. Forgiveness is one of the hardest things to do because the sins that need forgiving can be so damaging. They have wounded us so deeply that the mere idea of offering forgiveness to those who hurt us seems impossible. Forgiveness, in these cases, appears like letting people off the hook for their transgressions. The sharp pain in our hearts creates a barrier that prevents us from moving beyond our pain. Our pain and brokenness seem unending.

In the face of so much brokenness in ourselves and in our world, how should we respond? Should we deny it? Ignore it? Get even? Give up? God's Word says to forgive it. Forgiveness will never be easy. However, only through forgiveness can healing begin.

> "Forgiveness is God's invention for coming to terms with a world in which, despite their best intentions, people are unfair to each other and hurt each other deeply. He began by forgiving us. And he invites us all to forgive each other."
>
> —Lewis B. Smedes

Most of us can relate to many kinds of brokenness. Below are a few examples of situations in which forgiveness might be very difficult.

AREAS	SOURCES OF BROKENNESS
Emotional	• Abandonment by a father or mother • Infidelity, divorce, lying • Betrayal by a trusted friend or confidant
Physical	• Sexual or domestic abuse • Parental neglect of a child's physical needs • Assault or violence
Spiritual	• Misuse of authority by a church leader • Rejection or poor treatment by a church "family" • Major sins committed by a pastor • Private sins that damage a person's relationship with God
Financial	• Stealing, embezzlement, fraud • Failure to repay a debt or loan • Unfair loss of a job or employment discrimination
Social	• Name calling, insults, public humiliation • Loss of reputation from gossip and lies • Discrimination from prejudices, racism, or sexism • Bullying, cyber-bullying

Forgiveness Is Needed

Forgiveness exists because sin exists. Forgiveness is necessary because sin powerfully affects all areas of our lives. Forgiveness is not about ignoring evil, excusing it, or making light of it. On the contrary, forgiveness courageously faces sin and evil. Forgiveness acknowledges that a terrible wrong has been done and seeks to do something about it.

SIN IS REAL

No one needs to look far to see that there is sin in the world. We are born into a world where harmful patterns of sin persist in societies, communities, churches, and families. We may not even be aware of our own contribution to the cycles of sin. Because sin is in the world and in us, we need forgiveness even more.

If we claim to be without sin, we deceive ourselves and the truth is not in us. If we confess our sins, he is faithful and just and will forgive us our sins and purify us from all unrighteousness. If we claim we have not sinned, we make him out to be a liar and his word is not in us.—1 John 1:8–10

SIN IS DESTRUCTIVE

Sin breaks our communion with God and destroys our relationships with others. The first human sin brought death into the world for all to suffer the consequences. When someone hurts us, our pain and our sin begin a cycle of anger, violence, resentment, and revenge that increases over time. Only forgiveness can allow us to break this cycle.

Therefore, just as sin entered the world through one man, and death through sin, and in this way death came to all people, because all sinned.—Romans 5:12

Once you were alienated from God and were enemies in your minds because of your evil behavior.—Colossians 1:21

What causes fights and quarrels among you? Don't they come from your desires that battle within you? You desire but do not have, so you kill. You covet, but you cannot get what you want, so you quarrel and fight.—James 4:1–2a

GOD TAKES SIN SERIOUSLY

Scripture tells us that God is merciful and forgiving, but it also makes clear that God does not tolerate sin. Because sin is so harmful, it demands divine judgment, not mere dismissal.

And he passed in front of Moses, proclaiming, "The LORD, the LORD, the compassionate and gracious God, slow to anger, abounding in love and faithfulness, maintaining love to thousands, and forgiving wickedness, rebellion and sin. Yet he does not leave the guilty unpunished; he punishes the children and their children for the sin of the parents to the third and fourth generation."—Exodus 34:6–7

Forgiveness Is Possible

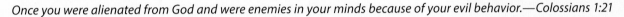

If judgment of sin were the last word on the matter, we would all stay trapped in our guilt and brokenness. If vengeance for every offense were the only option, we would forever remain separated from our Creator. But thank God he has provided another way—the way of forgiveness. Forgiveness does not erase the past, but it gives us a chance for a better future.

GOD DESIRES TO FORGIVE

The Old Testament contains many examples of God sending punishment for sinful acts. However, his withholding of judgment was for the purpose of bringing the people back to God so he could forgive them and restore the broken relationship. Though our actions deserve judgment, God desires to be merciful.

If my people, who are called by my name, will humble themselves and pray and seek my face and turn from their wicked ways, then I will hear from heaven and I will forgive their sin and will heal their land.—2 Chronicles 7:14

Perhaps when the people of Judah hear about every disaster I plan to inflict on them, they will turn from their wicked ways; then I will forgive their wickedness and their sin.—Jeremiah 36:3

The LORD is compassionate and gracious, slow to anger, abounding in love. He will not always accuse, nor will he harbor his anger forever; he does not treat us as our sins deserve or repay us according to our iniquities. For as high as the heavens are above the earth, so great is his love for those who fear him; as far as the east is from the west, so far has he removed our transgressions from us.—Psalm 103:8–12

JESUS MADE FORGIVENESS POSSIBLE

In the New Testament, we see God's desire to forgive expressed most clearly in the life and death of his Son. Jesus' sinless life and voluntary death atoned for the world's sins. He bore the ultimate judgment of sin so we don't have to. God forgives us because he loves us.

Therefore, my friends, I want you to know that through Jesus the forgiveness of sins is proclaimed to you.—Acts 13:38

But God demonstrates his own love for us in this: While we were still sinners, Christ died for us.—Romans 5:8

In him we have redemption through his blood, the forgiveness of sins, in accordance with the riches of God's grace. —Ephesians 1:7

For he has rescued us from the dominion of darkness and brought us into the kingdom of the Son he loves, in whom we have redemption, the forgiveness of sins. —Colossians 1:13–14

Forgiveness Is Available

When we place our faith in Jesus, we are declared free from divine condemnation and we stand forgiven of our sin. Forgiveness, not judgment, is the final word.

> "Forgiving love is a possibility only for those who know that they are not good, who feel themselves in need of divine mercy... [who] feel themselves as well as their fellow men convicted of sin by a holy God and know that the differences between the good man and the bad man are insignificant in his sight."
>
> —Reinhold Niebuhr

I, even I, am he who blots out your transgressions, for my own sake, and remembers your sins no more.—Isaiah 43:25

Therefore, there is now no condemnation for those who are in Christ Jesus, because through Christ Jesus the law of the Spirit of life has set you free from the law of sin and death.—Romans 8:1–2

Peter replied, "Repent and be baptized, every one of you, in the name of Jesus Christ for the forgiveness of your sins. And you will receive the gift of the Holy Spirit." —Acts 2:38

All the prophets testify about him that everyone who believes in him receives forgiveness of sins through his name.—Acts 10:43

Forgiveness Is Ongoing

Forgiveness is not a one-time thing. We need to continue to ask God for forgiveness for the wrongs we commit even after our initial acceptance of Jesus. In response to such generous forgiveness, God entrusts us with the responsibility and privilege to mirror his love by forgiving those who sin against us.

ASK FOR FORGIVENESS AS OFTEN AS NEEDED

As believers, we are made right with God through Jesus, yet old patterns of sin may still resurface. Sinful habits in our lives hurt others and impede a growing, vibrant relationship with God. We continue to be in need of God's forgiveness daily, and are instructed to ask forgiveness from anyone whom we have wronged.

My dear children, I write this to you so that you will not sin. But if anybody does sin, we have one who speaks to the Father in our defense—Jesus Christ, the Righteous One. He is the atoning sacrifice for our sins, and not only for ours but also for the sins of the whole world.—1 John 2:1–2

Therefore confess your sins to each other and pray for each other so that you may be healed.—James 5:16a

"God's forgiveness is unconditional; it comes from a heart that does not demand anything for itself, a heart that is completely empty of self-seeking. It is this divine forgiveness that I have to practice in my daily life. It calls me to keep stepping over all my arguments that say forgiveness is unwise, unhealthy, and impractical. It challenges me to step over all my needs for gratitude and compliments. Finally, it demands of me that I step over that wounded part of my heart that feels hurt and wronged and that wants to stay in control and put a few conditions between me and the one whom I am asked to forgive."

—Henri Nouwen

Therefore, if you are offering your gift at the altar and there remember that your brother or sister has something against you, leave your gift there in front of the altar. First go and be reconciled to them; then come and offer your gift.
—Matthew 5:23–24

FORGIVE OTHERS AS OFTEN AS NEEDED

God forgives us time and time again, and he calls us to do the same. There is no limit to how often or how many times we are to forgive others. God wants his forgiven people to be forgivers.

If your brother or sister sins against you, rebuke them, and if they repent, forgive them. Even if they sin against you seven times in a day, and seven times come back to you saying "I repent," you must forgive them.—Luke 17:3–4

Bear with each other and forgive one another if any of you has a grievance against someone. Forgive as the Lord forgave you. And over all these virtues put on love, which binds them all together in perfect unity.—Colossians 3:13–14

Ten Stories of Forgiveness

THE STORY	REFERENCE	KEY VERSE
Esau forgave his brother Jacob after years of estrangement.	Genesis 25:19–34; 27:1–28:9; 32:1–21; 33	But Esau ran to meet Jacob and embraced him; he threw his arms around his neck and kissed him. And they wept (33:4).
Joseph forgave his brothers who betrayed him.	Genesis 37–50	You intended to harm me, but God intended it for good to accomplish what is now being done, the saving of many lives (50:20).
David asked for God's forgiveness for his adultery with Bathsheba.	2 Samuel 11:1–12:25; Psalm 51	Wash away all my iniquity and cleanse me from my sin. For I know my transgressions, and my sin is always before me (Ps. 51:2–3).
Out of love, a forgiven woman anointed Jesus' feet.	Luke 7:36–50	Therefore, I tell you, her many sins have been forgiven—as her great love has shown. But whoever has been forgiven little loves little (v. 47).
The Parable of the Prodigal Son	Luke 15:11–32	But while he was still a long way off, his father saw him and was filled with compassion for him; he ran to his son, threw his arms around him and kissed him (v. 20).
A tax collector begged for mercy while a Pharisee failed to see his own need for forgiveness.	Luke 18:9–14	But the tax collector stood at a distance. He would not even look up to heaven, but beat his breast and said, "God, have mercy on me, a sinner" (v. 13).
Jesus did not condemn a woman caught in adultery.	John 8:1–11	"Then neither do I condemn you," Jesus declared. "Go now and leave your life of sin" (v. 11b).
Jesus asked the Father to forgive those who crucified him.	Luke 23:32–43	Father, forgive them, for they do not know what they are doing (v. 34).
Jesus restored Peter who had denied him three times.	John 13:31–38; 18:15–27; 21:15–19	Jesus asked [Peter] the third time, "Do you love me?" He said, "Lord, you know all things; you know that I love you." Jesus said, "Feed my sheep" (21:17).
Stephen asked God to forgive those who were stoning him.	Acts 7:54–60	Then he fell on his knees and cried out, "Lord, do not hold this sin against them." When he had said this, he fell asleep (v. 60).

The Parable of the Unmerciful Servant *Matthew 18:21–35*

Peter's Question: "Lord, how many times shall I forgive my brother or sister who sins against me? Up to seven times?" (v. 21). Peter probably thought his "seven times" suggestion was generous since the rabbis of the day taught that one should forgive only up to three times.

Jesus' Answer: "I do not say to you, up to seven times, but up to seventy times seven" (v. 22 NASB). If Peter is fishing for a cap on forgiveness, Jesus gives him an impossible limit, which is really no limit at all. Jesus explains why we should forgive with this story about a king and a servant who owes him a lot of money.

The Merciful King	The Unmerciful Servant
Is owed a massive debt of 10,000 bags of gold (v. 24). (This is a way of saying it is an incalculable sum, like saying "billions of dollars.")	Is owed a small debt (v. 28). (The debt the servant owes the king is about 600,000 times more than what the servant is owed by a fellow servant.)
Is moved to compassion by the servant's plea in which the servant promises to pay a debt which is clearly impossible for him to do (v. 26).	Becomes violent and chokes the servant who owes him, and refuses to listen when the servant pleads for mercy (v. 29).
Cancels the entire debt and lets the servant walk away a debt-free man instead of being sold into slavery as the law allowed (v. 27).	Throws his fellow servant into a debtor's prison (v. 30).

When the unmerciful servant's actions are exposed:

- The fellow servants are outraged and report his conduct to the king (v. 31).
- This time the king is moved to anger, not compassion (v. 34).
- The servant is called "wicked" by the king (v. 32).
- The king renews the debt and hands the servant over to jailers (v. 34).

The Lesson: "This is how my heavenly Father will treat each of you unless you forgive your brother or sister from your heart" (v. 35). Our debt to God is enormous, and his forgiveness is extravagant. In light of this, Jesus allows no excuse for withholding forgiveness from others.

Why Forgive?

FORGIVENESS FREES THE FORGIVER

Anyone who has been wronged knows that forgiveness is not easy. However, resentment and bitterness are damaging. If anger is allowed to fester it will spill over into other areas of life, destroying relationships and leading to a path of revenge.

> *Make every effort to live in peace with everyone and to be holy; without holiness no one will see the Lord. See to it that no one falls short of the grace of God and that no bitter root grows up to cause trouble and defile many.—Hebrews 12:14–15*

> *Finally, all of you, be like-minded, be sympathetic, love one another, be compassionate and humble. Do not repay evil with evil or insult with insult. On the contrary, repay evil with blessing, because to this you were called so that you may inherit a blessing.—1 Peter 3:8–9*

FORGIVE SO THAT YOU WILL BE FORGIVEN

If we want to be forgiven ourselves, we must extend that same forgiveness to others, allowing forgiveness to triumph over the desire to extract retribution.

> *For if you forgive other people when they sin against you, your heavenly Father will also forgive you. But if you do not forgive others their sins, your Father will not forgive your sins.—Matthew 6:14–15*

"Resentment is like a glass of poison that a man drinks; then he sits down and waits for his enemy to die." —Author Unknown

"Forgiveness is unlocking the door to set someone free and realizing you were the prisoner!" —Author Unknown

And when you stand praying, if you hold anything against anyone, forgive them, so that your Father in heaven may forgive you your sins.—Mark 11:25

Do not judge, and you will not be judged. Do not condemn, and you will not be condemned. Forgive, and you will be forgiven.—Luke 6:37

Speak and act as those who are going to be judged by the law that gives freedom, because judgment without mercy will be shown to anyone who has not been merciful. Mercy triumphs over judgment.—James 2:12–13

HEALING RELATIONSHIPS REQUIRES FORGIVENESS

Often the key to healing relationships begins with forgiveness. God is working in the world to reconcile fallen humans to himself through Christ, and he calls us to be ministers of reconciliation in this broken world.

> "Without forgiveness, there's no future."
>
> —Desmond Tutu, Anglican Archbishop who opposed apartheid (racial segregation) in South Africa

All this is from God, who reconciled us to himself through Christ and gave us the ministry of reconciliation: that God was reconciling the world to himself in Christ, not counting people's sins against them. And he has committed to us the message of reconciliation. We are therefore Christ's ambassadors, as though God were making his appeal through us. We implore you on Christ's behalf: Be reconciled to God.—2 Corinthians 5:18–20 (See also Romans 5:6–11)

Once you were alienated from God and were enemies in your minds because of your evil behavior. But now he has reconciled you by Christ's physical body through death to present you holy in his sight, without blemish and free from accusation—if you continue in your faith, established and firm, and do not move from the hope held out in the gospel.—Colossians 1:21–23a

If anyone has caused grief, he has not so much grieved me as he has grieved all of you, to some extent—not to put it too severely. The punishment inflicted on him by the majority is sufficient. Now instead, you ought to forgive and comfort him, so that he will not be overwhelmed by excessive sorrow. I urge you, therefore, to reaffirm your love for him.—2 Corinthians 2:5–8

FORGIVENESS IS A TESTIMONY OF GOD'S LOVE

The world tells us to "get even" or "make them sorry!" God says something quite different. God's love for all people motivates us to love others as well—even the most unlovable! When we forgive, we demonstrate God's love for a sinful world.

> "We forgive with no strings attached; that may require us to forgive repeatedly. When we do, we shock the world with God's power at work within us."
>
> —Rebecca Nichols Alonzo, who, at age seven, witnessed her mother's murder

But I tell you: Love your enemies and pray for those who persecute you, that you may be children of your Father in heaven. He causes his sun to rise on the evil and the good, and sends rain on the righteous and the unrighteous. If you love those who love you, what reward will you get? Are not even the tax collectors doing that? And if you greet only your own people, what are you doing more than others? Do not even pagans do that? Be perfect, therefore, as your heavenly Father is perfect.—Matthew 5:44–48

DOES FORGIVENESS MEAN RECONCILIATION?

A common reason people withhold forgiveness is that they think that forgiveness requires immediate and total reconciliation with the offender. People who have been hurt ask: If I forgive, does that mean I have to put myself back in the abusive situation? Must I force myself to be best friends again with the person who wronged me? Am I required to give the betrayer my full trust?

No, forgiveness is not the same as reconciliation. Forgiveness involves letting go of vengeance and hatred for being wronged. Reconciliation can be described as "restoration to harmony in relationship." One person can forgive, but it takes two people to restore a broken relationship. Forgiveness alone neither guarantees nor demands reconciliation. Often much more is needed before reconciliation can (or should) take place, for example: repentance, restitution of the wrong, gaining back trust, or evidence of genuine change. If forgiveness is taken to mean "going back" to the offender as if nothing ever happened, then people will end up only with a cheap imitation of reconciliation, far unlike the genuine harmony in a restored relationship described in Scripture (1 Thess. 5:11; Rom. 12:10).

 www.rose-publishing.com

DEALING WITH ANGER

Sometimes anger and bitterness prevent us from experiencing the freedom of forgiveness. The following steps can help us break free from the chains of anger.

1. Acknowledge God's complete forgiveness by grace (Col. 1:13–14).
   I am forgiven by the grace of God!

2. Be willing to confess your bitterness and resentment to God (Ps. 51:10–12).
   God, forgive my bitter attitudes and my anger toward _____.

3. Recognize that your anger is a violation of God's Word (Matt. 6:14–15) and choose to release the anger (Heb. 12:14–15).
   With the Holy Spirit's help, I choose to lay down this anger. I release my desire for revenge on _____.

4. Follow the Holy Spirit's leading as to whether you need to speak to the person you need to forgive (James 2:12–13).
   God, I ask for your Spirit to guide me into what I should do next.

Go through these steps repeatedly until words become experience.

How to Forgive

PRACTICE FORGIVENESS BEFORE IT'S NEEDED

A runner who finishes a marathon has gotten into the habit of running long before the start of the race. In the same way, if we want to be able to forgive the big stuff, we have to get into the habit of forgiving the small stuff. Forgiveness, like other virtues, takes daily cultivation.

> "That is the whole lesson: the sins of others you see, but your own sin you fail to see. In repentance, recognize God's mercy toward you; in this way alone will you be able to forgive."
>
> —Dietrich Bonhoeffer, German pastor and theologian who was imprisoned and executed for his opposition to Nazism

> *Get rid of all bitterness, rage and anger, brawling and slander, along with every form of malice. Be kind and compassionate to one another, forgiving each other, just as in Christ God forgave you.—Ephesians 4:31–32*

> *Above all, love each other deeply, because love covers over a multitude of sins. —1 Peter 4:8*

EXAMINE YOUR OWN SIN

Recognizing our own need for God's forgiveness enables us to see our offender's need for mercy. The practice of the Lord's Supper (Communion) reminds us that we are all flawed and sinful people in need of forgiveness. Self-righteousness will breed an unforgiving heart, but through humility we can learn to extend mercy to others.

> *He who conceals their sins does not prosper, but the one who confesses and renounces them finds mercy.—Proverbs 28:13*

> *But who can discern their own errors? Forgive my hidden faults.—Psalm 19:12*

> *Then he took the cup, gave thanks and offered it to them, saying, "Drink from it, all of you. This is my blood of the covenant, which is poured out for many for the forgiveness of sins."—Matthew 26:27–28*

GIVE UP YOUR RIGHT TO REVENGE

Anger is a natural response when we are harmed. But God's Word says to be careful that our anger does not result in taking revenge. We should not add sin upon sin, but leave the situation where it belongs—in God's hands. (See also 1 Thess. 5:15)

> *Do not say, "I'll pay you back for this wrong!" Wait for the LORD, and he will avenge you.—Proverbs 20:22*

> *In your anger do not sin: Do not let the sun go down while you are still angry, and do not give the devil a foothold. —Ephesians 4:26–27*

> *Bless those who persecute you; bless and do not curse…. Do not repay anyone evil for evil. Be careful to do what is right in the eyes of everyone. If it is possible, as far as it depends on you, live at peace with everyone. Do not take revenge, my friends, but leave room for God's wrath, for it is written: "It is mine to avenge; I will repay," says the Lord. On the contrary: "If your enemy is hungry, feed him; if he is thirsty, give him something to drink. In doing this, you will heap burning coals on his head." Do not be overcome by evil, but overcome evil with good.—Romans 12:14–21*

LOVING YOUR ENEMIES

Loving your "enemies" is to see them as fellow human beings who are loved by God and in need of his grace; but it is not to tolerate their abuse or invite them to hurt you again. The so-called "love" that ignores or allows such damaging sins is not really love at all.

LEARN FROM VETERAN FORGIVERS

There is no cookie-cutter way to forgive. Every situation is different. For instance, how to go about forgiving a close friend who has betrayed you will be different from how to forgive an unknown hit-and-run driver. We can gain wisdom in knowing how to deal with particular situations by taking note of Christians who have already walked the path of forgiveness. Their examples and guidance can give us a long-term view beyond the initial feelings of anger and pain.

Join together in following my example, brothers and sisters, and just as you have us as a model, keep your eyes on those who live as we do.—Philippians 3:17

Brothers and sisters, as an example of patience in the face of suffering, take the prophets who spoke in the name of the Lord. As you know, we consider blessed those who have persevered. You have heard of Job's perseverance and have seen what the Lord finally brought about. The Lord is full of compassion and mercy.—James 5:10–11

LET FORGIVENESS TAKE TIME

The apostle Paul compares the Christian life to a race that we have not yet finished. This side of heaven we may not be able to forgive to the extent that we want to because we are still imperfect people in an imperfect world. What we are called to do is to continue moving forward and not to give up.

Not that I have already obtained all this, or have already arrived at my goal, but I press on to take hold of that for which Christ Jesus took hold of me. Brothers and sisters, I do not consider myself yet to have taken hold of it. But one thing I do: Forgetting what is behind and straining toward what is ahead, I press on toward the goal to win the prize for which God has called me heavenward in Christ Jesus. All of us who are mature should take such a view of things. And if on some point you think differently, that too God will make clear to you. Only let us live up to what we have already attained.—Philippians 3:12–16

PRAY FOR YOUR ENEMIES

It might sound cliché to say "just pray about it," but there is nothing trite about praying for someone who has wronged you. Such prayers can have a powerful effect on the person praying. By the power of God's Spirit in us, through prayer, God can miraculously change our hatred into love.

But I tell you: Love your enemies and pray for those who persecute you, that you may be children of your Father in heaven.—Matthew 5:44–45a

In the same way, the Spirit helps us in our weakness. We do not know what we ought to pray for, but the Spirit himself intercedes for us through wordless groans.—Romans 8:26

But [the Lord] said to me, "My grace is sufficient for you, for my power is made perfect in weakness." … For when I am weak, then I am strong.—2 Corinthians 12:9–10

TRUST IN GOD'S GOODNESS

Placing a painful situation in God's hands is only possible if we allow ourselves to trust that God knows best. When we give it over to God, we will be surprised at the good he will bring out of any bad situation. The best example of God's goodness transcending evil is that of Jesus' death on the cross. What appeared to many to be the pointless crucifixion of an innocent man turned out to be the means whereby God provided forgiveness of sins for the world. Jesus trusted the Father that the way of forgiveness would be the best path.

To this you were called, because Christ suffered for you, leaving you an example, that you should follow in his steps. "He committed no sin, and no deceit was found in his mouth." When they hurled their insults at him, he did not retaliate; when he suffered, he made no threats. Instead, he entrusted himself to him who judges justly. "He himself bore our sins" in his body on the cross, so that we might die to sins and live for righteousness; "by his wounds you have been healed."—1 Peter 2:21–24

"Forgiveness stretches out over time, but you have to start out with the will to forgive. But the bitterness may reenter your mind from time to time, and then you have to think about forgiveness again."

—An Amish mother whose daughter was killed when a gunman opened fire in a schoolhouse

"When we are powerless to do a thing, it is a great joy that we can come and step inside the ability of Jesus."

—Corrie ten Boom, Holocaust survivor

WHAT THE BIBLE SAYS ABOUT MONEY

Money is a big thing in the world's eye, but from God's view it's a small thing. It's what we *do* with this small thing that makes a big, eternal difference. God cares about our faithfulness with what he has entrusted to us—whether it's a lot or a little. Jesus praised the poor widow who gave generously to God out of her meager income (Mark 12:41–44). Her outward act of exceeding faithfulness mirrored an inward spiritual reality of a heart set on the things of God.

> *"Small things are small things, but faithfulness with a small thing is a big thing."*
> —Hudson Taylor, Missionary to China

Jesus tells us to invest in the kingdom of God so that we will find genuine treasures far better than the fleeting, insignificant riches of this world (Matthew 6:19–21). As we remain faithful to God in our use of money, he will prove faithful to care for us through all life's financial ups and downs. Jesus reassures us with these words: "Seek first [God's] kingdom and his righteousness, and all these things will be given to you as well" (Matthew 6:33).

ATTITUDES TOWARD MONEY

People may have different attitudes toward money based on personal experience or how they were raised. But whatever one's feelings are about money and possessions, they need to be evaluated in light of what the Bible says. Looking at the diagram below, how do you view money in your life?

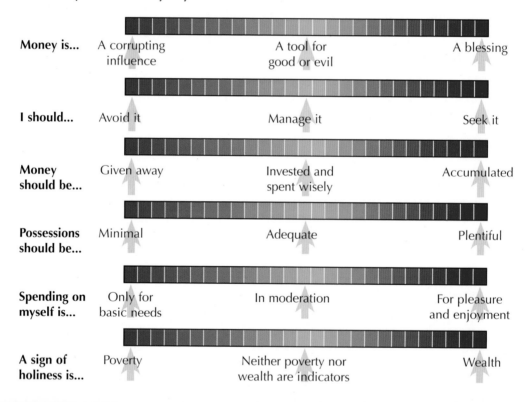

Money is...	A corrupting influence	A tool for good or evil	A blessing
I should...	Avoid it	Manage it	Seek it
Money should be...	Given away	Invested and spent wisely	Accumulated
Possessions should be...	Minimal	Adequate	Plentiful
Spending on myself is...	Only for basic needs	In moderation	For pleasure and enjoyment
A sign of holiness is...	Poverty	Neither poverty nor wealth are indicators	Wealth

FOR THE GLORY OF GOD

First Corinthians 10:31 says, "So whether you eat or drink or whatever you do, do it all for the glory of God." The use of money can be for the glory of God.

God Is the True Owner of Our Money.

In order to use money in ways that glorify God, it's important to first understand whose money it really is. God is the Creator and Owner of all things—including all money, property, and investments.

The earth is the LORD's and everything in it. —PSALM 24:1

©2014 Bristol Works, Inc.   www.rose-publishing.com

Yours, O LORD, is the greatness and the power and the glory and the majesty and the splendor, for everything in heaven and earth is yours. Yours, O LORD, is the kingdom; you are exalted as head over all. —1 CHRONICLES 29:11

"The silver is mine and the gold is mine," declares the LORD Almighty. —HAGGAI 2:8

Faithfulness Will Be Rewarded.

God is the Owner, but we are his managers whom he has entrusted with the things of this world. We are accountable to the true Owner to be faithful in our financial transactions.

His master replied, "Well done, good and faithful servant! You have been faithful with a few things; I will put you in charge of many things. Come and share your master's happiness!" —MATTHEW 25:23

Honor the LORD with your wealth, with the firstfruits of all your crops; then your barns will be filled to overflowing, and your vats will brim over with new wine. —PROVERBS 3:9–10

Give generously to [the needy] and do so without a grudging heart; then because of this the LORD your God will bless you in all your work and in everything you put your hand to. —DEUTERONOMY 15:10

> *"The everyday choices I make regarding money will influence the very course of eternity."*
> —Randy Alcorn, Christian author

Whoever can be trusted with very little can also be trusted with much, and whoever is dishonest with very little will also be dishonest with much. So if you have not been trustworthy in handling worldly wealth, who will trust you with true riches? And if you have not been trustworthy with someone else's property, who will give you property of your own? —LUKE 16:9–12

Then the King will say to those on his right, "Come, you who are blessed by my Father; take your inheritance, the kingdom prepared for you since the creation of the world. For I was hungry and you gave me something to eat, I was thirsty and you gave me something to drink, I was a stranger and you invited me in, I needed clothes and you clothed me, I was sick and you looked after me, I was in prison and you came to visit me." —MATTHEW 25:34–36

God's Agenda Matters More than Ours.

Any money God has entrusted to us has the potential to be used for our selfish ends or for God's agenda. Evangelist Billy Graham said, "Give me five minutes with a person's checkbook, and I will tell you where their heart is." If you want your heart to be set on the things of God, get into the habit of placing your money into things God cares about.

Do not store up for yourselves treasures on earth, where moth and rust destroy, and where thieves break in and steal. But store up for yourselves treasures in heaven, where moth and rust do not destroy, and where thieves do not break in and steal. For where your treasure is, there your heart will be also. —MATTHEW 6:19–21

But Zacchaeus stood up and said to the Lord, "Look, Lord! Here and now I give half of my possessions to the poor, and if I have cheated anybody out of anything, I will pay back four times the amount." Jesus said to him, "Today salvation has come to this house, because this man, too, is a son of Abraham. For the Son of Man came to seek and to save what was lost." —LUKE 19:8–9

From everyone who has been given much, much will be demanded; and from the one who has been entrusted with much, much more will be asked. —LUKE 12:48b

BLESSINGS FROM GOD

God is the ultimate Owner of all things, but he is no miser. The Bible shows him to be a generous Father who gives blessings to his children because he loves them.

God Blesses His Children.

God gave his chosen people in the Old Testament a land of affluence. Abundance of wealth is portrayed (particularly in the Old Testament) as a blessing from God and considered to be evidence of God's favor.

You open your hands and satisfy the desires of every living thing. —Psalm 145:16

For the Lord your God will bless you in all your harvest and in all the work of your hands, and your joy will be complete. —Deuteronomy 16:15

If you, then, though you are evil, know how to give good gifts to your children, how much more will your Father in heaven give good gifts to those who ask him! —Matthew 7:11

God Gives Generously So We Can Give Generously.

Our Father's gifts to us are not for hoarding, but for giving as he gives.

Whoever sows sparingly will also reap sparingly, and whoever sows generously will also reap generously. Each man should give what he has decided in his heart to give, not reluctantly or under compulsion, for God loves a cheerful giver. And God is able to make all grace abound to you, so that in all things at all times, having all that you need, you will abound in every good work.... You will be made rich in every way so that you can be generous on every occasion, and through us your generosity will result in thanksgiving to God. —2 Corinthians 9:6–11

Share with God's people who are in need. Practice hospitality. —Romans 12:13

Trusting God Is at the Center.

At the core of receiving blessing and giving back generously is our trust in God. Trust is an expression of faith that God will come through for us. It may not be in the way we expect, but he will work all things together for good because of his abundant love.

I am not saying this because I am in need, for I have learned to be content whatever the circumstances. I know what it is to be in need, and I know what it is to have plenty. I have learned the secret of being content in any and every situation, whether well fed or hungry, whether living in plenty or in want. I can do everything through him who gives me strength.... And my God will meet all your needs according to his glorious riches in Christ Jesus. —Philippians 4:11–13, 19

THE DANGER OF MONEY

Money can be a blessing used to honor God, but allowing it to become an idol corrupts our lives and harms our walk with God. When we covet and cling to money instead of using money to serve God, we begin to serve money itself.

Serving Money Takes Us Away from God.

Jesus personified money as a rival master to our real Master. Like the rich young man who did not follow Jesus because it meant giving up his money, serving "master Money" will tear us away from allegiance to God (Matthew 19:16-22).

Still others, like seed sown among thorns, hear the word; but the worries of this life, the deceitfulness of wealth and the desires for other things come in and choke the word, making it unfruitful. —Mark 4:18–19

No one can serve two masters. Either he will hate the one and love the other, or he will be devoted to the one and despise the other. You cannot serve both God and Money. —Matthew 6:24

Then Jesus said to his disciples, "I tell you the truth, it is hard for a rich man to enter the kingdom of heaven. Again I tell you, it is easier for a camel to go through the eye of a needle than for a rich man to enter the kingdom of God."
—Matthew 19:23–24

The Love of Money Leads to Destruction.

People who love money will do anything to get it. The grip that money can have over one's life can push one to resort to devious and exploitive means.

You want something but don't get it. You kill and covet, but you cannot have what you want. You quarrel and fight. You do not have, because you do not ask God. When you ask, you do not receive, because you ask with wrong motives, that you may spend what you get on your pleasures. —James 4:2–3

People who want to get rich fall into temptation and a trap and into many foolish and harmful desires that plunge men into ruin and destruction. For the love of money is a root of all kinds of evil. Some people, eager for money, have wandered from the faith and pierced themselves with many griefs. —1 Timothy 6:9–10

By your great skill in trading you have increased your wealth, and because of your wealth your heart has grown proud. —Ezekiel 28:5

Trust in God, Not Money.

Money's false promises are fleeting and ultimately unsatisfying. God's promises are eternal and always trustworthy.

Keep your lives free from the love of money and be content with what you have, because God has said, "Never will I leave you; never will I forsake you." —Hebrews 13:5

Money's False Promises	The Bible's Promises
SECURITY	Command those who are rich in this present world not to be arrogant nor to put their hope in wealth, which is so uncertain, but to put their hope in God, who richly provides us with everything for our enjoyment. —1 Timothy 6:17
POWER	So do not fear, for I am with you; do not be dismayed, for I am your God. I will strengthen you and help you; I will uphold you with my righteous right hand.... For I am the Lord, your God, who takes hold of your right hand and says to you, Do not fear; I will help you. —Isaiah 41:10, 13
PRIVILEGE AND SOCIAL STANDING	People will come from east and west and north and south, and will take their places at the feast in the kingdom of God. Indeed there are those who are last who will be first, and first who will be last. —Luke 13:29–30
SUCCESS	Has not God chosen those who are poor in the eyes of the world to be rich in faith and to inherit the kingdom he promised those who love him? —James 2:5
LOVE AND ATTENTION	The Lord your God is with you, he is mighty to save. He will take great delight in you, he will quiet you with his love, he will rejoice over you with singing. —Zephaniah 3:17
PEACE OF MIND	Come to me, all you who are weary and burdened, and I will give you rest. —Matthew 11:28
FREEDOM FROM CONSEQUENCES	Wealth is worthless in the day of wrath, but righteousness delivers from death. —Proverbs 11:4
HAPPINESS	Delight yourself in the Lord and he will give you the desires of your heart. —Psalm 37:4

WHY GIVE?

Giving Brings Freedom.

When we release our grip on money, we break free from the grip money has on our lives. Giving keeps us from spiraling down the destructive path of greed. If you want to be free from materialism and the love of money, start by giving.

Be on your guard against all kinds of greed; a man's life does not consist in the abundance of his possessions. —LUKE 12:15

Whoever loves money never has money enough; whoever loves wealth is never satisfied with his income. —ECCLESIASTES 5:10

What good will it be for a man if he gains the whole world, yet forfeits his soul? Or what can a man give in exchange for his soul? —MATTHEW 16:26

Giving Is Our Worshipful Obligation.

In the act of giving we worship God by acknowledging that it is ultimately God's money and it is his right to instruct us how to use it. Theologian Richard Foster suggests that rather than approaching the question of giving as "How much of my money should I give God?" we should ask, "How much of God's money should I keep for myself?"

"Will a man rob God? Yet you rob me. But you ask, 'How do we rob you?' In tithes and offerings. You are under a curse—the whole nation of you—because you are robbing me. Bring the whole tithe into the storehouse, that there may be food in my house. Test me in this," says the LORD Almighty, "and see if I will not throw open the floodgates of heaven and pour out so much blessing that you will not have room enough for it." —MALACHI 3:8–10

Then he will say to those on his left, "Depart from me, you who are cursed, into the eternal fire.... For I was hungry and you gave me nothing to eat, I was thirsty and you gave me nothing to drink, I was a stranger and you did not invite me in, I needed clothes and you did not clothe me, I was sick and in prison and you did not look after me." They also will answer, "Lord, when did we see you hungry or thirsty or a stranger or needing clothes or sick or in prison, and did not help you?" He will reply, "I tell you the truth, whatever you did not do for one of the least of these, you did not do for me." Then they will go away to eternal punishment, but the righteous to eternal life. —MATTHEW 25:41–46

And do not forget to do good and to share with others, for with such sacrifices God is pleased. —HEBREWS 13:16

Giving Makes Us Trust God.

Stockpiling money may be a sign of trusting in money rather than God. Giving helps focus one's eyes back on God, seeking him as the first priority and relying on him to supply our needs.

And why do you worry about clothes? See how the lilies of the field grow. They do not labor or spin. Yet I tell you that not even Solomon in all his splendor was dressed like one of these. If that is how God clothes the grass of the field, which is here today and tomorrow is thrown into the fire, will he not much more clothe you, O you of little faith? So do not worry, saying, "What shall we eat?" or "What shall we drink?" or "What shall we wear?" For the pagans run after all these things, and your heavenly Father knows that you need them. But seek first his kingdom and his righteousness, and all these things will be given to you as well. Therefore do not worry about tomorrow, for tomorrow will worry about itself. Each day has enough trouble of its own. —MATTHEW 6:28–34

Giving Is a Fundamental Part of Following Jesus.

Following Jesus requires earthly sacrifice for heavenly gain. Christian author Randy Alcorn said, "The more holdings we have on earth, the more likely we are to forget that we're citizens of another world ... and our inheritance lies there, not here."

And anyone who does not carry his cross and follow me cannot be my disciple.... Any of you who does not give up everything he has cannot be my disciple. —LUKE 14:27, 33

Give to everyone who asks you, and if anyone takes what belongs to you, do not demand it back. Do to others as you would have them do to you. —LUKE 6:29b–31

I tell you the truth, at the renewal of all things, when the Son of Man sits on his glorious throne, you who have followed me will also sit on twelve thrones, judging the twelve tribes of Israel. And everyone who has left houses or brothers or sisters or father or mother or children or fields for my sake will receive a hundred times as much and will inherit eternal life. —MATTHEW 19:28–29

Giving is a Privilege.

Whether we have been blessed with much or with little, we can be part of God's plan. Financial giving is one of many ways to do the Lord's work. As God has blessed you, you can bless others.

And now, brothers, we want you to know about the grace that God has given the Macedonian churches. Out of the most severe trial, their overflowing joy and their extreme poverty welled up in rich generosity. For I testify that they gave as much as they were able, and even beyond their ability. Entirely on their own, they urgently pleaded with us for the privilege of sharing in this service to the saints. —2 CORINTHIANS 8:1–4

We have different gifts, according to the grace given us. If a man's gift is prophesying, let him use it in proportion to his faith. If it is serving, let him serve; if it is teaching, let him teach; if it is encouraging, let him encourage; if it is contributing to the needs of others, let him give generously. —ROMANS 12:6–8a

All the believers were one in heart and mind. No one claimed that any of his possessions was his own, but they shared everything they had.... There were no needy persons among them. For from time to time those who owned lands or houses sold them, brought the money from the sales and put it at the apostles' feet, and it was distributed to anyone as he had need. —ACTS 4:32–35

Giving Comes from Love

Missionary Amy Carmichael said, "You can give without loving, but you cannot love without giving." God gave generously to us out of his great love, and we give generously out of our love for others.

This is how we know what love is: Jesus Christ laid down his life for us. And we ought to lay down our lives for our brothers. If anyone has material possessions and sees his brother in need but has no pity on him, how can the love of God be in him? Dear children, let us not love with words or tongue but with actions and in truth. —1 JOHN 3:16–18

Suppose a brother or sister is without clothes and daily food. If one of you says to him, "Go, I wish you well; keep warm and well fed," but does nothing about his physical needs, what good is it? In the same way, faith by itself, if it is not accompanied by action, is dead. —JAMES 2:15–17

PROVERBS ABOUT MONEY

Proverb	Scripture
BRIBERY	A greedy man brings trouble to his family, but he who hates bribes will live. —Proverbs 15:27
	A wicked man accepts a bribe in secret to pervert the course of justice. —Proverbs 17:23
DEBT	Do not be a man who strikes hands in pledge or puts up security for debts; if you lack the means to pay, your very bed will be snatched from under you. —Proverbs 22:26–27
	The rich rule over the poor, and the borrower is servant to the lender. —Proverbs 22:7
DILIGENCE	Lazy hands make a man poor, but diligent hands bring wealth. He who gathers crops in summer is a wise son, but he who sleeps during harvest is a disgraceful son. —Proverbs 10:4–5
ENVY	A heart at peace gives life to the body, but envy rots the bones. —Proverbs 14:30
FRAUD	Food gained by fraud tastes sweet to a man, but he ends up with a mouth full of gravel. —Proverbs 20:17
GENEROSITY	He who is kind to the poor lends to the Lord, and he will reward him for what he has done. —Proverbs 19:17
	A generous man will himself be blessed, for he shares his food with the poor. —Proverbs 22:9
HOARDING GOODS	People curse the man who hoards grain, but blessing crowns him who is willing to sell. —Proverbs 11:26
HONESTY IN BUSINESS	The wicked man earns deceptive wages, but he who sows righteousness reaps a sure reward. —Proverbs 11:18
	A fortune made by a lying tongue is a fleeting vapor and a deadly snare. —Proverbs 21:6
MODERATION	Do not wear yourself out to get rich; have the wisdom to show restraint. —Proverbs 23:4
PATIENCE	Dishonest money dwindles away, but he who gathers money little by little makes it grow. —Proverbs 13:11
REPUTATION	A good name is more desirable than great riches; to be esteemed is better than silver or gold. —Proverbs 22:1
STINGINESS	A stingy man is eager to get rich and is unaware that poverty awaits him. —Proverbs 28:22
SUCCESS	Humility and the fear of the Lord bring wealth and honor and life. —Proverbs 22:4
	Whoever trusts in his riches will fall, but the righteous will thrive like a green leaf. —Proverbs 11:28
TRUE WEALTH	How much better to get wisdom than gold, to choose understanding rather than silver! —Proverbs 16:16
WORK	He who works his land will have abundant food, but he who chases fantasies lacks judgment. —Proverbs 12:11

HOW TO HONOR GOD WITH MONEY

1. Ask God to help you depend on him instead of money.

You say, "I am rich; I have acquired wealth and do not need a thing." But you do not realize that you are wretched, pitiful, poor, blind and naked. I counsel you to buy from me gold refined in the fire, so you can become rich.... Those whom I love I rebuke and discipline. So be earnest, and repent. Here I am! I stand at the door and knock. If anyone hears my voice and opens the door, I will come in and eat with him, and he with me. To him who overcomes, I will give the right to sit with me on my throne. —Revelation 3:17–21a

But remember the Lord your God, for it is he who gives you the ability to produce wealth. —Deuteronomy 8:18a

2. Stay focused on what matters most.

Better a little with the fear of the LORD than great wealth with turmoil. Better a meal of vegetables where there is love than a fattened calf with hatred. —PROVERBS 15:16–17

Jesus replied: "Love the Lord your God with all your heart and with all your soul and with all your mind. This is the first and greatest commandment. And the second is like it: Love your neighbor as yourself." —MATTHEW 22:37–39

Family Budget

3. Remember that God is always faithful.

He who did not spare his own Son, but gave him up for us all—how will he not also, along with him, graciously give us all things? —ROMANS 8:32

"For I know the plans I have for you," declares the LORD, "plans to prosper you and not to harm you, plans to give you hope and a future." —JEREMIAH 29:11

4. Ask God for your needs.

Give me neither poverty nor riches, but give me only my daily bread. Otherwise, I may have too much and disown you and say, "Who is the LORD?" Or I may become poor and steal, and so dishonor the name of my God. —PROVERBS 30:8–9

5. Ask for wisdom in financial matters.

If any of you lacks wisdom, he should ask God, who gives generously to all without finding fault, and it will be given to him. —JAMES 1:5

6. Handle money honestly and responsibly.

Give everyone what you owe him: If you owe taxes, pay taxes; if revenue, then revenue; if respect, then respect; if honor, then honor. —ROMANS 13:7

7. Put your money to work for God's purposes.

Sell your possessions and give to the poor. Provide purses for yourselves that will not wear out, a treasure in heaven that will not be exhausted, where no thief comes near and no moth destroys. —LUKE 12:33

8. Be ready to give freely.

If there is a poor man among your brothers in any of the towns of the land that the LORD your God is giving you, do not be hardhearted or tightfisted toward your poor brother. —DEUTERONOMY 15:7

9. Practice being content with what you have.

But godliness with contentment is great gain. For we brought nothing into the world, and we can take nothing out of it. But if we have food and clothing, we will be content with that. —1 TIMOTHY 6:7–8

I have not coveted anyone's silver or gold or clothing. You yourselves know that these hands of mine have supplied my own needs and the needs of my companions. In everything I did, I showed you that by this kind of hard work we must help the weak, remembering the words the Lord Jesus himself said: "It is more blessed to give than to receive." —ACTS 20:33–35

10. Praise God for his blessings!

Praise the LORD. Blessed is the man who fears the LORD, who finds great delight in his commands. His children will be mighty in the land; the generation of the upright will be blessed. Wealth and riches are in his house, and his righteousness endures forever. Even in darkness light dawns for the upright, for the gracious and compassionate and righteous man. Good will come to him who is generous and lends freely, who conducts his affairs with justice. —PSALM 112:1-5

DO'S AND DON'TS WITH MONEY

Don't	Do
Don't love it! LUKE 16:13	**Love the Lord.** DEUTERONOMY 6:5
Don't think it will last. JEREMIAH 17:11	**Only the things of God will last.** MATTHEW 19:21
Don't think it can save you. PSALM 37:16–17	**Remember that only God can save you.** PSALM 27:1
Don't serve it. MATTHEW 6:24	**Serve the Lord.** 1 PETER 5:2; MARK 12:41–44
Don't envy others who have it. EXODUS 20:17	**Be content with what you have.** LUKE 3:14
Don't hoard it. JAMES 5:3–6	**Remember that God provides.** JOB 1:20–21; JAMES 4:13–15
Don't be foolish with it. PROVERBS 17:16	**Use it wisely.** PROVERBS 31:10–31
Don't think it can compensate for turmoil. PROVERBS 15:16–17	**Find peace in God.** ROMANS 15:13
Don't rely on it. PSALM 62:10	**Rely on the Lord.** PROVERBS 18:10–11
Don't think it can buy God's blessings. ACTS 8:9–24	**Find blessings by living for God.** 2 CORINTHIANS 6:10
Don't use it for fraud. MICAH 2:2	**Repay your debts with it.** PSALM 37:21
Don't oppress people to get it. PROVERBS 22:16; AMOS 2:6–7	**Work to get it.** 2 THESSALONIANS 3:9–11
Don't steal it. TITUS 2:9–10; EXODUS 20:15	**Handle it justly.** LEVITICUS 25:14; PSALM 112:5
Don't give special honor to those who have it. JAMES 2:2–6	**Give it to those in need.** MATTHEW 5:41–42
Don't use it dishonestly. PROVERBS 13:11	**Be trustworthy with it.** PROVERBS 11:1
Don't use it for evil. EZEKIEL 8:12–13	**Honor God with it.** PROVERBS 3:9–10
Don't extort it. EZEKIEL 22:29	**Earn it.** PROVERBS 13:4
Don't be greedy for it. LUKE 12:15	**Give it intentionally.** 1 CORINTHIANS 16:2
Don't worry about it. MATTHEW 6:34	**Know that God will take care of you.** PROVERBS 15:25

WHAT THE BIBLE SAYS ABOUT *Prayer*

PRAYER IS AN IMPORTANT PART OF HOW WE RELATE TO GOD. Many religions recognize the need for prayer, but what does the Bible say about it? Does God hear all our prayers? Do some people get special access to God? Is there a prayer technique that will get you what you want? God's Word answers these questions, and also gives us guidance as we struggle with tougher questions such as, Why didn't God answer my prayer? Why should I pray at all?

*T*hree Things to Know Before You Pray

1. **GOD CARES FOR YOU.** Because of God's unfailing love for us, we can bring anything and everything in our hearts to God in prayer. Prayer is a safe place of trust.

   Cast all your anxiety on him because he cares for you.—1 Peter 5:7

   I trust in God's unfailing love for ever and ever.—Psalm 52:8

2. **GOD HEARS YOUR PRAYERS.** God Almighty is listening. Because we are his beloved children, no prayer is too small for him to hear.

   He will respond to the prayer of the destitute; he will not despise their plea.—Psalm 102:17

   How gracious he will be when you cry for help! As soon as he hears, he will answer you.—Isaiah 30:19

   For the eyes of the Lord are on the righteous and his ears are attentive to their prayer.—1 Peter 3:12a

What Is Prayer?

At its base, prayer is talking with God. We can pray alone or in a group; silently or aloud; using a written prayer or a spontaneous one. But to be in prayer is more than just speaking words. Scripture portrays a life of continual prayer, meaning a kind of openness toward God in all we do (1 Thess. 5:17). Our entire lives should be prayers to God, exhibiting the praise and love of our Creator and Savior.

3. **YOU CAN PRAY WITH CONFIDENCE.** You don't have to be a prayer giant to come confidently to God in prayer. As believers, we can all equally approach God because of our unique standing in Jesus.

   In him [Jesus] and through faith in him we may approach God with freedom and confidence.—Ephesians 3:12

   Let us then approach God's throne of grace with confidence, so that we may receive mercy and find grace to help us in our time of need.—Hebrews 4:16

*W*hy Pray?

PRAYER IS IMPORTANT. God's Word instructs believers to make prayer a high priority. God wants to hear from his children.

   Devote yourselves to prayer.—Colossians 4:2

   I urge, then, first of all, that petitions, prayers, intercession and thanksgiving be made for all people.—1 Timothy 2:1 (Also see verse 8)

Prayer should not be regarded "as a duty which must be performed, but rather as a privilege to be enjoyed, a rare delight that is always revealing some new beauty."—E. M. Bounds

PRAYER DRAWS US CLOSE TO GOD. In prayer, we worship, confess our sins, bring our requests to God, and wait and listen for him to speak. In short, we enter deeply and directly into relationship with God. Through communion with God, our hearts and minds will be changed to be more like our Lord, and we will grow to know his perfect will for our lives.

> "Prayer is a strong wall and fortress of the church; it is a goodly Christian weapon."
> —Martin Luther

> *Do not conform to the pattern of this world, but be transformed by the renewing of your mind. Then you will be able to test and approve what God's will is—his good, pleasing and perfect will.*—Romans 12:2

> *So all of us who have had that veil removed can see and reflect the glory of the Lord. And the Lord—who is the Spirit—makes us more and more like him as we are changed into his glorious image.*—2 Corinthians 3:18 NLT

PRAYER IS POWERFUL. God not only hears our prayers, but he is acting on them. Our prayer requests bring about real change in the world and in the lives of the people we pray for.

> *Ask and it will be given to you; seek and you will find; knock and the door will be opened to you. For everyone who asks receives; the one who seeks finds; and to the one who knocks, the door will be opened.*—Matthew 7:7–8

> *If you believe, you will receive whatever you ask for in prayer.*—Matthew 21:22 (Mark 11:24; John 15:7, 16)

> *And the prayer offered in faith will make the sick person well....*
> *The prayer of a righteous person is powerful and effective.*—James 5:15–1

> *Dear friends, if our hearts do not condemn us, we have confidence before God and receive from him anything we ask, because we keep his commands and do what pleases him.*—1 John 3:21–22

> Prayer as a relationship is probably your best indication about the health of your love relationship with God. If your prayer life has been slack, your love relationship has grown cold."—John Piper

PRAYER BRINGS PEACE. When we are at our wit's end, Scripture tells us to turn all those anxieties over to God who will give us peace of mind.

> *Do not be anxious about anything, but in every situation, by prayer and petition, with thanksgiving, present your requests to God. And the peace of God, which transcends all understanding, will guard your hearts and your minds in Christ Jesus.*—Philippians 4:6–7

PRAYER PROTECTS US. We have Almighty God on our side! Jesus showed believers the importance of praying for protection and deliverance. (Also see 2 Cor. 10:4; Eph. 6:10–18.)

> *Jesus' prayer for his disciples: My prayer is not that you take them out of the world but that you protect them from the evil one.*—John 17:15

> *The Lord's Prayer: And lead us not into temptation, but deliver us from the evil one.*—Matthew 6:13

> *Jesus warns his disciples: Be always on the watch, and pray that you may be able to escape all that is about to happen, and that you may be able to stand before the Son of Man.*—Luke 21:36

The Prayers of Jesus

Jesus took time to pray to God the Father. Jesus "often withdrew to lonely places and prayed" (Luke 5:16) and he would pray for long stretches of time (Luke 6:12).

JESUS:

- Prayed for his followers. John 17:9
- Prayed for the children. Matthew 19:13
- Praised the Father in prayer. Matthew 11:25
- Prayed for himself. John 17:1
- Prayed for Simon Peter. Luke 22:32
- Thanked the Father in prayer. John 11:41; Luke 24:30
- Asked the Father to forgive sinners. Luke 23:34a
- Prayed with his last words on the cross. Luke 23:46
- Prayed that his Father's will be done. Matthew 26:39; Luke 22:42

Four Kinds of Prayer

There are many types of prayer. Below are several main categories of prayer. A person may pray one or all of these in a single prayer time, and in any order. You can remember these categories with the acronym ACTS.

Adoration

Prayer, first and foremost, ought to be about worship. God alone is worthy of undiluted praise. That would be true even if God never gave us a thing, and that is why adoration is distinct from thanksgiving. Notice that the Lord's Prayer begins with "Our Father in heaven, hallowed be your name" (Matt. 6:9). Holding up God's name for praise is our prime duty in prayer. Examples: 1 Chron. 29:10; 2 Chron. 6:26–27; Luke 2:37.

Confession

"Forgive us our sins, for we also forgive everyone who sins against us" (Luke 11:4). Knowing that human sin blocks communication with God, Jesus taught his disciples to pray this way to make sure that there are no stumbling blocks between God and them. Examples: 2 Chron. 7:14; Dan. 9:4–19; 1 John 1:8–9.

Thanksgiving

Thanksgiving is praise for something God has done for us or given to us—or for what we trust him to do. The apostle Paul thanked God for the believers in Philippi: "I thank my God every time I remember you. In all my prayers for all of you, I always pray with joy because of your partnership in the gospel from the first day until now" (Phil. 1:3–5). Examples: Ps. 100:4; 107:1; 118:21; Matt. 14:19; Eph. 1:15–16; 1 Thess. 1:2; 5:16–18; 1 Tim. 4:4.

Supplication (Also called Petition)

Our heavenly Father wants his children to bring their requests to him (Phil. 4:6). Jesus taught, "If you, then, though you are evil, know how to give good gifts to your children, how much more will your Father in heaven give good gifts to those who ask him!" (Matt. 7:11). Intercession is a type of supplication where we pray for the needs and concerns of others. And we should not just pray for our friends, but also "...pray for those who persecute you" (Matt. 5:44). Examples: Gen. 24:12–15; 1 Sam. 7:8.

How to Pray

PRAY ALWAYS. We should live in a constant attitude of prayer. John MacArthur, a Christian author and pastor, explains that praying continually means "you live your life and your experiences of life with a constant, close connection to the Lord and are drawn into his presence through everything." (Also see Ps. 1; Josh. 1:8.)

Rejoice always, pray continually [or "pray without ceasing"], give thanks in all circumstances; for this is God's will for you in Christ Jesus.—1 Thessalonians 5:16–18

PRAY ACCORDING TO GOD'S WILL. In all requests, we should keep the perspective that it is always "if the Lord wills." He is still in charge and knows best.

Now listen, you who say, "Today or tomorrow we will go to this or that city, spend a year there, carry on business and make money." Why, you do not even know what will happen tomorrow.... Instead, you ought to say, "If it is the Lord's will, we will live and do this or that."—James 4:13–15

This is the confidence we have in approaching God: that if we ask anything according to his will, he hears us. And if we know that he hears us—whatever we ask—we know that we have what we asked of him.—1 John 5:14–15

PRAY IN THE HOLY SPIRIT. Every time you pray, come with an open heart allowing God's Spirit in you to guide your prayers. Where we are inadequate, the Spirit knows exactly the right thing to say. (Also see Rom. 8:15–16; Eph. 5:18.)

And pray in the Spirit on all occasions with all kinds of prayers and requests. With this in mind, be alert and always keep on praying for all the Lord's people.—Ephesians 6:18

But you, dear friends, by building yourselves up in your most holy faith and praying in the Holy Spirit, keep yourselves in God's love as you wait for the mercy of our Lord Jesus Christ to bring you to eternal life.—Jude 20–21

We do not know what we ought to pray for, but the Spirit himself intercedes for us through wordless groans. And he who searches our hearts knows the mind of the Spirit, because the Spirit intercedes for God's people in accordance with the will of God.—Romans 8:26–27

> "Don't pray when you feel like it. Have an appointment with the Lord and keep it. A man is powerful on his knees." —Corrie Ten Boom

ASK IN FAITH—AND ALSO FOR FAITH. Faith may move mountains, but having that faith is often easier said than done. The Gospel of Mark tells a story of a father who wanted to fully believe that Jesus would answer his request to heal his son. The father cried out to Jesus, "I do believe; help me overcome my unbelief!" Even though this father had difficulty with faith, Jesus healed his son (Mark 9:14–29). Like this father, we too can pray for stronger faith.

Jesus replied, "Truly I tell you, if you have faith and do not doubt, not only can you do what was done to the fig tree, but also you can say to this mountain, 'Go, throw yourself into the sea,' and it will be done. If you believe, you will receive whatever you ask for in prayer."—Matthew 21:21–22

If any of you lacks wisdom, you should ask God, who gives generously to all without finding fault, and it will be given to you. But when you ask, you must believe and not doubt, because the one who doubts is like a wave of the sea, blown and tossed by the wind. That person should not expect to receive anything from the Lord.—James 1:5–7

PRAY IN JESUS' NAME. Jesus' death on the cross removed the "sin block" for all who believe. The lines of communication are now open for those who trust in Christ. This is what it means to pray in Jesus' name, for only through Jesus will any prayer be heard by God.

You did not choose me, but I chose you and appointed you so that you might go and bear fruit—fruit that will last—and so that whatever you ask in my name the Father will give you.—John 15:16

Until now you have not asked for anything in my name. Ask and you will receive, and your joy will be complete.—John 16:24

PRAY WITH A CLEAR MIND AND SELF-CONTROL.

The end of all things is near. Therefore be alert and of sober mind so that you may pray.—1 Peter 4:7

PRAY IN AGREEMENT WITH OTHER BELIEVERS.

Again, truly I tell you that if two of you on earth agree about anything they ask for, it will be done for them by my Father in heaven. For where two or three gather in my name, there am I with them.—Matthew 18:19–20

KEEP ON PRAYING. Persevere as you wait for the Lord to answer. Pray and don't give up.

Be joyful in hope, patient in affliction, faithful in prayer.—Romans 12:12

*H*ow Not to Pray

God does not expect us to be perfect to come to him in prayer, but he does expect us to be honest. Prayer should be the place where we meet God honestly and openly. The Bible tells us that the prayers that God does not accept are the prayers of hypocrisy.

PRAYERS THAT ARE SPOKEN TO PAT OURSELVES ON THE BACK (Luke 18:9–14).

"God, I thank you that I am not like other people—robbers, evildoers, adulterers—or even like this tax collector."—Luke 18:11

PRAYERS THAT ARE PRAYED ALL THE WHILE IGNORING GOD'S INSTRUCTIONS (Psalm 66:18–20). God cares more about whether we are following him and how we are treating others, rather than if we are simply "going through the motions" of prayer. Those prayers end up being empty and hindered (1 Peter 3:7).

If anyone turns a deaf ear to my instruction, even their prayers are detestable.—Proverbs 28:9

For I desire mercy, not sacrifice, and acknowledgment of God rather than burnt offerings.—Hosea 6:6

PRAYERS THAT ARE FOR SELFISH REASONS. God knows all desires and no secret is hidden from him. Real prayer is an attitude of the heart (1 Thess. 5:16–18).

You desire but do not have, so you kill. You covet but you cannot get what you want, so you quarrel and fight. You do not have because you do not ask God. When you ask, you do not receive, because you ask with wrong motives, that you may spend what you get on your pleasures.—James 4:2–3

PRAYERS THAT ARE LONG AND LOUD TO GET ATTENTION AND ADMIRATION FROM OTHER PEOPLE (Mark 12:40; Luke 20:47).

> "We may pray most when we say least, and we may pray least when we say most."
> —Augustine of Hippo

And when you pray, do not be like the hypocrites, for they love to pray standing in the synagogues and on the street corners to be seen by others. Truly I tell you, they have received their reward in full. But when you pray, go into your room, close the door and pray to your Father, who is unseen. Then your Father, who sees what is done in secret, will reward you. And when you pray, do not keep on babbling like pagans, for they think they will be heard because of their many words. Do not be like them, for your Father knows what you need before you ask him.—Matthew 6:5–8

The Lord's Prayer MATTHEW 6:9–13; LUKE 11:2–4

When Jesus' disciples wanted to know how to pray, he taught them a prayer that is known today as "The Lord's Prayer." But this prayer is not so much Jesus' prayer as it is our prayer—it is how Jesus wants all his followers to pray.

The Seven Petitions

		Petition	Meaning
"Your"	1	Our Father in heaven, hallowed be your name,	**God's holiness** comes first. We should set forth God's name as holy.
	2	your kingdom come,	**God's sovereignty** is a fact affirmed by believers. We pray for the day when the world will see God's rule.
	3	your will be done, on earth as it is in heaven.	**God's authority** extends over all his creation. We pray for his authority to be known and obeyed in all the earth.
"Us"	4	Give us today our daily bread.	**God's providence** for our daily needs means that we may pray in faith that God will provide what we need or a way to obtain what we need.
	5	And forgive us our debts, as we also have forgiven our debtors.	**God's forgiveness** of our sins (debts) is possible because of Jesus' sacrifice on the cross. We can expect to see God's mercy in our lives according to how merciful we are to others (Mark 11:25).
	6	And lead us not into temptation,	**God's protection** from the things that will trip us up and undo us is something we need to ask for. Whether in trial or out of trial, we should seek God's protection.
	7	but deliver us from the evil one.	**God's deliverance** from enemies and especially from death and the Devil are legitimate concerns. We can be confident in our prayers for deliverance because we are more than conquerors through Christ (Rom. 8:37).

When God Says No

Anyone who has made prayer a part of his or her life knows that not everything asked for in prayer is granted. Prayer requests are just that, "requests," not demands or magic words that will make something happen. God hears our prayers and makes them effective, but he ultimately decides how to answer them—and sometimes that answer is no. "No" is one of the shortest yet hardest words to hear. But what does God's "no" mean? Often his "no" is not a "No way!" or "Forget about it," but rather it is, "No, I have something better in mind."

MOSES *Deut. 3:23–27*
Moses asked to cross over the Jordan River to see the Promised Land. God said "No," but he let Moses view the land from the top of a mountain.

DAVID *2 Sam. 7*

King David asked to set up God's temple. God said "No," but promised to set up David's kingdom forever, and later allowed David's son, Solomon, to build God's temple.

MARY AND MARTHA *John 11*

Mary and Martha asked Jesus to come quickly and heal their dying brother, but instead Jesus waited until their brother died. Then Jesus did something beyond their wildest expectations: he raised their brother from the dead! He answered their hearts' longing in a different way than what they had asked for.

PAUL *2 Cor. 12:7–10*

Paul pleaded three times for God to free him from a problem (the "thorn in his flesh"), but God did not remove it. However, through accepting the problem, Paul found that God's grace was sufficient for him and that power is made perfect in weakness. Paul found a greater meaning in his unanswered prayer.

JESUS *Matt. 26:36–42; Mark 14:32–36; Luke 22:39–44; John 18:11*

Jesus' prayer in the Garden of Gethsemane is the only prayer Jesus made that was denied. He prayed, that if it were possible, the suffering he was about to experience would be avoided. Yet he also prayed, "not my will, but yours be done." This example should teach us that there are some things we ask for—good as they may seem—that are not God's will for us. Jesus accepted the Father's will that he should suffer on our behalf. And just look at the powerful results: the forgiveness of sins and Jesus' resurrection from the dead! In Jesus' case, as in ours, the ultimate outcome from God will be life out of death.

When God Seems Silent

Sometimes we pray for change in our lives or the lives of our loved ones, and yet nothing happens. We do what we can, but God seems silent. From our perspective, our prayers may look like they are falling on deaf ears. Should we keep praying? Jesus addresses this important concern through two parables.

THE PARABLE OF THE FRIEND IN NEED *Luke 11:5–13*

After Jesus teaches his disciples how to pray in the Lord's Prayer, he continues to instruct them through a story about a man who needs to borrow some food from a friend late at night for a visitor who is coming. Jesus says that the man will receive what he needs from his friend, not because his friend is so generous, but simply because of the man's persistence in asking.

The Lesson: God, who is far more generous than the friend, will surely supply our needs if we consistently ask him.

THE PARABLE OF THE PERSISTENT WIDOW *Luke 18:1–8*

"Jesus told his disciples a parable to show them that they should always pray and not give up" (v. 1). In this parable, a widow keeps coming back day after day to seek justice from a corrupt judge. Though the judge does not care about the woman's concern, he gets tired of her bothering him so he grants her justice.

The Lesson: If even a corrupt judge grants persistent requests, how much more will God who is just and cares for us bring about justice in our lives when we continue to call on him.

Waiting for God to Answer

As we pray for all the things we want and need and hope for, we must remember that prayer is learning what God wants for our lives. When we make God our top priority in prayer, our will begins to align with his will. As we stay connected to God, he will transform our hearts to his will (See John 15).

But seek first his kingdom and his righteousness, and all these things will be given to you as well.—Matthew 6:33 (Luke 12:31)

Take delight in the Lord, and he will give you the desires of your heart.... Be still before the Lord and wait patiently for him. —Psalm 37:3–7a

One thing I ask from the Lord, this only do I seek: that I may dwell in the house of the Lord all the days of my life, to gaze on the beauty of the Lord and to seek him in his temple.—Psalm 27:4

The Who, What, Where, When and Why of Prayers in the Bible

The Bible provides us with many examples of all kinds of people praying for all sorts of things—in all imaginable situations! These examples show us that we can pray anytime and anywhere.

Who prayed?

- A national leader (Moses) *Ex. 32:11–13, 31–32; Num. 14:13–19*
- A child (Samuel) *1 Sam. 3:10*
- A military commander (Joshua) *Josh. 7:6–9*
- A weak man, once strong (Samson) *Judg. 16:28*
- A childless wife (Hannah) *1 Sam. 1:10–11*
- Priests *2 Chron. 30:27*
- Foreigners from distant lands *2 Chron. 6:32–33*
- An elderly widow (Anna) *Luke 2:36–38*
- A man on his deathbed (Hezekiah) *Isa. 38:2–3*
- A prophet (Isaiah) *Isa. 6:8*
- A king and musician (David) *Ps. 139*
- A grieving man (Jeremiah) *Lam. 3*
- A rebellious man (Jonah) *Jon. 2:2–9*
- Frightened sailors *Jon. 1:14*
- An elderly priest (Zechariah) *Luke 1:13*
- A blind beggar (Bartimaeus) *Mark 10:47*
- Jesus' family (his brothers and mother) *Acts 1:14*
- The Son of God *John 17*
- A seeking Gentile (Cornelius) *Acts 10:31*
- Widows *1 Tim. 5:5*
- Worshipers in heaven *Rev. 11:15–18*

Why did they pray?

- Were afraid for their life (Moses) *Ex. 17:4–5*
- Felt betrayed by God (Moses) *Num. 11:10–15*
- A sister was ill (Moses for Miriam) *Num. 12:13*
- Feared enemy nations (Joshua) *Josh. 6–8*
- Wanted revenge (Samson) *Judg. 16:28*
- Experienced life-changing disasters (Job) *Job 1:20–21*
- Were thankful to God for a child (Hannah) *1 Sam. 2:1–10*
- Saw God fulfill his promise (Solomon) *1 Kings 8:23–53*
- Didn't know what to do (Jehoshaphat) *2 Chron. 20:1–12*
- Couldn't go on anymore (Elijah) *1 Kings 19:4*
- Had a big decision and move to make (Nehemiah) *Neh. 2:4*
- Were very depressed *Ps. 116:3–4*
- A boy was demon possessed (Jesus' teaching) *Mark 9:29*
- Were thankful for other believers (Paul) *Eph. 1:16; 1 Thess. 1:2*
- Had new church leaders appointed *Acts 6:6; 14:23*
- A woman had died (Peter for Tabitha) *Acts 9:40–42*
- A father was ill (Paul for Publius's father) *Acts 28:8*
- Were awaiting the Lord's return (John) *Rev. 22:20*

What did they pray for?

- To spare a wicked city (Abraham for Sodom) *Gen. 18:23–25*
- A bride (Abraham's servant) *Gen. 24:12–14*
- Protection from a brother (Jacob) *Gen. 32:9–12*
- Their grandsons (Jacob) *Gen. 48:15–16*
- Someone else to do the work (Moses) *Ex. 4:13*
- To see God (Moses) *Ex. 33:18*
- To see the Promised Land (Moses) *Deut. 3:23–25*
- A child to be raised from the dead (Elijah for a widow's son) *1 Kings 17:21*
- Parenting instructions (Samson's father) *Judg. 13:8*
- A sign from God (Gideon) *Judg. 6:17–18*
- More sunlight (Joshua) *Josh. 10:12*
- A son (Hannah) *1 Sam. 1:11*
- To know what God wants them to do (David) *2 Sam. 5:19–23*
- Thunder and rain (Samuel) *1 Sam. 12:16–17*
- Forgiveness for adultery and murder (David) *Ps. 51; 2 Sam. 12:16*
- Wisdom (Solomon) *1 Kings 3:9*

- A heart wholly devoted to God *Ps. 86:11*
- Fire from heaven (Elijah) *1 Kings 18:36–38*
- Success (Jabez) *1 Chron. 4:10*
- Protection for their city (Hezekiah) *2 Kings 19:14–19*
- Strengthened hands (Nehemiah) *Neh. 6:9*
- Revival *Ps. 85:6–7*
- Protection from Satan (Jesus) *John 17:15*
- New believers to receive the Holy Spirit (Peter and John for believers in Samaria) *Acts 8:15*

- To speak God's Word with boldness (Apostles) *Acts 4:24–30; Eph. 6:19–20*
- Salvation of the Jews (Paul) *Rom. 10:1*
- That other believers would do right *2 Cor. 13:7*
- That the eyes of one's heart may be opened *Eph. 1:18*
- Government leaders *1 Tim. 2:1–2*
- Good health (John for Gaius) *3 John 1:2*
- The gospel to be spread *2 Thess. 3:1*

Where did they pray?

- Outdoors (Abraham's Servant) *Gen. 24:11–12*
- On the battlefield (Joshua) *Josh. 7:6–9*
- At the altar (Solomon) *2 Chron. 6:12–14*
- In their room (Daniel) *Dan. 6:10*
- In bed *Ps. 63:6*

- Inside the belly of a whale (Jonah) *Jonah 2:2–9*
- On a mountainside (Jesus) *Luke 6:12; 9:28*
- At the temple (Pharisee and tax collector) *Luke 18:10*
- From prison (Paul and Silas) *Acts 16:25*
- On the beach (disciples) *Acts 21:5*

When did they pray?

- At midnight *Ps. 119:62; Acts 16:25*
- Three times a day (Daniel) *Dan. 6:10*
- All through the night (Samuel) *1 Sam. 15:11*
- Every morning *Ps. 5:3*
- At fixed times daily *Ps. 55:17*

- Very early in the morning (Jesus) *Mark 1:35*
- While nearly drowning (Peter) *Matt. 14:30*
- While being crucified (Thief on the cross) *Luke 23:42*
- While being martyred (Stephen) *Acts 7:59–60*
- During a period set apart for prayer *1 Cor. 7:5*

How did they pray?

- Sitting (David) *2 Sam. 7:18*
- Standing (Solomon) *1 Kings 8:22 (Also Mark 11:25)*
- Kneeling (Peter) *Acts 9:40 (Also Dan. 6:10; Eph. 3:14; 1 Kings 8:54)*
- Facing Jerusalem (Daniel) *Dan. 6:10*
- In whispers *Isa. 26:16*
- In silence (Hannah) *1 Sam. 1:13*
- In a loud voice (Ezra) *Ez. 11:13*
- Looking up (Jesus) *John 11:41*
- With face to the ground (Jesus) *Matt. 26:39*

- With hands toward heaven (Solomon) *1 Kings 8:22 (Also Ps. 28:2)*
- With bitter weeping (Hezekiah) *Isa. 38:2–3*
- With tears and crying (Ezra) *Ezra 10:1 (Also Jesus; Heb. 5:7)*
- With joy! (Paul) *Phil. 1:4*
- As a group (believers) *Acts 1:14*
- Alone (Jesus) *Matt. 14:23*
- In unison (believers) *Acts 4:24*
- Earnestly! (Paul, Silas, and Timothy) *1 Thess. 3:10*

"No learning can make up for the failure to pray. No earnestness, no diligence, no study, no gifts will supply its lack."—E.M. Bounds

©2014 Bristol Works, Inc.   www.rose-publishing.com

Spiritual Gifts

Gifts for Life

You've become a believer and, perhaps, even joined a church. Wonderful! Your wonderful and challenging journey has just begun. The church as God's people has existed for many hundreds of years. The church you're becoming part of has likely been around for a few years already. How do you, being new to Christianity and the different practices in your specific congregation, go about being an active member in the life of the church?

The good news is that God himself will help each believer fit into God's church. The way God does this is through the special empowering of the Holy Spirit. God not only promised to be with each of his people "to the very end of the age" (Matt. 28:20), but he also promised to give us all the tools we need to serve him and each other—"you will receive power when the Holy Spirit comes on you" (Acts 1:8).

Gifts for the Body

The apostle Paul used a helpful illustration to explain this important teaching. When he explained what the church is and how it works, he used the image of the body.

Paul taught in his letters that for the church to function correctly, each member of the "body" must perform a role. God prepared *ministries*. Ministries are activities believers do that serve and allow the church to grow and mature. These ministries exist for each believer. God empowers every believer that forms part of the church to participate in one or more of these ministries. Through the work of the Holy Spirit, God gives gifts— in the sense of "presents"—to each believer. These gifts are called "spiritual gifts" because they are directly connected to the work of the Holy Spirit. Through these gifts, the life and the ministry of the church occur.

Read on to discover presents from God that allow us to be active members of Christ's body.

> "For just as each of us has one body with many members, and these members do not all have the same function, so in Christ we, though many, form one body, and each member belongs to all the others."
>
> —Romans 12:4–5

GIFTS?

The English word *gift* has two meanings:

1. A special ability or talent—such as playing piano, learning languages, and so on.

2. Something that is given without a charge and freely—such as a *present* for a birthday.

These two definitions color the way we read the New Testament passage. For some of these ministries God did give special talents and abilities—for healings, miracles, or speaking in tongues. However, the emphasis of the New Testament is not on the abilities themselves but on how they function in the ministries (services) of the church.

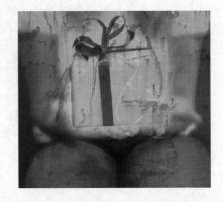

As we think about the spiritual gifts, we must keep in mind that what makes them spiritual is that they come from the Holy Spirit. And what makes them a gift is that the Holy Spirit freely gives them to us so we can use them in serving the body of Christ. Spiritual gifts are not meant to be stored or publicized. They are meant to be *used* for the service of the body.

THE REAL FORCE—THE HOLY SPIRIT

WHO IS THE SPIRIT?

The Holy Spirit is a person. The Spirit is God. Before his death and resurrection, Jesus promised his disciples to send the Spirit of truth, one who "will teach you all things and will remind you of everything I have said to you" (John 14:26). Jesus has not left his disciples alone. The Holy Spirit is with us.

WHAT DOES THE SPIRIT DO?

Besides giving us comfort as we wait for Jesus' return, the Spirit is actively moving within our lives.

THE HOLY SPIRIT ACTS IN THESE WAYS:

ADVOCATES (John 14:16)—"And I will ask the Father, and he will give you another advocate to help you and be with you forever." The Holy Spirit teaches, reveals, and interprets Jesus' words to his followers. The Holy Spirit is the divine presence with Jesus' followers.

CONVICTS (John 16:8–9)—"When he comes, he will prove the world to be in the wrong about sin and righteousness and judgment." The Holy Spirit will convince people of the need to repent from sin, that justice is only achieved through Christ, and that judgment of all humanity belongs to Jesus alone.

DRAWS TO CHRIST (John 16:14)—"He will glorify me because it is from me that he will receive what he will make known to you." The Holy Spirit leads people to Christ at all times.

TEACHES (John 14:26)—"But the Advocate, the Holy Spirit, whom the Father will send in my name, will teach you all things and will remind you of everything I have said to you."

SEALS (Eph. 1:13)—"And you also were included in Christ when you heard the message of truth, the gospel of your salvation. When you believed, you were marked in him with a seal, the promised Holy Spirit," Like a "seal of authenticity," the Holy Spirit marks us as God's property.

GUIDES (John 16:13)—"But when he, the Spirit of truth, comes, he will guide you into all the truth. He will not speak on his own; he will speak only what he hears, and he will tell you what is yet to come."

INTERCEDES (Rom. 8:26)—"In the same way, the Spirit helps us in our weakness. We do not know what we ought to pray for, but the Spirit himself intercedes for us through wordless groans."

EMPOWERS (Acts 1:8)—"But you will receive power when the Holy Spirit comes on you; and you will be my witnesses in Jerusalem, and in all Judea and Samaria, and to the ends of the earth."

These ministries identify the Holy Spirit's main function: to glorify Christ (John 16:14). Similarly, the primary function of our own ministries is *to glorify Christ*. The other critical function of our ministries—service—in the church is to allow the body to mature, to grow up. How do we reach this goal? Through the ministry of the Holy Spirit, especially his ministry of empowering believers, each Christian becomes an extension of God's own ministry among his people.

The Nurturing of the Body—Spiritual Gifts

One way the Holy Spirit empowers believers in the church is by creating ministries—opportunities to serve. Each believer contributes to the growth—both in numbers and in maturity—of the church. If the Holy Spirit is the "fire" that gives the body warmth and life, believers are the "members of the body" that keep it moving.

The Holy Spirit empowers believers to be part of these ministries. The spiritual gifts, then, are the tools we use to carry on those ministries. The function of the spiritual gifts is service. Paul's main interest in his letters to the early churches is to teach, guide, and help them to grow as the body of Christ.

FOUR LISTS of SPIRITUAL GIFTS in the BIBLE

EPHESIANS 4:11	ROMANS 12:6–8	1 CORINTHIANS 12:8–10	1 CORINTHIANS 12:28–30
Apostles	Prophecy	A word of wisdom	Apostles
Prophets	Service/serving	A word of knowledge	Prophets
Evangelists	Teaching	Faith	Teachers
Pastor-teachers (or pastors and teachers)	Encouragement	Healings	Miracles
	One who gives	Workings of miracles	Healings
	One who leads	Prophecy	Helps
	One who shows mercy	Distinguishing the spirits	Guidance
		Kinds of tongues	Speaking in tongues
		Interpretation of tongues	Interpreting tongues

Cessationism and Continuationism

One of the most debated issues in Christian theology is the question of what some people call the "extraordinary or miraculous" gifts of the Holy Spirit. These gifts are:

- APOSTLESHIP
- PROPHECY
- SPEAKING and INTERPRETING TONGUES
- WORKING of MIRACLES

MOST COMMON CHRISTIAN UNDERSTANDING of the GIFTS:

- Some believers hold firmly that these four gifts were limited to a period between Jesus' ascension and the death of the last Apostle, Jesus' beloved disciple John (about AD 90). People who hold this view are known as cessationists.

- Other Christians affirm the continuation of all of the gifts. They are continuationists.

- Many other believers would fall in an in-between category of being "open but cautious."

- Still other believers hold that some of the four gifts continue, while others have ceased.

Whatever view we take, we must remember that according to Paul, the spiritual gifts are meant to promote the unity of the body (1 Cor. 12:12; Eph. 4:12–13). In the letters of Paul, the unity of the body is necessary for the church's growth. The alternative, disunity and spiritual arrogance, tears down the church.

	Cessationists	Continuationists
DEFINITION	Cessation refers to the conviction that the extraordinary gifts that the Holy Spirit gives to the church ended with the closing of the apostolic age.	Continuation refers to the conviction that the Holy Spirit continues to grant extraordinary gifts to the church so it can continue its mission in the world.
MAIN POINTS	• The extraordinary gifts of the Holy Spirit were necessary to lay down the church's foundation—in other words, the teachings of the apostles. • Apostleship as a gift ended when the New Testament-era apostles died. Since the church has already been founded, the presence of apostles is no longer necessary. • Since the writings of the New Testament are finished, there is no need for new revelation. Thus, the gift of prophecy is no longer necessary. • Although God can and does do miracles, the gift of working of miracles by individuals has ended along with the gifts of apostleship and prophecy.	• Although the foundation work—for example, writing the New Testament—of apostles and prophets has ended, they had other functions—for example, planting new churches or bringing the gospel to people who've never heard it. • The extraordinary gifts of the Spirit aid the church in fulfilling its mission by providing encouragement, edification, and guidance. • Unlike prophecy as an office in the Old Testament, prophecy in the church is a gift that any believer can have, though some have a special gift in this area. Prophecy today does not reveal God's will the way the Scriptures did. Prophecy today communicates God's word to his people for encouragement, edification, and guidance. • Prophecy and all other gifts are dependent and subordinated to the authority of the Scriptures.

What is the Church?

The word *church* comes from a Greek word (*kuriaskos*) that means "belonging to the Lord." However, the most common word in the New Testament for *church* is *ekklesia*, which means "assembly, gathering." In the New Testament, it is used for the gathering of believers in specific places to worship and have fellowship together.

The church is made up of individuals. Yet, it is more than just the sum of individuals. It is a divine institution. The church is one (it is Christ's body) even if it can be found in many places and at different times. The church is universal. Christ's body is found throughout the world, and it is timeless. It contains all the people who have believed and those who will believe.

POWER and WEAKNESS

God empowers his people to carry on their ministries in the church. Spiritual gifts aren't only about the abilities one may have, but about what God is doing in and through the church and how we fit in. God is always active inside and outside the church. We must discern how he is active and ask him to empower us to be part of those activities.

The apostle Paul reminds us that our calling does not depend on who we are, what we have, and what we can do. God uses for his glory what we can offer. Yet, God is not limited to our personality and abilities. Surprisingly, according to Paul, God often calls us to serve him and others out of our weaknesses, even to the point of emphasizing that we are weak. It is in these cases that God's strength shines through our weaknesses. Paul concludes that, "For when I am weak, then I am strong" (2 Cor. 12:10). Paul teaches us that we must serve out of humility, dependence, and trust.

DESCRIPTION OF GIFTS

APOSTLE
1 Cor. 12:28–29; Eph. 4:11

We can speak of more than one kind of apostle in the New Testament. The first kind refers to those Jesus called and set apart, who witnessed his life and ministry. They are the first twelve disciples, although it also includes people like Paul and James (see 1 Cor. 9:1; 15:5–9; Gal. 2:9). A different type of apostle includes those who were especially appointed as missionaries to spread the gospel—for example, Barnabas (Acts 13:2–3; 14:14) and Silas (Acts 15:40; 1 Thess. 1:1, 2:6).

MIRACLES
1 Cor. 12:10, 28–29

For the apostle Paul, miracles existed to validate the message of the apostles—"I persevered in demonstrating among you the marks of a true apostle, including signs, wonders and miracles" (2 Cor. 12:12). Some examples of miracles in the New Testament are the judgment of Ananias and Sapphira (Acts 5:9–11) and the judgment of Elymas the magician (Acts 13:6–11). Many Christians believe that the need for these miracles for validation ended with the passing of the apostles. However, Christians affirm the possibility and existence of miracles from God today. Miracles strengthen the believers' faith. They build up the church.

EVANGELIST
Eph. 4:11

Though sharing the good news of the gospel is a privilege and responsibility of every believer, some people have the ability to present the message of salvation in a clear, simple, and engaging way. Those who fit in this ministry can provide leadership to all believers to carry on their task of evangelism.

TEACHING, PASTOR-TEACHER, *and* EXHORTATION
1 Cor. 12:28–29; Rom. 12:7-8; Eph. 4:11

Traditionally, the ministry of pastors is closely connected to that of teaching. In addition to caring for the members of each church, the other crucial role of pastors is to explain the apostolic teachings to believers. However, many people can thrive as teachers without having to become pastors. Teaching is a vital ministry of the body of Christ. Beyond giving information, teaching allows people to deepen their relationship with God. Furthermore, teaching equips believers to be aware of false teachings that they might encounter. Closely connected to other gifts, exhortation means that one comes alongside of someone with words of encouragement, comfort, consolation, and counsel to help them be all God wants them to be.

HEALINGS
1 Cor. 12:9, 28, 30

Connected to miracles, healings were also a demonstration of God's power that validated apostolic authority. The specific "office" of healer—if there was ever one—may have ended with the apostolic age. However, Christians continue to believe that God can and does heal as a response to prayer.

WORD of WISDOM *and* WORD of KNOWLEDGE
1 Cor. 12:8

We must understand these two gifts in the context of the whole letter. The Corinthian church seems to have struggled with being too impressed with, and attracted to, the more "flashy" gifts of tongues and prophecy. Although Paul does not deny their importance, he makes it clear that these gifts without love, wisdom, and knowledge are empty. Wisdom, the discerning and understanding of God's doings in the world and the way the world functions, is a critical ministry that allows all ministries and gifts of the church to work in harmony and unity. Knowledge allows believers to understand and explain God's revelation to others.

HELPING, SERVING, GIVING, *and* MERCY
1 Cor. 12:28, Rom. 12:7, 8

These different gifts are so closely related that some tend to assign them to the tasks of deacons. However, the overall context of these passages suggests that they are activities for all believers. These gifts are crucial for the maturity of the church. Service stands at the core of our calling. The practice of these gifts can be as varied as offering help to widows, orphans, and the poor, give aid for the daily activities in the church, and discerning when individuals or groups are in need of help to carry on their ministries.

FAITH
1 Cor. 12:9

This faith does not refer to "saving faith," which every believer has. Nor does it refer to the daily faith necessary for the Christian life (Eph. 2:8), which every believer is expected to exercise (Heb. 11). Rather, it refers to a faith that complements the other gifts and allows them to be daring and active. When the ministries of the church face odds that overwhelm most people, this ministry of faith challenges, encourages, and reminds people that we serve a powerful God who owns and controls all things.

LEADERSHIP *and* GUIDANCE
Rom. 12:8, 1 Cor. 12:28

Although traditionally these gifts have been related to the ministry of elders in the church, the context of the passages suggests that they are meant for all believers. These ministries are applicable to many areas of church life: goals for the church, teaching, evangelism, acts of mercy and service, and so on.

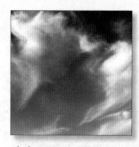

DISTINGUISHING BETWEEN SPIRITS
1 Cor. 12:10

In the context of the letter to the Corinthians, distinguishing (or discerning) between spirits may refer to two activities. One is the ability to recognize truth from error. In this sense, truth is a revelation from God, so this gift is the ability to discern when a prophecy actually comes from God. According to many believers, since God has stopped revealing his will in the same way he did in the Bible and since prophecies have stopped, this part of discerning is no longer necessary. However, the second activity is still important. It refers to the ministry that discerns when a teaching or a plan fits in with God's will, whether it comes from the leading of the Holy Spirit. It also includes the ability to discern when a new teaching contradicts the basic teachings of the Christian faith—for example, contradicts teaching on the Trinity, the person and ministry of Christ, the person and ministry of the Holy Spirit, the inspiration of the Scriptures.

TONGUES *and* INTERPRETATION *of* TONGUES
1 Cor. 12:10, 28, 30

The apostle Paul did not discourage speaking of tongues—in fact, he urged the Corinthian leaders to not forbid it (1 Cor. 14:39). However, Paul was correcting an error in the church. Some in the Corinthian church were too enchanted with the flashy gift of speaking in tongues. Paul reminds them that speaking in tongues without love is like a "resounding gong or a clanging cymbal." Paul's main concern is the edification of the church as a whole, as a body. He explains that speaking in tongues edifies the one speaking (1 Cor. 14:4). Thus, for the apostle Paul, speaking in tongues seems to be a secondary. Today, Christians are divided on whether the ministry of speaking in tongues has stopped or continues. Paul makes it clear that the unity of the body of Christ is far more important than speaking, or not speaking, in tongues.

SPIRITUAL GIFT QUESTIONNAIRE

This questionnaire is one of many tools to help you discern where you fit in the church's many ministries. It can help you to either learn or confirm areas of affinity—areas that you naturally tend to focus on. But as with most spiritual gifts tests, it is not meant to definitively *tell* you what your gift is. Simply knowing your spiritual gifts is not the goal, but rather knowing how to serve God as a member of Christ's body and serve are the real goals.

- *Ask God for guidance and wisdom to find your place in the church's ministry.*
- *Your life experience can be a good guide to find your interest and abilities.*
- *Be mindful of the needs of your church. Sometimes, God will call you to minister—serve—in places you might not prefer. The calling may be temporary or long term.*
- *Be ready, willing, and courageous. Obedience is challenging.*
- *Listen to the encouragement, wisdom, and guidance of other members of the body of Christ.*
- *Be prayerful about finding God's will for you.*

FOR EACH QUESTION, CHOOSE A RESPONSE BETWEEN 0 AND 3 AS FOLLOWS:

3 Consistently, almost always true   **2** Most of the time, usually true   **1** Some of the time, once in a while   **0** Not at all, never

---

1. _____ I am able to communicate effectively the message of salvation.

2. _____ I make critical decisions when necessary.

3. _____ I rejoice when meeting needs through sharing my possessions.

4. _____ I enjoy studying.

5. _____ I thrive when trusting God in difficult situations.

6. _____ I actively meet physical and practical needs.

7. _____ I can analyze events or ideas from different points of view.

8. _____ I naturally encourage others.

9. _____ I am acutely in tune with the emotions of other people.

10. _____ I am a cheerful giver.

11. _____ Yielding to God's will gives me great joy.

12. _____ It is very important for me to do things for people in need.

13. _____ I can identify those who need encouragement.

14. _____ I am sensitive to the hurts of people.

15. _____ I am sensitive to new truths and to how they apply to specific situations.

16. _____ I have experience with organizing ideas, resources, time, and people effectively.

17. _____ I am able to discern when sermons or teachings do not conform to the Scriptures.

18. _____ I can trust in God even in very difficult moments.

19. _____ I can discern where God wants a group to go and help it get there.

20. _____ I have the ability and desire to teach.

21. _____ I am sensitive to what people need.

22. _____ I have experience making effective and efficient plans for accomplishing the goals of a group.

23. _____ I can explain Scripture in simple and accessible ways.

24. _____ I spend time digging into facts.

25. _____ Sharing Christ with nonbelievers comes naturally to me.

26. _____ I can discern the motivation of persons and movements.

27. _____ I can delegate and assign meaningful work.

28. _____ I detect when people experience stress and distress.

29. _____ I desire to give generously and unpretentiously to worthwhile projects and ministries.

30. _____ I can relate God's truths to specific situations.

31. _____ I can organize facts into meaningful relationships.

32. _____ I can detect honesty when people share their religious experiences.

33. _____ I look for ways to encourage and comfort others around me.

34. _____ I am able to help people flourish in their ministries.

35. _____ I can make complex ideas and doctrines simple and accessible.

36. _____ I look for opportunities to establish relationships with non-believers.

Write your answer for each question, then add your answers for each gift. Pay attention to 2's or 3's. These are likely the gifts you are currently leaning toward.

GIFT	QUESTION NUMBER	YOUR ANSWER	TOTAL
Discernment	17		
	26		
	32		
Exhortation	8		
	13		
	33		
Evangelism	1		
	25		
	36		
Faith	5		
	11		
	18		
Giving	3		
	10		
	29		
Guidance	16		
	22		
	27		
Help/Serving	6		
	12		
	21		
Knowledge	4		
	24		
	31		
Leadership	2		
	19		
	34		
Mercy	9		
	14		
	28		
Teaching	20		
	23		
	35		
Wisdom	7		
	15		
	30		

Spiritual Disciplines

What are Spiritual Disciplines?

Understanding the power of sin over us will help us grasp the meaning and necessity for spiritual disciplines.

Sin

The Bible explains sin with several metaphors. Sin:

- Captures (Prov. 5:22; Heb. 12:1)
- Enslaves (Gen. 4:7; John 8:34; Rom. 7:14, 23; Gal. 3:22)
- Is deadly (Rom. 6:23; 5:12; Eph. 2:1)
- Is a sickness (Ps. 32:1–5; Isa. 53:5; Matt. 9:2, 5; 1 Peter 2:24)
- Is impurity (Zech. 13:1; Ps. 51:2; Isa. 1:18)
- Separates (Isa. 59:1–2; Eph. 2:12–16; 4:18)

Sin disguises itself as habits—that is, behaviors and thoughts that have become "second-nature." Many of the sins we commit come so naturally to us that we hardly notice them—whether they occur while driving on a busy freeway, having conversations about other people, abusing substances or other harmful things that may temporarily make us feel better. Habits require time and repetition to become entrenched. These habits enslave us, lead us to deadly consequences, make us sick, corrupt us, and ultimately separate us from God. We have to unlearn many of these behaviors and learn behaviors that are fit for the citizens of God's kingdom.

Spiritual disciplines are practices we do regularly that can help us change, with the power and grace of the Holy Spirit, our sinful habits into good habits that make us more like Christ and connect us closer to God.

Spiritual Disciplines and Salvation

We are saved by and through God's grace alone. We can do nothing to earn our salvation. Spiritual disciplines are not behaviors or practices that make us right with God in any way. They are tools that the Holy Spirit can use to renew our hearts. When we practice spiritual disciplines:

- We recognize that Jesus is the King of our lives.
- We acknowledge that we belong to him alone.
- We also seek to live out the fruit of the Spirit in our lives: love, joy, peace, patience, kindness, goodness, faithfulness, gentleness, and self-control (Gal. 5:22–23).

Spiritual disciplines *do not* help God to make our lives holy. Instead:

- They help us recognize God's callings and promptings in our lives, and identify those areas in our lives that still need to be renewed.
- They make us sensitive and humble to follow God's leading.
- They help us realize that we depend completely on God's grace at every moment and for everything.
- They train and equip us to respond in a worthy manner when life throws problems and storms at us.

"God has given us the Spiritual Disciplines as a means of receiving His grace and growing in Godliness. By them we place ourselves before God for Him to work in us."

—Donald S. Whitney, *Spiritual Disciplines for the Christian Life*

Spiritual Disciplines Should Be

- Instruments of God's grace which, through the Spirit, transform us daily into people who reflect Jesus' love, obedience, humility, and connection to God
- Activities that connect us deeply to other believers in our common desire to follow God's will
- A source of humility and dependence on God
- Experiences that enrich our lives and the lives of those around us
- Activities that occur in the context of God's whole body; spiritual disciplines, although often practiced alone, are not individualistic activities
- As much focused on building up God's body as building up each believer
- Practices that give us hope, despite our failings and limitations. We can hope that "he who began a good work in you will carry it on to completion until the day of Christ Jesus" (Phil. 1:6).
- Practices that permeate every area of our lives
- Disciplines that help us train for the life of faith, hope, and love to which Jesus has called us

Spiritual Disciplines Should Not Be

- Heavy loads of impossible, unrealistic, or unfair expectations for people
- Benchmarks to judge people's Christianity or maturity
- Individualistic attempts to be holy or perfect
- A measure of one's spiritual stature and strength
- A way to separate our "religiosity" from the rest of our lives
- A way to hide our sins with good works

Spiritual Disciplines and the Bible

Contemporary society is fascinated with spirituality. One can find all kinds of books about self-help or spiritual guidance and practices. How are Christian spiritual disciplines different from those offered in such books? The difference is simple, though profound.

POPULAR SPIRITUAL DISCIPLINES ARE:	BIBLICAL SPIRITUAL DISCIPLINES ARE:
For self-improvement	For the spiritual maturity of each person and the community as a whole
For self-realization—the fulfillment of one's abilities and potential	For realization of the fruit of the Spirit in one's life
For self-sufficiency	For dependence on God and interdependence with other believers within God's body
Based on one's own work and dedication	Based on the work of the Spirit in our lives, the support and encouragement of all believers, and the effort of each believer.

His divine power has given us everything we need for life and godliness through our knowledge of him who called us by his own glory and goodness.... For this very reason, make every effort to add to your faith goodness; and to goodness, knowledge; and to knowledge, self-control; and to self-control, perseverance; and to perseverance, godliness; and to godliness, brotherly kindness; and to brotherly kindness, love. For if you possess these qualities in increasing measure, they will keep you from being ineffective and unproductive in your knowledge of our Lord Jesus Christ.—**2 Peter 1:3, 5–8**

The Apostle Peter is clear: God has given us all we need, and we must make every effort to grow.

Spiritual Practice

Practicing spiritual disciplines is not easy. Jesus reminded the disciples that believers would experience hatred and persecution (John 15:18–25). Spiritual disciplines help us get ready for difficult moments: moments of persecution, temptation, doubt, and grief.

Moreover, spiritual disciplines help us to deepen our relationship with God. God does not wish a shallow, "good morning–see you later," type of relationship. God wishes to be in deep, satisfying, loving, transforming, and challenging relationships with us, individually and as a community of believers. Spiritual disciplines build in us the attitudes, emotions, thoughts, and actions that will promote the kind of relationship that our hearts yearn for.

Below is a list of common spiritual practices, by no means comprehensive, which many Christians have practiced throughout the centuries.

> "A disciplined person is someone who can do the right thing at the right time in the right way with the right spirit."
>
> —**John Ortberg,** *The Life You've Always Wanted: Spiritual Disciplines for Ordinary People*

1. **Bible Reading/Study**
2. **Prayer**
3. **Fasting**
4. **Worship**
5. **Service**
6. **Solitude**
7. **Discernment**
8. **Evangelism**

From Bad to Good Habits

1. **Know** your bad habits.
   - Pray that God will help you see the specific areas of your life that need changing;
   - Pray that God will give you the courage, strength, and help to face those areas.

2. **Confess** your weaknesses to God with a humble and hopeful heart.

3. **Submit** to God's call to change. Surrender your efforts and receive God's grace. Trust that God is with you and is helping you.

4. **Be accountable.**
   - Find one or more people you trust and ask them to pray with and for you about a specific area in your life that needs changing;
   - Allow them to be God's instruments in your life for that specific area.

5. **Train** to substitute a bad habit—sin—with a good habit—virtue.
   - If prayer is difficult for you, find a person who will pray with you, or begin a praying group that meets once a week.

6. **Be persistent.** Bad habits take a long time to form; it takes an equally long time to break them and acquire new habits.

7. **Be graceful** toward yourself and others.
   - It is highly possible that you will experience failure.
   - Remember, you are not changing just for your sake; you are allowing God's Spirit to work in your life.
   - Jesus gave his life for you. You are that valuable; God will patiently wait for you to get up and continue walking every time you stumble and fall.
   - Do not obsess over the actual change; it is not your job. The Holy Spirit is the one who renews and transforms us. Focus on the growing relationship with God. Let God be God and do what he does best: give you new life.

8. **Be grateful** for all the things you already are and have.
   - Thank God for every small change that occurs;
   - Thank God for every time you get up after a fall;
   - Thank the people around you for helping you along.

I. Scripture Reading and Studying

Biblical Basis and Examples

- Moses read the word of God to the people and commanded that it be read publicly—Ex. 24:7; Deut. 31:9–13
- Joshua was commanded to meditate on God's word day and night—Josh. 1:8
- Kings of Israel were to study the Scriptures—Deut. 17:18–19
- The longest psalm is a psalm about the value of knowing God's word—Ps. 119
- Paul required his letters be read publicly—Col. 4:16; 1 Thess. 5:27
- Paul urged Timothy to study the Word of God and handle it with care—2 Tim. 2:15
- The Ethiopian was reading God's Word and he became a follower of Jesus—Acts 8:27–40
- Jesus read the Bible and taught it to the people—Luke 4:16–21
- Jesus said the value of studying the Bible was to see that it spoke about him—John 5:39
- God's word is supposed to be close to the mouths and hearts of believers—Deut. 30:11–14; 32:47; Ps. 1:2; Rom. 10:8–11; Col. 3:16

The Disciplines Today

Jesus said: "I am the vine; you are the branches. If a man remains in me and I in him, he will bear much fruit; apart from me you can do nothing" (John 15:5).

- Reading the Bible is the best way to stay connected to God.
- Scripture reading is the lifeblood of the church. The Bible equips, trains, and empowers believers to fulfill God's calling (2 Tim. 3:17; 2 Peter 1:3–11; Heb. 13:21).
- Scripture reading and studying involves different activities: memorization, reflection, and transformative study.

Memorization

- When scuba divers face problems under water, they rely on their previous training to find a way out. When we face temptation or sudden grief, our "training" will kick in.
- All those verses we have memorized will come back; God will speak to us through them in unexpected ways.
- One of the best ways to memorize something is by finding partners who help and challenge you to work together.

Reflection

- It is often called *meditation*. It means that we allow the Bible to settle in our minds and hearts.

- We do this by thinking about it all day long, wondering what a passage or a verse means for us throughout the day's activities.
- Write a verse, or passage, on a small piece of paper and carry it along with you. If you are standing in line, waiting at a restaurant, or another short moment, take the paper out and think about how the text connects to your life at that specific moment.

Transformative Study

- Studying the Bible does not mean one becomes an expert in one passage or book. Studying the Bible means we dig deeply so we can be deeply transformed.
- The more we know about God, the more we can love him.
- God gave the Bible to the church. Reading and studying the Bible in community is most profitable.
- Traditionally, Christians have practiced this discipline by reading early in the morning, after meals, or before going to bed.
- Today there are many other opportunities for Bible reading, memorizing, and studying.
- The many hours we spend in transportation can be useful for listening to an audio recording of the Bible.
- The Internet is full of tools and helps for Bible reading and studying.

2. PRAYER

BIBLICAL BASIS AND EXAMPLES

- Many of the Psalms are prayers—for example, see Psalms 10, 59, 83, 86, and others
- The believer is to constantly be in an attitude of prayer—Luke 18:1; Eph. 6:18; Phil. 4:6; Col. 4:2; 1 Thess. 5:17; 1 Tim. 2:8
- Access to God through Jesus belongs to the believer—Heb. 4:16
- The manner of prayer calls for honest communication, not showy pretense or empty repetition—Eccl. 5:1–3; Matt. 6:5–7
- Prayer should not be done with an unforgiving attitude—Mark 11:25
- Prayer should be made in confident hope that God hears and knows our real needs—Matt. 7:7–11; Heb. 11:6

THE DISCIPLINES TODAY

- Prayer is commanded in the Bible. The discipline of prayer is a way to be obedient to this commandment.
- Often learning about the heroes of the faith is intimidating. Instead of being motivated, we might feel discouraged with the enormous challenge of their example.
- Who could fly a jet or run a marathon without much previous and rigorous training? No one is born knowing how to pray and being great at it.
- Learning to pray is a bit like learning to swim. It can only happen in the water, despite fears, insecurities, and doubts.
- Prayer requires *concentration* and *focus*.
  - Teaching ourselves to concentrate is one of the reasons we close our eyes.
  - But we need to close our ears and minds as well to the many distractions around us.
  - Spending a few minutes just to quiet mind and heart will help us achieve better concentration and focus.
- Prayer builds up our humility, dependence on God, and compassion for others.
- If praying on your own is difficult, make a "prayer date" with a friend you are comfortable with.
- Start by praying simple, short prayers—pray one minute, take a break and read or sing, then pray again.

- When you feel stuck, unmotivated, or without words—all very normal occurrences—pray a prayer from the Bible: a psalm, the Lord's Prayer (Matt. 6:9–13), Nehemiah's prayer (Neh. 1:5–11), Solomon's prayer (1 Kings 8:22–61).
- Your prayers do not have to be pretty—the Holy Spirit takes all of our prayers, pretty or not, and brings them before God the Father (Rom. 8:26–27).
- Make sure your prayers include, among other things, *praise* for God's greatness, *gratitude* for God's gifts, *petitions* for you and others, *confession* of your struggles and sins, and whatever the Spirit brings to your mind.
- The apostle Paul tells us to "pray continually" (1 Thess. 5:17). Is this even possible? Not immediately. Just as no one can run a marathon without training, no one can pray continually without training.
- Sometimes prayer is a "battleground." Prayer can be difficult and produce anxiety. Sometimes it is while praying that God reveals to us what needs changing, what needs to be done. Sometimes, prayer can be a painful mirror.
- Finally, our prayers are not primarily for changing God's mind about something; prayer changes our mind about who we are, what we need, and how we please God. Prayer is transformational.

3. Fasting

Biblical Basis and Examples

- The nation Israel fasted asking God's forgiveness—Judg. 20:26; 1 Sam. 7:6; Jer. 36:9; Ezra 8:21–23
- The city of Nineveh fasted asking God's forgiveness—Jonah 3:5–10
- Moses fasted when he received God's commandments—Ex. 34:28
- David fasted seeking God's forgiveness and guidance—2 Sam. 1:12, 3:35, 12:16–22
- Ezra fasted to ask God's forgiveness—Ezra 10:6
- Nehemiah fasted seeking God's favor—Neh. 1:4
- Daniel fasted seeking God's favor—Dan. 9:3, 10:2–3
- Anna fasted seeking God's favor and guidance—Luke 2:37
- Cornelius fasted seeking God's favor—Acts 10:30
- Paul fasted seeking God's guidance—Acts 9:9
- Jesus fasted in the wilderness seeking God's guidance—Matt. 4:2
- The manner of fasting is to be sincere, dedicated to God, without a public show—Matt. 6:16–18

The Disciplines Today

- Fasting may be the most neglected of all the spiritual disciplines today. It is easy to dismiss it as an old and quaint practice. But we miss an important and meaningful opportunity for spiritual growth.
- The central point of fasting is training for self-control (2 Peter 1:6; Gal. 5:23; 1 Peter 1:13).
- If we are to break the hold of habits—sin—in our lives, training for self-control is essential.
- Fasting is an effective approach to developing self-control because it deals with a very fundamental necessity of human existence: food.
- We need food to live; however, we can become enslaved by food—or other things we may need or simply want for our lives.
- If we are able to control things essential for life, we will be able to keep in check the things that are not essential for life.
- The practice of fasting fosters humility, reliance on God, compassion, gratitude, and self-control.
- Begin by fasting from food for a short period, such as skipping a meal. Build your fasting time up from there.

- As much as possible, use the time it takes to get or prepare food and eat it for prayer and Bible reflection.
- Fasting from food is the most obvious way to do it. However, you can also abstain from other things. For example, watching television (or other media) often consumes too much of our lives. That central place belongs to God alone.
- If you find you rely too much on caffeine to stay awake or for energy, it may be a good idea to fast from caffeine and be reminded that our dependence on God is sufficient.
- We can extend the same principle to many things around us: technology, music, sports, and so on.
- Internet, although a wonderful tool of communication, can absorb our time and attention in ways not even television could. Try a "media fast." Turning the computer off in order to be completely present in the lives of others has become a wonderful spiritual practice for many people today.

"First, let [fasting] be done unto the Lord with our eye singly fixed on Him. Let our intention herein be this, and this alone, to glorify our Father which is in heaven."

—(John Wesley, as found in the collection *Sermons On Several Occasions*)

4. WORSHIP

BIBLICAL BASIS AND EXAMPLES

- Worship must be to God and God alone—Ex. 20:1–6; Matt. 4:10
- Worship must be in Spirit and in truth—John 4:23–24
- Moses composed and taught a song about God to the people—Deut. 31:19–22; 32:1–47
- David danced in worship before the Lord—2 Sam. 6:14–16
- The entire book of Psalms is a book for worship—Ps. 8, 89, and 105 are examples
- Worship may be in a public place—Deut. 16:11; Luke 24:53
- It may be in a private residence—Acts 1:13–14; 5:42; 12:12; Rom. 16:5; Col. 4:15
- Worship may be done with instruments—Ps. 150
- It may be done in silence—Ps. 46:10; Hab. 2:20
- Worship may be done bowing or kneeling—Ps. 95:6
- It may be done upright or with hands raised—1 Tim. 2:8
- Paul tells believers to use psalms, hymns, and spiritual songs—Col. 3:16
- Believers are commanded to worship God regularly—Psalm 96:8–9; Heb. 10:25

THE DISCIPLINES TODAY

- Worship is more than an activity: it is an attitude—an attitude of awe and gratitude, of humble submission to God's greatness and grace, of obedience and love.
- Every activity and every relationship in our daily life can be a way to worship God.
- The spiritual discipline of worship is not limited to the activities we do on Sundays.
- We must train ourselves to recognize God's presence in the smallest of events and in the most casual of our relationships.
- This discipline will hone our humility, dependence on God, gratitude, obedience, and fellowship with God and our fellow believers.
- We can worship alone. However, worshiping with other believers has a way of connecting people in an incomparable way. Worship nurtures fellowship, promotes intimate relationships, and fosters the edification of Christ's body.
- Sunday worship is the best initial training ground for this discipline. As we continue developing this habit of worshiping God, we will see Sunday worship as the beginning of our worship, rather than as the only worship time.

- List your daily activities from dawn to bedtime. Reflect on how each of your activities and your attitudes toward them worship God. Sometimes they do not seem to worship God; is there any way you can make them worshipful?
- Take one event, activity, or relationship at a time and find ways it can bring worship to God. Perhaps all you need to do is dedicate the activity to God in prayer, or change an attitude toward a relationship that is difficult. Perhaps you need to stop an activity or event that does not glorify God.
- Just as prayer can occur all day long in the background of your mind and spirit, worshiping God occurs often unnoticed. If you make a habit of noticing and being mindful about God throughout your day, you will be able to express your joy, gratitude, sadness, frustration, anger, or love in different ways that bring worship to God.
- It is in this discipline that the previous disciplines are handy. You can express your worship through prayer, singing, or meditating on a Bible verse.

5. SERVICE

BIBLICAL BASIS AND EXAMPLES

- Jesus taught that true greatness is serving others—Matt. 20: 26–27; Mark 9:35
- Jesus illustrated the importance of service when he washed his disciples' feet —Mark 10:43–45; John 13:4–17
- Paul followed Jesus' example and taught the same—Acts 20:35; Rom. 15:1–3; 1 Cor. 10:24; 2 Cor. 4:5; Gal. 6:10
- Believers are to follow this example—Phil. 2:3–8; Eph. 2:8–10
- "… faith by itself, if it is not accompanied by action, is dead" (James 2:17)

> **"Resolved: that all men should live for the glory of God.**
>
> **Resolved second: that whether others do or not, I will."**
>
> —Jonathan Edwards

THE DISCIPLINES TODAY

- The discipline of service is not self-serving. Serving others to feel better, or to gain people's gratitude, becomes a self-serving activity. We give expecting nothing in return.
- Serving arises from our identity in Christ: we are his servants. Service is not what we do; it is who we are.
- Calling Jesus Lord means that we are his servants. Being a servant means that God called us to be of service.
- One of the ways to serve God is by serving people.
- Service is born of love and gratitude. It requires humility, strength, and love.
- Serving others can be exhausting and draining. One way to minimize this problem is by allowing the spiritual disciplines above to be the basis for our service. In addition, service in community also helps to minimize the problem of exhaustion and feeling burnt out.
- Like the other disciplines, training for service is a gradual process. The more we serve others, especially those with great need, the barriers that stay in our way of spiritual growth—pride, arrogance, indifference, fears, and insecurities—will slowly crumble.
- The practice of service begins by caring for one's own family (1 Tim. 5:8).
- Begin by serving those around you in small and unexpected ways. When they notice your service, be sure to give God the honor and the glory. Enjoy being a faithful servant (Matt. 25:21).

- Find ways to serve those with the greatest need in our society.
- Serving the people we like or feel comfortable with is easy. However, Jesus urges us to serve even if we are treated unfairly or unkindly.
- The apostle Peter (1 Peter 4:10–11) urges us to serve other believers in order to share in God's goodness. Service begins among Christians and extends to others as a way to show gratitude for God's own grace.
- In serving others, we become channels of God's love and compassion.
- When we serve others, we get to see Jesus' heart of love and compassion. Service becomes a spiritual experience beyond ourselves.

6. Solitude

Biblical Basis and Examples

- The prophets Moses, Elijah and Habakkuk retired to the wilderness to seek God's guidance—Ex. 3:1–6; 1 Kings 19:11–13; Hab. 2:1
- Jesus often withdrew to a solitary place to pray—Matt. 14:23; Mark 1:12, 35; Luke 5:16; 6:12; 9:18, 28
- Jesus taught the value of praying in private—Matt. 6:6
- Jesus advised the disciples to retire to a lonely place and rest—Mark 6:31
- The Apostle Paul went away to prepare for his ministry—Gal. 1:17

The Disciplines Today

- We live in a time of continuous visual and auditory stimulation: images and sound constantly come at us from many different sources.
- Often we miss God's voice and signals because we are distracted. We are busy people with busy lives.
- Just as our bodies need physical rest, our minds, hearts, and souls need intellectual, emotional, and spiritual rest.
- The problem with intellectual, emotional and spiritual rest is that they often require solitude and silence. We have grown so used to being surrounded by busyness, noise, and stuff that it is a great challenge to be in true solitude and silence.
- Like all disciplines, the habit of solitude takes time to form. It requires one step at a time.
- Begin by setting apart moments of quiet and reflection.
- Turn the radio off while driving in traffic. Allow that stressful time to be a moment of solitude, prayer, praise, and reflection.
- Solitude can be practiced by setting aside an hour, a day, a week, or any period of time that allows you to focus on God.
- Share with others the insights you gain during your moments of solitude. It will be an inspiration and example to others.

"Here then I am, far from the busy ways of men. I sit down alone; only God is here."
—John Wesley (1703–1791)

7. Discernment

Biblical Basis and Examples

- Discernment may include wisdom to understand the times—1 Chron. 12:32
- It may include wisdom to understand dreams—Gen. 41:25–39; Dan. 2:27–48
- It may include wisdom to make moral or judicial decisions—1 Kings 3:9–12
- Jesus told his followers to be wise but gentle—Matt. 10:16
- James tells believers to ask God for wisdom—James 1:5
- Discernment may at times run counter to prevailing human wisdom—1 Cor. 1:18–25
- It is useful to distinguish truth from falsehood and grow mature in the faith—Eph. 4:14; 2 Peter 2:1–22

The Disciplines Today

- Discernment is primarily a spiritual gift. However, all believers are called to be wise and discerning (Phil. 1:9–10).
- While some people in the church have a special gift for discernment, everyone in the church ought to be able to use discernment for at least two purposes:
  - To understand God's calling and will for our individual and collective lives.
  - To perceive and distinguish truth from falsehood.
- Discernment develops alongside the practice of all the previous spiritual disciplines.
- At a time when religions and pseudo-Christian cults are drawing away young people and uneducated Christians, correctly defining and recognizing beliefs is key.

- As a spiritual discipline, discernment depends entirely on the work of the Holy Spirit.
- We develop our ability to discern through prayer, Bible study and meditation, and fasting. As we become more sensitive to God's voice and promptings, our ability to discern God's plans and desires for our lives will increase.
- Discernment benefits greatly from the joint search for God's will within Christ's body. We are limited and imperfect beings; we are also skilled in self-deception. We may be convinced that God is leading in a specific direction. However, we could be deceiving ourselves. Having the joint discernment of God's people can keep us from this error.

Discernment: The Spirit-inspired ability to separate our imperfect will from God's perfect will in recognizing, judging, and choosing what is right, good, and pure from what is wrong, evil, and impure.

8. Evangelism

Biblical Basis and Examples

- Jesus charged his followers with the duty of spreading the gospel—Matt. 28:19–20
- The special ministry of evangelism is given to some—Eph. 4:11
- Peter tells believers to be ready to give a reasonable answer concerning the hope of the gospel—1 Peter 3:15

> **"There is not a square inch in the whole domain of our human existence over which Christ, who is Sovereign over all, does not cry: 'Mine!'"**
> —Abraham Kuyper, inaugural address at the dedication of the Free University of Amsterdam

The Disciplines Today

- Evangelism is a command for every person in the church.
- However, speaking about one's faith is not always a natural thing for many people.
- Practicing evangelism as a spiritual discipline will allow many Christians to grow more comfortable in sharing their faith.
- Just like our lives, all the spiritual disciplines are intimately related. They enrich each other and work in harmony.
- Evangelism feeds on all the spiritual disciplines mentioned above:
  - Scripture study: The more we know God, about God, and God's plans for humanity, the better we can share what God has done for us.
  - Prayer: Abundant life overflows our hearts and minds. The closer we are to God, the more life we can share with others.
  - Worship, fasting, and service can open doors to engage people in conversation about spiritual matters.
- We must also train ourselves to be God's instruments. It can be difficult to remember that we are not the ones convincing, transforming, or converting people. That is God's job. Our mission is to share with others what God has done. We do not "close the deal." Only God can do that.
- There are many evangelistic tools and programs that help believers obey Jesus' command to evangelize.
- Often, however, the best way to evangelize is by developing close relationships with people around us.

- Spiritual conversations are most natural in the context of close, intimate relationships.
- A spiritual conversation can be simply telling others your own story about when you first realized the importance of Jesus Christ in your life.

> **"Evangelism is a natural overflow of the Christian life…. But evangelism is also a Discipline in that we must discipline ourselves to get into the context of evangelism, that is, we must not just wait for witnessing opportunities to happen."**
> —Donald S. Whitney,
> *Spiritual Disciplines for the Christian Life*

One-Year Bible Reading Plan

Reading the Bible is an important practice of the Christian life. The Bible is the life-line of the believer. It gives us guidance, light, comfort, encouragement, correction, strength, and connection to God. However, where does one begin? It is helpful for the new believer, or even for a believer who has read the Bible on many occasions, to follow a structured format. By reading the Bible following different structures, God will show himself and his will to the believer in new and fresh ways. The following pages have three different arrangements that will help you read the Bible in one year. These arrangements will guide you during fifty-two weeks through daily, manageable sections. The three plans below provide ways to read the Bible that will open up new windows into God's Word. Each plan includes check boxes so you can keep track of your progress.

Plan One	Old/New Testament Psalms–Proverbs	Presents an Old Testament portion, a New Testament portion, a Psalm, and a section of Proverbs for each day.
Plan Two	One portion from each of seven key sections	Divides the Scriptures in seven traditional sections: Epistles, Law, History, Psalms, Poetry, Prophecy, Gospels.
Plan Three	Beginning to End	Guides one to read the whole Bible in order through the year.

Reasons to Study with Your Mind and Heart

To know God—God created the heaven and the earth and everyone in it (Genesis 1-3).

To enjoy and love God—Meditate on God's character, principles, and promises. Rejoice in his love, care, and forgiveness (Psalm 119:12-18, 160-162; 1 Timothy 6:17)

To know God's Word—The Scriptures were inspired by God. They teach us the truth and show us what is wrong in our lives. They straighten us out (2 Timothy 3:16).

To understand the Word—Jesus is called the Word because he is the ultimate communication from God. He existed from the beginning with God, he is God, and he created everything. He said that those who have seen him have seen the Father (John 1:1-3; 10:30; 12:44, 45; 14:7-9).

To learn direction in life—The Bible shows us what to do (Ps. 119:11).

To find comfort and hope—The Scriptures give us encouragement (Romans 15:4).

To let God expose our innermost thoughts and desires—His Word helps us see ourselves as we really are and convicts us of sin so that we repent and change (Hebrews 4:12-16).

To become pure and holy—Jesus prayed this for all believers that they would be set apart for God and his holy purposes (John 17:17-23).

To obey the Great Commandment—The more we know God, the more we can love him. The Great Commandment is to love God with all of our being and our neighbor as ourselves (Mark 12:29-31). And Jesus gave us a new commandment to love one another (John 13:34-35).

Reading Through the Bible: Helpful Tools

1. Study Bibles — A study Bible will help you by giving explanations, introductions, outlines, cross references and study notes. A good study Bible has a concordance, maps, and a topical index. Ask your pastor to recommend one.

2. Concordances — A concordance helps you look up any word in the Bible. It gives an alphabetical listing of key words, names, and topics, plus a list of verses that contain that word.

3. Bible Software — Bible concordances and other references are available on both desktop and hand held software. Enter a word or reference to quickly find and print out Bible verses in various versions. Complete Bible study libraries and study Bibles are available on computer software.

4. Bible Dictionaries — Look up words you don't understand, such as "grace," "redemption," or "faith." Expository dictionaries give you detailed meanings and explanations.

5. Bible Atlases, Maps, and Time Lines — On a map, locate where Bible events took place. Daniel was in Babylon. Babylon ruins are south of Baghdad today. On a time line, locate when Bible events took place. During the fierce Assyrian Kingdom, around 781 BC, Jonah went to Nineveh to warn the people to repent.

6. Bible Commentaries and Handbooks — First, study the Bible yourself. See what it means and how it applies to you. List questions you have. Later, you can read to see how Bible scholars explain it.

7. Special Bibles — Topical Bibles organize Scripture in special areas of interest, such as Salvation, Marriage, or Prayer. Interlinear Bibles compare original language (Hebrew or Greek) to modern language. Large-print Bibles are easy to read and helpful for many people.

Plan One: Old & New Testaments, Psalms, Proverbs

Wk	DAY 1	DAY 2	DAY 3	DAY 4	DAY 5	DAY 6	DAY 7
1	Gen 1:1–2:25 Matt 1:1–2:12 Ps 1:1–6 Prov 1:1–6	Gen 3:1–4:26 Matt 2:13–3:6 Ps 2:1–12 Prov 1:7–9	Gen 5:1–7:24 Matt 3:7–4:11 Ps 3:1–8 Prov 1:10–19	Gen 8:1–10:32 Matt 4:12–25 Ps 4:1–8 Prov 1:20–23	Gen 11:1–13:4 Matt 5:1–26 Ps 5:1–12 Prov 1:24–28	Gen 13:5–15:21 Matt 5:27–48 Ps 6:1–10 Prov 1:29–33	Gen 16:1–18:15 Matt 6:1–24 Ps 7:1–17 Prov 2:1–5
2	Gen 18:16–19:38 Matt 6:25–7:14 Ps 8:1–9 Prov 2:6–15	Gen 20:1–22:24 Matt 7:15–29 Ps 9:1–12 Prov 2:16–22	Gen 23:1–24:51 Matt 8:1–17 Ps 9:13–20 Prov 3:1–6	Gen 24:52–26:16 Matt 8:18–34 Ps 10:1–15 Prov 3:7–8	Gen 26:17–27:46 Matt 9:1–17 Ps 10:16–18 Prov 3:9–10	Gen 28:1–29:35 Matt 9:18–38 Ps 11:1–7 Prov 3:11–12	Gen 30:1–31:16 Matt 10:1–23 Ps 12:1–8 Prov 3:13–15
3	Gen 31:17–32:12 Matt 10:24–11:6 Ps 13:1–6 Prov 3:16–18	Gen 32:13–34:31 Matt 11:7–30 Ps 14:1–7 Prov 3:19–20	Gen 35:1–36:43 Matt 12:1–21 Ps 15:1–5 Prov 3:21–26	Gen 37:1–38:30 Matt 12:22–45 Ps 16:1–11 Prov 3:27–32	Gen 39:1–41:16 Matt 12:46–13:23 Ps 17:1–15 Prov 3:33–35	Gen 41:17–42:17 Matt 13:24–46 Ps 18:1–15 Prov 4:1–6	Gen 42:18–43:34 Matt 13:47–14:12 Ps 18:16–36 Prov 4:7–10
4	Gen 44:1–45:28 Matt 14:13–36 Ps 18:37–50 Prov 4:11–13	Gen 46:1–47:31 Matt 15:1–28 Ps 19:1–14 Prov 4:14–19	Gen 48:1–49:33 Matt 15:29–16:12 Ps 20:1–9 Prov 4:20–27	Gen 50:1–Ex 2:10 Matt 16:13–17:9 Ps 21:1–13 Prov 5:1–6	Ex 2:11–3:22 Matt 17:10–27 Ps 22:1–18 Prov 5:7–14	Ex 4:1–5:21 Matt 18:1–20 Ps 22:19–31 Prov 5:15–21	Ex 5:22–7:25 Matt 18:21–19:12 Ps 23:1–6 Prov 5:22–23
5	Ex 8:1–9:35 Matt 19:13–30 Ps 24:1–10 Prov 6:1–5	Ex 10:1–12:13 Matt 20:1–28 Ps 25:1–15 Prov 6:6–11	Ex 12:14–13:16 Matt 20:29–21:22 Ps 25:16–22 Prov 6:12–15	Ex 13:17–15:18 Matt 21:23–46 Ps 26:1–12 Prov 6:16–19	Ex 15:19–17:7 Matt 22:1–33 Ps 27:1–6 Prov 6:20–26	Ex 17:8–19:15 Matt 22:34–23:12 Ps 27:7–14 Prov 6:27–35	Ex 19:16–21:21 Matt 23:13–39 Ps 28:1–9 Prov 7:1–5
6	Ex 21:22–23:13 Matt 24:1–28 Ps 29:1–11 Prov 7:6–23	Ex 23:14–25:40 Matt 24:29–51 Ps 30:1–12 Prov 7:24–27	Ex 26:1–27:21 Matt 25:1–30 Ps 31:1–8 Prov 8:1–11	Ex 28:1–43 Matt 25:31–26:13 Ps 31:9–18 Prov 8:12–13	Ex 29:1–30:10 Matt 26:14–46 Ps 31:19–24 Prov 8:14–26	Ex 30:11–31:18 Matt 26:47–68 Ps 32:1–11 Prov 8:27–32	Ex 32:1–33:23 Matt 26:69–27:14 Ps 33:1–11 Prov 8:33–36
7	Ex 34:1–35:9 Matt 27:15–31 Ps 33:12–22 Prov 9:1–6	Ex 35:10–36:38 Matt 27:32–66 Ps 34:1–10 Prov 9:7–8	Ex 37:1–38:31 Matt 28:1–20 Ps 34:11–22 Prov 9:9–10	Ex 39:1–40:38 Mark 1:1–28 Ps 35:1–16 Prov 9:11–12	Lev 1:1–3:17 Mark 1:29–2:12 Ps 35:17–28 Prov 9:13–18	Lev 4:1–5:19 Mark 2:13–3:6 Ps 36:1–12 Prov 10:1–2	Lev 6:1–7:27 Mark 3:7–30 Ps 37:1–11 Prov 10:3–4
8	Lev 7:28–9:6 Mark 3:31–4:25 Ps 37:12–29 Prov 10:5	Lev 9:7–10:20 Mark 4:26–5:20 Ps 37:30–40 Prov 10:6–7	Lev 11:1–12:8 Mark 5:21–43 Ps 38:1–22 Prov 10:8–9	Lev 13:1–59 Mark 6:1–29 Ps 39:1–13 Prov 10:10	Lev 14:1–57 Mark 6:30–56 Ps 40:1–10 Prov 10:11–12	Lev 15:1–16:28 Mark 7:1–23 Ps 40:11–17 Prov 10:13–14	Lev 16:29–18:30 Mark 7:24–8:10 Ps 41:1–13 Prov 10:15–16
9	Lev 19:1–20:21 Mark 8:11–38 Ps 42:1–11 Prov 10:17	Lev 20:22–22:16 Mark 9:1–29 Ps 43:1–5 Prov 10:18	Lev 22:17–23:44 Mark 9:30–10:12 Ps 44:1–8 Prov 10:19	Lev 24:1–25:46 Mark 10:13–31 Ps 44:9–26 Prov 10:20–21	Lev 25:47–27:13 Mark 10:32–52 Ps 45:1–17 Prov 10:22	Lev 27:14–Num 1:54 Mark 11:1–26 Ps 46:1–11 Prov 10:23	Num 2:1–3:51 Mark 11:27–12:17 Ps 47:1–9 Prov 10:24–25

Plan One: Old & New Testaments, Psalms, Proverbs *continued*

Wk	DAY 1	DAY 2	DAY 3	DAY 4	DAY 5	DAY 6	DAY 7
10	Num 4:1–5:31 Mark 12:18–37 Ps 48:1–14 Prov 10:26	Num 6:1–7:89 Mark 12:38–13:13 Ps 49:1–20 Prov 10:27–28	Num 8:1–9:23 Mark 13:14–37 Ps 50:1–23 Prov 10:29–30	Num 10:1–11:23 Mark 14:1–21 Ps 51:1–19 Prov 10:31–32	Num 11:24–13:33 Mark 14:22–52 Ps 52:1–9 Prov 11:1–3	Num 14:1–15:16 Mark 14:53–72 Ps 53:1–6 Prov 11:4	Num 15:17–16:40 Mark 15:1–47 Ps 54:1–7 Prov 11:5–6
11	Num 16:41–18:32 Mark 16:1–20 Ps 55:1–23 Prov 11:7	Num 19:1–20:29 Luke 1:1–25 Ps 56:1–13 Prov 11:8	Num 21:1–22:20 Luke 1:26–56 Ps 57:1–11 Prov 11:9–11	Num 22:21–23:30 Luke 1:57–80 Ps 58:1–11 Prov 11:12–13	Num 24:1–25:18 Luke 2:1–35 Ps 59:1–17 Prov 11:14	Num 26:1–51 Luke 2:36–52 Ps 60:1–12 Prov 11:15	Num 26:52–28:15 Luke 3:1–22 Ps 61:1–8 Prov 11:16–17
12	Num 28:16–29:40 Luke 3:23–38 Ps 62:1–12 Prov 11:18–19	Num 30:1–31:54 Luke 4:1–30 Ps 63:1–11 Prov 11:20–21	Num 32:1–33:39 Luke 4:31–5:11 Ps 64:1–10 Prov 11:22	Num 33:40–35:34 Luke 5:12–28 Ps 65:1–13 Prov 11:23	Num 36:1–Deut 1:46 Luke 5:29–6:11 Ps 66:1–20 Prov 11:24–26	Deut 2:1–3:29 Luke 6:12–38 Ps 67:1–7 Prov 11:27	Deut 4:1–49 Luke 6:39–7:10 Ps 68:1–18 Prov 11:28
13	Deut 5:1–6:25 Luke 7:11–35 Ps 68:19–35 Prov 11:29–31	Deut 7:1–8:20 Luke 7:36–8:3 Ps 69:1–18 Prov 12:1	Deut 9:1–10:22 Luke 8:4–21 Ps 69:19–36 Prov 12:2–3	Deut 11:1–12:32 Luke 8:22–39 Ps 70:1–5 Prov 12:4	Deut 13:1–15:23 Luke 8:40–9:6 Ps 71:1–24 Prov 12:5–7	Deut 16:1–17:20 Luke 9:7–27 Ps 72:1–20 Prov 12:8–9	Deut 18:1–20:20 Luke 9:28–50 Ps 73:1–28 Prov 12:10
14	Deut 21:1–22:30 Luke 9:51–10:12 Ps 74:1–23 Prov 12:11	Deut 23:1–25:19 Luke 10:13–37 Ps 75:1–10 Prov 12:12–14	Deut 26:1–27:26 Luke 10:38–11:13 Ps 76:1–12 Prov 12:15–17	Deut 28:1–68 Luke 11:14–36 Ps 77:1–20 Prov 12:18	Deut 29:1–30:20 Luke 11:37–12:7 Ps 78:1–31 Prov 12:19–20	Deut 31:1–32:27 Luke 12:8–34 Ps 78:32–55 Prov 12:21–23	Deut 32:28–52 Luke 12:35–59 Ps 78:56–64 Prov 12:24
15	Deut 33:1–29 Luke 13:1–21 Ps 78:65–72 Prov 12:25	Deut 34:1–Josh 2:24 Luke 13:22–14:6 Ps 79:1–13 Prov 12:26	Josh 3:1–4:24 Luke 14:7–35 Ps 80:1–19 Prov 12:27–28	Josh 5:1–7:15 Luke 15:1–32 Ps 81:1–16 Prov 13:1	Josh 7:16–9:2 Luke 16:1–18 Ps 82:1–8 Prov 13:2–3	Josh 9:3–10:43 Luke 16:19–17:10 Ps 83:1–18 Prov 13:4	Josh 11:1–12:24 Luke 17:11–37 Ps 84:1–12 Prov 13:5–6
16	Josh 13:1–14:15 Luke 18:1–17 Ps 85:1–13 Prov 13:7–8	Josh 15:1–63 Luke 18:18–43 Ps 86:1–17 Prov 13:9–10	Josh 16:1–18:28 Luke 19:1–27 Ps 87:1–7 Prov 13:11	Josh 19:1–20:9 Luke 19:28–48 Ps 88:1–18 Prov 13:12–14	Josh 21:1–22:20 Luke 20:1–26 Ps 89:1–13 Prov 13:15–16	Josh 22:21–23:16 Luke 20:27–47 Ps 89:14–37 Prov 13:17–19	Josh 24:1–33 Luke 21:1–28 Ps 89:38–52 Prov 13:20–23
17	Judg 1:1–2:9 Luke 21:29–22:13 Ps 90:1–91:16 Prov 13:24–25	Judg 2:10–3:31 Luke 22:14–34 Ps 92:1–93:5 Prov 14:1–2	Judg 4:1–5:31 Luke 22:35–53 Ps 94:1–23 Prov 14:3–4	Judg 6:1–40 Luke 22:54–23:12 Ps 95:1–96:13 Prov 14:5–6	Judg 7:1–8:17 Luke 23:13–43 Ps 97:1–98:9 Prov 14:7–8	Judg 8:18–9:21 Luke 23:44–24:12 Ps 99:1–9 Prov 14:9–10	Judg 9:22–10:18 Luke 24:13–53 Ps 100:1–5 Prov 14:11–12
18	Judg 11:1–12:15 John 1:1–28 Ps 101:1–8 Prov 14:13–14	Judg 13:1–14:20 John 1:29–51 Ps 102:1–28 Prov 14:15–16	Judg 15:1–16:31 John 2:1–25 Ps 103:1–22 Prov 14:17–19	Judg 17:1–18:31 John 3:1–21 Ps 104:1–24 Prov 14:20–21	Judg 19:1–20:48 John 3:22–4:3 Ps 104:24–35 Prov 14:22–24	Judg 21:1–Ruth 1:22 John 4:4–42 Ps 105:1–15 Prov 14:25	Ruth 2:1–4:22 John 4:43–54 Ps 105:16–36 Prov 14:26–27

Plan One: Old & New Testaments, Psalms, Proverbs *continued*

Wk	DAY 1	DAY 2	DAY 3	DAY 4	DAY 5	DAY 6	DAY 7
19	1 Sam 1:1–2:21 John 5:1–23 Ps 105:37–45 Prov 14:28–29	1 Sam 2:22–4:22 John 5:24–47 Ps 106:1–12 Prov 14:30–31	1 Sam 5:1–7:17 John 6:1–21 Ps 106:13–31 Prov 14:32–33	1 Sam 8:1–9:27 John 6:22–42 Ps 106:32–48 Prov 14:34–35	1 Sam 10:1–11:15 John 6:43–71 Ps 107:1–43 Prov 15:1–3	1 Sam 12:1–13:23 John 7:1–30 Ps 108:1–13 Prov 15:4	1 Sam 14:1–52 John 7:31–53 Ps 109:1–31 Prov 15:5–7
20	1 Sam 15:1–16:23 John 8:1–20 Ps 110:1–7 Prov 15:8–10	1 Sam 17:1–18:4 John 8:21–30 Ps 111:1–10 Prov 15:11	1 Sam 18:5–19:24 John 8:31–59 Ps 112:1–10 Prov 15:12–14	1 Sam 20:1–21:15 John 9:1–41 Ps 113:1–114:8 Prov 15:15–17	1 Sam 22:1–23:29 John 10:1–21 Ps 115:1–18 Prov 15:18–19	1 Sam 24:1–25:44 John 10:22–42 Ps 116:1–19 Prov 15:20–21	1 Sam 26:1–28:25 John 11:1–54 Ps 117:1–2 Prov 15:22–23
21	1 Sam 29:1–31:13 John 11:55–12:19 Ps 118:1–18 Prov 15:24–26	2 Sam 1:1–2:11 John 12:20–50 Ps 118:19–29 Prov 15:27–28	2 Sam 2:12–3:39 John 13:1–30 Ps 119:1–16 Prov 15:29–30	2 Sam 4:1–6:23 John 13:31–14:14 Ps 119:17–32 Prov 15:31–32	2 Sam 7:1–8:18 John 14:15–31 Ps 119:33–48 Prov 15:33	2 Sam 9:1–11:27 John 15:1–27 Ps 119:49–64 Prov 16:1–3	2 Sam 12:1–31 John 16:1–33 Ps 119:65–80 Prov 16:4–5
22	2 Sam 13:1–39 John 17:1–26 Ps 119:81–96 Prov 16:6–7	2 Sam 14:1–15:22 John 18:1–24 Ps 119:97–112 Prov 16:8–9	2 Sam 15:23–16:23 John 18:25–19:22 Ps 119:113–128 Prov 16:10–11	2 Sam 17:1–29 John 19:23–42 Ps 119:129–152 Prov 16:12–13	2 Sam 18:1–19:10 John 20:1–31 Ps 119:153–176 Prov 16:14–15	2 Sam 19:11–20:13 John 21:1–25 Ps 120:1–7 Prov 16:16–17	2 Sam 20:14–21:22 Acts 1:1–26 Ps 121:1–8 Prov 16:18
23	2 Sam 22:1–23:23 Acts 2:1–47 Ps 122:1–9 Prov 16:19–20	2 Sam 23:24–24:25 Acts 3:1–26 Ps 123:1–4 Prov 16:21–23	1 Kings 1:1–53 Acts 4:1–37 Ps 124:1–8 Prov 16:24	1 Kings 2:1–3:2 Acts 5:1–42 Ps 125:1–5 Prov 16:25	1 Kings 3:3–4:34 Acts 6:1–15 Ps 126:1–6 Prov 16:26–27	1 Kings 5:1–6:38 Acts 7:1–29 Ps 127:1–5 Prov 16:28–30	1 Kings 7:1–51 Acts 7:30–50 Ps 128:1–6 Prov 16:31–33
24	1 Kings 8:1–66 Acts 7:51–8:13 Ps 129:1–8 Prov 17:1	1 Kings 9:1–10:29 Acts 8:14–40 Ps 130:1–8 Prov 17:2–3	1 Kings 11:1–12:19 Acts 9:1–25 Ps 131:1–3 Prov 17:4–5	1 Kings 12:20–13:34 Acts 9:26–43 Ps 132:1–18 Prov 17:6	1 Kings 14:1–15:24 Acts 10:1–23 Ps 133:1–3 Prov 17:7–8	1 Kings 15:25–17:24 Acts 10:24–48 Ps 134:1–3 Prov 17:9–11	1 Kings 18:1–46 Acts 11:1–30 Ps 135:1–21 Prov 17:12–13
25	1 Kings 19:1–21 Acts 12:1–23 Ps 136:1–26 Prov 17:14–15	1 Kings 20:1–21:29 Acts 12:24–13:15 Ps 137:1–9 Prov 17:16	1 Kings 22:1–53 Acts 13:16–41 Ps 138:1–8 Prov 17:17–18	2 Kings 1:1–2:25 Acts 13:42–14:7 Ps 139:1–24 Prov 17:19–21	2 Kings 3:1–4:17 Acts 14:8–28 Ps 140:1–13 Prov 17:22	2 Kings 4:18–5:27 Acts 15:1–35 Ps 141:1–10 Prov 17:23	2 Kings 6:1–7:20 Acts 15:36–16:15 Ps 142:1–7 Prov 17:24–25
26	2 Kings 8:1–9:13 Acts 16:16–40 Ps 143:1–12 Prov 17:26	2 Kings 9:14–10:31 Acts 17:1–34 Ps 144:1–15 Prov 17:27–28	2 Kings 10:32–12:21 Acts 18:1–22 Ps 145:1–21 Prov 18:1	2 Kings 13:1–14:29 Acts 18:23–19:12 Ps 146:1–10 Prov 18:2–3	2 Kings 15:1–16:20 Acts 19:13–41 Ps 147:1–20 Prov 18:4–5	2 Kings 17:1–18:12 Acts 20:1–38 Ps 148:1–14 Prov 18:6–7	2 Kings 18:13–19:37 Acts 21:1–17 Ps 149:1–9 Prov 18:8
27	2 Kings 20:1–22:2 Acts 21:18–36 Ps 150:1–6 Prov 18:9–10	2 Kings 22:3–23:30 Acts 21:37–22:16 Ps 1:1–6 Prov 18:11–12	2 Kings 23:31–25:30 Acts 22:17–23:10 Ps 2:1–12 Prov 18:13	1 Chron 1:1–2:17 Acts 23:11–35 Ps 3:1–8 Prov 18:14–15	1 Chron 2:18–4:4 Acts 24:1–27 Ps 4:1–8 Prov 18:16–18	1 Chron 4:5–5:17 Acts 25:1–27 Ps 5:1–12 Prov 18:19	1 Chron 5:18–6:81 Acts 26:1–32 Ps 6:1–10 Prov 18:20–21

Plan One: Old & New Testaments, Psalms, Proverbs *continued*

Wk	DAY 1	DAY 2	DAY 3	DAY 4	DAY 5	DAY 6	DAY 7
28	1 Chron 7:1-8:40 Acts 27:1-20 Ps 7:1-17 Prov 18:22	1 Chron 9:1-10:14 Acts 27:21-44 Ps 8:1-9 Prov 18:23-24	1 Chron 11:1-12:18 Acts 28:1-31 Ps 9:1-12 Prov 19:1-3	1 Chron 12:19-14:17 Rom 1:1-17 Ps 9:13-20 Prov 19:4-5	1 Chron 15:1-16:36 Rom 1:18-32 Ps 10:1-15 Prov 19:6-7	1 Chron 16:37-18:17 Rom 2:1-24 Ps 10:16-18 Prov 19:8-9	1 Chron 19:1-21:30 Rom 2:25-3:8 Ps 11:1-7 Prov 19:10-12
29	1 Chron 22:1-23:32 Rom 3:9-31 Ps 12:1-8 Prov 19:13-14	1 Chron 24:1-26:11 Rom 4:1-12 Ps 13:1-6 Prov 19:15-16	1 Chron 26:12-27:34 Rom 4:13-5:5 Ps 14:1-7 Prov 19:17	1 Chron 28:1-29:30 Rom 5:6-21 Ps 15:1-5 Prov 19:18-19	2 Chron 1:1-3:17 Rom 6:1-23 Ps 16:1-11 Prov 19:20-21	2 Chron 4:1-6:11 Rom 7:1-13 Ps 17:1-15 Prov 19:22-23	2 Chron 6:12-8:10 Rom 7:14-8:8 Ps 18:1-15 Prov 19:24-25
30	2 Chron 8:11-10:19 Rom 8:9-25 Ps 18:16-36 Prov 19:26	2 Chron 11:1-13:22 Rom 8:26-39 Ps 18:37-50 Prov 19:27-29	2 Chron 14:1-16:14 Rom 9:1-24 Ps 19:1-14 Prov 20:1	2 Chron 17:1-18:34 Rom 9:25-10:13 Ps 20:1-9 Prov 20:2-3	2 Chron 19:1-20:37 Rom 10:14-11:12 Ps 21:1-13 Prov 20:4-6	2 Chron 21:1-23:21 Rom 11:13-36 Ps 22:1-18 Prov 20:7	2 Chron 24:1-25:28 Rom 12:1-21 Ps 22:19-31 Prov 20:8-10
31	2 Chron 26:1-28:27 Rom 13:1-14 Ps 23:1-6 Prov 20:11	2 Chron 29:1-36 Rom 14:1-23 Ps 24:1-10 Prov 20:12	2 Chron 30:1-31:21 Rom 15:1-22 Ps 25:1-15 Prov 20:13-15	2 Chron 32:1-33:13 Rom 15:23-16:9 Ps 25:16-22 Prov 20:16-18	2 Chron 33:14-34:33 Rom 16:10-27 Ps 26:1-12 Prov 20:19	2 Chron 35:1-36:23 1 Cor 1:1-17 Ps 27:1-6 Prov 20:20-21	Ezra 1:1-2:70 1 Cor 1:18-2:5 Ps 27:7-14 Prov 20:22-23
32	Ezra 3:1-4:23 1 Cor 2:6-3:4 Ps 28:1-9 Prov 20:24-25	Ezra 4:24-6:22 1 Cor 3:5-23 Ps 29:1-11 Prov 20:26-27	Ezra 7:1-8:20 1 Cor 4:1-21 Ps 30:1-12 Prov 20:28-30	Ezra 8:21-9:15 1 Cor 5:1-13 Ps 31:1-8 Prov 21:1-2	Ezra 10:1-44 1 Cor 6:1-20 Ps 31:9-18 Prov 21:3	Neh 1:1-3:14 1 Cor 7:1-24 Ps 31:19-24 Prov 21:4	Neh 3:15-5:13 1 Cor 7:25-40 Ps 32:1-11 Prov 21:5-7
33	Neh 5:14-7:73a 1 Cor 8:1-13 Ps 33:1-11 Prov 21:8-10	Neh 7:73-9:21 1 Cor 9:1-18 Ps 33:12-22 Prov 21:11-12	Neh 9:22-10:39 1 Cor 9:19-10:13 Ps 34:1-10 Prov 21:13	Neh 11:1-12:26 1 Cor 10:14-33 Ps 34:11-22 Prov 21:14-16	Neh 12:27-13:31 1 Cor 11:1-16 Ps 35:1-16 Prov 21:17-18	Esther 1:1-3:15 1 Cor 11:17-34 Ps 35:17-28 Prov 21:19-20	Esther 4:1-7:10 1 Cor 12:1-26 Ps 36:1-12 Prov 21:21-22
34	Esther 8:1-10:3 1 Cor 12:27-13:13 Ps 37:1-11 Prov 21:23-24	Job 1:1-3:26 1 Cor 14:1-17 Ps 37:12-29 Prov 21:25-26	Job 4:1-7:21 1 Cor 14:18-40 Ps 37:30-40 Prov 21:27	Job 8:1-11:20 1 Cor 15:1-28 Ps 38:1-22 Prov 21:28-29	Job 12:1-15:35 1 Cor 15:29-58 Ps 39:1-13 Prov 21:30-31	Job 16:1-19:29 1 Cor 16:1-24 Ps 40:1-10 Prov 22:1	Job 20:1-22:30 2 Cor 1:1-11 Ps 40:11-17 Prov 22:2-4
35	Job 23:1-27:23 2 Cor 1:12-2:11 Ps 41:1-13 Prov 22:5-6	Job 28:1-30:31 2 Cor 2:12-17 Ps 42:1-11 Prov 22:7	Job 31:1-33:33 2 Cor 3:1-18 Ps 43:1-5 Prov 22:8-9	Job 34:1-36:33 2 Cor 4:1-12 Ps 44:1-8 Prov 22:10-12	Job 37:1-39:30 2 Cor 4:13-5:10 Ps 44:9-26 Prov 22:13	Job 40:1-42:17 2 Cor 5:11-21 Ps 45:1-17 Prov 22:14	Eccl 1:1-3:22 2 Cor 6:1-13 Ps 46:1-11 Prov 22:15
36	Eccl 4:1-6:12 2 Cor 6:14-7:7 Ps 47:1-9 Prov 22:16	Eccl 7:1-9:18 2 Cor 7:8-16 Ps 48:1-14 Prov 22:17-19	Eccl 10:1-12:14 2 Cor 8:1-15 Ps 49:1-20 Prov 22:20-21	Song 1:1-4:16 2 Cor 8:16-24 Ps 50:1-23 Prov 22:22-23	Song 5:1-8:14 2 Cor 9:1-15 Ps 51:1-19 Prov 22:24-25	Isa 1:1-2:22 2 Cor 10:1-18 Ps 52:1-9 Prov 22:26-27	Isa 3:1-5:30 2 Cor 11:1-15 Ps 53:1-6 Prov 22:28-29

Plan One: Old & New Testaments, Psalms, Proverbs *continued*

Wk	DAY 1	DAY 2	DAY 3	DAY 4	DAY 5	DAY 6	DAY 7
37	Isa 6:1-7:25 2 Cor 11:16-33 Ps 54:1-7 Prov 23:1-3	Isa 8:1-9:21 2 Cor 12:1-10 Ps 55:1-23 Prov 23:4-5	Isa 10:1-11:16 2 Cor 12:11-21 Ps 56:1-13 Prov 23:6-8	Isa 12:1-14:32 2 Cor 13:1-14 Ps 57:1-11 Prov 23:9-11	Isa 15:1-18:7 Gal 1:1-24 Ps 58:1-11 Prov 23:12	Isa 19:1-21:17 Gal 2:1-16 Ps 59:1-17 Prov 23:13-14	Isa 22:1-24:23 Gal 2:17-3:9 Ps 60:1-12 Prov 23:15-16
38	Isa 25:1-28:13 Gal 3:10-22 Ps 61:1-8 Prov 23:17-18	Isa 28:14-30:11 Gal 3:23-4:31 Ps 62:1-12 Prov 23:19-21	Isa 30:12-33:9 Gal 5:1-12 Ps 63:1-11 Prov 23:22	Isa 33:10-36:22 Gal 5:13-26 Ps 64:1-10 Prov 23:23	Isa 37:1-38:22 Gal 6:1-18 Ps 65:1-13 Prov 23:24	Isa 39:1-41:16 Eph 1:1-23 Ps 66:1-20 Prov 23:25-28	Isa 41:17-43:13 Eph 2:1-22 Ps 67:1-7 Prov 23:29-35
39	Isa 43:14-45:10 Eph 3:1-21 Ps 68:1-18 Prov 24:1-2	Isa 45:11-48:11 Eph 4:1-16 Ps 68:19-35 Prov 24:3-4	Isa 48:12-50:11 Eph 4:17-32 Ps 69:1-18 Prov 24:5-6	Isa 51:1-53:12 Eph 5:1-33 Ps 69:19-36 Prov 24:7	Isa 54:1-57:14 Eph 6:1-24 Ps 70:1-5 Prov 24:8	Isa 57:15-59:21 Phil 1:1-26 Ps 71:1-24 Prov 24:9-10	Isa 60:1-62:5 Phil 1:27-2:18 Ps 72:1-20 Prov 24:11-12
40	Isa 62:6-65:25 Phil 2:19-3:3 Ps 73:1-28 Prov 24:13-14	Isa 66:1-24 Phil 3:4-21 Ps 74:1-23 Prov 24:15-16	Jer 1:1-2:30 Phil 4:1-23 Ps 75:1-10 Prov 24:17-20	Jer 2:31-4:18 Col 1:1-17 Ps 76:1-12 Prov 24:21-22	Jer 4:19-6:15 Col 1:18-2:7 Ps 77:1-20 Prov 24:23-25	Jer 6:16-8:7 Col 2:8-23 Ps 78:1-31 Prov 24:26	Jer 8:8-9:26 Col 3:1-17 Ps 78:32-55 Prov 24:27
41	Jer 10:1-11:23 Col 3:18-4:18 Ps 78:56-72 Prov 24:28-29	Jer 12:1-14:10 1 Thess 1:1-2:8 Ps 79:1-13 Prov 24:30-34	Jer 14:11-16:15 1 Thess 2:9-3:13 Ps 80:1-19 Prov 25:1-5	Jer 16:16-18:23 1 Thess 4:1-5:3 Ps 81:1-16 Prov 25:6-8	Jer 19:1-21:14 1 Thess 5:4-28 Ps 82:1-8 Prov 25:9-10	Jer 22:1-23:20 2 Thess 1:1-12 Ps 83:1-18 Prov 25:11-14	Jer 23:21-25:38 2 Thess 2:1-17 Ps 84:1-12 Prov 25:15
42	Jer 26:1-27:22 2 Thess 3:1-18 Ps 85:1-13 Prov 25:16	Jer 28:1-29:32 1 Tim 1:1-20 Ps 86:1-17 Prov 25:17	Jer 30:1-31:26 1 Tim 2:1-15 Ps 87:1-7 Prov 25:18-19	Jer 31:27-32:44 1 Tim 3:1-16 Ps 88:1-18 Prov 25:20-22	Jer 33:1-34:22 1 Tim 4:1-16 Ps 89:1-13 Prov 25:23-24	Jer 35:1-36:32 1 Tim 5:1-25 Ps 89:14-37 Prov 25:25-27	Jer 37:1-38:28 1 Tim 6:1-21 Ps 89:38-52 Prov 25:28
43	Jer 39:1-41:18 2 Tim 1:1-18 Ps 90:1-91:16 Prov 26:1-2	Jer 42:1-44:23 2 Tim 2:1-21 Ps 92:1-93:5 Prov 26:3-5	Jer 44:24-47:7 2 Tim 2:22-3:17 Ps 94:1-23 Prov 26:6-8	Jer 48:1-49:22 2 Tim 4:1-22 Ps 95:1-96:13 Prov 26:9-12	Jer 49:23-50:46 Titus 1:1-16 Ps 97:1-98:9 Prov 26:13-16	Jer 51:1-53 Titus 2:1-15 Ps 99:1-9 Prov 26:17	Jer 51:54-52:34 Titus 3:1-15 Ps 100:1-5 Prov 26:18-19
44	Lam 1:1-2:22 Philem 1:1-25 Ps 101:1-8 Prov 26:20	Lam 3:1-66 Heb 1:1-14 Ps 102:1-28 Prov 26:21-22	Lam 4:1-5:22 Heb 2:1-18 Ps 103:1-22 Prov 26:23	Ezek 1:1-3:15 Heb 3:1-19 Ps 104:1-23 Prov 26:24-26	Ezek 3:16-6:14 Heb 4:1-16 Ps 104:24-35 Prov 26:27	Ezek 7:1-9:11 Heb 5:1-14 Ps 105:1-15 Prov 26:28	Ezek 10:1-11:25 Heb 6:1-20 Ps 105:16-36 Prov 27:1-2
45	Ezek 12:1-14:11 Heb 7:1-17 Ps 105:37-45 Prov 27:3	Ezek 14:12-16:41 Heb 7:18-28 Ps 106:1-12 Prov 27:4-6	Ezek 16:42-17:24 Heb 8:1-13 Ps 106:13-31 Prov 27:7-9	Ezek 18:1-19:14 Heb 9:1-10 Ps 106:32-48 Prov 27:10	Ezek 20:1-49 Heb 9:11-28 Ps 107:1-43 Prov 27:11	Ezek 21:1-22:31 Heb 10:1-17 Ps 108:1-13 Prov 27:12	Ezek 23:1-49 Heb 10:18-39 Ps 109:1-31 Prov 27:13

Plan One: Old & New Testaments, Psalms, Proverbs *continued*

Wk	DAY 1	DAY 2	DAY 3	DAY 4	DAY 5	DAY 6	DAY 7
46	Ezek 24:1–26:21 Heb 11:1–16 Ps 110:1–7 Prov 27:14	Ezek 27:1–28:26 Heb 11:17–31 Ps 111:1–10 Prov 27:15–16	Ezek 29:1–30:26 Heb 11:32–12:13 Ps 112:1–10 Prov 27:17	Ezek 31:1–32:32 Heb 12:14–29 Ps 113:1–114:8 Prov 27:18–20	Ezek 33:1–34:31 Heb 13:1–25 Ps 115:1–18 Prov 27:21–22	Ezek 35:1–36:38 James 1:1–18 Ps 116:1–19 Prov 27:23–27	Ezek 37:1–38:23 James 1:19–2:17 Ps 117:1–2 Prov 28:1
47	Ezek 39:1–40:27 James 2:18–3:18 Ps 118:1–18 Prov 28:2	Ezek 40:28–41:26 James 4:1–17 Ps 118:19–29 Prov 28:3–5	Ezek 42:1–43:27 James 5:1–20 Ps 119:1–16 Prov 28:6–7	Ezek 44:1–45:12 1 Peter 1:1–12 Ps 119:17–32 Prov 28:8–10	Ezek 45:13–46:24 1 Peter 1:13–2:10 Ps 119:33–48 Prov 28:11	Ezek 47:1–48:35 1 Peter 2:11–3:7 Ps 119:49–64 Prov 28:12–13	Dan 1:1–2:23 1 Peter 3:8–4:6 Ps 119:65–80 Prov 28:14
48	Dan 2:24–3:30 1 Peter 4:7–5:14 Ps 119:81–96 Prov 28:15–16	Dan 4:1–37 2 Peter 1:1–21 Ps 119:97–112 Prov 28:17–18	Dan 5:1–31 2 Peter 2:1–22 Ps 119:113–128 Prov 28:19–20	Dan 6:1–28 2 Peter 3:1–18 Ps 119:129–152 Prov 28:21–22	Dan 7:1–28 1 John 1:1–10 Ps 119:153–176 Prov 28:23–24	Dan 8:1–27 1 John 2:1–17 Ps 120:1–7 Prov 28:25–26	Dan 9:1–11:1 1 John 2:18–3:6 Ps 121:1–8 Prov 28:27–28
49	Dan 11:2–35 1 John 3:7–24 Ps 122:1–9 Prov 29:1	Dan 11:36–12:13 1 John 4:1–21 Ps 123:1–4 Prov 29:2–4	Hos 1:1–3:5 1 John 5:1–21 Ps 124:1–8 Prov 29:5–8	Hos 4:1–5:15 2 John 1:1–13 Ps 125:1–5 Prov 29:9–11	Hos 6:1–9:17 3 John 1:1–14 Ps 126:1–6 Prov 29:12–14	Hos 10:1–14:9 Jude 1:1–25 Ps 127:1–5 Prov 29:15–17	Joel 1:1–3:21 Rev 1:1–20 Ps 128:1–6 Prov 29:18
50	Amos 1:1–3:15 Rev 2:1–17 Ps 129:1–8 Prov 29:19–20	Amos 4:1–6:14 Rev 2:18–3:6 Ps 130:1–8 Prov 29:21–22	Amos 7:1–9:15 Rev 3:7–22 Ps 131:1–3 Prov 29:23	Obad 1:1–21 Rev 4:1–11 Ps 132:1–18 Prov 29:24–25	Jonah 1:1–4:11 Rev 5:1–14 Ps 133:1–3 Prov 29:26–27	Mic 1:1–4:13 Rev 6:1–17 Ps 134:1–3 Prov 30:1–4	Mic 5:1–7:20 Rev 7:1–17 Ps 135:1–21 Prov 30:5–6
51	Nah 1:1–3:19 Rev 8:1–13 Ps 136:1–26 Prov 30:7–9	Hab 1:1–3:19 Rev 9:1–21 Ps 137:1–9 Prov 30:10	Zeph 1:1–3:20 Rev 10:1–11 Ps 138:1–8 Prov 30:11–14	Hag 1:1–2:23 Rev 11:1–19 Ps 139:1–24 Prov 30:15–16	Zech 1:1–21 Rev 12:1–17 Ps 140:1–13 Prov 30:17	Zech 2:1–3:10 Rev 13:1–13:18 Ps 141:1–10 Prov 30:18–20	Zech 4:1–5:11 Rev 14:1–20 Ps 142:1–7 Prov 30:21–23
52	Zech 6:1–7:14 Rev 15:1–8 Ps 143:1–12 Prov 30:24–28	Zech 8:1–23 Rev 16:1–21 Ps 144:1–15 Prov 30:29–31	Zech 9:1–17 Rev 17:1–18 Ps 145:1–21 Prov 30:32	Zech 10:1–11:17 Rev 18:1–24 Ps 146:1–10 Prov 30:33	Zech 12:1–13:9 Rev 19:1–21 Ps 147:1–20 Prov 31:1–7	Zech 14:1–21 Rev 20:1–15 Ps 148:1–14 Prov 31:8–9	Mal 1:1–4:6 Rev 21:1–22:21 Ps 149:1–150:6 Prov 31:10–31

Plan Two: The Seven Biblical Sections

	Epistles	The Law	History	Psalms	Poetry	Prophecy	Gospels
Wk	DAY 1	DAY 2	DAY 3	DAY 4	DAY 5	DAY 6	DAY 7
1	Rom 1–2	Gen 1–3	Josh 1–5	Ps 1–2	Job 1–2	Isa 1–6	Matt 1–2
2	Rom 3–4	Gen 4–7	Josh 6–10	Ps 3–5	Job 3–4	Isa 7–11	Matt 3–4
3	Rom 5–6	Gen 8–11	Josh 11–15	Ps 6–8	Job 5–6	Isa 12–17	Matt 5–7
4	Rom 7–8	Gen 12–15	Josh 16–20	Ps 9–11	Job 7–8	Isa 18–22	Matt 8–10
5	Rom 9–10	Gen 16–19	Josh 21–24	Ps 12–14	Job 9–10	Isa 23–28	Matt 11–13
6	Rom 11–12	Gen 20–23	Judg 1–6	Ps 15–17	Job 11–12	Isa 29–33	Matt 14–16
7	Rom 13–14	Gen 24–27	Judg 7–11	Ps 18–20	Job 13–14	Isa 34–39	Matt 17–19
8	Rom 15–16	Gen 28–31	Judg 12–16	Ps 21–23	Job 15–16	Isa 40–44	Matt 20–22
9	1 Cor 1–2	Gen 32–35	Judg 17–21	Ps 24–26	Job 17–18	Isa 45–50	Matt 23–25
10	1 Cor 3–4	Gen 36–39	Ruth	Ps 27–29	Job 19–20	Isa 51–55	Matt 26–28
11	1 Cor 5–6	Gen 40–43	1 Sam 1–5	Ps 30–32	Job 21–22	Isa 56–61	Mark 1–2
12	1 Cor 7–8	Gen 44–47	1 Sam 6–10	Ps 33–35	Job 23–24	Isa 62–66	Mark 3–4
13	1 Cor 9–10	Gen 48–50	1 Sam 11–15	Ps 36–38	Job 25–26	Jer 1–6	Mark 5–6
14	1 Cor 11–12	Ex 1–4	1 Sam 16–20	Ps 39–41	Job 27–28	Jer 7–11	Mark 7–8
15	1 Cor 13–14	Ex 5–8	1 Sam 21–25	Ps 42–44	Job 29–30	Jer 12–16	Mark 9–10
16	1 Cor 15–16	Ex 9–12	1 Sam 26–31	Ps 45–47	Job 31–32	Jer 17–21	Mark 11–12
17	2 Cor 1–3	Ex 13–16	2 Sam 1–4	Ps 48–50	Job 33–34	Jer 22–26	Mark 13–14
18	2 Cor 4–5	Ex 17–20	2 Sam 5–9	Ps 51–53	Job 35–36	Jer 27–31	Mark 15–16
19	2 Cor 6–8	Ex 21–24	2 Sam 10–14	Ps 54–56	Job 37–38	Jer 32–36	Luke 1–2
20	2 Cor 9–10	Ex 25–28	2 Sam 15–19	Ps 57–59	Job 39–40	Jer 37–41	Luke 3–4
21	2 Cor 11–13	Ex 29–32	2 Sam 20–24	Ps 60–62	Job 41–42	Jer 42–46	Luke 5–6
22	Gal 1–3	Ex 33–36	1 Kings 1–4	Ps 63–65	Prov 1	Jer 47–52	Luke 7–8
23	Gal 4–6	Ex 37–40	1 Kings 5–9	Ps 66–68	Prov 2–3	Lamentations	Luke 9–10
24	Eph 1–3	Lev 1–3	1 Kings 10–13	Ps 69–71	Prov 4	Ezek 1–6	Luke 11–12
25	Eph 4–6	Lev 4–6	1 Kings 14–18	Ps 72–74	Prov 5–6	Ezek 7–12	Luke 13–14
26	Phil 1–2	Lev 7–9	1 Kings 19–22	Ps 75–77	Prov 7	Ezek 13–18	Luke 15–16
27	Phil 3–4	Lev 10–12	2 Kings 1–5	Ps 78–80	Prov 8–9	Ezek 19–24	Luke 17–18
28	Col 1–2	Lev 13–15	2 Kings 6–10	Ps 81–83	Prov 10	Ezek 25–30	Luke 19–20
29	Col 3–4	Lev 16–18	2 Kings 11–15	Ps 84–86	Prov 11–12	Ezek 31–36	Luke 21–22
30	1 Thess 1–3	Lev 19–21	2 Kings 16–20	Ps 87–89	Prov 13	Ezek 37–42	Luke 23–24
31	1 Thess 4–5	Lev 22–24	2 Kings 21–25	Ps 90–92	Prov 14–15	Ezek 43–48	John 1–2

Plan Two: The Seven Biblical Sections *continued*

		Epistles	The Law	History	Psalms	Poetry	Prophecy	Gospels
Wk		**DAY 1**	**DAY 2**	**DAY 3**	**DAY 4**	**DAY 5**	**DAY 6**	**DAY 7**
32		2 Thess	Lev 25–27	1 Chron 1–4	Ps 93–95	Prov 16	Dan 1–6	John 3–4
33		1 Tim 1–3	Num 1–4	1 Chron 5–9	Ps 96–98	Prov 17–18	Dan 7–12	John 5–6
34		1 Tim 4–6	Num 5–8	1 Chron 10–14	Ps 99–101	Prov 19	Hosea 1–7	John 7–9
35		2 Tim 1–2	Num 9–12	1 Chron 15–19	Ps 102–104	Prov 20–21	Hosea 8–14	John 10–12
36		2 Tim 3–4	Num 13–16	1 Chron 20–24	Ps 105–107	Prov 22	Joel	John 13–15
37		Titus	Num 17–20	1 Chron 25–29	Ps 108–110	Prov 23–24	Amos 1–4	John 16–18
38		Philemon	Num 21–24	2 Chron 1–5	Ps 111–113	Prov 25	Amos 5–9	John 19–21
39		Heb 1–4	Num 25–28	2 Chron 6–10	Ps 114–116	Prov 26–27	Obadiah	Acts 1–2
40		Heb 5–7	Num 29–32	2 Chron 11–15	Ps 117–118	Prov 28	Jonah	Acts 3–4
41		Heb 8–10	Num 33–36	2 Chron 16–20	Ps 119	Prov 29–30	Micah	Acts 5–6
42		Heb 11–13	Deut 1–3	2 Chron 21–24	Ps 120–121	Prov 31	Nahum	Acts 7–8
43		James 1–3	Deut 4–6	2 Chron 25–28	Ps 122–124	Eccl 1–2	Habakkuk	Acts 9–10
44		James 4–5	Deut 7–9	2 Chron 29–32	Ps 125–127	Eccl 3–4	Zephaniah	Acts 11–12
45		1 Peter 1–3	Deut 10–12	2 Chron 33–36	Ps 128–130	Eccl 5–6	Haggai	Acts 13–14
46		1 Peter 4–5	Deut 13–15	Ezra 1–5	Ps 131–133	Eccl 7–8	Zech. 1–7	Acts 15–16
47		2 Peter	Deut 16–19	Ezra 6–10	Ps 134–136	Eccl 9–10	Zech. 8–14	Acts 17–18
48		1 John 1–3	Deut 20–22	Neh 1–4	Ps 137–139	Eccl 11–12	Malachi	Acts 19–20
49		1 John 4–5	Deut 23–25	Neh 5–9	Ps 140–142	Song 1–2	Rev 1–6	Acts 21–22
50		2 John	Deut 26–28	Neh 10–13	Ps 143–145	Song 3–4	Rev 7–11	Acts 23–24
51		3 John	Deut 29–31	Esther 1–5	Ps 146–148	Song 5–6	Rev 12–17	Acts 25–26
52		Jude	Deut 32–34	Esther 6–10	Ps 149–150	Song 7–8	Rev 18–22	Acts 27–28

Plan Three: Beginning to End

DAY	VERSE	DAY	VERSE	DAY	VERSE	DAY	VERSE	DAY	VERSE
1	Gen 1–3	39	Num 1–3	77	Ruth 1–4	115	1 Chron 16–18	153	Job 37–39
2	Gen 4–6	40	Num 4–6	78	1 Sam 1–3	116	1 Chron 19–21	154	Job 40–42
3	Gen 7–9	41	Num 7–9	79	1 Sam 4–6	117	1 Chron 22–25	155	Ps 1–5
4	Gen 10–12	42	Num 10–12	80	1 Sam 7–9	118	1 Chron 26–29	156	Ps 6–10
5	Gen 13–15	43	Num 13–15	81	1 Sam 10–12	119	2 Chron 1–3	157	Ps 11–15
6	Gen 16–18	44	Num 16–18	82	1 Sam 13–15	120	2 Chron 4–6	158	Ps 16–20
7	Gen 19–21	45	Num 19–21	83	1 Sam 16–18	121	2 Chron 7–9	159	Ps 21–25
8	Gen 22–24	46	Num 22–24	84	1 Sam 19–21	122	2 Chron 10–12	160	Ps 26–30
9	Gen 25–27	47	Num 25–27	85	1 Sam 22–24	123	2 Chron 13–15	161	Ps 31–35
10	Gen 28–30	48	Num 28–30	86	1 Sam 25–27	124	2 Chron 16–18	162	Ps 36–40
11	Gen 31–33	49	Num 31–33	87	1 Sam 28–31	125	2 Chron 19–21	163	Ps 41–45
12	Gen 34–36	50	Num 34–36	88	2 Sam 1–3	126	2 Chron 22–24	164	Ps 46–50
13	Gen 37–39	51	Deut 1–3	89	2 Sam 4–6	127	2 Chron 25–27	165	Ps 51–55
14	Gen 40–42	52	Deut 4–6	90	2 Sam 7–9	128	2 Chron 28–30	166	Ps 56–60
15	Gen 43–46	53	Deut 7–9	91	2 Sam 10–12	129	2 Chron 31–33	167	Ps 61–65
16	Gen 47–50	54	Deut 10–12	92	2 Sam 13–15	130	2 Chron 34–36	168	Ps 66–70
17	Ex 1–3	55	Deut 13–15	93	2 Sam 16–18	131	Ezra 1–3	169	Ps 71–75
18	Ex 4–6	56	Deut 16–18	94	2 Sam 19–21	132	Ezra 4–6	170	Ps 76–80
19	Ex 7–9	57	Deut 19–21	95	2 Sam 22–24	133	Ezra 7–10	171	Ps 81–85
20	Ex 10–12	58	Deut 22–24	96	1 Kings 1–3	134	Neh 1–3	172	Ps 86–90
21	Ex 13–15	59	Deut 25–27	97	1 Kings 4–6	135	Neh 4–6	173	Ps 91–95
22	Ex 16–18	60	Deut 28–30	98	1 Kings 7–9	136	Neh 7–9	174	Ps 96–100
23	Ex 19–21	61	Deut 31–34	99	1 Kings 10–12	137	Neh 10–13	175	Ps 101–105
24	Ex 22–24	62	Josh 1–3	100	1 Kings 13–15	138	Est 1–3	176	Ps 106–110
25	Ex 25–27	63	Josh 4–6	101	1 Kings 16–18	139	Est 4–6	177	Ps 111–115
26	Ex 28–30	64	Josh 7–9	102	1 Kings 19–22	140	Est 7–10	178	Ps 116–120
27	Ex 31–33	65	Josh 10–12	103	2 Kings 1–3	141	Job 1–3	179	Ps 121–125
28	Ex 34–36	66	Josh 13–15	104	2 Kings 4–6	142	Job 4–6	180	Ps 126–130
29	Ex 37–40	67	Josh 16–18	105	2 Kings 7–9	143	Job 7–9	181	Ps 131–135
30	Lev 1–3	68	Josh 19–21	106	2 Kings 10–12	144	Job 10–12	182	Ps 136–140
31	Lev 4–6	69	Josh 22–24	107	2 Kings 13–15	145	Job 13–15	183	Ps 141–145
32	Lev 7–9	70	Judg 1–3	108	2 Kings 16–18	146	Job 16–18	184	Ps 146–150
33	Lev 10–12	71	Judg 4–6	109	2 Kings 19–21	147	Job 19–21	185	Prov 1–3
34	Lev 13–15	72	Judg 7–9	110	2 Kings 22–25	148	Job 22–24	186	Prov 4–6
35	Lev 16–18	73	Judg 10–12	111	1 Chron 1–6	149	Job 25–27	187	Prov 7–9
36	Lev 19–21	74	Judg 13–15	112	1 Chron 7–9	150	Job 28–30	188	Prov 10–12
37	Lev 22–24	75	Judg 16–18	113	1 Chron 10–12	151	Job 31–33	189	Prov 13–15
38	Lev 25–27	76	Judg 19–21	114	1 Chron 13–15	152	Job 34–36	190	Prov 16–18

Plan Three: Beginning to End *continued*

DAY	VERSE		DAY	VERSE		DAY	VERSE		DAY	VERSE		DAY	VERSE
191	Prov 19–21		226	Jer 10–12		261	Hos 1–3		296	Mark 13–16		331	2 Cor 1–3
192	Prov 22–24		227	Jer 13–15		262	Hos 4–6		297	Luke 1–3		332	2 Cor 4–6
193	Prov 25–27		228	Jer 16–18		263	Hos 7–10		298	Luke 4–6		333	2 Cor 7–9
194	Prov 28–31		229	Jer 19–21		264	Hos 11–14		299	Luke 7–9		334	2 Cor 10–13
195	Eccl 1–3		230	Jer 22–24		265	Joel 1–3		300	Luke 10–12		335	Gal 1–3
196	Eccl 4–6		231	Jer 25–27		266	Amos 1–3		301	Luke 13–15		336	Gal 4–6
197	Eccl 7–9		232	Jer 28–30		267	Amos 4–6		302	Luke 16–18		337	Eph 1–3
198	Eccl 10–12		233	Jer 31–33		268	Amos 7–9		303	Luke 19–21		338	Eph 4–6
199	Song 1–4		234	Jer 34–36		269	Obadiah		304	Luke 22–24		339	Phil 1–4
200	Song 5–8		235	Jer 37–39		270	Jonah 1–4		305	John 1–3		340	Col 1–4
201	Isa 1–3		236	Jer 40–42		271	Mic 1–3		306	John 4–6		341	1 Thess 1–5
202	Isa 4–6		237	Jer 43–45		272	Mic 4–7		307	John 7–9		342	2 Thess 1–3
203	Isa 7–9		238	Jer 46–48		273	Nah 1–3		308	John 10–12		343	1 Tim 1–3
204	Isa 10–12		239	Jer 49–52		274	Hab 1–3		309	John 13–15		344	1 Tim 4–6
205	Isa 13–15		240	Lam 1–3		275	Zeph 1–3		310	John 16–18		345	2 Tim 1–4
206	Isa 16–18		241	Lam 4–5		276	Hag 1–2		311	John 19–21		346	Titus 1–3
207	Isa 19–21		242	Ezek 1–3		277	Zech 1–3		312	Acts 1–3		347	Philemon
208	Isa 22–24		243	Ezek 4–6		278	Zech 4–6		313	Acts 4–6		348	Heb 1–3
209	Isa 25–27		244	Ezek 7–9		279	Zech 7–10		314	Acts 7–9		349	Heb 4–6
210	Isa 28–30		245	Ezek 10–12		280	Zech 11–14		315	Acts 10–12		350	Heb 7–9
211	Isa 31–33		246	Ezek 13–15		281	Mal 1–2		316	Acts 13–15		351	Heb 10–13
212	Isa 34–36		247	Ezek 16–18		282	Mal 3–4		317	Acts 16–18		352	James 1–3
213	Isa 37–39		248	Ezek 19–21		283	Matt 1–3		318	Acts 19–21		353	James 4–5
214	Isa 40–42		249	Ezek 22–24		284	Matt 4–6		319	Acts 22–24		354	1 Peter 1–5
215	Isa 43–45		250	Ezek 25–27		285	Matt 7–9		320	Acts 25–28		355	2 Peter 1–3
216	Isa 46–48		251	Ezek 28–30		286	Matt 10–12		321	Rom 1–3		356	1 John 1–3
217	Isa 49–51		252	Ezek 31–33		287	Matt 13–15		322	Rom 4–6		357	1 John 4–5
218	Isa 52–54		253	Ezek 34–36		288	Matt 16–18		323	Rom 7–9		358	2–3 John; Jude
219	Isa 55–57		254	Ezek 37–40		289	Matt 19–21		324	Rom 10–12		359	Rev 1–3
220	Isa 58–60		255	Ezek 41–44		290	Matt 22–24		325	Rom 13–16		360	Rev 4–6
221	Isa 61–63		256	Ezek 45–48		291	Matt 25–28		326	1 Cor 1–3		361	Rev 7–9
222	Isa 64–66		257	Dan 1–3		292	Mark 1–3		327	1 Cor 4–6		362	Rev 10–12
223	Jer 1–3		258	Dan 4–6		293	Mark 4–6		328	1 Cor 7–9		363	Rev 13–15
224	Jer 4–6		259	Dan 7–9		294	Mark 7–9		329	1 Cor 10–12		364	Rev 16–18
225	Jer 7–9		260	Dan 10–12		295	Mark 10–12		330	1 Cor 13–16		365	Rev 19–22

24 Ways to Explain the Gospel

Some concepts and ideas in the Bible are difficult to express in words. Things like love, forgiveness, sin, and others are very abstract and complex. Metaphors make abstract concepts easier to understand. By using common experiences—such as gardening, becoming ill, joining a family, becoming a citizen, or having debt—metaphors allow people to connect with the concepts at a personal level.

The gospel is about the good news of Jesus: Jesus has come to save us. It is important to explore, learn, appropriate, and use the illustrations the Bible itself uses to explain what Jesus accomplished on the cross.

What does "salvation" mean? How does the Bible explain it? How do we explain it to others? The following pages list twenty four illustrations of salvation in the Bible.

> A **metaphor** is a figure of speech in which a word or phrase, literally denoting one kind of object or idea, is used in place of another to suggest a likeness or analogy between them.
>
> An **illustration** is an example or instance that helps explain and make something clear.

Removing the Veil

The Bible is God's revelation to humans (2 Tim. 3:16). That means that in the Bible we meet and get to know who God is and what he has done. Revelation means that something hidden is unveiled so it is open to be seen. We can only know God if he lifts the veil from our eyes so we can know him and his actions.

- The Lord Jesus spoke about "the secrets of the kingdom of God" (Luke 8:10). The Apostle Paul wrote about the mysteries God revealed to us in Jesus (Rom. 16:25; Eph. 1:9; 3:6; Col. 1:26).
- These secrets and mysteries are now revealed in the Scriptures. However, not all mysteries are revealed (Deut. 29:29). God lifted the veil far enough to let us see: who God is, what he has done in history, Jesus' work of salvation, and our need for that salvation.

Metaphor	NAVIGATION	Jesus came to seek and save the lost. He promises to guide us to the right destination (Luke 19:10).
Positive	FOUND	• The lost have been returned (1 Peter 2:25). • The Good Shepherd seeks the lost sheep (Matt. 18:12). • Jesus came to save what was lost (Luke 19:10). • Joy in heaven for the found (Luke 15:1–7) • Joy over the lost who is found (Luke 15:11–32)
Negative	LOST	• We were lost (Isa. 53:6; Jer. 50:6; Mark 6:34).
Illustrations		• The sense of being lost, especially in a hostile environment, produces many and strong emotions: fear, anxiety, anger, and disappointment. • The final problem is that lost people are incapable of reaching their destination. • Jesus reorients us toward our correct destination: God's kingdom. When Jesus saves us, we begin to walk in the direction that will lead us to our final destination in God's presence.

Metaphor	VISION	Jesus promises to open our eyes so we can see him and God's wonders (Isa. 42:7).
Positive	SIGHT	• Jesus opened the eyes of his disciples (Luke 24:31). • Jesus came to give sight (Luke 4:18–19; John 9:39).
Negative	BLINDNESS	• Sin is blindness (John 9:39-41). • Blind guides lead others astray (Matt. 23:16–17). • People blinded to the gospel (2 Cor. 4:4).
Illustrations		• In the Bible, physical blindness was a metaphor for spiritual blindness. • Jesus used this metaphor to teach about the gospel (see John 9) • In the ancient world, only the "gods" were able to heal blindness. • Jesus restores both physical and spiritual sight to people. • Spiritual blindness has different causes: fear, unbelief, pride, greed, hatred, and egocentrism. Spiritual blindness prevents us from seeing God's doings in the world.

Metaphor	PURITY	Jesus promises to cleanse us completely from our sins (Heb. 9:14).
Positive	PURE/CLEAN	• Jesus purifies his people (Titus 2:14). • Jesus' blood purifies us from sin (1 John 1:9).
Negative	IMPURITY/ DIRTY	• Jesus did not call us to be impure (1 Thess. 4:7). • We were slaves to impurity (Rom. 6:19).
Illustrations		• Cleanliness and dirtiness are daily experiences in life. The idea of cleaning something to make it acceptable is easy to visualize. • We clean our homes, our clothing, our bodies to make them presentable and pleasant for others. • Sin corrupts and makes people impure. • People cannot make themselves clean of this pollution on their own. • However, God cleans us with Jesus' blood to make us acceptable, pleasant to himself.

Sin

- Disobeying God's law in deed or attitude is a common definition of sin. The Bible uses illustrations to explain the meaning of sin.
- One of these illustrations is the idea of missing the mark. The most common words for sin in the Old and the New Testaments have the basic meaning of someone missing the mark. When people disobey, rebel, or act on their iniquity, their actions and thoughts miss the mark of God's Law. Acting or thinking in a way that contradicts God's Law leads us in a path away from God.

Metaphor	KNOWLEDGE	Jesus gives us the knowledge of God to be saved, to grow and mature, and live a life that pleases God (1 Tim. 2:4; 2 Tim. 2:25).
Positive	UNDERSTANDING	• Jesus gives the knowledge of salvation (Luke 1:77). • The Spirit gives understanding of what Christ has done (1 Cor. 2:12). • We have wisdom from God (Eph. 1:8, 17; Col. 2:2–3; James 1:5).
Negative	IGNORANCE	• Lack of knowledge causes destruction (Hos. 4:6). • Life apart from God is a life of ignorance (1 Peter 1:14). • Foolishness separates us from God (Jer. 5:21; 10:8; Titus 3:3).
Illustrations		• The knowledge the Bible refers to here is not only mental knowledge. It also means intimate knowledge. It is a knowledge that affects the mind and the heart. • To truly get to know a person, reading a biography, hearing from other people, or spending a few minutes with a person is not enough. One needs time and energy to develop a relationship. After that time, one knows the other person. • It is not only book knowledge that allows us to know God and obtain salvation; we need deep, relational knowledge of Jesus. • The Holy Spirit gives us this knowledge primarily through the Scriptures, prayer, and fellowship with other believers.

Metaphor	MILITARY	Jesus has promised to give us lasting peace (John 14:27).
Positive	PEACE	• Peace with God through faith in Jesus (Rom. 5:1) • Jesus destroyed barriers of hostility (Eph. 2:14–22). • Jesus has defeated the powers of this world (1 Cor. 15:24–28). • Believers are also victorious (Rom. 8:31–39).
Negative	WAR	• We were God's enemies (Rom. 5:10; Col. 1:21). • We were under the dominion of darkness (Col. 1:12–14). • We were followers of the Devil and his ways (Eph. 2:1–7).
Illustrations		• Life often feels like a battle: a battle with our own struggles and sin (Rom. 7:21–25), with external influences and pressures. • Yet, Jesus' victory on the cross has defeated all the powers that bind and limit humanity: sin and death are defeated; Satan and his hosts are defeated. • Jesus' death on the cross was D-Day for God's people. In the famous day in World War II, the Allies overtook the beaches of Normandy and changed the course of the war. Jesus mortally wounded Satan and sealed his fate.

Metaphor	**AGRICULTURAL**	By being connected to Jesus, God's people have new life, can be fruitful, and have an abundant life.
Positive	**CONNECTION**	• God is portrayed as a caring gardener (Isa. 5:1–7). • Jesus allows us to be saved by grafting us into the tree to become part of his people (Rom. 11:24). • God's people are like trees planted by streams of water (Ps. 1:3). • Only by being connected to Jesus, the true vine, can we bear fruit (John 15:1–8).
Negative	**SEPARATION**	• By pruning Israel, God allowed Gentiles to become part of God's people (Rom. 11:17–21). • People without Jesus are like chaff that the wind blows away (Ps. 1:4). • No one can bear fruit apart from Jesus (John 15:4, 5–6).
Illustrations		• Gardening has become a more common urban activity—and continues to be vital in rural communities. Grafting and pruning are common activities in gardening. • Gardeners, professional and amateur, understand how important pruning is for the care and productivity of plants. • Like a gardener caring for his plants, God cares for his people. • God takes each of us, lifeless chaff, and grafts us into the tree of his people to give us new life. • Being saved is like being a plant, which is cared for and fruitful, in God's garden.

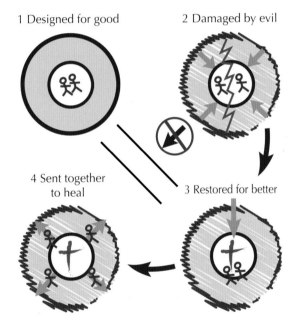

1 Designed for good

2 Damaged by evil

4 Sent together to heal

3 Restored for better

James Choung's Four Circles illustration shows God's original intention for his creation. God made humans to be and do good. However, sin affected our ability to do good. We became self-centered and enslaved to sin. Our sin breaks our relationship with God, nature, and one another.

Jesus came to restore humanity. His death on the cross liberated us from the slavery of sin and death.

Being free from sin, believers can become ambassadors of God. God is sending believers to heal relationships by preaching the good news of Jesus to a lost humanity.

Humans cannot move from circle 2 to 4 because sin has opened a gap that separates God from humans. Only through Christ is it possible to reach God.

Metaphor	**FAMILY**	Through Jesus, believers become children of God and can call him, "Abba, Father" (Gal. 4:6).
Positive	**ADOPTION**	• Christians become part of God's family (Rom. 8:15; Eph. 1:5). • Have the full rights of a son (Gal. 4:5). • Receive the assurance that God will resurrect believers' bodies.
Negative	**ORPHAN**	• The orphan, along with the widow and the poor, are the most vulnerable and needy in society (Deut. 10:18; James 1:26–27). • Life apart from God is like that of an orphan: full of uncertainty, danger, and lack of love (Hos. 14:1–3).
Illustrations		• Orphans are some of the most neglected, unprotected, and unloved people in societies throughout history. • Family connections were decisive for survival and a chance to succeed. • Christians call God "Father" because God has adopted us into his family. • The word *Abba* is a close affectionate term like *daddy*. • Now, regardless of who our family is, whether they are good or not, we all have one, good Father.

Metaphor	LEGAL	In Jesus we find complete forgiveness so God "will tread our sins underfoot and hurl our iniquities into the depths of the sea" (Micah 7:19).
Positive	FORGIVENESS	• Sins are forgiven forever (Jer. 31:34; Heb. 8:12). • Forgiveness comes from God's grace (Eph. 1:7). • God desires for everyone to be forgiven (1 Tim. 2:4).
Negative	CRIME AND PUNISHMENT	• A compassionate but just God (Num. 14:18) • God punishes sin (Lam. 3:39). • God is the ultimate judge (Prov. 24:12; Rom. 14:12).
Illustrations		• Most people, at one point in their lives, have had to deal with a legal issue—a parking ticket, a dispute in court, the selling of a home, or other more serious cases. • While not pleasant, we understand that the legal requirements and process is necessary and healthy. • The Bible uses this metaphor to show both the necessity and the rightness of Jesus' ministry of forgiveness and eventual judgment. • The legal consequences of sin are so big and eternal that we cannot deal with it on our own. Jesus is the only person who can and has done something about it. • His death on the cross has made it possible for us to receive God's forgiveness. • The Bible presents Jesus' work as an advocate on our behalf. He is our "defense lawyer" (Heb. 7:25; 1 John 2:1, 9).

Metaphor	BIOLOGY	Jesus promises us a new and abundant life (John 10:10).
Positive	LIFE	• Abundant life (John 5:24–26) • Bread of life (John 6:35) • God wants us to be fruitful (John 15:8; Col. 1:10).
Negative	DEATH	• Deserving death (Rom. 1:32) • Death through Adam (Rom. 5:12–14) • Sin causes lack of fruit (Gen. 3:16–19; Luke 3:9; John 15:2).
Illustrations		• Death is a human reality. But Jesus offers life, eternal life. • As a metaphor, death represents the end of all possibilities and hope. People live as if they were dead, without hope and separated from God. • Jesus offers abundant life. Jesus offers a new opportunity to live life like God intended it from the beginning. • Jesus raised Lazarus from the dead (John 11). Besides being a miracle, it also illustrates what Jesus can and does for people: He gives new life. • As we receive new life, God wants us to be fruitful and share this new life with the people around us.

Metaphor	AMBULATORY—RELATED TO WALKING	Jesus promises to walk alongside us: "And surely I am with you always, to the very end of the age" (Matt. 28:20).
Positive	STANDING/WALKING	• Walking on the path of righteousness (Prov. 8:20; 12:28) • The path of life revealed (Acts 2:28; Ps. 16:11) • Jesus keeps us from falling (Jude 1:24).
Negative	FALLING/STUMBLING	• Those burdened by sin stagger and fall (Isa. 3:8). • Those who do not know Christ will stumble over him (Rom. 9:32, 33; Isa. 8:14). • Unbelief in Jesus causes us to fall (1 Peter 2:8; Luke 20:18).
Illustrations		• Walking in God's paths is a common metaphor in the Bible. • Walking brings to mind the idea of movement and journey, the satisfactions and benefits of traveling as well as the difficulties involved in it. • As we walk, we learn, grow, and move forward. • However, walking requires a direction, lest it becomes a mere wandering. • One way to understand sin is that one misses the mark, or one's destination. • Jesus gives us a new orientation. • The Holy Spirit is our compass, and the Scriptures our map. • Only by walking alongside Jesus can we reach God, our true destination.

Metaphor	LIGHT	Jesus is the light that shines on our path toward God (John 12:46).
Positive	LIGHT	• Jesus is the light of the world (John 8:12). • Jesus' light shines in our hearts (2 Cor. 4:4–6). • Children of light (Eph. 5:8). • Jesus has rescued us from darkness (Col. 1:13). • Putting aside the deeds of darkness (Rom. 13:12).
Negative	DARK	• People living in darkness have seen a great light (Matt. 4:16). • Humans have loved darkness (John 3:19).
Illustrations		• A campfire in the wilderness provides light, warmth, safety, and sustenance. • The light helps campers to find their way back to the camp. It provides warmth for the night. It keeps wild animals away. It cooks food and purifies water. • In a similar way, Jesus provides us with guiding light, warmth, safety, and sustenance for our journey of life.

Metaphor	HEALTH	Jesus promises to be our physician and heal our minds, hearts, and souls (Mark 2:17).
Positive	HEALING	• Through Jesus' sacrifice, we are healed from our sins (Isa. 53:5; 1 Peter 2:24). • Prayer and confession to be healed (James 5:16) • God forgives our sins and heals our illness (Ps. 103:3).
Negative	ILLNESS	• Sickness (Matt. 9:2, 5; 1 Peter 2:24)
Illustrations		• The common experience of illness offers many possibilities to illustrate Christ's work. • "It is not the healthy who need a doctor but the sick…" Jesus used these words to describe his own ministry. The prophet Isaiah had promised: "No one living in Zion will say, 'I am ill'; and the sins of those who dwell there will be forgiven" (Isa. 33:24). • There are illnesses that our body can fight off alone. There are others, however, that require help. There are personality faults and character issues that one can deal with. There is a deep, moral problem, called sin, that only one physician can cure: Jesus.

Metaphor	TRUTH	Jesus offers the only truth that can lead us to God (John 14:6).
Positive	CORRECT/ TRUE	• Salvation as knowledge of the truth (1 Tim. 2:4) • The gospel is the word of truth (Eph. 1:13; John 17:17). • The truth of the gospel makes us free (John 8:32). • The Holy Spirit leads us to the truth (John 16:13).
Negative	ERROR/FALSE	• False prophets deceive and lead astray (Ezek. 13:1–23; Matt. 24:11, 24). • False teachings lead to destruction (2 Peter 2:1–2).
Illustrations		• Traveling without a map can lead to an exciting adventure or a disastrous end. A map is helpful when we follow its instructions. A correct map will lead us faithfully. An incorrect map will lead us astray. • The words of the gospel lead us correctly to our final destination.

Metaphor	RELATIONSHIP	Jesus promises to be more than our master. He promises to be our friend (John 15:15).
Positive	FRIEND	• Jesus gave his life for his friends (John 15:13). • We show our friendship through our obedience (John 15:14).
Negative	ENEMY	• We were God's enemies (Rom. 5:10; Col. 1:21); in Jesus, we are reconciled with God. • Jesus will defeat his enemies (1 Cor. 15:25).
Illustrations		• Sin has created a gap between God and humans. • This gap is enmity between God and us. • Jesus became a bridge that allows us to walk over to God. • Then, we can have a relationship with God as his friends.

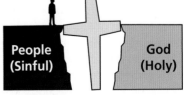

This drawing illustrates how Jesus' work on the cross allows sinful people to begin a relationship with God and be rescued from eternal death.

Metaphor	ECONOMIC	Jesus bought each believer at a price; the sale is final (1 Cor. 6:20; 7:23).
Positive	PAYMENT	• Offered himself as ransom (payment) on our behalf (Matt. 20:28; Heb. 9:15) • His sacrifice on the cross paid in full the debt that sin caused.
Negative	DEBT	• Sin caused a "debt" with God—Jesus cancels this debt (Col. 2:14). • The price for redemption is high (1 Peter 1:19).
Illustrations		• Difficult economic times make the burden of debts a very concrete reality. Although we often ignore it, the burden of sin is much heavier. • Getting rid of the huge weight of financial debt would allow people to start over, be wiser, and live better. Similarly, when Jesus lifts the weight of sin from us through his death, we are free to live life to the fullest. Jesus offers the opportunity to live without the burden of sin so we can live the abundant life that Jesus promises.

Redemption

- Redemption refers to the payment one offers for the deliverance of someone or something.
- In the ancient world, redemption was related to the freedom of prisoners of war and slaves. In this sense, God redeemed Israel from Egypt with power.
- The New Testament uses this metaphor to explain what Jesus accomplished on the cross. Jesus redeemed us from the power of sin and evil. His blood was the price he paid to make us free. The price for our freedom from sin and death was too high for any human to pay. Jesus alone was able to make the only and final payment for our redemption. Jesus' redemption is a free offer to every person.

Metaphor	FREEDOM	Jesus has promised to make us free from all bondage (John 8:36).
Positive	DELIVERANCE	To free us to: • New life (Rom. 6:4) • Freedom to serve (Gal. 5:1, 13) • Eternal life (John 10:28)
Negative	SLAVERY	To free us from: • Sin (Rom. 6:18) • The curse of the law (Gal. 4:3–5) • The fear of death (Heb. 2:14–15)
Illustrations		• Many things bind us: self-interest, addictions, broken relationships, anger and bitterness, destructive pasts, and debts. Sin captures our minds and hearts. Only a miracle can break those bonds. • Jesus breaks these bonds and gives us new life. This new life gives us the freedom to serve God, to become the people God wants us to be.

Metaphor	NATIONAL	Jesus allows us to become citizens of the kingdom of heaven.
Positive	CITIZEN	• Fellow citizens (Eph. 2:19) • Citizens of heaven (Phil. 3:20)
Negative	ALIEN	• Alien to a sinful world (1 Peter 2:11) • People looking for a country of their own (Heb. 11:13) • Longing for our real home (2 Peter 3:13)
Illustrations		• Being a citizen of a country provides identity, security, and rootedness. • Christians are citizens of God's kingdom. Our loyalties are to God and his will. • In a globalized world, where people move so fast and everywhere, the concept of citizenship takes new meanings. • Our identity, security and sense of community do not depend on the place or culture in which we were born. Rather, it depends on the values of the kingdom of God.

Citizenship in the Roman World

- The concept of Roman citizenship is the background for the Apostle Paul's use of citizenship as an illustration of salvation. The Apostle Paul was a Roman citizen by birth (Acts 22:25–29).
- Access to Roman citizenship was limited and difficult to obtain. Although many people achieved, earned, or were granted Roman citizenship, their citizenship was of a secondary kind. Even this secondary type of citizenship provided many rights and protections. In the Roman Empire, when slaves were freed, they became citizens.

Metaphor	**HUMAN DEVELOPMENT**	Jesus promises to complete the transforming work of maturity in each believer (Phil. 1:6).
Positive	**MATURITY**	• Parable of the Sower (Luke 8:14) • Becoming mature (Eph. 4:13) • Perseverance to maturity (James 1:4) • No longer foolish (Titus 3:3)
Negative	**IMMATURITY**	• Idols made by humans are foolishness (Jer. 10:8). • In need of teaching (Rom. 2:20) • Ignorance of God's will (Eph. 5:17)
Illustrations		• One of the effects of sin is that it stunts growth. God intended humans to live a full life. Sin does not allow us to reach our true potential. It makes people act like fools, in immature ways. • Sin has stunted our growth. Although we claim wisdom, our sin has made us fools (Rom. 1:22). • When Jesus cares for us, we become like trees planted by abundant waters that have the maturity to stand during droughts (Ps. 1:1).

Metaphor	**CREATION**	Jesus gives us the opportunity to be born again, to be a new creation. It is more than a fresh start. It is the right start (John 3:16–18).
Positive	**NEW CREATION**	• Jesus used the language of being born again (John 3:3, 7; 1 Peter 1:23). • Those born of God are children of God (1 John 3:9–10). • Christians are a new creation (2 Cor. 5:17; Gal. 6:15). • Jesus is presented as the second Adam (Rom. 5:15–17). • Jesus is the firstborn of the new creation (1 Cor. 15:27; 2 Cor. 5:17; Col. 1:15; Phil. 3:21).
Negative	**OLD CREATION**	• Sin transformed all of creation (Gen. 3:18; Rom. 8:22). • Sin entered through Adam's disobedience (Rom. 5:12–14). • This creation will pass and God will make all things new (Rev. 21:1; 2 Peter 3:13). • Nothing of the old creation can enter the kingdom of God (John 3:5).
Illustrations		• Jesus illustrated this point with a common object of his time: an unshrunk cloth to patch an old garment (Matt. 9:16). • The illustration is clear: when the garment is washed, the patch will shrink and tear the garment beyond repair. The old and the new do not mix with each other. • In the same way, God's grace requires a new heart (Ezek. 36:26). • Just as God makes us a new creation, God will make all things new one day (Rev. 21:1).

Creation to New Creation

Human Nature	What	When	Where	Who
Innocent	Good heart (Gen. 1:31)	In the beginning (past time)	In Eden (in paradise)	In Adam (our first parent)
Fallen	Corrupt heart (Gen. 3:19; 6:5,11,12; Rom. 3:9–19)	Upon the first sin (present time)	Upon the Earth (a wilderness outside Eden)	Upon all humanity
Redeemed	Transformed heart (Rom. 12:1–2)	At Christ's death and resurrection (present time)	At Calvary (outside the city of Jerusalem)	At conversion (all who are in Christ)
Perfect	Pure heart (Matt. 5:8; Heb. 12:14)	The age to come (future time)	The new heavens and earth (in the New Jerusalem)	God's people (believers in Christ, the last Adam)

For it is by grace you have been saved, through faith—and this not from yourselves, it is the gift of God— not by works, so that no one can boast.

—Ephesians 2:8–9

Metaphor	RESCUE	Jesus promises to rescue and keep us safe forever (Deut. 31:6; Heb. 13:5).
Positive	SAVED	• Jesus came to save the world (John 3:17). • Saves us from our sins (Eph. 2:1–9). • Saves us from God's just wrath (Rom. 5:9). • Saves us from death (Heb. 2:14–15). • Whoever believes in Jesus will not perish (John 3:16). • Jesus gives eternal life (John 10:28).
Negative	PERISHING	• God does not want anyone to perish (2 Peter 3:9). • Eternal Death (Matt. 25:41, 46; Matt. 7:13; Rev. 20:14–15) • Gehenna (Garbage Dump) (Matt. 5:22, 29, 30; 10:28; 18:9; 23:15, 33; Mark 9:43–47; Luke 12:5)
Illustrations		• Jesus speaks of the wicked perishing in "Gehenna." • Gehenna is another word for hell, but it was also the garbage dump of the city of Jerusalem, where garbage was continually burning. • Our sin had broken us and made us useless to God. • We were ready for the garbage dump. • Jesus came to rescue us from the never-ending trash pile. • Jesus' cross stands as a bridge that leads us to eternal safety.

Evangelism Plans

These four evangelism plans are ways to illustrate the gospel so its message is easier to understand. These four plans have helped millions of Christians around the world to bring the message of the gospel in a simple yet effective way.

Four Spiritual Laws (Campus Crusade for Christ)	➤ God loves you and offers a wonderful plan for your life (John 3:16; 10:10). ➤ Humans are sinful and separated from God. Thus, they cannot know and experience God's love and plan for their lives (Rom. 3:23; 6:23). ➤ Jesus Christ is God's only provision for humanity's sin. Through Jesus, you can know and experience God's love and plan for your life (Rom. 5:8; John 14:6). ➤ We must individually receive Jesus Christ as Savior and Lord; then we can know and experience God's love and plan for our lives (John 1:12; Eph. 2:8–9).
Bridge to Life (Navigators)	➤ The Bible teaches that God loves all humans and wants them to know him (John 10:10; Rom. 5:1). ➤ But humans have sinned against God and are separated from God and his love. This separation leads only to death and judgment (Rom. 3:23; Isa. 59:2). ➤ But there is a solution: Jesus Christ died on the cross for our sins (the bridge between humanity and God) (1 Peter 3:18; 1 Tim. 2:5; Rom. 5:8). ➤ Only those who personally receive Jesus Christ into their lives, trusting him to forgive their sins, can cross this bridge. Everyone must decide individually whether to receive Christ (John 3:16; John 5:24).
Steps to Peace with God (Billy Graham Crusade)	➤ Step 1. God's Plan ⇒ Peace and Life (Rom. 5:1; John 3:16; 10:10) ➤ Step 2. Humanity's Problem ⇒ Separation (Rom. 3:23; 6:23; Isa. 59:2) ➤ Step 3. God's Remedy ⇒ The Cross (1 Tim. 2:5; 1 Peter 3:18; Rom. 5:8) ➤ Step 4. Human Response ⇒ Receive Christ (John 1:12; 5:24; Rom. 10:9)
The Romans Road of Salvation	➤ Human Need (Rom. 3:23) ➤ Sin's Penalty (Rom. 6:23) ➤ God's Provision (Rom. 5:8) ➤ The Person's Response (Rom. 10:9)

BIBLE FAVORITES: OLD TESTAMENT

JOSEPH

◼ GOD IN THE LIFE OF JOSEPH

The story of Joseph (Genesis 30–50) teaches about faith and trust, and God's power in times of suffering. It's also a thrilling story of a 17-year-old boy who was …

+ Favored by his father
+ Resented by his ten older brothers
+ Thrown into a pit in the wilderness
+ Sold into slavery and never returned home

Later — just when it appeared his life was improving — he was:

+ Stalked by someone powerful and vengeful
+ Falsely accused and imprisoned
+ Abandoned in jail without friends or supporters to defend him
+ Forgotten by people who owed him a favor

But throughout the misery, God was there with Joseph.

Joseph's story gives hope on four levels:

1. Personal: God has a purpose in our suffering. God grew Joseph from immaturity to strength and mercy.

2. Family: God used bad circumstances to save Joseph's family and change attitudes.

3. Nationally: God used Joseph's misfortunes to save many lives and set up the rest of the biblical story that leads to the saving of the world through Christ.

4. Beyond: God used this event to bring blessing to the world long past biblical days. We, too, are part of God's larger plan that calls for patience and trust during times of suffering. Just as God blessed Joseph's faithfulness, God will bless our faithfulness.

◼ BEGINNING OF THE PROMISE (Read Gen. 12:1–3)

This story begins long before Joseph's birth. It begins with his great-grandfather, Abraham, a nomadic sheep and goat herder who lived in the dry, hot region of the Middle East known then as Canaan and today as Israel.

Although Joseph is the main character, the story is really about God's promise to Abraham's descendants.

> *God appeared to Abraham and made two promises:*
> + *I will make you a great nation.*
> + *All the nations of the earth will be blessed by you. (Gen. 12:1–2)*

God's promise to Abraham changed the direction of humanity. Human disobedience and rebellion turned God's creation upside down. Instead of being a good and blessed creation, human rebellion resulted in a cursed creation and a cursed history (see Gen. 1–3).

God promised Abraham to start a new history of blessing with him and his family.

God's promise lies with a family; it is not an ideal family—it resembles many families today, with struggles, deep problems, sadness, and grief.

Question: God gave Abraham some specific promises. What are some promises in the Bible that God gives to everyone who believes in him?

◼ A DYSFUNCTIONAL FAMILY

The story of Joseph begins in Gen. 37:1, with his father Jacob "in the land of Canaan." This simple statement is a reminder that God is implementing his promise to Abraham. Then the biblical story introduces Joseph and his brothers. It is immediately clear that their relationships are broken and that the potential for conflict is great.

◻ PLAYING FAVORITES (Read Gen. 37:1–4)

Joseph is Jacob's youngest and favorite son. This favoritism is evident in a few short lines in the story.

Two main clues of this favoritism:

1. The "coat of many colors," or "richly ornamented robe," was a gift from Jacob to Joseph. Whatever the robe was, it was a special and precious garment indicating that Joseph was not meant for a life of fieldwork like the other sons.

2. The other telling comment is of "a bad report" (see box) Joseph brings about his brothers. Jacob foolishly sends the favored son to check on his brothers. By this time, Joseph's actions and attitudes have hurt his relationship and angered his brothers.

◻ JOSEPH'S DREAM (Read Gen. 37:5–11)

Joseph's ten older brothers resent their father's favoritism as much as Joseph's attitude. Young Joseph fails to understand the depth of his brothers' loathing toward him. With little tact and wisdom, Joseph shares his dreams with his family. One night, Joseph dreams that his brothers and parents bow before him. The Bible does not say that Joseph's dreams come from God. In fact, we do not know that is the case until the end of the story, when the dreams become reality. It is also the straw that breaks the camel's back for his brothers.

> The Bible describes a similar robe in only one other place, 2 Sam. 13:18. There Tamar, King David's daughter, wears a similar robe and we read, "for this was the kind of garment the virgin daughters of the king wore" (2 Sam. 13:18).

> The expression *"bad report"* is also used in Ps. 31:13, Jer. 20:10, and Ezek. 36:3, where it is used for the whispering of hostile people.

The Wages of Deceit

Jacob's relationship with his sons reflects a lifetime of deceit. Jacob deceived Isaac, his father, for his blessing—cheating his brother Esau out of a blessing that was rightfully Esau's. Jacob fled his brother's anger and traveled to Haran to live with his uncle Laban (Gen. 27). There, Jacob fell in love with Laban's youngest daughter, Rachel. However, Laban tricked Jacob into working seven years for his daughter, but he gave his oldest daughter, Leah, to Jacob in marriage. Jacob had to work another seven years for Rachel.

Jacob's love for Rachel was always greater than his love for Leah. However, God granted Leah many sons from Jacob, whereas Rachel was not able to give birth. Rachel finally bore a son to Jacob, Joseph (Gen. 29:31–30:24). Jacob's love for Joseph became an extension of his love for Rachel.

◻ DECEIVING THE DECEIVER (Read Gen. 37:12–36)

The strained relationships among family members anticipate a potentially tragic ending. Jacob sends Joseph to check on his brothers who are herding sheep far away—an unwise decision considering the previous "bad report" from Joseph and the already weak relationships among his children. Joseph's brothers find a perfect opportunity to be rid of their youngest brother. The brothers throw Joseph in a pit and want to kill him. Reuben hopes to rescue Joseph, but Judah, one of two eldest brothers, argues that it is better to make some money from the deal. Instead of killing him, they sell Joseph to a trading caravan going to Egypt. Joseph, although alive, ends up as a slave in Egypt. Jacob is cruelly deceived by his sons, who return with a bloodied coat/robe and a terrible lie: Joseph is dead.

Question: Perhaps Joseph's brothers felt they had gotten away with a clever deception. But the Bible tells us that God is the Lord of Justice. Can you think of another story from the Bible that illustrates God's eventual triumph over wicked actions?

The Promise in Danger

Can God's promise to Abraham (or any other promise) ever be in danger? Absolutely not. God is always faithful to his promises. However, in times of trouble, it is difficult to remember this truth and easy to assume the worst. No, the promise is not in danger; though Joseph might find it difficult to believe while being dragged away from his family and into slavery. As readers, we can do nothing but weep along with Jacob: weep for Jacob's pain, for Joseph's fate, and for the brothers' hardness.

▣ A STORY WITHIN A STORY (Read Gen. 38)

Right in the middle of the story of Joseph, the Bible pauses and tells a separate story.

Joseph's brother Judah, now a grown man with three sons, tries to deceive his daughter-in-law, Tamar, by promising to follow the biblical laws that will protect her but actually refusing to carry them out. As time goes by, Tamar realizes she has been denied her proper rights; she turns around and deceives Judah.

In a family with a history of lying and violence, betrayal and hatred, how did God change Judah's heart? Judah had to admit that his actions had been wrong—far worse than his daughter-in-law's. He admitted that Tamar was more righteous than he was. Judah, a man unable to regret his mistreatment of his brother Joseph and his father, who lies and does injustice to his daughter-in-law, is a changed man. He is finally able to confess his error and make things right for Tamar.

While Joseph is in Egypt, God starts the change in Joseph's brothers.

Question: Joseph probably had no idea that God was working in the lives of his family members, but God knew what he was doing. What is an example from your own experience in which God was working in a way that was hidden from you at the time?

Judah and Tamar by Horace Vernet

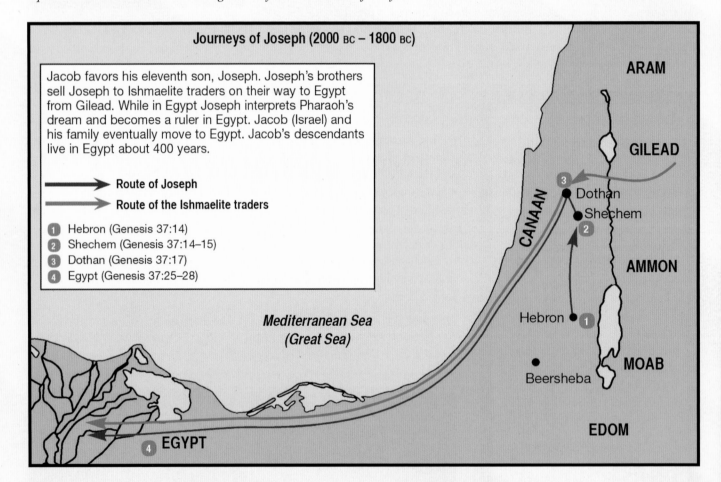

Journeys of Joseph (2000 BC – 1800 BC)

Jacob favors his eleventh son, Joseph. Joseph's brothers sell Joseph to Ishmaelite traders on their way to Egypt from Gilead. While in Egypt Joseph interprets Pharaoh's dream and becomes a ruler in Egypt. Jacob (Israel) and his family eventually move to Egypt. Jacob's descendants live in Egypt about 400 years.

➡ **Route of Joseph**
➡ **Route of the Ishmaelite traders**

1. Hebron (Genesis 37:14)
2. Shechem (Genesis 37:14–15)
3. Dothan (Genesis 37:17)
4. Egypt (Genesis 37:25–28)

ARAM

GILEAD

CANAAN

3 Dothan
Shechem
2

AMMON

Hebron 1

Mediterranean Sea (Great Sea)

Beersheba

MOAB

EDOM

4 **EGYPT**

▣ FROM POWERLESS TO POTIPHAR'S (Read Gen. 39:1–6)

Joseph goes from being the beloved son to being sold as a powerless slave in a powerful Egyptian officer's home. Potiphar is the captain of Pharaoh's bodyguard. In spite of this terrible reversal of fortunes, Scripture tells us, "The Lord was with Joseph." We do not know if Joseph, the shepherd boy, knew the language. It is unlikely that he was educated at the level of Egyptian upper class, but the Bible is clear that Joseph does not give up. He works hard and contributes to Potiphar's household. Every small responsibility he handles is successful. Over time, Potiphar realizes that the Lord is with this slave, and Potiphar puts Joseph in charge of everything he owns.

☐ REJECTION AND REVENGE (Read Gen. 39:7–19)

Potiphar's wife wants Joseph to sleep with her, but Joseph refuses, calling her proposed actions
- a breach of his responsibilities
- a betrayal of Potiphar who has trusted him
- a sin against God

She will not take no for an answer, so she stalks him. Day after day she talks with him, trying to seduce him. But one day, they are in the house alone and she grabs his clothing. Her grip must have been strong, because to get away he had to shed that garment and run outside. This final rejection leads her to revenge. She calls out to the men in the household and claims she has been attacked. When Potiphar hears, he is angry and throws Joseph in jail.

Question: Even when Joseph did what was right, he still received punishment as though he were guilty! Jesus said, "Blessed are those who are persecuted for righteousness sake for theirs is the kingdom of heaven" (Matt. 5:10). How do you understand Joseph's story in light of these words? How do you understand your own story?

☐ FROM POTIPHAR'S TO PRISON (Read Gen. 39:20–23)

Joseph is not given a trial; he is unfairly thrown into a jail for the king's prisoners. Scripture says he was there for many years. It was another reversal of fortunes. A good man treated wrongly, framed, betrayed by his employer's wife despite his flawless performance.

No one would blame Joseph for becoming angry and bitter, but he didn't. However, "the Lord was with Joseph" (Gen. 39:2). Joseph used his administrative skills to help, and over time was put in charge of all the prisoners and the prison organization. He found favor with the chief jailer, whose confidence in Joseph was so high that he didn't even supervise Joseph.

Question: What are some common reactions and emotions people have when they suffer injustice? How is it possible to avoid becoming bitter when treated unfairly?

☐ MORE HOPES DASHED (Read Gen. 40)

Two new prisoners from Pharaoh's household were placed in the jail for offending their master. Joseph was put in charge of them and took care of them for a long time. One night both men had troubling dreams, and in the morning Joseph noticed they were sad because there was no one to explain the dreams to them. Joseph told them that interpretations of dreams belonged to God and if they told him, he would explain it.

☐ THE CUPBEARER AND BAKER'S DREAM

	Dream	Interpretation from God
Cupbearer	A vine with three branches producing grapes. Grapes were squeezed and the juice given to Pharaoh.	In three days Pharaoh will give you back your job.
Baker	Carrying three baskets of bread for Pharaoh on his head. Birds came and ate them.	In three days Pharaoh will have you executed.

Interesting points:
- Joseph noticed that the men were troubled in the morning and asked about it. He who had been insensitive to his brothers' feelings now cared about others.
- Joseph gave credit to God rather than to himself, despite having a reputation as a clever man.
- Joseph asked the cupbearer to remember him and asked for help to get him out of jail.

Within three days both predictions come true. The cupbearer is restored to his place of privilege and the baker is executed. But the cupbearer forgets about Joseph, and Joseph continues to live in a dungeon several more years.

Questions: Even in prison, Joseph used his gifts to bless others. What are some difficult circumstances in your life in which you can use your gifts to bless others?

■ PHARAOH'S DREAM (Read Gen. 41:1–36)

One night Pharaoh has two dreams that none of his magicians and wise men can interpret.

Dream 1	Seven cows come out of the Nile River. They are sleek and fat and grazing. Seven more cows come out of the Nile. These are ugly and gaunt. They eat the sleek fat cows.
Dream 2	Seven ears of plump good grain appear on one single stalk. Then seven thin and scorched ears sprout up and swallow the plump ears.

Suddenly the cupbearer remembers Joseph and tells about the Hebrew slave who interpreted his own dream two years before. Pharaoh calls for Joseph. Joseph has to shave and change clothes from his prison garb. Pharaoh says, "I have heard it said about you, that when you hear a dream you can interpret it." Joseph replied, "It is not in me; God will give Pharaoh a favorable answer."

When Joseph hears the dreams, he calls them parallels having the same message.

Interpretation

After seven years of abundance in the land of Egypt, seven years of famine will ravage the land. The double dream means that God will surely do this and do it soon.

Recommendation

Pharaoh should find a wise supervisor to put in charge. Then appoint overseers who will collect and store one fifth of the annual food harvests in Egypt for the seven good years. This reserve will keep the people of Egypt from perishing.

Questions: It is easy to become overly confident and start taking credit for the good that happens in our lives. In what ways can a person give credit to God?

■ WHAT A DIFFERENCE A DAY MAKES

(Read Gen. 41:37–57)

Pharaoh sets Joseph over all Egypt, gives him his signet ring of authority, clothes him in fine linen and emblems of power, and puts him in a chariot and makes him his second-in-command.

For 13 years, Joseph has been a slave in Egypt and now he is second in command, and given every honor of status and fame and a notable marriage. At age 30, he is given the responsibility to travel through Egypt and supervise the storage of grain in locations owned by Pharaoh. He is so successful and the abundance is so great that even he can no longer keep track of the massive amounts of harvest.

■ JOSEPH'S BROTHERS IN EGYPT (Read Gen. 42:1–44:34)

Just then, Joseph's brothers arrive in Egypt on a mission to save their family from starvation. This surprise encounter sparks a series of events that transforms Joseph and his brothers' lives forever.

As his brothers arrive and bow down to the Egyptian lord, Joseph recognizes his brothers, but they do not recognize him. The statement reminds the readers of the brothers asking their father to *recognize* (the Hebrew word means *recognize*, "examine" in the NIV) Joseph's bloodied garment (Gen. 37:32). This recognition brings Joseph's memories back like a flood. As his son Manasseh's name reminds us, Joseph had been able to forget his difficult past (see Gen. 41:51; Manasseh probably means "to forget"). Now, the memories, the pain, the anger, and the doubts arise with renewed impetus.

Of Dreams and Gods

Dreams were important in the ancient world, especially in Egypt. The Egyptians had texts that priests would use to interpret dreams. Dreams were windows into the world of the gods. For this reason, priests were the people who could best interpret them.

When Pharaoh asks Joseph to interpret his dreams, Joseph replies, "I cannot do it, but God will give Pharaoh the answer he desires" (Gen. 41:16). Joseph claims that his God, the God of the Bible, can do something Pharaoh's gods have failed to do. Joseph is confident because, as he said before, "Do not interpretations belong to God?" (Gen. 40:8). It is an astonishing claim. Although the Egyptians were quite open to other people's gods, they were confident their own gods were superior. Joseph's claim suggests that the interpretation of dreams belongs to God because revelation through dreams comes from God! Joseph is proclaiming God's superiority over the Egyptians gods.

Part of God's promise to Abraham finds fulfillment through Joseph here. However, another important part of God's promise was that Abraham's descendants would make a great nation. This part of the promise implies a people and a land. The story is not over, the promise is still incomplete.

Joseph Accuses His Brothers

Joseph speaks harshly to the brothers and accuses them of being spies. This is not a light issue; the brothers understand immediately that they are in mortal peril. The Egyptian lord does not have to offer proofs for his accusation and could execute them at any moment with a simple command. Sheer terror makes them tell the truth about themselves: "We are all the sons of one man. Your servants are honest men, not spies." Their claim is another way to say they have clan responsibilities.

Joseph tests their claim of being honest men and accuses them again of being spies. The brothers insist, "Your servants were twelve brothers, the sons of one man, who lives in the land of Canaan. The youngest is now with our father, and one is no more" (Gen. 42:13). Joseph learns more about his family—his father is still alive and there is a new member of the family, Benjamin.

In this brief episode we can imagine a divided Joseph: a man full of anger and overwhelmed with memories but also full of wisdom and responsibility. Joseph is a changed man. However, if Joseph is changed, have his brothers changed at all? Are they still the same foolish men, willing to destroy a person's life to quench their anger?

Question: Joseph had the opportunity and the means either to take revenge or to hope for reconciliation. Whether a person chooses to get even or seek peace will make all the difference. How have you seen these different choices play out in real life situations?

Joseph Tests His Brothers

Joseph tests his brothers more than once, first by hiding his true identity, then by making them leave Simeon as a guarantee that they would return with their youngest brother. The brothers fail to persuade their father to let them bring Benjamin with them to Egypt. Jacob, a broken man, bitterly reminds them of Joseph—Jacob refuses to trust them with Benjamin's life for he fears the ending will be as tragic as that of Joseph's. Reuben makes a proposal: the lives of his two children for the life of Benjamin. Jacob has already lost two children (Joseph and Simeon). Why would he risk losing Benjamin and two grandchildren? Reuben's proposal is reckless. Jacob decides not to send Benjamin with them.

Since the famine is so severe, Jacob's sons need to return to Egypt. Judah steps forward and makes a wise suggestion. If something happens to Benjamin, Judah accepts the guilt and responsibility himself. It is a wise and mature proposal. In the ancient world, a verbal promise was not a thing lightly taken. Verbal commitments were a guarantee of action. Because of Judah's promise, Jacob reluctantly accepts; the twelve brothers are on their way back to Egypt.

Joseph continues the charade. He knows his brothers will return for his brother Simeon; but would they do the same for Benjamin?

Through yet another test, Joseph forces his brothers to demonstrate the kind of men they have become. When Benjamin is falsely found guilty of stealing a silver cup, Joseph quickly and angrily issues the punishment: Benjamin is to remain as his slave. But Judah steps up and demonstrates his moral quality and maturity. He explains to Joseph his own promise to Jacob. He says, "Now then, please, let your servant remain here as my lord's slave in place of the boy, and let the boy return with his brothers" (Gen. 44:33).

Judah has changed; he is no longer the self-centered man who once chose personal gain over his brother's safety, and personal security over his daughter-in-law's righteous claim.

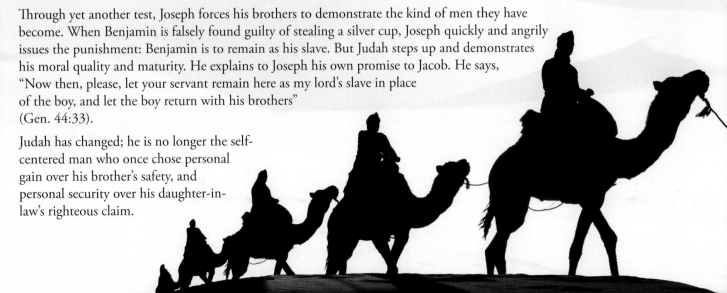

◻ RECONCILIATION IN EGYPT (Read Gen. 45:1–50:26)

Joseph cannot control himself and reveals his identity. While Joseph is moved to tears, his brothers are terrified when they finally recognize him. Joseph makes the wise and powerful statement: "But God sent me ahead of you to preserve for you a remnant on earth and to save your lives by a great deliverance. So then, it was not you who sent me here, but God" (Gen. 45:7–8). Joseph and Pharaoh invite Jacob and everyone in his family to come to Egypt.

Before leaving Canaan, the land God had promised to Abraham, Jacob has a dream. In the dream, God tells him, "I am God, the God of your father…. Do not be afraid to go down to Egypt, for I will make you into a great nation there. I will go down to Egypt with you, and I will surely bring you back again" (Gen. 46:3–4). God is renewing his promise to Abraham. God will make Abraham's descendants into a great nation *in* Egypt. Then, God will give this new nation a land where God will dwell with them.

Years later, after Jacob's death, Joseph's brothers still wonder if now Joseph will take revenge against them. Instead, Joseph says, "Don't be afraid. Am I in the place of God? You intended to harm me, but God intended it for good to accomplish what is now being done, the saving of many lives" (Gen. 50:19–20).

Question: Why is forgiveness often so difficult? What are the benefits of forgiving someone who has hurt you?

◻ THE GOD WHO WAS THERE

Joseph	• Joseph moved from Canaan to Egypt. • He moved from being a spoiled, foolish young man to being a wise man. • He moved from anger and forgetfulness to forgiveness and restoration. • He is redeemed from his sufferings in Egypt. • He is redeemed from being the victim of violence and injustice from his brothers. • He is redeemed from his own anger and memories. • He is redeemed by learning wisdom and trusting in God.
Jacob	• Jacob moved from being the deceiver to being deceived. • He moved from the joy of his favorite son to the tragedy of his supposed death. • He moved from being a man defeated to being a man with a future. • He is redeemed by receiving God's renewed promise. • Though he had become a broken man, God's gracious acts through Joseph allow Jacob to have a renewed sense of hope for the future. • This hope includes the promises that God made to Abraham.
Joseph's Brothers	• They moved from their wicked deeds to willingness to accept their responsibility. • They are redeemed from their early, evil ways.
Judah	• Judah moved from being a man merely concerned with his own well-being to one willing to accept the consequences of his actions. • Later, when Jacob blesses his children, Judah receives this blessing: "The scepter will not depart from Judah, nor the ruler's staff from between his feet" (Gen. 49:10). • From Judah, King David would be born, and later, Jesus, the promised Messiah, the one who fulfilled God's promises. • Judah is redeemed from his previous egotism. • He becomes the leader of the children of Israel. • Through him, the Messiah is born.

Through Joseph's life, we can learn how God moves in the lives of his people. Throughout the story, we find God at crucial moments. He is not always acting directly, but his presence is constant, causing or enabling all possible movement: geographic, moral, from foolishness to wisdom. Through the movement in Joseph's story, God redeems a broken family.

Although this story does not explain every case of suffering and grief, it instructs us on how to acquire the necessary wisdom that will allow us to face such experiences. The Bible recognizes that doctrinal statements are not enough to deal with suffering and grief. Wisdom allows us to see life from God's perspective. When we can see life through wisdom, we can trust that God will allow "neither death nor life, neither angels nor demons, neither the present nor the future, nor any powers, neither height nor depth, nor anything else in all creation, will be able to separate us from the love of God that is in Christ Jesus our Lord" (Rom. 8:38–39) and that "all things God works for the good of those who love him…" (Rom. 8:28).

Question: Everyone has experienced some sort of trouble in life. What has happened to you that has later turned into a benefit?

Joseph's Family Tree

The story of Joseph is part of the larger story of how God fulfilled his promise to Joseph's great-grandfather, Abraham. Just like his father had done, Jacob blessed his children before dying (the brief sentence below summarizes Jacob's blessings to each of his children in Gen. 49:1–27). The traditional list of Israel's twelve tribes includes Joseph's sons, Ephraim and Manasseh, but not Joseph. Jacob adopted Joseph's sons as his own children (Gen. 48:5–20). By doing this, Jacob exalted Joseph to his own level as a patriarch of the Tribes of Israel, and granted his children a sharing in the promises God made to Abraham. (Because Levi's descendants became the priestly tribe, they did not partake in the distribution of the promised land. Thus, they are not counted in the twelve tribes of Israel.)

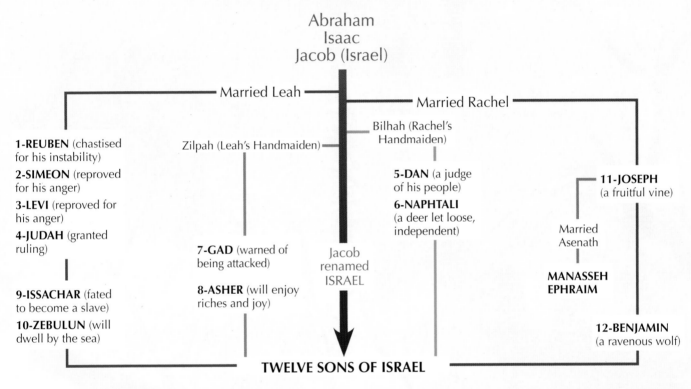

Abraham
Isaac
Jacob (Israel)

Married Leah — Married Rachel

1-REUBEN (chastised for his instability)
2-SIMEON (reproved for his anger)
3-LEVI (reproved for his anger)
4-JUDAH (granted ruling)

Zilpah (Leah's Handmaiden)

Bilhah (Rachel's Handmaiden)

5-DAN (a judge of his people)
6-NAPHTALI (a deer let loose, independent)

11-JOSEPH (a fruitful vine)

Married Asenath

MANASSEH
EPHRAIM

7-GAD (warned of being attacked)
8-ASHER (will enjoy riches and joy)

Jacob renamed ISRAEL

9-ISSACHAR (fated to become a slave)
10-ZEBULUN (will dwell by the sea)

12-BENJAMIN (a ravenous wolf)

TWELVE SONS OF ISRAEL

Life of Joseph Time Line

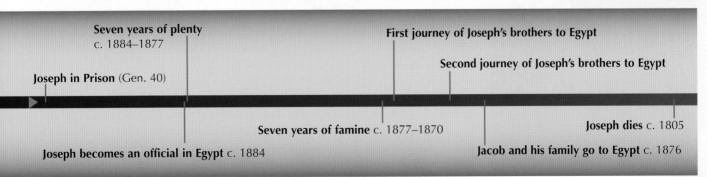

Abraham c. 2166–1991 BC
Some scholars place Abraham's birth at 1952 BC. In this case, biblical events through Joseph would slide to the right 214 years.

Jacob flees to Haran c. 1929

Joseph sold into slavery c. 1897

Joseph in Potiphar's home (Gen. 39)

Abrahamic Covenant

Joseph is born c. 1914

Jacob (Israel) c. 2005–1859

Judah and Tamar (Gen. 38—unsure of date)

Isaac c. 2066–1886

Ishmael c. 2080–1943

Joseph's dreams (Gen. 37:1–11)

(continued below)

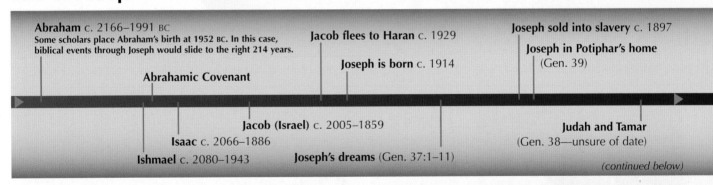

Seven years of plenty c. 1884–1877

First journey of Joseph's brothers to Egypt

Second journey of Joseph's brothers to Egypt

Joseph in Prison (Gen. 40)

Seven years of famine c. 1877–1870

Joseph dies c. 1805

Joseph becomes an official in Egypt c. 1884

Jacob and his family go to Egypt c. 1876

Moses

*Since then, no prophet has risen in Israel like Moses, whom the LORD knew face to face, who did all those miraculous signs and wonders the LORD sent him to do in Egypt, to Pharaoh and to all his officials and to his whole land. **For no one has ever shown the mighty power or performed the awesome deeds that Moses did in the sight of all Israel.** —Deuteronomy 34:10–12*

- ➣ A baby in danger became a liberator.
- ➣ A man who disliked the limelight became a leader.
- ➣ An 80-year-old shepherd faced a mighty Pharaoh.
- ➣ A man slow of speech became a prophet.
- ➣ A husband and father became a priest.
- ➣ A simple, humble man became God's servant.
- ➣ The life of this man changed the life of a nation-to-be.

Moses was perhaps the most important person in the Old Testament. His life was bound to the life of God's people, the children of Israel, and to God himself. In a special way, Moses represented Israel to God and God to Israel. Thus, learning about Moses means learning about God's people and about God himself.

The Hebrew People

Moses was born in Egypt to a Hebrew slave family.

- The Hebrew people had originally come to Egypt about 400 years before, after a time of famine. Jacob (also known as Israel) and his sons moved to Egypt, where Jacob's son Joseph had become the second most important ruler after Pharaoh.

- After Joseph died, the Israelites were thriving. God was fulfilling his promise to Abraham to give him many descendants and bless them (Gen. 17:4–7): "The Israelites were fruitful and multiplied greatly and became exceedingly numerous, so that the land was filled with them" (Ex. 1:7).

- However, eventually Egypt's pharaohs forgot Joseph and worried about the great strength of the Hebrew people. Besides enslaving the children of Israel, the Pharaoh, moved by fear, began a murderous policy to control the Israelite population growth. By the Pharaoh's decree, all male newborns were to be thrown into the Nile River.

- It seemed as though Pharaoh had the upper hand. However, God planned to make Abraham's descendants fruitful and a great nation. Pharaoh opposed God's will and plan. God was behind the scenes, engineering a great deliverance for his people.

THE BIRTH OF HOPE

In that time of grief, suffering, and danger, Moses was born. Although Pharaoh had intended to destroy Israel and frustrate God's plans to bless them, God worked through the most unexpected people to save the child. The baby's mother put the baby in a basket in the Nile to save him. The baby's sister Miriam wisely talked Pharaoh's daughter into giving the baby back to his mother to raise him. In contrast to the Pharaoh's evil intentions, his own daughter's tender and compassionate heart became a tool for the baby's salvation.

Thus the child Moses was born to a slave family, rescued by a noble person, nurtured by his own slave mother, and educated as a member of the Egyptian nobility. As we read the story of Moses' birth and rescue, we understand that God was working behind the scenes. What we might miss is that Moses' own story anticipated what was about to happen to Israel.

Moses	Israel
Moses came out of the Nile River miraculously "reborn."	Israel miraculously came out of the Red Sea as a people with a new identity.
Moses became aware of the injustice and acted to save his people (Ex. 2:11–12).	God heard and was concerned with the fate of his people; he acted decisively to save his people.
Moses had to flee the anger of Pharaoh into the wilderness (Ex. 2:15).	Israel had to flee Egypt into the wilderness (Ex. 14:8–9).
Moses met God at the burning bush on Mt. Sinai (Ex. 3:1).	Israel met God while camping around the base of Mt. Sinai (Ex. 19:1–2).
Moses, an Egyptian (Ex. 2:19), became the deliverer of some troubled shepherds.	God chose Moses, the shepherd, to deliver his people from Egypt.

Moses' Name

- The Hebrew name *Moses* sounds like the Hebrew verb for "to draw out."

- Pharaoh's daughter named the child Moses because "I drew him out of the water" (Ex. 2:10)

- But the name *Moses* has an Egyptian meaning as well and is found in many Egyptian names: Ra-messes, Thut-mose, Ah-mose.

- The first part of each name is related to an Egyptian deity (Ra, Thut, Ah). The second part of each name (*messes/mose*) means "boy" or "son." Moses can be an Egyptian name meaning *boy*, *son*, or *child*.

DIVINE APPOINTMENT

In a fit of anger, Moses killed an Egyptian who was mistreating an Israelite. His life changed radically. After being a noble, Moses became a fugitive. Fleeing into the wilderness, he began a new life: a new home, a new clan, a wife and children, a new profession as shepherd. He remained with Reuel, the Medianite high priest, and married his daughter, Zippora. In time, Gershon, his son, was born (Ex. 2:22).

Meanwhile, back in Egypt, the cruel pharaoh died—but another equally ruthless pharaoh took his place, and the Hebrew people cried out to God under their burdens. Exodus notes that God entered the scene directly: he listened, remembered, and acted in favor of his people (Ex. 2:23–25).

God called out to Moses from a burning bush on Mt. Sinai (Ex. 3:4).

> God identified himself as the God of Moses' forefathers. With reverence, Moses removed his sandals because God's presence made the ground holy (Ex. 3:5).

> God announced that he had seen his people's misery and was sending Moses to bring them out of Egypt. Moses protested that he was not the right person for the job. God offered signs that he would be with him:

- Israel would worship God on the same mountain (3:12).

- God revealed his own name to Moses (3:14).

- God would perform great wonders (3:20).

- Israel would not leave Egypt empty-handed (3:21).

- God showed his power by changing Moses' staff into a snake (4:2–4).

- God made Moses' hand leprous and restored it back to health (4:6–7).

Insight

Moses' encounter with God at the burning bush revealed much about God, Moses, and the children of Israel.

- God is faithful to his promises—he had not forgotten his covenant with Abraham.

- God chose and equipped Moses to be his special representative to Egypt to free his people.

- Moses' role became defined as that of an intermediary between God and Israel. From this moment on, Moses spoke to God on behalf of the children of Israel and to Israel on behalf of God.

CLASH OF THE GODS

When Moses went to see the Pharaoh, he confronted a person who the Egyptians considered a divinity. In the eyes of the Egyptians, it would seem that a foreign god was challenging their own god, Pharaoh. A clash of the gods was the natural result. Having grown up in the Egyptian court, Moses' fear and hesitancy make sense: he was an 80-year-old humble shepherd, how could he confront a "divine being"? On the surface, Moses and Aaron were facing the Pharaoh and his magicians; yet, at another level of reality, the God of Moses, the Lord, the Creator of heaven and earth, was facing the false gods of the Egyptians.

Pharaoh stubbornly refused to allow his Hebrew slaves to leave the country. The Scriptures tell us that God was also behind Pharaoh's hardened heart. Pharaoh's obstinacy happened so that Moses, and the children of Israel, would know that the Lord, the God of Abraham, Isaac, and Jacob, is the real and only God (Ex. 4:5; 9:16). As God had foreseen, Pharaoh opposed Moses and worsened the life conditions of the Israelites by denying them straw to make their bricks, making it much more difficult to meet their quotas.

As God challenged and defeated the gods of Egypt with each plague, Moses and the people of Israel witnessed God's power over creation, the gods of Egypt, and Egypt itself. For example, God defeated Ra, the sun-god, one of Egypt's main gods, in the ninth plague: Darkness.

Insight

Through the exodus experience, God created a people for himself. In time, he started a relationship with this people that would define the rest of God's involvement with humanity.

Christ's work on the cross is the miracle that brings us salvation and defines believers as a new people. "This salvation, which was first announced by the Lord, was confirmed to us by those who heard him. God also testified to it by signs, wonders and various miracles, and gifts of the Holy Spirit distributed according to his will" (Heb. 2:3–4).

Aaron

Aaron was Moses' and Miriam's brother and the first High Priest of Israel. God assigned Aaron to be Moses' assistant (4:14–17). As Moses' assistant (4:14–17), Aaron served throughout the Exodus and the journey through the wilderness. As the High Priest, Aaron was in charge of the Tabernacle and all the activities around it. Despite his closeness to God and Moses, Aaron committed a terrible sin when he agreed to build an idol—the Golden Calf—for Israel (Ex. 32:1–10).

Aaron died in the wilderness, and the community mourned him for 30 days (Num. 20:22-29). The New Testament contrasts Aaron's imperfect priesthood with Jesus' perfect priesthood (Heb. 5:2–5; 7:11–12).

AGENT OF DELIVERANCE

In the last, decisive plague, God killed the firstborns in all the land of Egypt, including Pharaoh's own son. Pharaoh, a broken man, allowed Israel to leave Egypt. As God had promised, the Israelites left Egypt with Egyptian silver, gold, and clothing (Ex. 3:21–22; 12:35–36).

However, Pharaoh changed his mind and chased the Israelites to kill them (Ex. 14:5).

With a column of fire separating them, Pharaoh's troops trapped Israel against the Red Sea. Moses took charge in the midst of the Israelites' doubts and fears. God promised to fight for the Israelites. As they crossed the Red Sea in a mighty miracle of deliverance, a new people was born: God's people, a nation in formation. Just as baptism symbolizes a new beginning in the life of the Christian, the crossing of the Red Sea was a new beginning for Israel as a people (1 Cor. 10:1–2). Pharaoh's army disappeared as the waters closed in on them. God's deliverance was complete.

DIVINE PRESENCE

As the Israelites moved away from the sea toward Sinai, they rejoiced for their liberation (Ex. 15:1–21), grumbled and complained against Moses and Aaron (16:3; 17:3), and disobeyed God's instructions (16:20, 27). The Israelites asked for the basics for life: food and water. God provided in a miraculous way. For food, God gave them manna and quail. As for the water, God instructed Moses to strike a rock to give water to the Israelites (17:6).

Even after seeing God's providence over and over, the Israelites ask the question that highlights a central issue in the book of Exodus, the whole Bible, and the life of Moses: "Is the Lord among us or not?" (17:7). One of the central themes of the book of Exodus is God's presence among his people.

God's Presence with Moses

God's double revelation to Moses on Mount Sinai (Ex. 3 and 19) established that God's presence was with Moses.

The battle against the Amelekites in Exodus 17 shows that God's presence with Moses represented God's presence with the Israelites. When Moses held his staff above his head, the Israelites defeated the Amelekites. When Moses lowered his arms to rest them, the fate of the battle turned against Israel. This event illustrates Moses' intercession in favor of Israel, and God's presence with Moses.

When the Israelites arrived at the foot of Mount Sinai, God made it clear that his demonstration of power—the thunder, lightning, and the thick cloud—had a specific purpose: "so that the people will hear me speaking with you and will always put their trust in you" (19:9).

Moses represented God to the people of Israel. God's presence with Moses was a sign for the Israelites to know that God was with them as well. Moses' authority and guidance represented God's own authority and guidance.

Stan Stein

God's presence with Moses remained the visual sign of God's presence with Israel until the Israelites built the Tabernacle. The Tabernacle, then, became the visual representation of God's presence in the midst of his people (Ex. 25:8). In a late Jewish tradition, the term *shekinah* became associated with God's presence. *Shekinah* is derived from a Hebrew word meaning "dwelling." God's presence, the *shekinah*, was represented by a cloud during the day and the column of fire during the night.

THE COVENANT AT SINAI

The Tabernacle, God's visible presence with Israel, also symbolized God's willingness to travel with his people through their wilderness journey. The wilderness, itself a symbol of the chaos and lifeless forces that oppose God, was a training ground for Israel to learn what it meant to be God's people. God had promised to be with them and live with them. However, God is holy, whereas the Israelites lived with many impurities and sin. How could they live in the presence of a holy God?

For the purpose of teaching Israel how to live as God's people in his presence and in the Promised Land, God gave Moses the Ten Commandments. The covenant at Sinai became the basis for God's relationship with Israel.

Moses was a kind of mediator of this covenant. When he climbed the mountain, he was representing the Israelites before God. When he descended the mountain, Moses was representing God to the people. The essence of the covenant remains, though the

> ### The Ten Commandments
>
> The Ten Commandments are a summary of the agreement (covenant) that God made with Israel at Sinai. Israel agreed to keep (obey) the terms of their agreement (stipulations of the covenant) and God agreed to be their God and King (bless, protect, and provide for them).

basis for it has changed. That is, in the old covenant, God inscribed the words of the covenant on stone; Israel would treasure them and keep them close to their hearts and minds forever. Their entire life should have been determined by these words.

Insight

In Christ, we can enjoy a relationship with God like the one Moses enjoyed. God revealed himself in a special way through Christ. Because of the presence of the Holy Spirit in us, we have direct access to God!

But humans are forgetful and rebellious. The Israelites broke the terms of the agreement on repeated occasions. For that reason, God had promised to instead inscribe his Law in people's hearts (Deut. 30:6) and send a perfect mediator of a new covenant, the Messiah, Jesus (Heb. 9:15).

Jesus as Mediator

Sin separates humans from God. We can only relate to him indirectly, through covenants, sacrifices, and human intercessors (priests and prophets). As the perfect priest and prophet, Jesus is the only mediator we need. As a prophet, he communicated God's will through his teachings and ministry (Heb. 1:1–2). As a priest, he offered the only perfect sacrifice that could bring us back to God (Heb. 10:10–14). The letter to the Hebrews makes it clear that Jesus is a mediator like Moses but superior to him.

- 1 Timothy 2:5: *For there is one God and one mediator between God and men, the man Christ Jesus.*

- Hebrews 9:15: *For this reason Christ is the mediator of a new covenant, that those who are called may receive the promised eternal inheritance—now that he has died as a ransom to set them free from the sins committed under the first covenant.*

LEADING THROUGH THE WILDERNESS

The Israelites spent 26 months camped at the feet of Mt. Sinai (Num. 10:11). They learned what it meant to be God's people and how to live with God's presence in their midst (most of the instructions in the book of Leviticus).

Organized as an army, Israel traveled from Sinai to the Promised Land. God, as Israel's King, led the march through the wilderness and dwelt in the middle of the Israelite camp. At different times during the journey, both Israel and Moses rebelled and expressed their discontent.

The Twelve Spies

As the Israelites approached the Promised Land, God instructed Moses to send twelve men to explore the land. Their report confirmed all that God had promised: a land flowing with milk and honey! However, they also brought bad news: the people in the land were too strong. Filled with fear despite the assurances from Moses, Joshua, and Caleb, the Israelites rebelled and refused to follow God's instructions to conquer the land. God's punishment was terrible: that whole generation would die in the wilderness, except for Joshua and Caleb. The Israelites wandered in the wilderness for 40 years. Joshua and Caleb, the two faithful spies who trusted God, were the only two from that generation who entered the Promised Land.

Korah's Rebellion

Korah, a Levite, incited a rebellion against Aaron and Moses' leadership. Korah said to Moses and Aaron, "You have gone too far! The whole community is holy, every one of them, and the LORD is with them. Why then do you set yourselves above the LORD's assembly?" Moses turned to God to find out his will, and God again communicated very clearly: As the rebel group gathered around the tents of Korah, Dathan, and Abiram, "the earth opened its mouth and swallowed them and their households, and all those associated with Korah" (Num. 16:32).

The complaints of Israel and Moses are different: while Israel rebelled against God's authority, Moses' complaining came from a secure relationship of friendship. Because God treated Moses as a friend, Moses could appeal to God's own promises and honor (see Ex. 32:11–13; and Num. 14:13–19). These remarkable examples force us to wonder why God punished Moses and Aaron so severely in Numbers 20:12: "But the LORD said to Moses and Aaron, 'Because you did not trust in me enough to honor me as holy in the sight of the Israelites, you will not bring this community into the land I give them.'"

Water from the Rock

The Scriptures make it clear that Moses did something that offended God; something so serious that God severely punished him. What was his sin? These are some possible answers:

1. It is possible that Moses' speech to the Israelites (Num. 20:10) was the offense. God commanded Moses to speak to the rock—not the people (Num. 20:8).

2. It is possible that Moses was claiming for himself the miracle he was about to perform: "... must we bring you water out of this rock?" (Num. 20:10).

3. It is possible that Moses was supposed to speak to the rock, not strike it.

4. It is possible that Moses' sin was a combination of the last three options—or that the Scriptures tell us only that God punished Moses and Aaron and the reason behind the punishment, but not the precise offense.

How exactly did Moses' action show lack of trust and failure to give honor to God? Let us remember that God performed a similar miracle before in Exodus 17:1–7. There, at the rocky wilderness of Sinai, the people quarreled with Moses and asked for water. God ordered Moses to use his staff to strike the rock. Before the elders of the Israelites, Moses struck the rock and water came gushing out. In Numbers 20, the need for water arose once again. This time, however, God ordered Moses to speak to the rock.

Moses' sin might be a question of expectations. The people expected God to deliver them from their thirst in the same way he had done it before. Yet, the Bible is clear that we cannot put God in a box; that God is and does far more than we can imagine.

Perhaps giving the Israelites water by speaking to the rock was a miracle they were not expecting; such a miracle could have had a stronger effect on their faith. By repeating the way the miracle was done previously, Moses "robbed" glory from God's miraculous provision. Preventing God from acting in new and sometimes surprising ways may reflect a lack of faith and trust in God's goodness and wisdom.

Moses Strikes the Rock by James Tissot, c. 1896-1902

LOCATION OF MT. SINAI

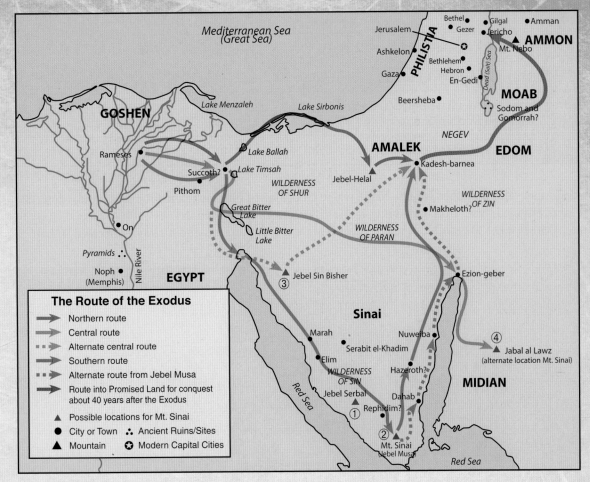

Traditionally, many people believe that Mount Sinai is found in the southern part of the peninsula. However, some scholars believe that the mountain might be found in the northern part of the peninsula or, even, outside of the peninsula in what was one location for ancient Midian. These are the four most common suggestions for the location of Mount Sinai.

① In the south, *Jebel* (Mount) *Serbal*   ③ In the north, *Jebel Sin Bisher*

② In the south, *Jebel Musa*   ④ Outside of the Sinai Peninsula, in Midian, *Jebel el-Lawz*

LAST WISHES AND DEATH

At the end of 40 years' journey, Moses and a new generation of the children of Israel arrived at the eastern border of the Promised Land.

This new generation did not witness firsthand God's mighty acts of salvation in Egypt nor his revelation at Sinai. They also needed to be instructed in what it meant to be God's people. Their identity, based on God's Law, would protect them as they entered the Promised Land and would guide them as they became a nation. Joshua, the faithful spy, was chosen to succeed Moses as leader.

At the edge of the Promised Land, at the end of the wilderness wanderings and of Moses' life, Moses instructed Israel.

Moses' instructions to the Israelites in the book of Deuteronomy can be summarized as follows:

Insight

Moses stood at the edge of the Promised Land; he could see it but could not enter it. Yet, Moses died full of hope for what he could witness. It is similar for Christians. We stand at the edge of the Promised Land, but cannot enter it quite yet. Until we do, we continue to wander in this life, knowing that although we are not of this world, the Lord has sent us into this world to serve him while we await for his return (John 17:13–19).

About God	God is one.	4:1–40; 6:4
	God is faithful and merciful.	1:8, 19–46; 7:1–26; 8:1–20; 9:1–10:11
	God is powerful.	2:1–3:11; 4:1–40; 7:1–26
About Israel	God chose Israel.	4:5–9; 10:14–15; 14:1–2, 21
	The land God promised to Israel is good.	1:25; 6:10–11; 8:7–13; 11:8–15
	Israel must love, serve, fear, and obey God.	6:5; 10:12–13; 13:4
	Israel must not have other gods (idolatry); rather, Israel must serve and worship God properly.	4:9–31; 5:6–10; 7:1–5; 8:19–20; 12:1–32; 13:1–18
	God's Law is meant for all areas of life in the Land.	12:1–27:26

After instructing Israel, Moses climbed Mount Nebo, where God allowed him to see the Promised Land. Moses did not enter the land, but died there. God buried him in the valley, east of the Jordan. Moses did not die of old age, nor of sickness; rather, "Moses was 120 years old when he died. His eye was undimmed, and his vigor unabated" (Deut. 34:7).

Jews across the Red sea by Wilhelm Kotarbinski, 1890

MOSES AND CHRIST JESUS

Because Moses is so significant, the writer of the letter to the Hebrews uses him to highlight Jesus' ministry. It's almost as if the writer were making the argument: if Moses, being this important, falls short before Jesus, and you believe Moses, shouldn't you believe Jesus even more?

Moses' life illustrates the human need for a mediator. Moreover, his life points to the life of that Mediator we need: Jesus Christ.

Moses' life shows a God full of grace and mercy, compassion and love, yet also holy and just. His life shows us the possibilities for a full relationship with God, a relationship in which we are no longer servants but friends (John 15:14–15).

Finally, Moses' life points to Christ in some other important ways:

Moses	Christ
Surrounding the birth of Moses, Pharaoh killed innocent children in Egypt—Ex. 1:22.	Surrounding the birth of Jesus, King Herod killed innocent children in Bethlehem—Matt. 2:16.
Moses had to flee his native land because of Pharaoh's persecution—Ex. 2:15.	Jesus had to flee his native land because of Herod's persecution—Matt. 2:14.
Pharaoh died and Moses returned after he was told: "All the men are dead that sought your life"—Ex. 4:19.	Herod died and Jesus returned after "…those who sought the child's life are dead"—Matt. 2:20–21.
Moses fasted 40 days before he delivered God's words to the people—Ex. 34:28.	Jesus fasted 40 days before he began to preach—Matt. 4:2, 17.
Moses was on a mountain for the blessing of the commandments—Ex. 19:20.	Jesus was on a mount when he gave his Beatitudes and commandments—Matt. 5:1–12.
Moses' own people question his authority—Ex. 2:14.	Jesus' own people question his authority—Matt. 13:54–55.
The dividing of the Red Sea took place under Moses' command—Ex. 14:15–22.	Jesus walked on the sea and calmed the storm—Matt. 14:22–32.
A cloud overshadowed Moses, Aaron and Miriam and the voice of God was heard—Num. 12:5–8.	A cloud overshadowed Peter, James and John with Jesus, and the voice of God was heard—Matt. 17:1–5.
Moses' face shown with God's glory—Ex. 34:30.	Jesus face shown with God's glory—Matt. 17:2.
God promised to raise up a prophet like Moses—Deut. 18:15.	Jesus Christ is the prophet that God promised; yet, he is even greater than Moses—Heb. 3:1–6.
Moses brought God's people to the border of the Promised Land—Num. 33:1–56; Deut. 1:5.	Jesus brings God's people into Paradise—Luke 23:43.

Time Line of Moses' Life

Dating the Exodus event is very difficult. Scholars have proposed two different possible dates for the Exodus: A "high" and a "low" date. In this pamphlet, we follow the traditional "high" date.

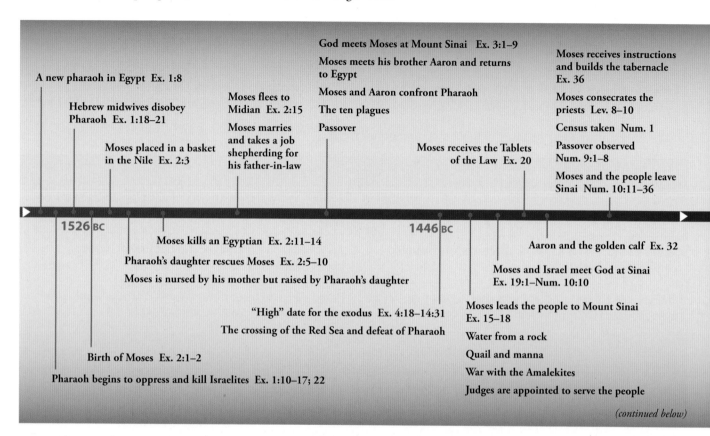

A new pharaoh in Egypt Ex. 1:8

Hebrew midwives disobey Pharaoh Ex. 1:18–21

Moses placed in a basket in the Nile Ex. 2:3

Moses flees to Midian Ex. 2:15

Moses marries and takes a job shepherding for his father-in-law

God meets Moses at Mount Sinai Ex. 3:1–9

Moses meets his brother Aaron and returns to Egypt

Moses and Aaron confront Pharaoh

The ten plagues

Passover

Moses receives instructions and builds the tabernacle Ex. 36

Moses consecrates the priests Lev. 8–10

Census taken Num. 1

Passover observed Num. 9:1–8

Moses and the people leave Sinai Num. 10:11–36

Moses receives the Tablets of the Law Ex. 20

1526 BC

1446 BC

Moses kills an Egyptian Ex. 2:11–14

Pharaoh's daughter rescues Moses Ex. 2:5–10

Moses is nursed by his mother but raised by Pharaoh's daughter

Aaron and the golden calf Ex. 32

Moses and Israel meet God at Sinai Ex. 19:1–Num. 10:10

Moses leads the people to Mount Sinai Ex. 15–18

"High" date for the exodus Ex. 4:18–14:31

The crossing of the Red Sea and defeat of Pharaoh

Water from a rock

Quail and manna

War with the Amalekites

Judges are appointed to serve the people

Birth of Moses Ex. 2:1–2

Pharaoh begins to oppress and kill Israelites Ex. 1:10–17; 22

(continued below)

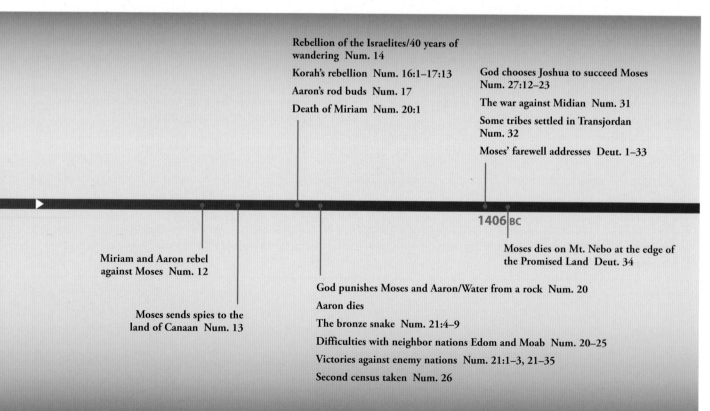

Rebellion of the Israelites/40 years of wandering Num. 14

Korah's rebellion Num. 16:1–17:13

Aaron's rod buds Num. 17

Death of Miriam Num. 20:1

God chooses Joshua to succeed Moses Num. 27:12–23

The war against Midian Num. 31

Some tribes settled in Transjordan Num. 32

Moses' farewell addresses Deut. 1–33

1406 BC

Miriam and Aaron rebel against Moses Num. 12

Moses dies on Mt. Nebo at the edge of the Promised Land Deut. 34

Moses sends spies to the land of Canaan Num. 13

God punishes Moses and Aaron/Water from a rock Num. 20

Aaron dies

The bronze snake Num. 21:4–9

Difficulties with neighbor nations Edom and Moab Num. 20–25

Victories against enemy nations Num. 21:1–3, 21–35

Second census taken Num. 26

David

A MAN AFTER GOD'S OWN HEART

King David's humanity is clear and compelling to any reader. Modern readers, centuries after his time, can still relate to his story. The Bible presents a realistic picture of a man who loved God, became a great instrument in God's plans, and was deeply flawed. David is a person we can easily relate to.

Although David's victories are exciting and stir our imaginations, David's failures and humility are what make him a powerful character and his life so meaningful. David's life shows that human weakness is the perfect opportunity for God's grace, power, strength, forgiveness, justice and holiness to shine incomparably.

SAMUEL—LAST OF THE JUDGES

In order to understand David's role in the story of Israel, we must see him in contrast to Israel's previous leaders.

- Forty years before David, Samuel was the last of the judges who brought order and unity as God's priest and prophet.
- Samuel symbolized God's own willingness to hear his people—*Samuel* means "God has heard."
- The people asked him to give them a king , an act that seemed to show disrespect for the Lord.
- He was hesitant, but God directed him to grant their request.
- He anointed Israel's first king, Saul—the name *Saul* means, "The one who was requested."
- Later he brought God's judgment against Saul when Saul rebelled against the Lord.
- He anointed David to be king instead of Saul.

> **The Judges**
> When God brought Israel out of Egypt, Israel was not a nation yet. It was, rather, a group of tribes. When they arrived in the Promised Land, the land was distributed among the Israelites. At that point, each tribe governed itself separately. When a crisis arose, God would choose special leaders to fight in favor of God's people. They received a special calling; often God's Spirit empowered them in special ways to carry on a special task.

The Prophet Samuel fresco painting.

"We want a king over us. Then we will be like all the other nations, with a king to lead us and to go out before us and fight our battles." When Samuel heard all that the people said, he repeated it before the LORD. The LORD answered, "Listen to them and give them a king." —1 Sam. 8:19–22

SAUL, FIRST (AND FAILED) KING OF ISRAEL

- Saul was "without equal among the Israelites..." (1 Samuel 9:2).
- Under his leadership, the Philistine threat was weakened but not eliminated.
- Saul was reluctant to become king. After Samuel anointed him, Saul returned to his regular activities (1 Sam. 11:5).
- Saul led Israel's armies to battle to save the city of Jabesh (1 Sam. 11).
- After an impressive victory, the people of Israel accepted Saul as their king.
- Saul made bad decisions that threatened his own kingship.

Why was Asking for a King a Bad Idea?

- The Tribes of Israel were without a king because God himself was their King. He governed them through the Law (Torah, the first five books of the Bible) and through the leadership of chosen people: judges, priests, prophets at crucial times.
- Israel was a chosen nation. God chose Israel to be his own treasured possession (Ex. 19:5). Israel should not have been like the nations around them (this is the theme of the whole book of Deuteronomy; see, for example, chapters 7 and 8).
- One of the purposes of the Law (Torah) was to help Israel be different from the peoples who lived around them (Deut. 7).

CALL OF DAVID—THE SINGING SHEPHERD

- God rejected Saul because of his rebelliousness.
- God sent Samuel to anoint the new chosen king of Israel.
- When Samuel visited David's father Jesse, Samuel expected the new king to be like Saul: impressive and imposing. Yet, God led the prophet to the last son: a small, young shepherd boy.
- After Samuel anointed him, David went back to his sheep.
- Although God had rejected Saul and anointed David as the new king, Saul continued to be king for sometime—perhaps for another 15 years or so.
- During that time, David came to be part of the royal court as a musician.
- David's music helped Saul find relief from his anguish.

It is good to know that God looks deep in our innermost being, that he knows our secrets, both the great goodness and great evil we are capable of doing. Still, Jesus came to die for each of us so we can become like David: people after God's own heart!

THE BATTLE IS THE LORD'S

- Just as Saul was tested, David needed to be tested as well.
- Saul's life was filled with fear and depression.
- When the Philistines challenged Israel, the king of Israel had to lead God's armies to victory.
- However, when the mighty Philistine hero, Goliath, challenged the Israelites to fight him, all cowered in terror (1 Sam. 17:11).
- Saul failed again to lead Israel's armies.
- During this battle, Jesse, David's father, sent David to check on his older brothers at the field of battle (1 Sam. 17:17–19).
- As he arrived and heard the commotion in the camp, David was surprised with the Philistine's defiance of God's army.
- With great courage and faith, David accepted the challenge and stepped forward to fight the Philistine.

Contrasting Warriors

The Bible's description of Goliath is important. It stands in contrast to David.

> **Israel's Singer of Songs**
>
> David was called "Israel's singer of songs." David was gifted artistically as well as with weaponry. Among the many Psalms that are attributed to him are some that form key prophetic texts in the New Testament. Psalm 16:10 is quoted by both Peter and Paul as prophetically fulfilled in Christ's resurrection (Acts 2:27, 13:35). Psalm 110:1 is the most quoted Old Testament verse in the New Testament, and 110:4 figures heavily in the book of Hebrews as pointing to the superior priesthood Christ exercised on our behalf. Jesus himself uses Psalm 110:2 to baffle his critics concerning the question of the Messiah's identity (Matt. 22:41–46).

> Ancient armies often allowed a fight between champions to decide the fate of the battle. However, behind the military practice was the understanding that it was not only champions fighting. Rather, the gods themselves fought on behalf of each army. At stake was more than just a battle: the name (or fame) of the Lord himself was on the line.

Opponent	Goliath	David
Description	Terrifying, giant warrior	Shepherd boy
Height	Nearly nine feet tall	Unknown and unimpressive
Weapons	Sword, spear, and javelin of bronze and iron; armor weighing about 125 pounds	Shepherd's staff and sling, five pebbles; a heart of faith and complete trust in the Lord

"Who is this uncircumcised Philistine that he should defy the armies of the living God?" (17:26).

David's answer showed his utter confidence in his God: "You come against me with sword and spear and javelin, but I come against you in the name of the Lord Almighty, the God of the armies of Israel, whom you have defied" (17:45). The battle ended before it had even started. Like many other parts of the Bible show, no one and nothing can stand against the Lord of creation (see Ex. 15:1–18).

FRIENDS TO THE END

Among the many events that make David's life unique, his friendship with Jonathan, King Saul's son, stands out:

✦ The two became friends after David's triumph over Goliath.

✦ The Scripture says, "Jonathan became one in spirit with David, and he loved him as himself" (1 Sam. 18:1).

✦ The friendship was costly to Jonathan. At his own risk, Jonathan protected David on more than one occasion. Although King Saul was out to kill David, Jonathan remained true to his bond. Jonathan protected David by giving him advanced knowledge of Saul's plans.

✦ Before fleeing from Saul's court, David promised to be kind to Jonathan's descendants. They parted as friends with many tears.

✦ Jonathan died in battle against the Philistines along with his father. David expressed his deep sorrow and love for Jonathan in a poem called "The Lament of the Bow" (2 Sam. 1:17–27). The words, "Your love for me was wonderful, more wonderful than that of women," reflect this deep friendship of precious and rare value.

Jonathan's Token to David by Leighton

ATTITUDES OF THE HEART

Saul's Attitude Toward David		David's Attitude Toward Saul	
Saul was jealous	1 Sam. 18:9	David remained respectful	1 Sam. 18:18
Saul attempted to make David fail	1 Sam. 18:11	David obeyed Saul's command	1 Sam. 18:5
Saul tried to kill David	1 Sam. 19:1–24	David refused to kill Saul	1 Sam. 24:6; 26:9–12
"I have treated you badly"	1 Sam. 24:17	"You have treated me well"	1 Sam. 24:17

HOW THE MIGHTY HAVE FALLEN

David's life took an unpredictable turn. David became an outlaw, escaping Saul's many attempts to kill him (1 Sam. 22:1–2). The Bible describes a difficult, if exciting, time in exile from his land. David's life went from being an independent fighter, to being in the midst of the Philistines—acting like a madman to avoid being killed (1 Sam. 27)—to serve as a mercenary for the Philistine king Achish (1 Sam. 29).

While Saul remained acting king of Israel, especially in the Northern Tribes. David increased his influence and power, especially in the Southern Tribes. After Saul's death, David strengthened his position in the Southern Tribes and became king of Judah. In the North, Saul's son Ishbosheth became king over Israel (2 Sam. 2:8–9). During two years (2 Sam. 2:10), the two kingdoms warred with each other, but "David grew stronger and stronger, while the house of Saul grew weaker and weaker" (2 Sam. 3:1).

David Contemplating the Head of Goliath by Orazio Gentileschi

Of Fools and Fair Women

During David's outlaw years, as he struggled to survive the elements and a hostile, insane king, he must have had a difficult time maintaining the compassion and civility necessary for kingly service. The story of David and Abigail shows David's sensitivity to his own failings and serves as another reminder of what made him "a man after God's own heart": "May you be blessed for your good judgment and for keeping me from bloodshed this day and from avenging myself with my own hands." (See 1 Sam. 25.)

SAUL'S DECLINE AND DAVID'S RISE TO POWER

Saul	David
Saul hunted down David to kill him. The king neglected his task of protecting the land against its enemies, especially the Philistines.	David fled Saul fearing for his life. The young warrior continued to fight and defeat the Philistines.
Saul's relationships with his family suffered from the king's increasing rage.	David reaffirmed and strengthened his relationship with Jonathan, Saul's eldest.
Saul consulted a medium to conjure Samuel because the Lord did not answer him.	David constantly inquired the Lord for his next decision (1 Sam. 23:2, 4; 30:8).
Saul took his own life to avoid falling into the hands of the Philistines	David lamented the death of Saul and Jonathan. He became the king of Israel.
Saul's heir Ishbosheth was assassinated.	David executed the murderers of Ishbosheth.

DAVID'S VICTORIES

Because of his focus on the Northern territories and his obsession to capture David, King Saul never conquered Jerusalem. Since the times of Joshua, the Israelites had been unable to conquer the city (see Josh. 15:63). The city belonged to a

Jebusite tribe (2 Sam. 5:6–15). The leaders of Jerusalem were very confident in the strength of the city. They bragged that even blind people could repel David's attack (2 Sam. 5:6). However, with a brilliant military move, David conquered the city and made it his own.

Conquering Jerusalem was David's first action as king of Israel. Jerusalem was important because:

1. Jerusalem was important for David as the new king of all Israel. Hebron was a traditional seat of power for the Southern Tribes. David had to unify the North and the South.

2. Jerusalem became a symbol of the unity of the kingdom of Israel. Eventually, Jerusalem, David's city (2 Sam. 5:7), became God's city as well (2 Chron. 6:6).

David's victory against the Philistines was David's second action as king of Israel. Throughout this time, David continued to inquire of the Lord for guidance (2 Sam. 5:19). God continued to give David victory after victory. Another important victory was for David to bring the ark of the covenant to Jerusalem. Although the actual transport of the ark to Jerusalem proved tragic with the death of Uzzah, eventually David brought it to Jerusalem with great celebration and joy (2 Sam. 6). Bringing the ark to Jerusalem showed David's commitment to God. The ark represented God's presence. David recognized that God himself was the King of Israel. He recognized that all authority and blessings proceeded directly from God's presence.

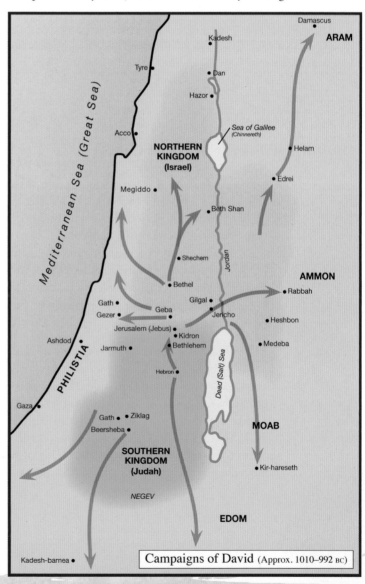

Campaigns of David (Approx. 1010–992 BC)

GOD'S COVENANT WITH DAVID

The high point of David's life came in a moment when David experienced some peace. "The Lord had given him rest from all his enemies around him" (2 Sam. 7:1; see Deut. 3:20; 12:10; 25:19). During moments of respite, David wondered about a house for the Lord. The prophet Nathan first agreed that David should build a temple. God, however, directed the prophet to bring a different message to the king. David would not build the house of God. Rather, God would build a house for David! It was a reversal of what David expected. This reversal plays on two meanings of the expression building a house: (1) Building an actual temple ("the house of God"); (2) building a dynasty ("the house of David").

God's dwelling place

The Bible makes it clear that God chose Jerusalem, Zion, to be his dwelling place on earth. Just like he had chosen to live in the midst of his people in the wilderness after the Exodus, God chose to continue living in their midst. However, David was not to build it. First Chronicles 22:8 states the reason: David was a man of war with much blood on his hands. Instead, Solomon, David's son, would build the temple (1 Chronicles 22:9).

David's house

Another characteristic of ancient kings was that they established dynasties, or houses. The principle that the Israelite king would not be like the kings of the other nations still applied. God's promise did not intend to be merely for David. The establishment of David's house had enormous implications for God's own plans. God made a covenant with David to use his family line to bring about a change unlike any other in history. Through David's lineage, the Messiah, God's own Son, would be born to redeem the world. This promise was also God's confirmation of David as Israel's king.

A KING-SIZED SIN

As David rejoiced in his victories and blessings, he stayed home while his troops went out to fight against the Amelakites. During an idle stroll, David saw a beautiful woman bathing and lusted after her. The woman was Bathsheba, daughter of one and wife of another of David's most trusted men (known as "The Thirty," 2 Sam. 23:34, 39). What the king desired, the king got. When Bathsheba became pregnant, David tried to hide his sin by making Uriah, Bathsheba's husband, sleep with her. When Uriah refused to do so because of his military responsibilities, David stepped up his plans. He plotted to kill Uriah in the field of battle. After Uriah died as a soldier and Bathsheba mourned him, she became David's wife. "But the thing David had done displeased the Lord" (2 Sam. 11:27). God sent the prophet Nathan to confront David. Although David thought he had gotten away with his crimes, Nathan's clever story caused David to discover and recognize his sin (2 Sam. 12:1–12).

> **Family Ties**
> Bathsheba also happened to be the granddaughter of Ahithophel, David's counselor who later betrayed David by siding with Absalom in his rebellion.

David's sin was terrible: coveting, adultery, abuse of his authority, and finally murder. In the ancient world, kings had absolute authority. If they desired to take a plot of land (or someone's wife or house), they just did it (see 1 Kings 21). Saul attempted to act like any other king by ignoring Samuel's instructions: he acted as a law unto himself. David, on the other hand, knew he had committed a terrible sin and tried to hide it. He knew he was below God's law and accountable to it. Despite David's foolishness, God's will mattered to him. David showed his repentance by confessing his sin (2 Sam. 12:13), fasting and praying (2 Sam. 12:16–23).

Both David and Saul did great evil before God. However, the effects on Saul and David's role in God's plans were very different. Saul's rebelliousness cut him out of his role as king. David's sins brought about a terrible punishment but did not affect his role in God's plans to bring the Messiah through his lineage.

A man after God's own heart

God punished David's sin. The punishment was as terrible as the sin. The prophet Nathan, who had brought great words of assurance and affirmation to David (2 Sam. 7), brought the dire news to the king. Because of his violent acts, "the sword will never depart from your house" (2 Sam. 12:10). In addition, the baby that was still to be born would also die (12:14). David's agony is reflected in Psalm 51. Despite the severe punishment, God forgave David! (2 Sam. 12:13). God's amazing grace accepted David's repentance, faith, and regret.

David is one of us: people who have sinned, sought, and found God's forgiveness.

Bathsheba Goes to King David
by Cecchino del Salviati

DAVID'S FAMILY TREE

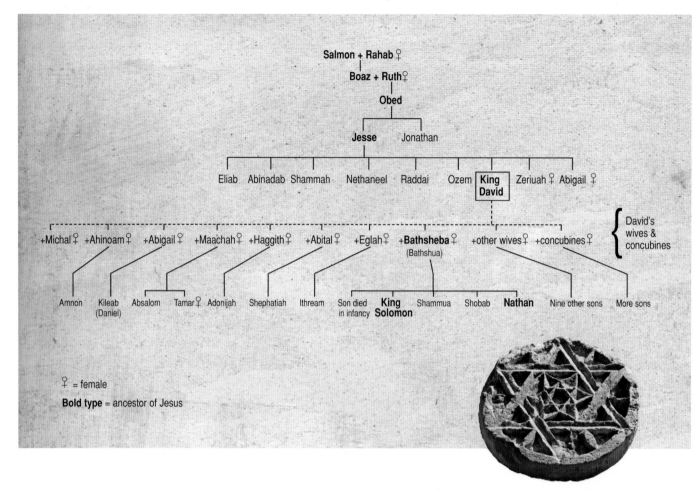

Salmon + Rahab ♀
Boaz + Ruth ♀
Obed
Jesse   Jonathan

Eliab   Abinadab   Shammah   Nethaneel   Raddai   Ozem   **King David**   Zeriuah ♀   Abigail ♀

+Michal ♀   +Ahinoam ♀   +Abigail ♀   +Maachah ♀   +Haggith ♀   +Abital ♀   +Eglah ♀   +**Bathsheba** ♀ (Bathshua)   +other wives ♀   +concubines ♀

} David's wives & concubines

Amnon   Kileab (Daniel)   Absalom   Tamar ♀   Adonijah   Shephatiah   Ithream   Son died in infancy   **King Solomon**   Shammua   Shobab   **Nathan**   Nine other sons   More sons

♀ = female
Bold type = ancestor of Jesus

The Sword Will Never Depart

The Bible provides sorrowful examples of God's punishment happening in David's family throughout the generations.

Reference	Event	Result
2 Sam. 13	Amnon raped Tamar.	Absalom killed Amnon.
2 Sam. 14–18	Absalom rebelled against David and tried to take over the kingdom.	David had to escape Jerusalem. Absalom took over the kingdom and made David's concubines his. Absalom dies later escaping David's armies.
1 Kings 1	Before David died, Adonijah declares himself as the new king of Israel.	God chose Solomon as the new king. However, the kingdom would eventually be divided into two kingdoms (1 Kings 12–14).

AN INGLORIOUS ENDING

After much struggle and grief, David arrived at the end of his life. Through the book of Samuel, David had been a strong man of war and authority. However, in 1 Kings 1:1–4, King David is an old man, incapable of staying warm, and out of touch with what is happening in his kingdom.

David's last kingly act was choosing the next king of Israel. Instead of choosing Adonijah, the oldest son alive (and who was already acting as though he was the next king), David chose Solomon. Although the book of Kings is not clear why David made this choice, the book of Chronicles states that God himself had chosen Solomon (1 Chron. 22:6–10).

A GLORIOUS FORESHADOWING

Through David's life, we can see God setting up history for the coming of Christ. Many events in David's life point to the life of Jesus Christ, the Messiah.

David	Christ
David was pursued by Saul, the rejected king of Israel (1 Sam. 19).	Jesus was pursued by Herod, the illegitimate king of Judah (Matt. 2:13–18).
David's enemies came after him, but were overpowered by the Holy Spirit (1 Sam. 19:18–24).	Jesus' enemies came to arrest him and were overpowered by the Holy Spirit at Jesus' word (John 18:1–11).
David had a friend and advocate in Jonathan who spoke up for David at the risk of his own life (1 Sam. 20).	Jesus had an advocate in John the Baptist who spoke up for Jesus at the risk of his own life (John 3:22–30).
David was tempted and fell (2 Sam. 11).	Jesus was tempted and did not fall (Heb. 4:15).
Even with David's imperfections, God loved David and made a covenant with him (2 Sam. 7:11–16).	Christ, in his love for humanity, made a new covenant (Matt. 26:28; Heb. 12:24).
David's son, Solomon, whose name means "Peace," inherited David's throne (1 Kings 1:29–30).	David's offspring, Jesus, is called the Prince of Peace and he holds David's throne forever (Isaiah 9:6; Luke 1:31–33).

When we see David's life in the light of this great truth, we can have hope to believe that our own lives, too, point to Christ, and joy in the Lord of history who makes wonderful stories out of us.

ANOINTED ONES

David, the great king of Israel, is one of the most important characters in the Bible. David was a powerful warrior, an insightful musician, and a hero of the faith. He is also important for his connection to Christ.

God promised to build a house for David (2 Sam. 7:8–16). God meant that David's lineage would endure forever. God fulfilled his promise with the birth of Solomon. However, the greatest fulfillment of this promise is the birth of Jesus Christ.

The words *Messiah* and *Christ* mean *anointed*. That is, when God chose a person for some task, that person would have been anointed with oil. Anointment symbolized God's choice, empowerment, and favor on the person anointed. People were anointed for specific tasks. Over time, it became clear that God's plans included a special Messiah. God anointed Jesus to be King and Savior of humanity.

All human rulers were flawed and sinful; but Christ, although fully human, was flawless: "...one who has been tempted in every way, just as we—yet was without sin" (Hebrews 4:15). Through Christ's obedience, death, and resurrection, God would forgive and make a people for himself. In Christ, all of God's promises and plans come to pass.

Time Line of David's Life
Events in approximate order. Exact dates unknown.

- David is born (1041 BC)
- Saul becomes jealous of David's popularity and success
- Saul's son Jonathan declares lifelong friendship with David
- David commands some of King Saul's troops
- David marries King Saul's daughter, Michal
- Saul tries to kill David; David lives in exile
- Saul takes Michal and marries her to another man
- David gathers a band of soldiers; they fight Israel's enemies
- Saul's armies chase David
- David becomes an outlaw
- David kills Goliath (1022 BC)
- Samuel anoints David as king

- Abner, cousin of King Saul, supports Saul's son Ishbosheth until insulted
- David rules in Hebron 7 years and 6 months (1011 BC)
- Six sons born to David, including Absalom and Adonijah
- David made king of Judah at age 30 in Hebron; Ishbosheth (Saul's son) made king of Israel by Abner
- King Saul and son Jonathan die in battle with Philistines (1011 BC)
- David marries Abigail and Ahinoam
- Nabal refuses hospitality to David
- David spares Saul's life
- Samuel dies (1013 BC)
- David lives among the Philistines
- David spares Saul's life a second time

(continued below)

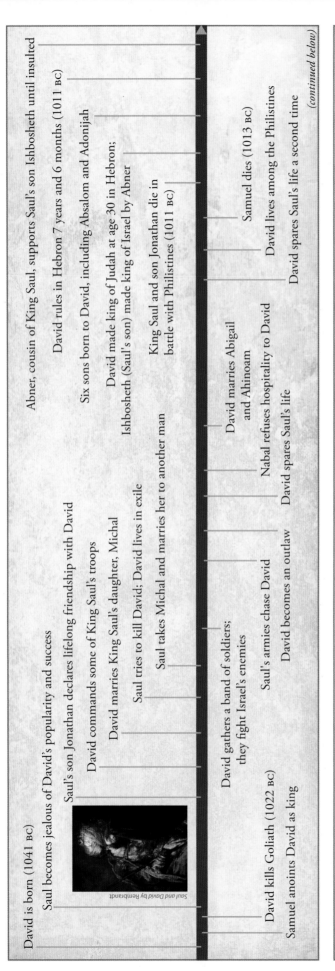

Saul and David by Rembrandt

David by Caravaggio

Death of King Saul by Elie Marcuse

- Ishbosheth murdered by own generals
- David marries four more wives and takes several concubines, has more children
- David orders the ark of the covenant to be returned to Shiloh from Kiriath Jearim
- David defeats the Philistines at Baal Perazim
- David made king of Israel; conquers Jerusalem and makes it his capital; rules 33 years (1005 BC)

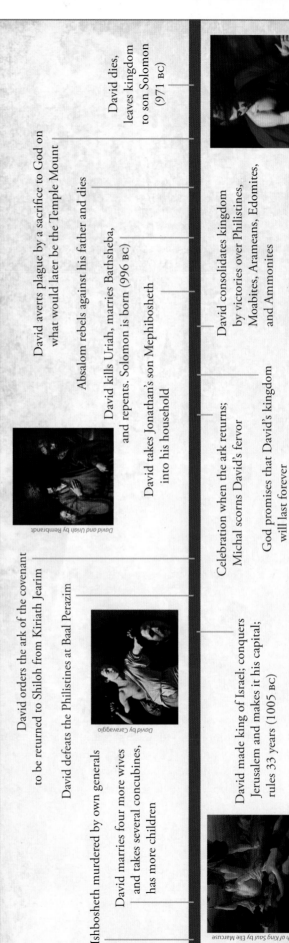

David and Uriah by Rembrandt

David with the Head of Goliath by M. Stanzione

- David averts plague by a sacrifice to God on what would later be the Temple Mount
- Absalom rebels against his father and dies
- David kills Uriah, marries Bathsheba, and repents. Solomon is born (996 BC)
- David takes Jonathan's son Mephibosheth into his household
- Celebration when the ark returns; Michal scorns David's fervor
- God promises that David's kingdom will last forever
- David consolidates kingdom by victories over Philistines, Moabites, Arameans, Edomites, and Ammonites
- David dies, leaves kingdom to son Solomon (971 BC)

ESTHER

CHOSEN FOR A TIME SUCH AS THIS

When the opposition seems unbeatable, does God care? Am I alone in this world, with its suffering, injustice, and pain? Where can I go to resign when life becomes too tough? How can I risk my reputation, comfort, and future to rescue others?

These are questions that come up in the life of Esther.

It's easy to dismiss Queen Esther as a lucky young woman who won the heart of the king. But realistically, she was a woman with a tragic background and dangerous secret that could cost her life and her family's. She was married to a king who destroyed peoples' lives on a whim and had a history of killing people close to him. Worse still, the king's favorite counselor and chief advisor was a mortal enemy of Esther's family. Esther had to keep a low profile, keeping her secret, hoping he wouldn't make the connection.

For Esther, life was unfair. But her story brings hope to all who face trouble by showing how God works even through the fears and dangers.

CHARACTER	GENEALOGY	ACTIONS IN HISTORY
King Ahasuerus (Xerxes)	Persian king Son of Darius I of the royal Persian line	The king in the Book of Esther Invaded Greece, but later defeated by Greece Assassinated by courtiers
Queen Vashti	Queen of King Xerxes May be Amestris, daughter of Otanes	Loses her position as queen for disobeying the king's orders
Mordecai	Son of Jair (Esther 2:5) of the first royal line of Israel (Kish/Saul 1 Sam. 9:1)	Raised his cousin Esther Prevents the assassination of the king Becomes the king's main advisor
Esther	Mordecai's cousin	Lost both of her parents; raised by her cousin. Wins over the king to become queen in a dangerous time Saves the Jewish people from genocide
Haman	Born of the royal line of the Amalekites (line of King Agag) an important detail.	King's main advisor Plots the destruction of all the Jews in the Persian Empire Is hung on the gallows

THE MISSING CHARACTER

Yet the missing character in the book of Esther is the one who has the largest role: God, conspicuous by his absence, who uses the actions of the human characters to shape all of history.

• God worked through the Persian king's own weaknesses to preserve the Jewish people.

• God worked through the courage of Mordecai and Esther to keep the Jewish people from harm and redeem a family name (1 Samuel 9:1; 15).

• God overturned Haman's evil plans, and fulfilled a 500-year-old prophecy of judgment on the Amalekites (Haman's ancestors) (1 Samuel 15:1–3).

POMP IN THE PERSIAN PALACE

This story takes place in the Persian royal court in Susa—a world of power where decisions, obsessions, and whims of the people with power in this world affect thousands. The book of Esther presents a childish, whimsical, unpredictable, and dangerous King Xerxes who acts in a drunken stupor, thoughtlessly punishes his own queen, is easily swayed by advisers

SUSA

Susa (Shushan in the Old Testament) is an ancient city in Iran today. Some of the oldest written records referenced this city. As Empires appeared and disappeared, Susa became Akkadian, Babylonian, Assyrian, Persian, Macedonian, Parthian, Roman, and Muslim.

In the 6th century BC, King Cyrus' son, Cambyses II, transferred the capital of the Persian government from Pasargadae to Susa. His son, Darius I (Xerxes' father), extended and improved a road from Susa to Asia Minor in the West and to India in the East. This road was known as the "Royal Road." The road was crucial for Imperial communication and commerce. Several centuries later the Royal Road became part of the "Silk Road" that joined the West to India and China.

around him, and is a danger to his people. However, these very qualities generate not only the main crisis in the book, but also its solution.

The book opens with Queen Vashti refusing to obey the king who wants to parade his beautiful wife in front of his banquet guests. On the urging of his advisors, the king deposes Vashti, leaving himself without a queen. Vashti's act of defiance sets up a series of events that will include conspiracy, pride, lies, murderous plots, unexpected heroism, and deliverance. A beleaguered, young Jewish woman is placed in a position of power and responsibility. The future of her people, endangered by a vindictive and ancient enemy of God's people, Haman, the Agagite, is in her hands. But, where is God in all of this? Are the Jews in Persia, and in many other places of the ancient world, all alone?

PERSIA

Persia became the dominant power of the ancient world in the 6th century BC. Under the leadership of Cyrus the Great, the Persian Empire (also known as the Achaemenid Empire) conquered Babylon in 539 BC. Besides being a brilliant warrior and conqueror, Cyrus was also a great politician. He created a policy to send people previously conquered in Babylonian and Assyrian times back to their homelands.

The Bible portrays Cyrus as God's instrument to free and restore the Jews to the Promised Land (Ezra 1:1–6, 6:1–5; Isaiah 44:23–45:8; 2 Chronicles 36:22–23). Thus, a group of Jews returned to Jerusalem to rebuild the walls and the temple around 515 BC. Other Jews, like Mordecai and Esther, remained in Persia.

The Persians remained in power until 330 BC when Alexander the Great, the Macedonian conqueror, defeated the armies of Darius III and occupied Persepolis, the capital of the Persian Empire.

The "Cyrus Cylinder" proclaims Cyrus as the legitimate king of Babylon. It also describes how Cyrus won the respect and favor of the Babylonian priests when he restored the temples in Babylon.

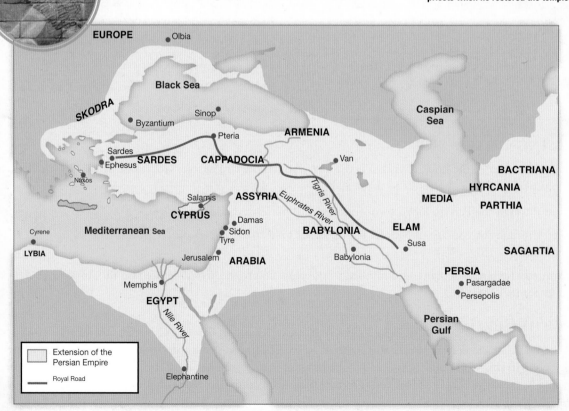

EUROPE
Olbia
Black Sea
SKODRA
Sinop
Byzantium
Pteria
ARMENIA
Caspian Sea
Sardes
SARDES
CAPPADOCIA
Van
Ephesus
Naxos
BACTRIANA
HYRCANIA
Salamis
ASSYRIA
Euphrates River
Tigris River
MEDIA
PARTHIA
CYPRUS
Damas
Sidon
Tyre
BABYLONIA
ELAM
Cyrene
Mediterranean Sea
Susa
SAGARTIA
LYBIA
Jerusalem
ARABIA
Babylonia
PERSIA
Memphis
Pasargadae
Persepolis
EGYPT
Nile River
Persian Gulf
Elephantine

Extension of the Persian Empire
Royal Road

Hebrew Name	Meaning	Alternate Name	Meaning
Daniel	God is my judge	Belteshazzar	Bel protect his life. (Bel is another name for Marduk.)
Hadassah	Myrtle	Esther	Star
(No Jewish name mentioned)		Mordecai	Related to the Babylonian chief god Marduk

ONE QUEEN, TWO IDENTITIES

After Vashti is stripped of her crown, the king finds a new queen: a young, beautiful woman whose identity seems irrelevant at the time. Her name is Esther. On Mordecai's instructions, Esther hides her Jewish identity and successfully blends into the Persian culture. The king is so pleased with his new queen that he throws a great banquet in her honor and proclaims a holiday throughout all the provinces.

BEAUTY SECRETS

Everything we know about Esther's personality is derived from her actions and the responses of people around her. The expression "won his favor" (2:9, 15) is a clue to Esther's personality. The common expression is for someone to "find favor" with a king. However, Esther "won" the king's favor, showing Esther as active and purposeful. She is no passive and powerless observer in this story; rather, she shows herself to be daring, intelligent, and strong despite having been orphaned in her youth.

But before Esther won the king's favor, she won the favor of the man in charge of all the virgins. Hegai "quickly" provided Esther with the diet and beauty treatments required, and even advanced her to the best spot in the harem! Clearly, Esther showed pleasing qualities that wore well with those who mattered. But the depth of her ability to choose wisely and to trust worthy advice is shown in her willingness to rely on Hegai's advice as to what to bring with her when it was Esther's turn to go in to the king. And the payoff is big—the king is so pleased that he crowns Esther as his new queen.

In the dangerous atmosphere of the Persian court, where conspiracies were thick and executions routine, Esther's apparent serenity stands out. She "won the favor of everyone who saw her." Her life must have seemed charmed—until the royal shoe dropped.

KING XERXES
(486-465 BC)

- Called Ahasuerus in the Bible

- Known for his war against the Greeks: Despite his famous loss at the Battle of Thermopylae in 480 BC (the basis for the famed Leonidas of Sparta and his 300 warriors), Xerxes led his armies to sack Athens.

- A year later, however, the Greeks expelled the Persian army from the Greek islands to Asia Minor.

- Much of the information about this war comes from the accounts of the historian Herodotus.

Why Were the Jews in Persia?

In 722 BC the powerful king of Assyria, Sargon II, conquered and destroyed Samaria. Almost two hundred years later, Nebuchadnezzar, king of Babylon, conquered the kingdom of Judah.

From 597 BC through 586 BC, Nebuchadnezzar systematically undermined Judah until he destroyed Jerusalem and its temple.

To avoid rebellion and exert complete dominance, both Assyria and Babylonia deported people. By uprooting people from their land and their gods, they were easier to control. Some of the Jews who were taken from their homes during these years went to Persia.

God's presence in the Jerusalem temple was a direct source of assurance and security for the Israelites, God's chosen people. If God was with them and dwelt among them, who could dare challenge them? However, the Babylonians not only conquered them but also destroyed their temple. Because every region had its own local gods, wars were also representations of divine wars. In conquering Judah, the Babylonians could claim that their god, Marduk, was superior to the Jewish God, Yahweh—a tremendous spiritual blow to the Jews (see for example 2 Kings 18:31–35).

Exiled Jews not only lost their homes and their land, but also the certainty of God's presence. In light of this desperation and spiritual grief, the words of the prophet Isaiah echo powerfully: "Comfort, comfort my people, says your God" (Isaiah 40:1).

When King Cyrus allowed the Jews to return to Jerusalem about 70 years later, an event Isaiah prophesied as God's own action (Isaiah 44:28–45:13), many who had already begun a new life in exile stayed in Babylon and Persia.

WHY DID MORDECAI REFUSE TO BOW?

The text does not specify the reasons for Mordecai's refusal.

Possible reasons:

- Mordecai's religious conviction that only God deserves praise, or

- A reflection of the ancient enmity between the Amalekites and Israelites. Mordecai's refusal provides the excuse for Haman's hatred and homicidal plans.

INTRIGUE IN THE PERSIAN COURT

Esther's cousin Mordecai, a Jew from the tribe of Benjamin, holds a high post at the royal residence. Mordecai overhears two guards plotting to kill the king, which he reports to Queen Esther who exposes the plot. The Bible relays this event without giving it much importance, but it turns out to be crucial in the climax of the story. Not only does the event determine Mordecai's future, it shows the intolerant reaction that the king has to betrayal and deception—he hangs the two guards on gallows.

Because of Mordecai's position of high visibility in the royal residence, Haman, an Amalekite and the king's closest advisor, notices Mordecai. Haman is a vain and conceited man and the mortal enemy of the Jews. Haman determines that everyone should treat him as royalty. However, Mordecai refuses to bow down before him. Haman persuades the king to approve an edict he has written to annihilate all the Jews—men, women, and children—in every province of Persia.

A QUEEN'S COURAGE

When Haman's plan for the Jews' destruction becomes public, Mordecai laments, and the Jews join him. Mordecai turns to Queen Esther to save the Jews by pleading with the king. Mordecai gives this message to Esther: "And who knows but that you have come to royal position for such a time as this."

Esther requests that Mordecai and the Jews join her in a three-day fast, after which she submits to whatever is to happen: "I will go to the king, even though it is against the law. And if I perish, I perish" (Esther 4:14, 16). Esther's memorable words are born from faith and fear. She is afraid of the unpredictable nature of the king who could legally have her executed for approaching him without being called. She has faith that someone above the powerful king himself is in control. In either case, these words show Esther's courage and willingness to risk her life for her people.

Esther relied on this courage for the next crucial steps. After days of severe fasting (and the implied accompanying prayer) Esther approaches the king, but instead of anger from this unpredictable man, she is met with his favor.

Just as this whole story begins at a banquet, Esther plans to appeal to the king at a banquet. Unexpectedly, Esther does not express her request to the king at the first banquet. Instead, she asks him and Haman to return for a second banquet.

AN ANCIENT FEUD

The Amalekites were semi-nomadic people, descendants of Esau (Genesis 36:11–12).

They became one of Israel's most bitter enemies.

They made an unexpected attack against Israel at Sinai (Exodus 17:8–16).

King Saul's failure to destroy the Amalekites, especially their King Agag, was one of the main reasons God eventually rejected Saul as king of Israel (1 Samuel 15).

The enmity between the descendants of Agag and Saul, Amalekites and Benjaminites, became an essential part of Esther's story in the Persian court.

Haman was Agag's descendant (Esther 3:1).

Mordecai was a Benjaminite (Esther 2:5).

FASTING TURNS TO FEASTING

The repetition of Esther's banquets parallels the king's banquets earlier in the story.

THE KING'S BANQUETS	ESTHER'S BANQUETS
The king calls Queen Vashti to the banquet, but she refuses to come.	Esther invites the king and Haman to a banquet; they agree to go.
The king becomes furious and listens to bad advice.	The king is pleased and generous toward Esther.
The king rejects Vashti as his queen.	The king confirms Esther as his queen by his willingness to grant her any favor. Esther invites the king and Haman to a second banquet.
Esther wins the king's favor to become queen.	Having the king's favor, Esther reveals her request and Jewish identity to the king. The king becomes furious and condemns Haman.
As a celebration, the king gives a great banquet in honor of Esther.	Queen Esther and her people are thus saved from Haman's evil plans. They celebrate with feasting and establish the Feast of Purim to commemorate the event.

ROYAL HUMILIATION

Between Esther's two banquets, another important event takes place. Haman's wife and friends advise him to build gallows and ask the king to hang Mordecai on them. Haman is so prideful and confident of his success that he builds the gallows, but Haman is doomed.

Meanwhile, back at the palace, the king has insomnia. To help him sleep, the king orders the chronicles of his reign to be read to him. By apparent coincidence, the chronicles contain the record of Mordecai exposing the plot to kill the king. When the king is reminded of this event, he wishes to follow tradition by rewarding the hero. Instead of deciding on his own how to reward Mordecai, the indecisive king looks around for someone to ask how to do this. Although Haman is actually approaching the king to request the execution of Mordecai, the king requests Haman's advice on how to honor a hero! In an ironic reversal Haman is bitterly humiliated when the king orders him to follow his own advice and honor Mordecai as a hero!

Haman returns home to receive a harsh warning from his wife and advisors: "Since Mordecai, before whom your downfall has started, is of Jewish origin, you cannot stand against him" (Esther 6:13). Before Haman can respond, the king's officers hurry him off to Esther's second banquet.

Such a reversal of fortune is an illustration of this prayer in the Bible: "He raises the poor from the dust and lifts the needy from the ash heap; he seats them with princes and has them inherit a throne of honor" (1 Samuel 2:8).

CHARACTER	TRAITS	LIFE LESSONS
King Xerxes	Foolish, rash, and acts in fits of anger	"A wise man fears the LORD and shuns evil, but a fool is hotheaded and reckless" (Proverbs 14:16). "Everyone should be quick to listen, slow to speak and slow to become angry, for a man's anger does not bring about the righteous life that God desires" (James 1:19–20).
Esther	Humble, faithful, and courageous even though fearful	"The LORD preserves the faithful, but the proud he pays back in full. Be strong and take heart, all you who hope in the LORD" (Psalm 31:23–24). "Humble yourselves before the Lord and he will lift you up" (James 4:10).
Haman	Prideful and arrogant	"Pride goes before destruction, a haughty spirit before a fall" (Proverbs 16:18). "There is no wisdom, no insight, no plan that can succeed against the LORD" (Proverbs 21:30).
Mordecai	Dedicated, and was used as an instrument of justice	"The LORD works righteousness and justice for all the oppressed" (Psalm 103:6). "Rescue the weak and needy; deliver them from the hand of the wicked" (Psalm 82:4).

IRONY AND DESPAIR

At Esther's second banquet, she chooses to express her request. When Esther reveals her Jewish identity and Haman's plot to destroy her and her people, the king's anger is not surprising. Haman realizes his doom at once.

The king leaves the room in a fit of rage. In the meantime, Haman realizes his only chance to escape alive. He falls over Esther in despair, seeking her favor. Haman had wanted all to bow down to him, now Haman is begging for his life. Haman's wife had already anticipated this "falling" (Esther 6:13). As this happens, the king enters the room.

The king accuses Haman of attempting to molest Esther. How could the king misunderstand Haman's intentions? Did he need a further reason to condemn him? This scene is parallel to the conspiracy Mordecai discovered earlier in chapter 2. There, the king made sure the information was correct before condemning the guards who had conspired against him. Here, Haman falling over the queen gives King Xerxes the perfect excuse to avoid investigation. In the ancient world, taking a king's wife or concubine was a claim to the throne (for example, that is what Absalom did with David's concubines in 2 Samuel 16:21–22). In another "coincidence," one of the servants happens to remember that Haman had built an enormous gallows to hang Mordecai. Ironically, Haman is hung on those very gallows.

PURIM CELEBRATIONS TODAY

Purim today is a minor festival which many Jews no longer celebrate. For those who do celebrate it as a religious holiday, it is a joyous celebration of God's grace and liberation, with parties, food, and gifts. During the service at the synagogue, as the story of Esther is read, people hiss and boo every time Haman's name is mentioned and cheer when Mordecai's name is mentioned. There are four main traditions people observe for Purim:

- listening to a reading of the Book of Esther,

- giving of gifts—usually food, pastries, or other sweets,

- giving charity to the poor as a way to express gratitude to God,

- eating a special meal in community to celebrate God's saving actions.

One of the special foods for this festival is a pastry called *hamantaschen*. They are triangle-shaped cookies filled with fruit (prune, dates, apricot) or a mixture of poppy seeds. In some traditions, the name *hamantaschen* refers to Haman's hat (or ears) which fell when he was executed.

HUMAN CHOICES AND GOD'S SOVEREIGNTY	
Human choices are real and have consequences.	God works through human choices.
Human choices do not and cannot deter God's action or his plan.	God does not approve evil but may use it to further his ultimate plan of salvation and judgment for the world.
We are foolish to think we can thwart God.	Wisdom is shown in acting according to God's principles.

ONE MORE REQUEST

Although the king's fury subsides after Haman's hanging (7:10), the original decree to destroy the Jews is still in force. Esther requests one more favor of the king. The request is similar to Haman's own request in chapter 3. The king's response is equally indifferent in both cases: he leaves the writing of the decree to someone else. Since "no document written in the king's name and sealed with his ring can be revoked" (8:8), the king allows Mordecai and Esther to write another edict to spare the Jews from destruction. Mordecai receives the king's signet ring, which grants him the same status that Haman previously enjoyed. Mordecai and Esther write the edict in the name of the king sealed with the signet ring. The narratives of the writing and communication of both edicts are parallel.

Each edict produces a reaction from the city of Susa—the Persian capital—and the Jewish people. In the first edict, "the city of Susa was bewildered" (3:15) and "there was great mourning among the Jews" (4:3). But upon news of the second edict, "the city of Susa held a joyous celebration" and for the Jews it was a time of "happiness and joy, gladness and honor" (8:15–16).

Chapter 9 commemorates the salvation of the exiled Jews in the Persian Empire. It recognizes the reversal of fortunes (9:1). The Jews moved from lament and mourning to rejoicing and celebration: "I will turn their mourning into gladness; I will give them comfort and joy instead of sorrow" (Jeremiah 31:13). This event became an annual festival, similar to the Passover. Although God saved his people on many occasions, only a few are remembered with festivals.

Important historical and cultural events in the 5th century BC (499–400 BC)		
APPROX. DATE	**ISRAEL/MESOPOTAMIA**	**GREECE/EGYPT/CHINA**
500–450 BC	Judah continues in exile in Babylon and Persia. The first group of exiled Jews returns to Jerusalem with Ezra and Nehemiah (around 458 BC). Around 486 BC, Xerxes I of Persia makes Esther his queen. Xerxes I is assassinated in 465 BC. Persia continues its expansion to the West and faces the Greeks.	Confucius teaches throughout China around 495 BC. Egypt is under Persian rule. The Battle of Thermopylae between the Persians and the Spartan King Leonidas occurs in 480 BC. After the Greeks defeat the Persians, the First Peloponnesian War begins between Athens and Sparta in 457 BC. Lives of Pericles, Athenian politician; Sophocles, Euripides, Aristophanes, Greek dramatists; Herodotus, historian; Hippocrates, physician; Anaxagoras and Socrates, philosophers.
449–400 BC	This is where the Bible ends its history of Israel. Persia administers the land of Israel.	The Second Peloponnesian War begins in 431 BC. Sparta defeats Athens in 404 BC.

REVERSAL OF FORTUNE

The great reversal in Susa is still remembered in the feast of Purim, which is celebrated between February and March. The word Purim comes from a Hebrew word meaning "lot" (pur). Ironically, Haman used the word first. Haman chose the date when the Jews would be destroyed by casting a lot (something like dice). On the very date that Haman had planned for the destruction of the Jews he lost his life, showing that coincidence does not exist, but God is in control of what happens. "The lot is cast into the lap, but its every decision is from the Lord" (Proverbs 16:33).

The story ends with a brief epilogue highlighting Mordecai's position in Persia. It reassures the reader that the Jews were safe and prosperous even in this distant land.

GOD'S PRESENCE AND ABSENCE

An important question arises when reading the book of Esther: Where is God in this story? The name of God or any explicit reference to him is missing. The apparent absence of God is more than an oversight. It is a theological point, one that is expressed through the literary medium. The Jews in exile had to answer crucial questions about themselves: Were they still part of God's people? Could they lay claim to God's promises to Abraham? Was God with them? In the past, God had manifested himself with power in miracles of salvation and liberation. Would God also act there in Persia, away from the land God had promised Abraham?

The book provides a series of events when things first fell apart and then came together. For the person of faith, those who know God's actions in history, God is present and active in the story. As shown above, there are different ways the writer reminds readers of God's actions: subtle references to Exodus, Joseph, and the Judges. One of the best clues, however, is Esther herself.

Throughout biblical history, God chooses the least likely person. The stories in the book of Judges show God choosing unlikely heroes: Ehud, Deborah and Jael, Gideon, and so on. Esther is a heroine because she acted in unexpected ways for her people. She surpassed everyone's expectations. Although the text does not explicitly state that her actions were born of faith, her obedient and courageous attitude, her willingness to follow Mordecai's advice to help the Jews, and her own wise choices demonstrate a person who knew how God acted in history. Esther stands in contrast to King Xerxes who in weakness relied on bad advice; Mordecai stands in contrast with Haman who devilishly offered bad advice.

God's presence and his behind-the-scenes activity are also known as "divine providence," that is, God's continuous care for his creation. As the exiled Jews wondered about God's presence, the Scriptures show that his presence and care were there all along. God fulfilled his promise to Abraham: "I will make you into a great nation, and I will bless you; I will make your name great, and you will be a blessing. I will bless those who bless you, and whoever curses you I will curse; and all peoples on earth will be blessed through you" (Genesis 12:2–3).

THE GREATEST REVERSAL

Although the reversal of fortunes in Esther was extraordinary, it was not the greatest reversal God has prepared. The greatest reversal came in the most unexpected way: in a humble king who was born in a barn, who rode a donkey, who lived with the poor, ate with tax collectors, became a friend to prostitutes, and died a humiliating death on the cross. In Jesus Christ, God produced the greatest reversal of history since creation itself. He is creating a new people, changing lives, and using humble, Esther-like people to bring about even more reversals. God defeated an arrogant, evil enemy who thought himself victorious. And one day this great reversal will end with a wonderful climax: a new heaven and a new earth (Revelation 21:1). In that day, God "will wipe every tear from their eyes. There will be no more death or mourning or crying or pain, for the old order of things has passed away" (Revelation 21:4).

Although God is never truly absent (for the Spirit is always present), often in moments of grief and suffering one feels as if God were far away. At the moment of greatest need and suffering on the cross, Jesus lamented God's absence (Matthew 27:46). Jesus, in his full humanity, also experienced and suffered God's apparent absence.

The book of Esther is a reassurance, not only for the Jews in exile, but also for Christians who "are still in the world … but are not of the world" (John 17:11, 15). An assurance that even when God seems to be absent from our world or suffering, he is ever present, interested, and ready to act. The book of Esther affirms in narrative form what the Apostle Paul affirmed in his letter to the Romans:

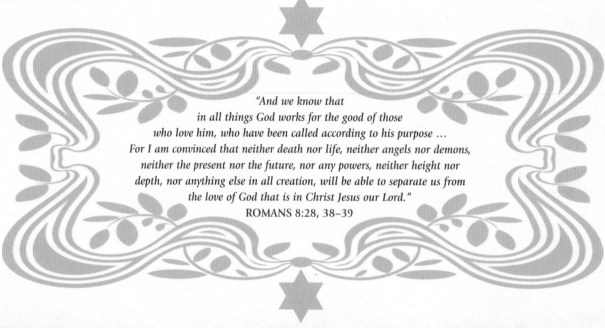

*"And we know that
in all things God works for the good of those
who love him, who have been called according to his purpose …
For I am convinced that neither death nor life, neither angels nor demons,
neither the present nor the future, nor any powers, neither height nor
depth, nor anything else in all creation, will be able to separate us from
the love of God that is in Christ Jesus our Lord."*
ROMANS 8:28, 38–39

COURAGE FOR DANGEROUS TIMES

Esther: Orphan, despised minority, exiled captive, beauty queen, trophy wife. Yet what defined Esther and gave her a place in history was the faithfulness and courage of her character, as shown in action. What lessons might we search out from her elegant story?

Esther was faithful and courageous in dangerous times.

Think of the last time you felt afraid. What did you do in response to your fear?

Why do you think God allows us to feel afraid and face danger?

Power is a noticeable theme in the book of Esther.

How have you seen people use and abuse their power?

What kinds of power do you have in your life?

What can you do to make sure you are using power wisely and not harmfully?

The book of Esther contains many reversals of fortune and power.

What reversals have you experienced in your own life?

In what ways was God working through those changes?

What do the reversals in the book of Esther teach us about hope?

RUTH

FROM TRAGEDY TO TRIUMPH

Life can throw us unexpected and painful surprises. For many of us, or for people we love, life can change in a single moment: a tragic car accident, an ill-timed jump into a pool, a catastrophic tornado or hurricane, or a broken relationship that drags us and others through horrible and sad experiences. Even worse, one terrible event might bring about another. As the saying goes, "when it rains, it pours." When events overturn our lives, we can get lost in grief and hurt. We might even experience a loss of identity and lose sight of those things that make us who we are. It is a time of disorientation.

The Old Testament story of Ruth and Naomi explores the problems of loss and identity. The answers the book offers contain much wisdom for our lives today. The book of Ruth is a love story. It is a love story between Ruth and Boaz, and one that illustrates the love between God and his people. It is a story that portrays God and his unfailing love and ceaseless loyalty.

In capable hands, stories are powerful tools. They appeal to both our emotions and our intellect. In the story of Ruth we encounter loss and suffering, disappointment and disorientation, uncertainty and bitterness. But we also find good news; we find love, commitment, perseverance, hope, and God's powerful and tender hand throughout. It is a story about transformation, about God turning our "wailing into dancing" (Ps. 30:11).

SCENE 1:

A TRAGIC STORY IN A FOREIGN LAND
(RUTH 1:1–22)

WHAT'S IN A NAME? "In the days when the judges ruled . . ." marks the setting for the story (Ruth 1:1). It sends the readers back to a time when "Israel had no king; everyone did as they saw fit" (Judg. 21:25). Israel's social and spiritual life was a mess. The time of the judges was known for its cycle of disobedience, repentance, God's intervention, gratitude, and back to disobedience. Although the text does not say that the famine was a punishment from God, the mention of the days of the judges makes this connection possible.

Whatever the case, we find a man from Bethlehem—the name *Bethlehem* means "house of bread"—leaving town and heading to the foreign land of Moab because of the famine. Already we know that things are not the way they are supposed to be. The "house of bread" is running out of bread. The Hebrew word for *bread* and *food* is the same.

The names of the man and his family increase the likelihood that we are in for a surprising story. The man's name, *Elimelek*, most likely means "my God is king." In those times, one of the main functions of a king was to provide security and food for his people. A good king made sure his people did not suffer hunger. Moreover, the names of Elimelek's sons suggest that the story will take a tragic turn. *Mahlon* means something equivalent to "sickly" and *Kilion* to "weakly." With those names, we suspect that they won't be in the story for too long. Elimelek's wife's name seems to be the only good news; *Naomi* means "pleasant." But in a story that promises surprises, we can anticipate a great surprise for Naomi as well.

DEATH AND THE AFTERMATH

In three short verses, we read that Elimelek died and, after ten years, so did Mahlon and Kilion. "And Naomi was left without her two sons and her husband" (Ruth 1:5). Before moving on, however, let's pause to fully appreciate the full effect of those few words.

In the cultural world during the times of the Old Testament, women were valued only by their connection to a man. Unmarried women derived their value from their fathers and married women from their husbands. Their security and safety depended on the husband's ability to provide for them. When a married woman lost her husband, as Naomi did, her value declined steeply, and her safety and security depended on her sons. When Naomi lost her sons as well, she became destitute. Now she was on a social level below servants. Making matters worse, she was a foreigner in a kingdom other than her own, one of the lowliest of the low.

The turn of fortunes for Naomi is total and paralyzing. Her life is overturned. It reminds us of another biblical character whose life was overturned: Job. However, Naomi was a woman; her life is even worse off than Job's because she has no one to turn to for help. "The LORD's hand has turned against me!" (Ruth 1:13).

A QUESTION OF LOYALTY

Naomi is not the only one in this position. Naomi's daughters-in-law, Ruth and Orpah, are in a similar predicament. They are also widows. Although the text never states it, Ruth and Orpah do not or cannot have children—ten years of marriage to Naomi's sons did not produce children for either woman. By cultural tradition, both women were attached to Naomi, their mother-in-law, to share her fate. Naomi, however, graciously releases them from their cultural duty and encourages them to go back to their mothers, to at least have the possibility of a future. After some argument, Orpah decides to go back. Ruth, however, decides to stay with her mother-in-law. It is a courageous decision, and one that comes from a deep love, commitment, and loyalty to Naomi. Naomi calls this love *hesed* ("kindness;" Ruth 1:8), a Hebrew word that is more often used to describe God's love, commitment, and loyalty toward Israel.

> DON'T urge me to leave you or to turn back from you. Where you go I will go, and where you stay I will stay. Your people will be my people and your God my God. Where you die I will die, and there I will be buried. May the LORD deal with me, be it ever so severely, if even death separates you and me. —Ruth 1:16–17

Ruth leaves her home, her identity, and her possibility of a favorable future, and joins Naomi in what could only be a future filled with more suffering. Yet, her actions are just what Naomi needs. Naomi leaves Moab, and when she is back in Bethlehem she says, "I went away full, but the LORD has brought me back empty. Why call me Naomi? The LORD has afflicted me; the Almighty has brought misfortune upon me" (1:21). Naomi changes her name; she is now "Mara," which means bitter (1:20).

THE LIFE OF DESTITUTION

Returning to Bethlehem must have been a very difficult decision for Naomi to make. All that she was had died in Moab. But she heard that "the LORD had come to the aid of his people by providing food for them" in Bethlehem (Ruth 1:6). Naomi understood that life for her back in her village of Bethlehem would be better. God commanded the Israelites to protect the weakest people in the community: "Do not deprive the foreigner or the fatherless of justice, or take the cloak of the widow as a pledge. Remember that you were slaves in Egypt and the LORD your God redeemed you from there. That is why I command you to do this" (Deut. 24:17–18; also Ex. 22:22). The second chapter of Ruth opens with a hopeful reminder: "Naomi had a relative on her husband's side, a man of standing . . . whose name was Boaz" (2:1).

LEARN to do right; seek justice. Defend the oppressed. Take up the cause of the fatherless; plead the case of the widow. —Isa. 1:17

However, life for Ruth in Bethlehem would not be any easier: She is female, a foreigner, barren, and widowed. Yet her commitment was firm and exemplary. She took it upon herself to care for her sorrowful mother-in-law. "As it turned out" (2:3), the text tells us, perhaps with a knowing smile and a wink, that Ruth just happened to be getting her grain in a plot of land that belonged to Boaz.

SCENE 2:

A NEW LIFE, A NEW HOPE
(RUTH 2:1—23)

BOAZ, A WORTHY MAN These three Hebrew words, *ish gibbor hayil*, are used to describe Boaz in Ruth 2:1. Translated sometimes as "a man of standing" or "a worthy man," these words offer clues to the character of Boaz. The first part of the expression *ish gibbor* means "man mighty in," and *hayil* can mean "strength, power, ability, honor, wealth," depending on the context. In this social context, the expression means a man strong in wealth, ability, and honor. In other words, Boaz is a man well respected and known for his character and leadership. The name *Boaz* probably means "in strength." Socially, Boaz stands galaxies away from Ruth's own social status.

We also learn about Boaz's spiritual character when he arrives at his field and greets his servants. Boaz is a pious and well-liked person; his servants' love for him suggests that he is a fair and honest person. He is so in touch with his servants that he even notices a new person following his harvesters. He approaches Ruth and makes an offering that speaks volumes about his character. Boaz greets his servants with, "The LORD be with you!" (2:4). Indeed, the Lord's presence becomes evident in Boaz's own righteous and compassionate character toward his servants and Ruth. Boaz makes offers to Ruth worthy of his character:

- Permission to stay in his field,

- Permission to be with his servants,

- Protection from the men in the field,

- Provision to share in the water of his workers.

Although the first offer fulfills the command to provide for the poor (Lev. 19:9; 23:22; Deut. 24:19), Boaz went far beyond the requirements of the law. Ruth's social condition places her below even the poor Israelites following the harvesters. Not only that, but providing his protection to her from the men reminds us that women then, as often is the case today, are easy targets for abuse and violence. However, Boaz offered more than protection; he made Ruth, for all practical purposes, part of his household. Again, Ruth was socially far below Boaz's servants, but now she is to share in their water. Further, Boaz invites Ruth to his own table to share his bread. It is more than a generous gesture; it is a righteous and compassionate deed.

However, Boaz is not finished with showcasing his character. Unknown to Ruth, he orders his servants to leave extra grain, and even stalks of wheat, for Ruth to pick up. Ruth ends up with about thirty pounds of grain to take home! According to documents from Babylon around that time, harvesters would take home one or two pounds a day. Ruth took home more than ten times the salary of a harvester! In addition, she took home leftover cooked grain for Naomi. While the great amount of grain Ruth brought back home was impressive, for a hungry Naomi the sight of already cooked grain was a blessing beyond words. Ruth's care and commitment soothed Naomi's bitterness and grief.

A DEEP LOVE Why did Boaz act in such a way toward Ruth? The answer, in part, is that he acted from his own commitment and character. The answer is also found in his own words. Ruth bows down with her face to the ground—as a person in her social standing would be expected—and asks, "Why have I found such favor in your eyes that you notice me—a foreigner?" (Ruth 2:10). Boaz answers, "I've been told all about what you have done for your mother-in-law since the death of your husband . . ." (2:11). Boaz is moved to compassion because of Ruth's own loyalty and commitment to Naomi. Ruth's love and commitment to Naomi exemplify the attitude that God's people should have toward those in need. Ruth's unrelenting and selfless love toward Naomi enraptured Boaz.

In the times of the Bible, marriage was more an economic than a romantic affair. Boaz had nothing to gain from courting a foreign woman from the lowest rung of the social ladder. And that is exactly what makes Boaz's actions even more extraordinary—a man doing what is right without expecting anything in return! Boaz's loving actions were a response to Ruth's own loving commitment and loyalty to Naomi. Although not at the same social level, Ruth is his match on a spiritual level.

WHOSE HESED?

With great joy, Naomi receives Ruth's gifts and cries out: "Blessed be the man who took notice of you!" (Ruth 2:19). Naomi had bitterly complained that God's noticing her had brought much affliction (1:21). When she learns that the man's name is Boaz, a light comes on in her mind: "He has not stopped showing his kindness to the living and the dead" (2:20). Who is the "he" referring to? Boaz or the Lord? It's not clear, though it probably refers to both. In Boaz's *hesed* Naomi recognizes the Lord's *hesed*.

HESED Most of the time in the Old Testament, *hesed* is used in connection to a covenant, such as marriage, as it is here in the book of Ruth. It means that people are willing to fulfill their covenant obligations and go beyond them for the sake of an important relationship. *Hesed*, then, suggests taking loyalty, commitment, compassion, and love a step beyond what is simply required.

After so much heartbreak and bitterness, Naomi finds comfort through the loving and compassionate acts of Ruth and Boaz. Although the text does not say it this way, we can recognize that God has reached out and touched Naomi through Ruth and Boaz. We would expect God to use his people this way. Boaz, after all, is an Israelite of impeccable character and reputation. But Ruth . . . well, notice the way Ruth is introduced in this chapter: "And Ruth the Moabite . . ." (2:2) and "She is the Moabite who came back from Moab . . ." (2:6). She is a Moabite, one of Israel's most ferocious enemies, and a pagan—remember that Naomi asked her to return to her gods and her family (1:15). Indeed, Boaz behaves the way all Israelites should. Ruth, although not from Israel, also behaves as an Israelite should!

SCENE 3:

A DECISIVE ENCOUNTER
(RUTH 3:1–18)

A PLAN FOR RUTH As she realizes that God is blessing her, Naomi's grief is diminished. But Naomi is still empty, and Ruth's future is still precarious. They are still poor, widowed, childless, and, in Ruth's case, a foreigner. With her renewed hope, Naomi reciprocates Ruth's *hesed* with a plan of her own. What will happen to Ruth if Naomi dies? Her prospects are even grimmer without her mother-in-law. Having witnessed the righteous character of her relative Boaz, Naomi makes a rather risky plan. Ruth is to approach Boaz in the middle of the night, after a time of celebration following the harvest, while he sleeps outside the city, where the threshing floor was most likely located. With any other man, such a plan would be a recipe for disaster. However, relying on Boaz's righteous character, Naomi is sure that Ruth will be safe.

RUTH AND PROVERBS

In the Hebrew Old Testament, the book of Ruth follows the book of Proverbs. By being there, the book of Ruth connects the last poem in Proverbs—"the wife of noble character" in Proverbs 31:10–31—and Ruth. The poem in Proverbs begins with the words *eshet hayil*: "A wife of noble character who can find?" (Prov. 31:10). The answer is Ruth. Ruth is the *eshet hayil*, the woman of noble character.

NAOMI'S LOYALTY Naomi explains her plan to Ruth and concludes: "He will tell you what to do" (Ruth 3:4). Ruth replies, "I will do whatever you say" (3:5). With this plan, Naomi is showing her *hesed* to Ruth: Naomi is seeking a husband for Ruth—a husband would assure a future for Ruth. However, Naomi needs to include the land in the marriage deal to entice a man such as Boaz to marry Ruth. By giving up her rights to the land, Naomi is taking a great risk. Once married, Ruth and the land would belong to Boaz. Naomi could end up with nothing, she could be completely

Boaz Pouring Six Measures of Barley into Ruth's Veil (Rembrandt)

destitute. Yet, Naomi knows Ruth's character and trusts in her *hesed*. Now more than ever, Naomi's future is tied to Ruth's. Filled with risks, this plan depends on Ruth's *hesed* and, as it turns out, on Boaz's *hesed* as well.

RUTH AND BOAZ

However, Ruth does not follow Naomi's instructions entirely. Instead, after waking up Boaz, she says, "Spread the corner of your garment over me, since you are a guardian-redeemer of our family" (Ruth 3:9). Boaz does not react in anger to Ruth's daring actions. He replies, "The LORD bless you, my daughter. This kindness [*hesed*] is greater than that which you showed earlier . . ." (3:10). It is not completely clear to what Boaz is referring by the earlier *hesed*. However, something Ruth has done has caused a great impression on Boaz.

Ruth's request to "spread the corner of your garment" is a term that readers should recognize. In Ezekiel, the prophet used the image of marriage to illustrate God's relationship with Israel. The prophet used the same expression, "I spread the corner of my garment over you . . ." (Ezek. 16:8) as a symbolic gesture for the marriage covenant. Ruth is asking Boaz to marry her—a very daring request from a woman to a man. However, the words Ruth uses reflect Boaz's own words back in his field in Ruth 2:12: "under whose *wings* [God's] you have come to take refuge." (The words *wings* and *corner* are the same word in Hebrew.) Being covered by Boaz's garment represents God's own covering of Ruth. However, Ruth not only requests Boaz to marry her, but she goes beyond her own needs and future and requests that Boaz also redeem (buy back) Elimelek's land for Naomi, which would then provide a secure future for Naomi. Ruth's ability to think beyond herself and consider her mother-in-law's needs shows her commitment to Naomi.

Ruth's requests to Boaz include two important social protections in the law: the levirate marriage and the guardian-redeemer. These two ancient practices had a very practical social and theological purpose: to assure both the safety of descendants and the possession of ancestral family land. Ancient Israelites derived much of their identity as God's people from these two social realities. Sons were to carry the family name and the land, which was the concrete expression of God's promises to Abraham. To this point, Ruth's explicit identity has been that of a foreign woman who accompanies her Israelite widowed mother-in-law. To the reader, it has become increasingly clear that Ruth behaves just as an Israelite should. In chapter 3 of Ruth, it is also clear that Boaz shares that view, since he has praised her *hesed* twice now. Furthermore, it has become clear to others in the city that Ruth is more than a foreigner: "All the people of my town know that you are a woman of noble character" (3:11). "Noble character" translates from a Hebrew expression that connects Ruth with Boaz: *eshet hayil*. Boaz was first introduced in the book as an *ish gibbor hayil*. Once again, the text presents Ruth at the same spiritual level as Boaz, an extraordinary claim in a male dominated world!

AN UNEXPECTED RESULT

Although Boaz promises to do as Ruth has requested, Boaz unexpectedly informs her that a closer relative has the rights of the guardian-redeemer (Ruth 3:12). However, Boaz assures Ruth that if the nameless relative is not willing to exercise his right, Boaz will do it. As a visible assurance of his promise to Ruth, Boaz gives her "six measures of barley" (3:15) to fill her shawl. Symbolically, Ruth and Naomi had come to Bethlehem with empty hands, but now Ruth's hands are full. Naomi responds with caution and wisdom: "Wait, my daughter, until you find out what happens" (3:18).

LEVIRATE MARRIAGE AND GUARDIAN-REDEEMER

Levirate Marriage: A provision in the Mosaic law which guaranteed that the lineage of a man will continue. The nearest kinsman would marry the widow of a man who dies without a son (Deut. 25:5–10). The term *levirate* comes from a Latin word *levir*, which means "brother-in-law." In addition, this law provided protection for a widow who could be in danger to become indigent.

Guardian-Redeemer: Also known as "Kinsman-Redeemer." When an Israelite man experienced hard times, his nearest relative was required to help him. The Guardian-redeemer would buy the land of the needy relative to prevent it from becoming the possession of someone outside the clan (Lev. 25:25).

SCENE 4:

FROM EMPTINESS TO FULLNESS
(RUTH 4:1–15)

RESOLUTION AT THE GATES After the private conversation that Ruth initiated, the scene moves again to the public sphere. In the public sphere, Ruth and Naomi are voiceless and powerless. Boaz becomes their voice. He is a man of strength, of noble character, of great standing in the community. However, rather than bullying others to get his way, or using his own social capital to accomplish his plans, Boaz acts with wisdom. Boaz trusts in God's *hesed*. Although not explicitly affirmed, God's presence throughout the story is apparent. When Boaz goes up to the town gate, the nameless guardian-redeemer happens to come along. God is working behind the scenes, so this turn of events is not merely luck.

The names of the main characters are important in the story. However, the relative "guardian-redeemer" remains nameless. This nameless Israelite is willing to redeem the land that belonged to Elimelek, Kilion, and Mahlon, possibly because of the financial benefits that come with it. However, Boaz reminds him, "On the day you buy the land from Naomi, you also acquire Ruth the Moabite, the dead man's widow" (Ruth 4:5). Notice how Boaz presents Ruth. To this point, Boaz has spoken of Ruth with much admiration and praise: her demonstration of *hesed* toward Naomi is noteworthy, and she is described as a woman of noble character, one who any Israelite male would be blessed to marry. But here, Boaz introduces her as "the Moabite," a foreigner who belongs to one of Israel's most hated enemy kingdom.

And she is also described as "the dead man's widow," not only a foreigner—and, although not explicitly said, also childless. Presented this way, Ruth is not a desirable partner but a financial liability. The nameless relative relinquishes his right to redeem Naomi's land. Although not doing anything illegal or immoral, this relative fails to do *hesed* to Naomi. While obeying the law, he was not willing to walk the extra mile that *hesed* would demand.

REMOVING a sandal was a symbolic act that signaled a change of status. When people expressed pain, they would tear their clothing, and changing into rough clothing would symbolize their low emotional state. When women became widows, such as Naomi and Ruth, they would wear clothing that reflected this new social status. And before going to see Boaz, Ruth changed her clothing to indicate her new status as one who is open for marriage. Boaz subsequently covers Ruth as a symbol for marriage.

In the public sphere, Boaz forced the hand of the nameless relative. By means of what seems to have been a formalized ritual, the relative transfers all rights to Boaz. This transfer was made official with an offering of clothing. Here, at the gate, the piece of clothing is a sandal. This symbolic act formalizes the transaction, and the elders witness it: "We are witnesses" (4:11) and bless the foreign woman, "May the LORD make the woman who is coming into your home like Rachel and Leah . . ." (4:11). The elders praise Ruth at the gate, just as Proverbs affirms, "Honor her for all that her hands have done, and let her works bring her praise at the city gate" (Prov. 31:31).

FROM EMPTINESS TO FULLNESS Boaz married Ruth, and "the LORD enabled her to conceive, and she gave birth to a son" (Ruth 4:13). This is a story of redemption through *hesed*. God could have done wonders with Naomi and Ruth; he could have come in an awesome storm and talked to them, as he did with Job. He could have sent a powerful prophet, as he did with the widow of Zarephath and the prophet Elijah. But he didn't. Instead, quietly behind the scenes, God allowed his people to represent him. Boaz's *hesed* represented God's own *hesed*. Boaz's loving, courageous, compassionate, and righteous actions represented God. And Ruth's own courageous, loving, daring, and loyal actions, along with her commitment to Naomi's God, show a way to go beyond the written law and seek the kingdom of God and its righteousness. Ruth becomes a model for what *hesed* looks like—not just for women, but for all of God's people.

Naomi is no longer "*Mara*"; she is no longer bitter or empty. Now, "Naomi has a son!" (4:17). Naomi's identity has radically changed. Ruth's identity is equally changed. She is no longer a foreign widow. She is now married to a man of noble character; she is a mother; and she is being compared to great women of Israel: Rachel, Leah, and Tamar (4:12). Ruth is now an Israelite woman, a woman of noble character, the mother of Obed, the ancestor of the great King David, and, eventually, of the Messiah Jesus (Matt. 1:5–16). God's *hesed* transforms and renews people!

GOD'S HESED
"This is how God showed his love among us: He sent his one and only Son into the world that we might live through him" (1 John 4:9). God's love is so much more than a feeling or an emotion—it is an action. The letter of John teaches us as much. We know about God's immense love in that he *sent* his own Son to give us life. That is the main quality of *hesed*. It is action that is born from commitment, loyalty, compassion, and love. If Ruth, Boaz, and Naomi illustrate it for us, Jesus Christ perfects it with his obedience and sacrifice. God's *hesed* in Christ gives us new life, makes us a new creation, and enables us to imitate Ruth, Boaz, Naomi, and, especially, Jesus. May our *hesed* be like that of Ruth, Boaz, Naomi, and Jesus!

WE LOVE *because he first loved us. Whoever claims to love God yet hates a brother or sister is a liar. For whoever does not love their brother and sister, whom they have seen, cannot love God, whom they have not seen. And he has given us this command: Anyone who loves God must also love their brother and sister.* —1 John 4:19–21

Psalms

Central to the Lives of God's People

In the psalms, we find words that express the deepest longings of our hearts: the aching of our souls when we experience loss, the exuberant joy of knowing ourselves forgiven, and the deep gratitude of God's amazing grace. God's people have sung, recited, memorized, and shared the psalms for thousands of years. The psalms are central in the lives of God's people.

The psalms are songs of praise, thanksgiving, lament, wisdom, blessing, and more. They provide us with models for our own spiritual lives. When pain has robbed us of words and meaning, the psalms provide us with words to scream to God for help and solace. When joy has filled our hearts so thoroughly, the psalms help us express our gratitude and our praise to God who is the fountain of all goodness.

However, the psalms do not give us step-by-step instructions for how to pray and give praise to God. Instead, the psalms *show* us how to praise and pray. As the fourth-century theologian Athanasius famously wrote, "Most of Scripture speaks *to* us; the Psalms speak *for* us."

The book of Psalms is for all of God's people. Although the psalms are important for our individual spiritual lives, they are the songs and prayers of a community, God's community. If we are to engage in the life of the kingdom of God, we must learn the language, the character, and the values of the kingdom of God.

The psalms are filled with teachings about God: who God is and how he relates to his people and nations. In their teachings, the psalms anticipate and prefigure the coming of God's promised Messiah, the one who would bring justice and righteousness to the world.

The book of Psalms can transform our minds by teaching us new and exciting things about our awesome God; it can transform our hearts by giving us words to understand strong and complex feelings; and it can transform our spirits by pointing us to the right way to praise God through our words and actions.

Background

The book of Psalms is a collection of collections. These collections were put together at different times and for purposes we might never know. One hundred and sixteen psalms have a title. It is likely that the titles were not part of the original writings and were added at later dates. However, these titles do provide helpful information. Each title reveals some details about a psalm's author, historical background, melody, use during worship, and other information.

Names for Psalms

The English word "psalms" comes from the title used in the Greek translation of the Old Testament, called the Septuagint. The Greek word *psalmos* was used to translate the Hebrew word *mizmor*, which could mean "song." The Hebrew title of the book of Psalms *tehillim* means "praises."

Authors of the Psalms

According to the titles, some of the named psalm authors are: David (73 times), Asaph (12 times), the sons of Korah (11 times), Solomon (2 times), Jeduthun (4 times), and Heman, Etan, and Moses (1 time each).

Dates of the Psalms

The poems were collected over a long period. Most were composed between the time of David (around 1000 BC) and the time of Ezra (450 BC).

In the times when the Scriptures were written, most people could not read and write. Yet the psalms still were important in people's lives. The psalms were sung (81:1–2; 144:9; 147:7), and they played a critical role in the worship at the temple (47:1; 118:27; 132:7; 149:3).

SOME FAVORITE PSALMS

Comfort:
23, 27, 42, 130

Deliverance:
13, 120, 126, 142

Confession:
27, 51, 78, 90

Forgiveness:
25, 32, 51, 103, 143

Protection:
23, 86, 91, 121, 145

Sadness and Sorrow:
42, 43, 88

Help in Times of Trouble:
70, 71, 74, 80, 83

Worry, Anxiety, and Anguish:
23, 40, 55, 91, 102, 145

The Psalm and the Psalter

Psalms are not only individual songs or prayers. They also have been placed together in one collection. When the many songs and prayers were put together, along with an introduction (Ps. 1) and a conclusion (146–150), the book of Psalms became a learning tool for God's people.

Monks of Ramsey Psalter, England, c. 1310

Scholars do not fully understand the way the individual psalms were placed in the Psalter (another name for the book of Psalms). However, we can make a few important observations that can help us understand the psalms as a collection.

 ### The Collection Is Divided into Five Books.

The five-book division seems to connect the Psalter with the Pentateuch—the first five books of the Bible. One of the main functions of the Pentateuch (in Hebrew, the *Torah*), was to instruct the Israelites how to be God's people. The psalms are also meant to be a book of instruction. They instruct us how to worship God, how to address God when we experience suffering or joy, and how to recognize the feelings that move us toward or away from God. The book of Psalms instructs God's people to be wise in all areas of life: spiritual, emotional, and moral—both individually and as a people.

 ### The Beginning and the Ending

Psalms 1 and 2 form a two-step introduction to the whole book. Two blessings frame this introduction: Ps. 1:1, "Blessed is the one who…" and Ps. 2:12, "Blessed are all who take refuge in him." These two psalms, a wisdom song and a royal song, set the tone of the psalms as a collection. For God's people, who would be conquered by the Babylonians and taken into exile for 70 years, the psalms became a way to relearn their identity as God's people. The psalms, with their powerful movement from grief to joy, from lament to praise, teach wisdom for life. The psalms show that trust in God's goodness and faithfulness, even in times of suffering and grief, leads people to a new vision and understanding of life at the other side of suffering, which is a life of praise as Psalm 150 shows.

 ### Each of the Five Books Ends with a Doxology.

A doxology is a prayer or song that praises God for his power and glory. At its core, the psalms are songs that teach us how to bring glory to God. The doxologies move from praising God (Ps. 41:13; 72:19; 89:52) to inviting all the people to join in the celebration (Ps. 106:48) to that wonderful closing psalm that has become an example of praise and celebration of who God is (Ps. 150).

Book I	Ps. 1–41	Prayers of lament and expressions of confidence in God.
Doxology	Ps. 41:13	Praise be to the LORD, the God of Israel, from everlasting to everlasting. Amen and Amen.
Book II	Ps. 42–72	Communal laments; ends with a royal psalm.
Doxology	Ps. 72:19	Praise be to his glorious name forever; may the whole earth be filled with his glory. Amen and Amen.
Book III	Ps. 73–89	Intense and bleak prayers of lament and distress.
Doxology	Ps. 89:52	Praise be to the LORD forever! Amen and Amen.
Book IV	Ps. 90–106	Answers to the bleakness of book III. The theme of "The Lord Reigns."
Doxology	Ps. 106:48	Praise be to the LORD, the God of Israel, from everlasting to everlasting. Let all the people say, "Amen!" Praise the LORD.
Book V	Ps. 107–150	This book declares that God is in control, will redeem his people, and praises God's faithfulness and goodness.
Doxology	Ps. 150	…Praise the Lord!

🕊 The Psalms Show a Movement from David to God.

The first three books in the Psalter highlight God's covenant with David. The last two books emphasize God's kingship. The Scriptures have not rejected David's kingship. On the contrary, the theological point of the psalms is that God will be faithful to his promise to David: to always have one of his descendants on the throne of Israel (2 Sam. 7:5–16). However, instead of a human king, God himself would fulfill the promise to David. This shift suggests that hope should not be placed on human institutions but on God's merciful and mighty acts. The teaching about the coming of the Messiah arises from this view of God's kingship.

King David, Westminster Abbey Psalter c. 1200

Types of Psalms—Knowing the Genres in the Psalms

A genre is a particular kind of writing—or painting, or music, for example—that shares specific elements of content and form. Most of the time we read the psalms in a devotional way. This type of reading is refreshing for our spirits and leads us closer to God and other fellow believers. However, other times we may want to explore a given psalm more deeply. In those times, knowing about its genre will help us in our spiritual exploration. Each main genre below lists a sample of representative psalms:

🕊 The Hymn of Praise

- The beautiful and glorious songs of praise to God characterize these psalms. These hymns highlight God's character and deeds, such as his goodness, majesty, and virtue (Ps. 8; 19; 29; 33; 65; 100; 145), or his righteous kingship over all of creation (47; 93–99).

- The psalmist acknowledges that God is great and worthy of praise. These psalms praise God as creator (Ps. 8; 18; 104; 148), as protector and benefactor of his people (66; 111; 114; 149; 199), and as the Lord of history (33; 103; 113; 117; 145–147).

🕊 Psalms of Lament

- The psalms of lament outnumber any other type of psalm. This fact might reflect the messiness of life, or the many reasons for suffering and sadness. However, the psalms do not typically end in lament. They move from lament to praise, from grief to joy.

- The conclusion of the psalms, the magnificent hallelujah songs (Ps. 146–150), reflect that with God, all tears will be dried, all sufferings will turn to joy, and all injustices will receive the proper and righteous response.

- There are individual prayers of lament (13; 22; 31; 42–43; 57; 139; etc.) and community laments (12; 44; 80; 85; 90; 94).

- These prayers provide us with the language to ask God to intervene in our favor. They might include a plea to God for help, the specific cause of the suffering, a confession of faith or innocence, a curse of the enemies, confidence in God's response, and a song of thanksgiving for God's intervention. Prayers of lament may include one or more of these elements.

Detail, Psalter of St. Gallen, c. 890, Latin

🕊 Songs of Thanksgiving

- These songs focus on thanking God for his answer to a specific request. The request is not always explicit in the song, though it seems that they are connected to laments.

- Songs of thanksgiving can also be individual (32; 34; 92; 116; 118; 138) or communal (107; 124).

Songs Related to the Temple

- Some songs were to remind the community of their covenant with God (Ps. 50; 81). These covenant renewal celebrations occurred in the temple.

- Other songs, royal psalms, make mention of King David or his descendants (2; 18; 110). They point to God as the King and the temple as his throne.

- Songs of Zion celebrate God's presence with his people (46; 84; 122). It appears that the singing of these psalms took place during the worship at the temple in Jerusalem.

Teaching Psalms

- Songs have a unique way of teaching the people who hear and sing them.

- The wisdom psalms use traditional wisdom themes—for example, the fear of the Lord and advice for a good life—to guide and shape the view of those singing them (37; 49; 73).

- Closely related to the wisdom psalms, other psalms praise the wonders of God's law and encourage God's people to obey it and delight in it (1; 19; 119).

Other Genres

- Psalms of Confidence (11; 23; 63; 91; 121).

- Psalms of Creation (8; 104; 148).

- Songs of Zion (46; 48; 76; 84; 122).

- Historical Psalms (78; 105; 106; 135; 136).

- Royal Psalms (2; 18; 20; 21; 45; 72; 101; 110).

- Wisdom Psalms (1; 37; 49; 73; 112; 127; 128; 133).

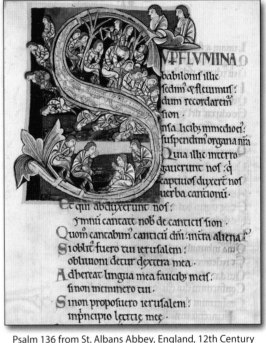

Psalm 136 from St. Albans Abbey, England, 12th Century

Reading the Psalms as Poetry

Poetry expresses deep and complex feelings and truths that may lie beyond normal speech. Short lines, powerful and vivid images, and conciseness characterize Hebrew poetry. However, interpreting a poem is like explaining a joke. Poetry is not supposed to be explained, but experienced. We understand a poem, then, when our emotions and our wills are moved as the poem desires: to joy, to compassion, to forgiveness, to repentance, to comfort, and so on. Analysis of biblical poetry is only a tool that allows us to enter into the world of the poem. However, understanding does not happen until we allow ourselves to experience the emotional and spiritual effects of each poem.

Reading Poetry

Most English poetry relies on rhyme and meter, as well as images and wordplay, to communicate the message. Old Testament poetry does not rely on rhyme, and there is a long-standing argument among scholars on whether Hebrew poetry has a meter or not. Nevertheless, the two most important characteristics of Hebrew poetry are terseness and parallelism.

Terseness

Terseness is the ability to express many complex ideas with only a few words. It is the most outstanding characteristic of Hebrew poetry. Typically, there are two or three short lines that make up a stanza. The ways in which those poetic lines relate to each other are an important tool for the poet's message.

🕊 Parallelism

As we read Old Testament poetry, we are struck by how much repetition there is. That is because poetic lines have parallelism. Parallelism means the second line of the verse repeats or advances the thought of the first line in some way. Determining how this movement occurs allows us to understand the sense and meaning of the poem.

There are different kinds of parallelism. Knowing that there is parallelism might be more important than knowing all the different kinds of parallelism. However, recognizing the main types of parallelism will illustrate how Hebrew poetry works.

Similar Parallelism

In similar parallelism, the second line can explain, specify, focus, or intensify the thought of the first line.

A *You have searched me, Lord,*
B *and you know me.* (Ps. 139:1)

A and B are the two lines that make up the first verse. The affirmation of the first line, that God has searched the poet, is further explained in the second line, B. When God searches for us, it is not as when we do a Google search. It means that God knows us, an intimate knowledge that grows in a relationship.

A *The LORD Almighty is with us;*
B *The God of Jacob is our fortress.* (Ps. 46:7)

Nonnberg Psalter Initial, c. 1255, Germany

The confession in the first line is extraordinary and is equivalent to Immanuel, which means "God is with us" and is one of Jesus' names! The second line explains what that powerful statement means. We know that God is with us because the God of Jacob is our fortress. It is an affirmation of trust and commitment.

Contrasting Parallelism

In contrasting, or antithetical parallelism, the second line moves the thought by offering a contrast with the first line.

A *Some trust in chariots and some in horses,*
B *but we trust in the name of the LORD our God.* (Ps. 20:7)

The verse contrasts two kinds of trust: one in human strengths that seem desirable and the other in the name of the Lord, which is another way to say the fame or reputation of God. The contrast emphasizes the point of the entire psalm: because of God's faithfulness and power, the safety of God's people, including the king, is assured.

Complementary Parallelism

In some poems, the following lines complement the thought or idea of the first line.

A *Have mercy on me, my God,*
B *have mercy on me,*
C *for in you I take refuge.* (Ps. 57:1)

A *I called to the LORD , who is worthy of praise,*
B *and I have been saved from my enemies.* (Ps. 18:3)

In both examples, the last lines finish the thought. In the first example, the third line gives the reason for mercy; it is called a motivational clause, in which the psalmist gives reasons for God to act. In the second example, the second line makes the result of the calling explicit: salvation.

Ways to Read the Psalms

Reading the Bible does not require advanced studies, but we should understand that there are different ways to read the Bible that produce different results. Reading devotionally, theologically, and communally are three different manners with three different goals.

Reading Devotionally

Reading devotionally has the goal of deepening and enriching our relationship with God, individually and as a group. It is the time when we tell God what is in our hearts and minds, and when we pay attention to what God has in mind for each of us. It is a time for loving communication between God and us.

Reading devotionally means reading prayerfully. Some people combine their reading with their prayer. The psalms are ideal for this type of devotional reading. Choose a psalm, for example, Psalm 23. And, as you read it, use the words of the psalm to pray to God:

"The Lord is my shepherd . . ." *You, Lord, are my shepherd.* "I lack nothing . . ."
Thank you, God, that I lack nothing; for you have given me all that I need . . . And so on.

An important part of a devotional reading is memorization. For hundreds of years, believers have memorized the Scriptures, especially the psalms. Memorization is a tool that God uses to speak to us. When we are grasped by sorrow, despair, anguish, fear, or temptation, all of those memorized verses will come back to us. God speaks to us through them in unexpected ways. They become anchors for our wandering minds and hearts. The words of God dwell in our minds and hearts, shaping and transforming us: "I remembered my songs in the night. My heart meditated and my spirit asked . . ." (Ps. 77:6).

Reading Theologically

With in-depth study of the Scriptures, we attempt to understand the larger historical, literary, and theological connections and ramifications of a text or book of the Bible. It is an important intellectual activity with a helpful role in the life of the church.

The importance of in-depth Scripture reading is clear every Sunday when pastors preach. Their insights and wisdom come from a careful and deep study of the Scriptures. However, this type of Bible reading is not only for pastors or scholars. All Christians must learn how to examine the Scriptures deeply and carefully. Good study will open new windows and understandings about the Word, God, and the world. The two main reasons for honing our in-depth Bible study skills are:

1. The Holy Spirit can more easily transform our minds and hearts in deep, powerful ways.

2. We can recognize when truth is distorted, twisted, or denied.

Reading the Bible theologically means that we pay attention, to whatever degree possible for each of us, to the history, the literature, and the theology of the book and the text we are studying. With the aid of other tools, you should also learn some history of and about the events the Bible describes. This history study will give you a context for understanding the biblical writings. Learn to pay attention to the literary side of the Scriptures—in the case of the psalms, its poetry.

We can begin to make theological connections. What does the text teach us about God, about humanity, about the world? Are there any theological connections with other parts of the Scripture? How do we read that particular psalm in light of Christ's cross and his resurrection? Are there any connections between the teachings of the psalm and that of the New Testament?

Reading Communally

Reading in groups can enhance our understanding and foster spiritual communion with others. Two ways the psalms have been used in community are in prayers and in songs. For most of the history of the church, the psalms have been part of worship services, shaped the prayers of communities, and transformed people by providing the vocabulary of faith through hymns.

Singing the psalms shapes the spiritual life of God's people, and the act of singing involves our whole beings: it forces us to be fully attentive, engages us with others singing around us, captures and transforms our emotions, and makes our bodies (voice, eyes, breathing, and body posture) full participants. Singing the psalms is a discipline too valuable for the church to forget or ignore.

Reading Some Important Psalms

Psalm 13

How long, Lord? Will you forget me forever?
How long will you hide your face from me?
How long must I wrestle with my thoughts
and day after day have sorrow in my heart?
How long will my enemy triumph over me?
(Ps. 13:1–2)

This is a song of lament. The psalmist inquires with great urgency of God, "How long, Lord?" The psalm begins with six piercing questions. Readers who know that parallelism plays a part in the composition of the psalm can better appreciate the important ways these questions relate to each other.

The questions move from the simple, initial question of "how long"; to asking God to stop hiding from the psalmist; to expressing the root problem: the threat of an enemy. The psalm does not give any details about the dangers the psalmist faced. However, the cry for help is easy to relate for most anyone.

The questions connect God's absence with the suffering of the psalmist. However, the answer to his suffering lies in God, and that is the basic confession of the psalm. "Although I'm in trouble, I trust in God's goodness," the psalmist is saying. So, the psalmist asks God to be present: "Look on me and answer . . ." The psalmist's solutions "look, answer, and give light" progressively move the psalm toward a final solution: to receive God's light "or I will sleep in death" (13:3). Giving light here is a metaphor for life. Light is the basis of natural life; God's light, then, is the basis for our lives, both physical and spiritual.

In addition, the psalmist offers motivations for God's action. If God does not act promptly, the psalmist's enemy will boast of the victory. God's name, his honor and reputation, will be tarnished if that happens. Moses argued similarly with God after the golden calf event in the desert (see Ex. 32:11–14).

The psalm ends in a beautiful and powerful expression of trust and confidence. The basis for trusting God is his "unfailing love" (Ps. 13:5). Because of this trust in God's goodness, the psalmist ends with a commitment to praise God. In six short and beautiful verses, the psalmist has shown to us the movement from grief to joy, from danger to salvation, from lament to praise.

Psalm 23

The LORD is my shepherd, I lack nothing.
He makes me lie down in green pastures,
he leads me beside quiet waters,
he refreshes my soul.
He guides me along the right paths
for his name's sake. (Ps. 23:1–3)

Perhaps the most well known and loved of all the psalms, Psalm 23 holds a special place in people's minds and hearts. Present in the psalm are two main images: the shepherd and the host. In our experience, those two images do not seem to go together well. However, when the psalm was composed, a shepherd was the protector and caretaker of both his sheep and of a traveler passing by. Hospitality while travelling the wilderness is crucial for life. God is portrayed as both the caring shepherd and a hospitable host.

In the first verse, the second phrase, "I lack nothing" states the result of the first phrase. Because "The Lord is my shepherd," we can say that, "I lack nothing." The next three verses elaborate on what it means to lack nothing. In a beautiful and memorable play with the imagery of shepherding life, the psalmist conveys the reasons for his complete confidence. In Old Testament times, "shepherd" was a metaphor for king. The psalmist's statement of trust, then, is for God as King. And the Shepherd-King provides for all the needs of the wanderer traveler.

As a gracious host, the Shepherd provides the full protection and welcoming that his tent—his house—can offer. Unlike the temporary safety and welcome that people can offer, the divine host offers a permanent, full, and certain safety and welcome to those who place trust in him.

Psalm 100

Shout for joy to the LORD, all the earth.
Worship the LORD with gladness;
come before him with joyful songs.
Know that the LORD is God.
It is he who made us, and we are his;
we are his people, the sheep of his pasture. (Ps. 100:1–3)

This is a hymn of praise celebrating God's faithfulness to his covenant. The psalm begins with a call to celebrate. This is an exuberant sort of celebration (the kind of celebration that rock stars or sports heroes often get). And it is a call for all the earth to join in the celebration.

"Shout for joy" is a general celebration of joy; "worship the LORD" is a more specific kind of celebration: the worship that happens at the temple, for example. "Come before him" is another way of saying: enter the temple, in the case of Jerusalem. The celebration of God happens on God's own terms. And, finally, "know that the LORD is God." Knowing refers to the intimate knowledge that spouses or close friends possess, and that grows in relationships. This relationship begins by understanding who we are in relationship to God: he is the creator and we are the creatures. But—and this is one of the amazing statements of the psalm—God's people are God's sheep. They are under the special protection of God!

The second part of the psalm is parallel to the first part, another three commands that explain what to do once one is at the temple: "Enter his gates . . . give thanks . . . and praise his name." The movement plays on the relationship between thanksgiving and praise. Praise arises from thanksgiving. And gratitude arises from recognizing who God is. We know who God is by what he has done. The last two poetic lines explain it: "the LORD is good . . ." We also know that the lines are parallel. So we can conclude that being good means that "his love endures forever" (the Hebrew word used here is *hesed*). Further, "the LORD is good" also means that God is faithful to his promises. Because he is faithful, we can rest assured that we are safe in God's hands (Ps. 100:4–5).

HESED

Most of the time in the Old Testament, *hesed* is used in connection to a covenant, such as marriage. It means that people are willing to fulfill their covenant obligations and go beyond them for the sake of an important relationship. *Hesed*, then, suggests taking loyalty, commitment, compassion, and love a step beyond what is simply required.

The Psalms and the New Testament

When Jesus said that all of the Scriptures spoke of him, he specifically mentioned the Psalms (Luke 24:44). It is not surprising then to find that the New Testament writers quote many of the Psalm's texts. The table shows some of these important quotations and what they say about the Messiah.

Psalm	What It Says of Jesus
2:1–12	Jesus is the Messiah, King and Son of God.
16:1–11	Jesus will rise from the dead.
22:1–31	Jesus will be forsaken, mocked, become thirsty, be pierced in hands and feet, have his clothes divided and gambled over, but conquer death to God's everlasting praise.
31:1–24	Jesus will commit his spirit into the hands of God and gain victory over those who oppress him.
40:1–17	Jesus will become human to fulfill the law for us just as it was written.
41:9–13	A close friend will betray Jesus, but Jesus will triumph in the end.
45:6–7	Jesus is crowned above all others and worshiped as God.
69:7–21	Because of his zeal, his own people will despise Jesus. He will be given gall and vinegar.
72:1–19	Jesus as David's son will be king forever.
110:1–6	Jesus will rule at God's right hand as Lord and High Priest.
118:1–29	Jesus will gain victory over his enemies and death. Although he is rejected, God will establish him as the one "who comes in the name of the Lord" (Ps. 118:26).

Proverbs: A Guide to Godly Living

"An apple a day keeps the doctor away..." We all have heard or used some of these pithy sayings at one point or another. They express popular wisdom about the world that anyone can understand and apply. Their content expresses an observation about nature or society or advice concerning behavior or making choices.

People understand that following the advice of these wise sayings will help one to live a better life. Part of their effectiveness lies in their brevity—they are easy to remember. These sayings are most effective when we quote them at the right moment and in the right circumstances.

> Proverbs are short, memorable sayings that generalize on human experience to communicate an experiential truth.

Although we all recognize that these bits of wisdom are helpful, they are not universal or always applicable. While generally "an apple a day keeps the doctor away," we all know that some serious illnesses require immediate medical attention. In other words, we all recognize the limits of popular wisdom.

In the following pages, we will learn about biblical proverbs from the book of Proverbs: their background, hints and steps for interpretations, main themes, and connections with the New Testament and the church today.

Who Wrote the Book?

- Proverbs 1:1, 10:1, and 25:1 affirm that King Solomon, King David's son, was the main author.
- Proverbs 25:1 also affirms that "the men of Hezekiah king of Judah" copied them.
- The book also recognizes other contributors: Wise men (22:17; 24:23), Agur (30:1), and Lemuel (31:1). Nothing is known about these writers.
- We read in 1 Kings 4:32 that Solomon wrote three thousand proverbs.

wisdom

Wisdom is often defined as "the ability to make godly choices." In the Bible, wisdom is tightly connected to creation. The way God created the universe has a direct effect on the way nature and society behave. In an important sense, wisdom is the ability to see life and the world the way God sees them. Wisdom is practical knowledge that allows people to live fully.

proverb

Proverb is a short, memorable saying that communicates an observation of the world or experience that helps one live better. The Hebrew word behind it is *mashal*. Among its meanings are: to rule and to compare or liken. The wisdom of proverbs helps wise people to master the art of godly living, as well as to discern how our lives and our behavior are connected with God's creation.

fear of the Lord

The Bible is clear that "the fear of the Lord is the beginning of knowledge" (1:7). In the Bible, the starting point of wisdom and its end-goal are an all-embracing relationship with God, the LORD of the covenant. The fear of the LORD is not a sense of terror but of reverence. In other words, it is a deep sense of who God is and who we are in relation to him. It is a deep understanding that God is the creator, sustainer, savior, judge, and owner of the whole universe. This knowledge is a relational knowledge that affects our behavior. The psalmist explains, "The Lord delights in those who fear him, who put their hope in his unfailing love" (Ps. 147:11). Fearing the LORD, then, takes the form of trust: trust in God's faithfulness to his promises as creator, redeemer, savior, and judge.

How Is the Book Arranged?

The structure of the book gives us an overview of the content and themes. The main sections of the book of Proverbs are:

1. Introduction to the book (1:1–7)
2. Instructions and warnings (1:8–9:18)
3. First collection of Solomon's proverbs (10:1–22:16)
4. First collection of the words of the wise (22:17–24:22)
5. Second collection of the words of the wise (24:23–34)
6. Second collection of Solomon's proverbs (25:1–29:27)
7. The words of Agur (30)
8. The words of Lemuel (31:1–9)
9. Poem of the virtuous woman (31:10–31)

Main Themes in the Book of Proverbs

1 Wisdom   We can read the whole book as an appeal to choose wisdom over all other things.

God created wisdom (8:22–23)	*The Lord brought me forth as the first of his works, before his deeds of old; I was appointed from eternity, from the beginning, before the world began.*
God used wisdom to create the universe (8:24–31)	*Then I was the craftsman at his side. I was filled with delight day after day, rejoicing always in his presence.*
God reveals and is the source of wisdom (2:6–7; 30:5–6)	*For the Lord gives wisdom, and from his mouth come knowledge and understanding (2:6–7).*
The beginning of wisdom is "fear of the Lord" (1:7; 2:5; 9:10; 10:27; 14:27; 15:16, 33; 16:6; 19:23; 22:4; 23:17)	*The fear of the Lord is the beginning of knowledge, but fools despise wisdom and discipline (1:7).*
Wisdom is desirable over all things (4:7–9; 8:10–11)	*Choose my instruction instead of silver, knowledge rather than choice gold, for wisdom is more precious than rubies, and nothing you desire can compare with her (8:10–11).*

2 Understanding Humanity   Wisdom teaching is directed to all people. Proverbs is an invitation to accurately identify the source of all wisdom, neither over- nor underestimating human wisdom. In the book of Proverbs we learn about humans:

Humans are God's creation (29:13)	*The poor man and the oppressor have this in common: The Lord gives sight to the eyes of both.*
Humans delude themselves (12:15; 14:12; 16:2; 25; 28:26)	*There is a way that seems right to a man, but in the end it leads to death.*
The heart is central and reveals humanity's true character (27:19)	*As water reflects a face, so a man's heart reflects the man.*
Humans are inherently foolish (22:15)	*Folly is bound up in the heart of a child, but the rod of discipline will drive it far from him.*

3 Description of a wise person

Wisdom is not something easily taught. As with many important things, it is easier to show what a wise person looks like than describe wisdom. Wise people are recognized by their:

Character

They are righteous (13:5–6; 12:17)	*The righteous hate what is false, but the wicked bring shame and disgrace. Righteousness guards the man of integrity, but wickedness overthrows the sinner (13:5–6).*
Loyal (16:6)	*Through love and faithfulness sin is atoned for; through the fear of the LORD a man avoids evil.*
Humble (3:5, 9; 8:17; 28:13; 21:4)	*He who conceals his sins does not prosper, but whoever confesses and renounces them finds mercy (28:13).*
Teachable (12:1, 15; 3:1; 10:14; 15:12; 17:10; 18:15)	*The heart of the discerning acquires knowledge; the ears of the wise seek it out (18:15).*
Self-controlled and not rash (17:27; 14:29, 30; 19:2)	*A man of knowledge uses words with restraint, and a man of understanding is even-tempered (17:27).*
Forgiving (10:12; 17:9; 14:9; 20:22; 24:29)	*Do not say, "I'll do to him as he has done to me; I'll pay that man back for what he did" (24:29).*
Thoughtful (13:16; 14:8, 15, 16; 22:5)	*A simple man believes anything, but a prudent man gives thought to his steps. A wise man fears the LORD and shuns evil, but a fool is hotheaded and reckless (14:15–16).*
Is honest (12:22)	*The LORD detests lying lips, but he delights in men who are truthful.*
Does not boast (27:2)	*Let another praise you, and not your own mouth; someone else, and not your own lips.*
Does not reveal secrets (17:9; 20:19)	*He who covers over an offense promotes love, but whoever repeats the matter separates close friends (17:9).*
Does not slander (6:12)	*A scoundrel and villain, who goes about with a corrupt mouth.*
Is peaceful (12:16)	*A fool shows his annoyance at once, but a prudent man overlooks an insult.*

Speech

Words have power (10:11; 12:18)	*Reckless words pierce like a sword, but the tongue of the wise brings healing (12:18).*
Limits of words (14:23; 28:24; 26:18–19)	*Like a madman shooting firebrands or deadly arrows is a man who deceives his neighbor and says, "I was only joking!" (26:18–19).*

Relationship with Wife

He recognizes she is from God (18:22; 19:14)	Houses and wealth are inherited from parents, but a prudent wife is from the LORD (19:14).
Acknowledges as his crowning glory (12:4; 31:28)	He who finds a wife finds what is good and receives favor from the LORD (12:4).
Is faithful to her (5:15–20; 6:29)	Drink water from your own cistern, running water from your own well. Should your springs overflow in the streets, your streams of water in the public squares? Let them be yours alone, never to be shared with strangers. May your fountain be blessed, and may you rejoice in the wife of your youth (5:15–18).

Relationship with Children

Acknowledges the need for wisdom in their lives (1–9)	*My son, do not forget my teaching, but keep my commands in your heart, for they will prolong your life many years and bring you prosperity (3:1–2).*
Recognizes children's natural condition (22:15)	*Folly is bound up in the heart of a child, but the rod of discipline will drive it far from him.*
Children can be trained (19:18; 22:6)	*Train a child in the way he should go, and when he is old he will not turn from it (22:6).*
Recognizes that foolish children are in danger and wisdom can help (20:20)	*If a man curses his father or mother, his lamp will be snuffed out in pitch darkness.*
Loves children and disciplines them (13:24)	*He who spares the rod hates his son, but he who loves him is careful to discipline him.*

Relationships with Other People

Chooses kind friends (22:24–25)	*Do not make friends with a hot-tempered man, do not associate with one easily angered, or you may learn his ways and get yourself ensnared.*
Values and is loyal to friends (27:10; 17:17)	*Do not forsake your friend and the friend of your father, and do not go to your brother's house when disaster strikes you—better a neighbor nearby than a brother far away (27:10).*
Behaves fairly and justly with all (3:27–28)	*Do not withhold good from those who deserve it, when it is in your power to act. Do not say to your neighbor, "Come back later; I'll give it tomorrow"—when you now have it with you.*
Is considerate (25:17)	*Seldom set foot in your neighbor's house—too much of you, and he will hate you.*
Lives in peace (3:29; 25:8–9)	*Do not plot harm against your neighbor, who lives trustfully near you (3:29).*

Possessions

Recognizes the proper value of money (30:7–9; 11:4)	*Wealth is worthless in the day of wrath, but righteousness delivers from death (11:4).*
Wisdom is better than riches (15:16; 16:8, 16; 22:1)	*How much better to get wisdom than gold, to choose understanding rather than silver! (16:16).*
Honors God with possessions and recognizes that blessings come from God (3:9–10; 10:22; 14:24)	*Honor the Lord with your wealth, with the firstfruits of all your crops; then your barns will be filled to overflowing, and your vats will brim over with new wine (3:9–10).*
Recognizes that foolish behavior leads to poverty (6:6–11; 10:4–5; 21:17; 26:13–15), as do injustice and oppression (13:23; 16:8; 22:16)	*He who loves pleasure will become poor; whoever loves wine and oil will never be rich (21:17).* *He who oppresses the poor to increase his wealth and he who gives gifts to the rich—both come to poverty (22:16).*
Is generous with possessions (3:27–28; 11:24; 28:27; 29:7)	*The righteous care about justice for the poor, but the wicked have no such concern (29:7).*
Is kind to animals (12:10)	*A righteous man cares for the needs of his animal, but the kindest acts of the wicked are cruel.*

A good man leaves an inheritance for his children's children,
but a sinner's wealth is stored up for the righteous.

4 Kingship

In the world of ancient Israel, the king represented the people. Kings were meant to model attitudes, behaviors, and character that all people should display in their lives. Jesus, the King of kings, plays this role when he shows us what it means to be God's children. Thus, the king should:

Know his place (21:1)	The king's heart is in the hand of the Lord; he directs it like a watercourse wherever he pleases.
Be wise (8:15–16)	By me kings reign and rulers make laws that are just; by me princes govern, and all nobles who rule on earth.
Be righteous (25:5)	Remove the wicked from the king's presence, and his throne will be established through righteousness.
Be just (28:8; 29:4, 14)	If a king judges the poor with fairness, his throne will always be secure (29:14).
Have self-control (31:1–7)	[D]o not spend your strength on women, your vigor on those who ruin kings. "It is not for kings, O Lemuel—not for kings to drink wine, not for rulers to crave beer (31:3–4).
Be compassionate (31:8–9)	"Speak up for those who cannot speak for themselves, for the rights of all who are destitute. Speak up and judge fairly; defend the rights of the poor and needy."
Be surrounded by godly people (16:13; 22:11)	He who loves a pure heart and whose speech is gracious will have the king for his friend (22:11).

genre **Genre** refers to the sorting of written texts into categories. Separating texts in genres is helpful for understanding the ways different texts work internally, as well as the settings in which they were used. For example, we have different expectations from a letter from a bank than we do a letter from a loved one. Each type of letter produces certain expectations and prompts a specific response.

The Bible contains different genres: narrative, prophecy, poetry, wisdom, apocalyptic literature, gospel, letters, history, and others. Each general genre is subdivided into smaller types. Wisdom, for example, is subdivided into proverbs, instructions, speeches, and advice. Knowing the genre helps us know the intention for the text.

Wisdom Literature

As "an apple a day" illustrates, proverbs do not occur exclusively in the Bible. The book of Proverbs is an example of a wider category of wisdom literature. In ancient Egypt and Mesopotamia, wisdom played an important role. In those societies, wisdom belonged to the royal court. Wise teachers instructed their royal students for important positions within the kingdom. From scribes to nobles, wisdom taught the proper—wise—behavior in the court, correct speech, and an understanding of society and the world that allowed them to serve the ruler effectively.

Wisdom Literature in the Bible

The book of Proverbs is an example of a wider category of wisdom books in the Old Testament.

Wisdom Books	Wisdom Themes in Other Books
• Job • Proverbs • Ecclesiastes	• Song of Songs • Psalms (for example, 1, 19, 34, 49, 78, 119) • Genesis (1–2, 37–50) • Amos and Isaiah • Daniel

Biblical wisdom literature shares themes, vocabulary, and genres with this international wisdom tradition. The chart shows some important differences between the wisdom of the Bible and that of the world around ancient Israel.

	Egypt and Mesopotamia	Old Testament
Focus	Anthropocentric (human-centered) The main interest was on finding ways for people to be successful in life. Material success was emphasized.	Theocentric (God-centered) The main focus is on the God who created with order. Success in life is connected to human relationship with God.
God	Since these societies were polytheistic, their wisdom depended on a personal god or a number of other gods. Each god provided some wisdom.	The Bible declares that the LORD alone is God. God is the source of all wisdom because he himself created wisdom and created the universe with wisdom.
Audience	The main audience for wisdom teachers were court officials and royalty.	Wisdom is meant for all people. Although Proverbs emphasize "sons," the other wisdom books make it clear that wisdom is for all.
Goal	Help civil servants to be effective and successful in their work and life in general.	Teach people to love wisdom by having a correct relationship with God, by understanding the order with which God created the universe, and by recognizing the limits of human wisdom.

Parallelism

Parallel lines are an important feature of biblical proverbs. English proverbs normally have one line—"a penny saved is a penny earned." Hebrew proverbs normally have two lines—"A fool finds pleasure in evil conduct, but a man of understanding delights in wisdom" (10:23).

The sense of the proverb is found in the interplay of these lines.

Parallelism means that the second line of the verse advances the thought of the first line in some way. Determining how this movement occurs allows us to understand the sense and meaning of the proverb. There are different kinds of parallelism; the following examples are the most common types of parallelism in the book of Proverbs.

Kings take pleasure in honest lips; they value a man who speaks the truth (16:13).	In this example, we find these parallels: 1. Kings are the main subject of the whole verse. 2. Taking pleasure is parallel to value. However, valuing something is a step beyond merely taking pleasure. 3. Honest lips is parallel to a man who speaks the truth. Although both expressions mean the same, the second one further specifies what honest lips are. 4. Some call this type of parallelism synonymous parallelism.
A fool finds pleasure in evil conduct, but a man of understanding delights in wisdom (10:23).	1. This verse presents a contrast which provides the parallelism. 2. A fool is contrasted with a man of understanding. 3. Another parallel is the action of each person: one finds pleasure whereas the other delights. The two concepts are closely related, though the first one seems more impulsive. 4. The true contrast is on what each one finds delight in: the fool finds pleasure in evil conduct, while the man of understanding delights in wisdom. 5. The final contrast is the key to the verse. Like the rest of Proverbs, the book invites its readers to delight in wisdom. Some call this contrasting parallel antithetical parallelism.
Better a meal of vegetables where there is love than a fattened calf with hatred (15:17)	1. Another important form of parallelism is often called "better than" proverbs. 2. These proverbs explain why wisdom is superior to folly. 3. In the book of Proverbs, riches can be a blessing from God. But not all riches are desirable. When riches are accompanied by hatred, then poverty with love is preferable.

Lady Wisdom and Lady Folly

The function of the book of Proverbs is to persuade and instruct. First, the book invites readers to make a decision. The choice is not only a rational one; it involves desires and emotions, as well as intelligence and discernment. The writer attempts to capture the reader's will by appealing to the imagination.

In the first nine chapters, the book addresses a "son." For young men, the choice of the right woman is life changing. Proverbs invites its readers to make an equally life-changing choice. Choosing wisdom over folly changes people's lives in a powerful way.

> Although the book addresses men only, as was traditional in ancient societies, its lessons are meant for all of God's people.

Wisdom and Folly are characterized as women. The readers "hear" from both Lady Wisdom and Lady Folly. Their invitations become alternatives between life and death. When reading the book of Proverbs, we must allow it to touch our emotions and our wills. We must allow ourselves not just to choose Lady Wisdom but also to love and pursue her.

Proverbs in Context

Although we can read each proverb separately, biblical proverbs were placed, by divine will, in a specific book context. Proverbs is part of a larger conversation with the other "wisdom books." Proverbs, Job, and Ecclesiastes balance and complement each other's views about wisdom, God, creation, humanity, and every important topic of the Bible.

A superficial reading of the book of Proverbs could suggest that the world functions with a perfect retribution theology: good things happen to good people, and bad things happen to bad people. As tempting as that might be to believe, the story in the book of Job calls us to be cautious. While Job's three friends argue individually that God rewards the righteous and punishes the wicked, Job continues to defend his own innocence. As readers, we know from the introduction in chapters one and two that Job is being used and abused by Satan, with God's authorization.

Job pleads for an audience with the creator. When he gets one, Job does not receive answers but a series of questions from God. God shows that he alone is wise; Job humbly recognizes the limits of his own wisdom, and declares, "Surely I spoke of things I did not understand, things too wonderful for me to know" (Job 42:3). At the end, God justifies and restores Job. He also rebukes Job's friends for their foolishness. Just as the book of Proverbs is an invitation to fall in love with Lady Wisdom, the book of Job is a reminder that we should not fall in love with our own wisdom.

Proverbs Today

Should we read the Proverbs today? Yes! And not only should we read them, but we need to allow the beauty and desirability of Lady Wisdom to captivate our imaginations and wills. The consequences of our efforts will be evident in:

1. Life
2. Health
3. Riches
4. Fulfillment and satisfaction
5. Relationships
6. Joy
7. Peace
8. Hope
9. Knowledge of and love for the world
10. Greater appreciation of God's wisdom in our lives

We will also be able to know and relate better to Jesus, "who has become for us wisdom from God…" (1 Cor. 1:30). In Jesus, God reveals the extent, depth, and power of his wisdom.

Reading Proverbs

Since the wisdom in the book of Proverbs is important for our lives today, how can we study it profitably? Below are common mistakes we make when reading the book and some suggestions for studying Proverbs.

Common mistakes when reading Proverbs

1. *Ignoring the genre of the book.* Biblical proverbs are not promises, nor are they universal, timeless truths. Although there are wonderful truths to learn from them, and some clarification on doctrinal matters, the role of the proverbs is to challenge our minds, hearts, and wills.

2. *Isolating individual proverbs from the rest of the book and Bible.* If we read only, "Lazy hands make a man poor, but diligent hands bring wealth" (Proverbs 10:4), we would get the impression that laziness is the cause for poverty. However, the book of Proverbs also makes it clear that other reasons exist. "He who oppresses the poor to increase his wealth and he who gives gifts to the rich—both come to poverty" (Proverbs 22:16) suggests that oppression and lack of opportunities are also causes of poverty.

3. *Forgetting the limits of wisdom.* The most evident limit is that proverbs are not adequate for every occasion. Reading and applying the sayings of the book requires wisdom: "Like a thornbush in a drunkard's hand is a proverb in the mouth of a fool" (26:9) and "A man finds joy in giving an apt reply—and how good is a timely word" (15:23). The wisdom of the proverbs are limited by their genre and good timing for their use. Also, although the proverbs reveal some of God's wisdom, our wisdom to understand and apply it is limited. Knowing that Jesus is the fullness of God's wisdom is a reminder that the wisdom we find in the book of Proverbs is limited.

Suggestions for reading the book of Proverbs

1. Remember that the meaning of individual proverbs is determined by the whole book's message.

2. Be sensitive to the metaphors and other literary devices in the book. Be especially attentive to the parallelism of lines.

3. Discern the specific message of the proverb. Then identify the contexts in which that particular proverb is applicable. Not all proverbs are applicable to all occasions. Part of what it means to be a wise person is knowing when and how wisdom is applicable.

4. Use commentaries to help you interpret cultural or literary issues. Proverbs uses imagery and customs that require knowledge of the ancient world.

5. If studying a theme in the book of Proverbs, like riches or discipline, read the entire book of Proverbs in more than one translation. Make notes of verses or sections that relate to the theme you are interested in. Then gather all the relevant verses and organize them in a way that makes the theme clear and does justice to the overall theme and message of the book of Proverbs.

6. The proverbs call us not to simply gain more knowledge but to become wiser in our words and actions. Search for a person who might be a good illustration of the wisdom you are studying. Remember that Jesus is the best illustration of God's wisdom.

Recommended Reading

Gordon D. Fee and D. Stuart, How to Read the Bible for All Its Worth. Grand Rapids: Zondervan, 2003.

Tremper Longman III. How to Read Proverbs. Downers Grove: InterVarsity Press, 2002.

Derek Kidner. Proverbs. Tyndale Old Testament Commentary Series. Downers Grove: InterVarsity Press, 1964.

Allen Ross. Proverbs. The Expositor's Bible Commentary. Grand Rapids: Zondervan, 1991.

Bruce Waltke. Proverbs 1:1–15:29. NICOT. Grand Rapids: Eerdmans, 2004.

Bruce Waltke. Proverbs 15:30–31:31. NICOT. Grand Rapids: Eerdmans, 2005.

JONAH

Have you ever felt anxious about having to confront someone with a truth that might cause conflict or hostility? The prophet Jonah's anxiety was not about telling a truth from God to a city; his anxiety came from the realization that the city just might repent!

The story of Jonah is best known for the time the prophet spent inside a fish. However, the story and its message are more than a three-day fish story! Although the hapless prophet has received the most attention, this is a story about a compassionate, merciful, and powerful God. The book of Jonah is an exciting invitation to meet a God that surprises, moves, challenges, and changes us in new and powerful ways.

JONAH IN BIBLICAL HISTORY

We first meet Jonah in the book of Kings (2 Kings 14:25). There, Jonah prophesies during the reign of King Jeroboam II around the beginning of the 8th century (790–760 BC).

This period of history is significant in the life of ancient Israel and the kingdoms around it. The enemy empires of Egypt and Assyria were experiencing urgent internal crises that kept them near home, far away from the edges of their territory. With this temporary freedom, Israel experienced times of prosperity. The prophets Amos and Micah's ministries occurred during these times.

During the reign of Jeroboam II, Jonah spoke a prophecy: King Jeroboam II would restore the boundaries of Israel (2 Kings 14:25). But in the book of Jonah, his task is quite different. This prophetic book is not promising new military victories.

THE STORY

1 God calls Jonah: Jonah Flees

God called the prophet Jonah from the northern kingdom of Israel to deliver a message to the city of Nineveh. It's a most unexpected calling: "Go to the great city of Nineveh and preach against it…" (Jonah 1:2).

At first glance, it appears to be great news: God's judgment is about to fall on the hated enemies. Surprisingly, however, the text informs us, "the prophet ran away from the Lord" (Jonah 1:3). Why did he do that? It makes no sense. Yet, Jonah's actions unleash a series of events that challenge us as believers.

Have you ever felt like "hiding" from God when he interrupts your life? Hiding from God doesn't mean one flees to the end of the world. Sometimes getting lost in our busyness is enough to hide. Have you ever tried to hide or make excuses when you sense God might be trying to tell you something?

ASSYRIA

After a period of decline, the Assyrian king Ashurnasirpal II (reigned 883–859 BC) began to expand the kingdom. His famous palace reliefs depict his campaigns. His descriptions are gory and display great cruelty; he describes cutting off the hands, feet, noses, ears, and lips of his prisoners. One of his military strategies was to induce terror in his conquered territories and neighbors. This policy continued until the times of kings:

- ⚜ Tiglath-pileser III (reigned 747–727 BC),
- ⚜ Shalmaneser V (reigned 726–722 BC),
- ⚜ Sargon II (reigned 721–705 BC, and responsible for the destruction of Samaria), and
- ⚜ Sennacherib (reigned 704–681 BC, who conquered most of Judah but never the city of Jerusalem).

The Assyrians became known for their cruelty and ruthlessness as military conquerors. Israel, like all the small kingdoms of the area, held no love for the Assyrians.

NOWHERE TO HIDE

Attempting to run away from God is a rather foolish thing to do.

Yet, that is precisely what Jonah did. Jonah attempted to escape God by fleeing to "Tarshish"—as if saying that he went to the end of the world, since most scholars believe that Tarshish was at the end of the known world back in Jonah's times. Jonah boarded a ship on its way to deep sea. It was a cargo ship, on which the crew were non-Israelite merchants. On his way to Tarshish, however, God cast a storm that threatened to destroy the ship.

In their desperation, the sailors cast their cargo off the ship. Besides lightening the ship, it is also possible that the sailors were offering a sacrifice to the ancient god of the sea—in Hebrew, the word *yam* means "sea" and was also the ancient name of the god of the sea.

> *"Where can I go from your Spirit? Where can I go from your presence?" Ps. 139:7*

In the meantime, Jonah went to the "belly" of the ship to take a deep nap. It was as if Jonah was "dead" asleep, as if the "belly" of the ship were the grave itself. Jonah's passivity contrasts with the sailors' frantic activity. As the sailors attempted to discover the cause of their predicament, they turned to Jonah. As he informed them of his identity as a prophet, Jonah presented a powerful testimony: "I am a Hebrew and I worship the LORD, the God of heaven, who made the sea and the dry land" (1:9). The common expression is "the God of heaven and earth," which means the God of the whole creation. Yet, Jonah makes a point of introducing God as creator of the dry land and sea. Jonah means God is in control of all things, even the chaos of the sea!

> *The word "cast" is important. The sailors "cast" their merchandise and "cast" Jonah off the ship.*

What an amazing evangelist! But, wait, Jonah was trying to flee God and now he's witnessing? If Jonah *knew* these things about God, why would he try to flee at all?

One way we "flee" or "run away" from God is by pretending he's not around to see what we do or don't do. Have you ever acted as if there were no God?

But the sea continued to be rough and the threat of drowning remained. Jonah's solution to the threat was to be cast over to the sea. Despite their best efforts, the sailors could not control the ship. After the sailors make a surprising prayer to the Lord (shouldn't the prophet be the one invoking the name of God instead of the pagan sailors?), they complied with Jonah's request. They cast him to the sea, which became peaceful once again. Their lives saved, the sailors *feared* the Lord, *offered* a sacrifice, and *made* vows. Their actions are surprising and refreshing. The Lord's prophet should be the one *fearing* God, *offering* his obedience as sacrifice, and *making* vows by proclaiming God's message. Yet, the sailors, who had asked for help from their gods, are the ones displaying behavior that should characterize God's people. The sailors display behavior that today we'd call "conversion." God's miracles, along with Jonah's unwitting testimony, produced extraordinary results. God's amazing grace can soften and transform the hardest of hearts! (Ezek. 36:26).

Have you ever experienced God's grace in a way that melts your rebellion, soothes your pain, or sweetens your sadness?

TARSHISH

The exact location of Tarshish is unknown, as is the meaning of the Hebrew word. However, some clues from biblical references to this name help us make an educated guess.

Some scholars suggest that the name refers to a place west of Israel in the Mediterranean. Some suggest it was an ancient Phoenician colony, perhaps as far as modern-day Spain. Others suggest it is located somewhere in Africa, perhaps in the Red Sea. Others still suggest that it's not a specific place. Rather, it refers to the activity of deep sea traveling using large, heavy cargo ships.

The origin of the name is not clear either. One of the most common suggestions among scholars is that the meaning of the word might be related to melting metals. Based on this, some scholars translate the word as "refinery." Others suppose that it is connected to the mining activities of the place. Whatever its exact location and meaning, the word clearly conveyed the idea of distance. Jonah, by fleeing to Tarshish, was attempting to reach "the end of the world" to escape God.

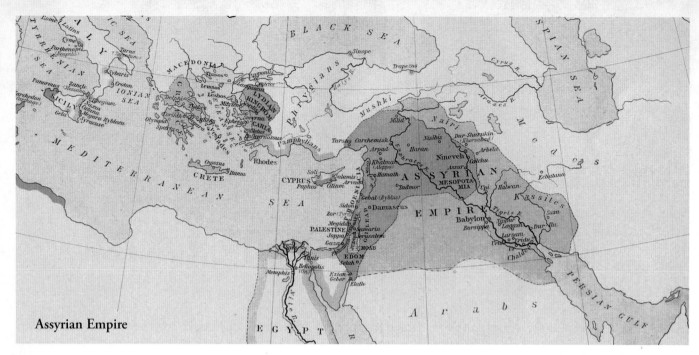

Assyrian Empire

2 ▶ God Provides a Fish for Jonah: Jonah Prays

If God showed mercy to the sailors, he also showed mercy to Jonah: "the Lord provided a huge fish to swallow Jonah" and save him from drowning. Jonah spent three days and three nights in the belly of the fish! There, Jonah prayed to God. In his prayer, Jonah testifies to God's deliverance, remembers the trouble he's in, and vows to worship God. Jonah's prayer has interesting connections with the actions of the sailors in chapter one.

Sailors (Chapter 1)	Jonah (Chapter 2)
Pleaded to God (1:14)	Pleaded to God (2:2)
God's response (1:15): Salvation	God's response (2:2) Recounting of the problem and salvation
God cast a great wind on the sea (1:4)	God cast Jonah into the sea (2:3)
The storm threatened the ship (1:4)	The waves, currents, and waters threatened Jonah's life (2:3, 5)
The sailors prayed to their gods (1:5)	Jonah looked toward God's holy temple (2:4, 7)
The sailors experienced the worthlessness of their gods and turned to God	Jonah affirmed that faith in God is superior to faith in idols (2:8)
The sailors feared God, offered a sacrifice, and made vows (1:16)	Jonah vowed to worship God and offer sacrifices (2:9)

The book of Jonah is about a compassionate and merciful God. The experience of the sailors and Jonah show that God acts with compassion and grace to all people. Their experience shows that human prayer and repentance move God to compassion.

To the sailors, Jonah confessed that the Lord is "the God of heaven, who made the sea and the dry land" (1:9). In his prayer, Jonah makes another powerful confession: "Salvation comes from the Lord" (2:9). Whether to pagan sailors or a rebellious prophet, God's grace and compassion are available to all.

At the end of the chapter, just as God had prepared the fish, now he commands it to release Jonah.

3 God Sends Jonah to Nineveh: Jonah Preaches

God ordered Jonah to go to Nineveh. The instructions in chapter 3 are less specific than before:

"Go to the great city of Nineveh and preach against it, because its wickedness has come up before me" (1:2)	"Go to the great city of Nineveh and proclaim to it the message I give you" (3:2)

This time, Jonah goes to Nineveh in obedience to God. The book turns its focus on the city. The text tells us that Nineveh was a "very large city." The description, "it took three days to go through it" (3:3) seems to refer to the city's size and importance. Jonah visits the city and preaches God's announcement: "Forty more days and Nineveh will be overthrown" (3:4). Jonah's message does not seem to leave any room for discussion. God will destroy Nineveh. It seems inevitable and decisive.

However, the next verse is surprising: "The Ninevites believed God" (3:5). It's not clear whether Jonah was supposed to go around the whole city (the full three days), but the preaching of one day's journey (3:4) was enough! The Ninevites, including the king of Nineveh, believed God and repented. The extent of their repentance is shown by the extent of their fast: Even the animals of the city fasted and were covered with sackcloth. Jonah's message didn't seem to leave any room for repentance; it was a message of judgment. Yet, the king showed an unexpected faith: "Who knows? God may yet relent and with compassion turn his fierce anger so that we will not perish" (3:9).

> The book of Jonah is not, after all, about Nineveh's repentance, as important as that event is. Rather, it is about Israel's own lack of repentance. Israel witnessed God's miracles to the Patriarchs, in the Exodus, the conquest of the Promised Land, in David and Solomon's kingdoms. Yet, Israel chose rebellion and unfaithfulness.

Jonah didn't even have the chance to walk through the whole city before the city repented. Unintentionally, Jonah became the most effective preacher ever! What a wonderful testimony of God's grace reaching to the ends of the world. The text informs us, "When God saw what they did and how they turned from their evil ways, he relented and did not bring on them the destruction he had threatened" (3:10). What did they see or know that persuaded them to repent and hope for God's mercy?

This final act of repentance and compassion would have been a wonderful ending for the story. The Ninevites repented, and God's glorious compassion shone through brighter than the sun. Nineveh's repentance is not a complete surprise; it parallels that of the sailors. What is surprising is that the book doesn't end here!

4 God Talks with Jonah: Jonah's Reactions

The book's last chapter presents a series of conversations between God and the disgruntled prophet. At this point, we get an explanation for Jonah's attempt to flee from God in chapter one: "I knew that you are a gracious and compassionate God, slow to anger and abounding in love, a God who relents from sending calamity" (4:2). Think about that: Jonah fled because he knew God was compassionate! Shouldn't a prophet of the Lord celebrate and appreciate God's grace and compassion?

There are at least two explanations for Jonah's angry reaction:

1. Jonah refused to share God's blessings with other people. Jonah's limited vision desired to keep God and God's blessings for Israel alone.

2. Jonah's prophetic understanding allowed him to see that Nineveh would act as God's instrument of judgment against Israel in the future.

Jonah's Limited Vision

Jesus' parable of the creditor and the two debtors in Luke 7:41–43 might help us understand the source of Jonah's problem. In the parable, Jesus concludes that those who are forgiven much will have a correspondingly greater love. Having witnessed God's compassion, fulfilled promises, forgiveness, and love through their history, the Israelites' gratitude and love for God and others should be evident. Yet, Jonah reacts with anger! How can we make sense of this reaction?

Remains of Nergal gate in Nineveh

In his prayer to God, Jonah says, "I knew that you are a gracious and compassionate God, slow to anger and abounding in love, a God who relents from sending calamity" (4:2). Jonah is alluding to a wonderful text from Exodus: "The LORD, the LORD, the compassionate and gracious God, slow to anger, abounding in love and faithfulness, maintaining love to thousands, and forgiving wickedness, rebellion and sin. Yet he does not leave the guilty unpunished; he punishes the children and their children for the sin of the parents to the third and fourth generation" (34:6–7). This is a central confession in Israel. In his prayer, Jonah emphasizes God's grace and forgiveness as the reason for not wanting to go to Nineveh.

God's Compassion to All, Even Nineveh

God's prophets understood the historical, social, and political climate of their times and how they connected with God's plans. Jonah had correctly diagnosed the spiritual darkness in the city of Nineveh. He knew that its sin offended God. And Jonah knew that God's holiness would move the Lord to act decisively to correct that darkness. Jonah understood God's holiness and righteousness.

Jonah also understood that God is merciful and compassionate—that's why he alluded to Exodus. What he *misunderstood* or refused to accept was that God would extend such mercy and compassion to people other than Israel!

Jonah's dejection about the fate of Nineveh is evident in his request to die: "take away my life, for it is better for me to die than to live" (4:3). What could Jonah mean with this request? Let's remember Jonah's prayer in chapter 2. In his lament, Jonah affirms that being separated from God is the worst experience ("I have been banished from your sight"), yet his hope remained on God's promise to be with his people ("yet I will look again toward your holy temple"). What changed so much to make Jonah wish to die? God's relenting of his punishment against Nineveh? Jonah and the Israelites of his time were intelligent; they were perfectly able to *understand* God's will. In fact, they had been told by God that Abraham's descendents would be a source of blessing to *other* nations.

Perhaps this analogy will help us understand what happened. It was similar to a child who's been told all of his life that he's special and the most perfect being in the world, well deserving of all good things. This child will most likely become a spoiled child filled with disregard for others and expecting others to treat him with deference. Israel expected God and other nations to treat them as special. They were special but not for who or what they were (Deut. 7:7) but because God loved them first (Deut. 7:8; 1 John 4:10). Yet, we humans tend to be possessive; we pretend to own those who love us and we love. The Israelites pretended to possess and deserve God's love. They claimed exclusivity over God's attentions and regard. But God is clear that's not the case: "'Are not you Israelites the same to me as the Cushites?' declares the Lord. 'Did I not bring Israel up from Egypt, the Philistines from Caphtor and the Arameans from Kir?'" (Amos 9:7).

God's intention to bless all the nations is first seen in his promise to bless Abraham: "...and all peoples on earth will be blessed through you" (Gen. 12:3). Throughout the prophets, God reminded Israel that his blessing would extend to all the nations. Around the time of Jonah, God revealed to Isaiah that God would bless all the nations, even the hated enemies of Israel: Assyria and Egypt: "The LORD Almighty will bless them, saying, 'Blessed be Egypt my people, Assyria my handiwork, and Israel my inheritance'" (Isa. 19:25).

HISTORICAL BACKGROUND: GOD'S DEALINGS WITH NINEVEH

In the book of Jonah, the acts of contrition that God saw in the people of Nineveh moved him to have compassion and to relent his judgment on the city. Although it's very difficult to establish a date for the events in the book of Jonah, it is possible that they occurred early in the eighth century (700s BC). About a century later, sometime before 612 BC, the prophet Nahum spoke about the destruction of the powerful and proud city of Nineveh, which happened in 612 BC. Around the time of Jonah, God had already revealed to Isaiah that Assyria and its king would be punished for "the willful pride of his heart and the haughty look in his eyes" (Isa. 10:12).

Future Role of Nineveh

As a prophet, Jonah understood history from God's perspective. Prophets understood the historical events around them in light of God's activity in the world. Jonah knew that all the things happening around him were God's doing. But what were the purposes of the events at Nineveh, and how did those purposes relate to Jonah's anger? Perhaps Jonah knew more about Nineveh than what appears at first.

Around Jonah's time, God had been sending prophets to Israel calling them to repentance and faithfulness. God was also beginning to reveal to his prophets that he would use the powerful and ruthless Assyrian empire to punish Israel's unfaithfulness (see, for example, Isa. 10:5–6). If Nineveh experienced God's judgment, would Israel's future change? Was this future judgment against Israel that drove Jonah to anger?

JONAH'S ANGER

"Is it right for you to be angry?" (4:4), asked God. It is a short but disarming question. The answer to this question seems clear—it's a rhetorical question. Rather than answering the question, the book of Jonah offers an extended explanation. Jonah went out of the city and found a place to sit. After building a simple shelter, Jonah waited to see "what would happen to the city" (4:5). Jonah seemed to be expecting quite a spectacle. God provided a leafy plant that shaded Jonah from the scorching sun. Jonah claimed that he knew God would forgive and so fled away to Tarshish (4:2). Yet, he set camp to enjoy the view as if thinking, "who knows, maybe God will actually destroy them," which contrasts with Nineveh's king's faith in God's compassion in 3:9: "Who knows? God may yet relent and with compassion turn his fierce anger so that we will not perish."

> ### ISAIAH 10:5–6
>
> "Woe to the Assyrian, the rod of my anger, in whose hand is the club of my wrath! I send him against a godless nation [Israel], I dispatch him against a people who anger me, to seize loot and snatch plunder, and to trample them down like mud in the streets."

Yet, God provided—as he had provided a fish to rescue Jonah—a worm that ate and destroyed the plant. Without its shade, Jonah's misery returned: "It would be better for me to die than to live" (4:8).

God's concrete lesson with the plant and the worm is meant to make Jonah realize his mistake—similar to Nathan's parable to David (2 Sam. 12:1–14) or Jesus' parable about the Good Samaritan to the Pharisees (Luke 10:25–37).

God inquires again from Jonah: "Is it right for you to be angry about the plant?" and Jonah's answer is unexpected: "It is" (4:9).

Was it self-centeredness on Jonah's part? Was Jonah depressed? Did his loyalty to his homeland blind him to God's actions? Why would he challenge God? We don't have a definite answer. However, God addressed Jonah's anger. Jonah is angry about the death of the plant, yet he did not "tend it or make it grow" (4:10). Then God asks, "And should I not have concern for the great city of Nineveh, in which there are more than a hundred and twenty thousand people who cannot tell their right hand from their left—and also many animals?"

Jesus called us to love our enemies. What might happen if we love them?

"And should I not have concern for the great city of Nineveh, in which there are more than a hundred and twenty thousand people who cannot tell their right hand from their left—and also many animals?"

God's question ends the book of Jonah. How should we answer it? In verse four, the answer to God's question seemed clearly to be no. However, Jonah answered it as "yes" (4:9). Should God worry about people other than his covenant people? The answer is so obviously yes.

RIGHT AND LEFT HANDS

It is hard to know exactly what the expression "cannot tell (or know) their right hand from their left" means. The expression might refer to the lack of ability to distinguish good from evil. For this reason, some scholars have suggested that it refers to little children. Another possibility is that the expression might point to the Ninevites' helplessness to choose what is right—often, the expression is connected to the obedience of God's law (see, for example, Prov. 4:27; Deut. 5:32, 28:14). In his second response to Jonah, God does not mention Nineveh's repentance as the reason for showing compassion. Rather, with the question, God shows Jonah that his relenting from punishing Nineveh was a result of his pity for his creation. Just like before, the rhetorical question at the end of the book shows that God's grace extends beyond Israel simply because God is merciful and compassionate. God's desire to save humans extends to the whole world. For that reason, Jesus sent all of his disciples—his followers—to proclaim the good news that, in Jesus, salvation is possible. He sent us to all the world, including those who we might think of as our enemies.

Did Jonah misunderstand God's grace? Did he simply not want to share it with others? Was he worried about Israel and Assyria's role in its future, or was he too self-centered to care about anyone else? The problem doesn't seem to have been only that Jonah didn't understand something. Rather, it seems that Jonah wanted God to meet Jonah's expectations about Nineveh. Jonah wanted to manipulate God. God couldn't possibly treat a pagan and savage nation with the same concern as he did Israel itself. Jonah's national interests were above God's own love and compassion.

But God's amazing grace is above human plans, desires, or attempts to manipulate it. The book of Jonah shows a God active in the world, sovereign over nature and nations, holy and just, graceful and compassionate.

The book of Jonah shows that God is active in the world and wants to be a blessing—even to unexpected people and places. How is God inviting you to join him in this mission in the world?

THE SIGN OF JONAH IN THE GOSPELS

The Gospels of Matthew and Luke both mention Jonah. The writers apply the story of Jonah in slightly different ways. When the Pharisees ask for a sign to prove that Jesus is not performing miracles by the power of Beelzebub, Jesus responds that they will be given only "the sign of Jonah."

The Gospel of Matthew (12:39-40)	The Gospel of Luke (11:29-30)
The sign of Jonah pointed to Jesus' burial and resurrection.	The sign of Jonah refers to Jonah's judgment sermon against Nineveh.
• Just as Jonah spent three days in the belly of the fish, Jesus would spend three days in the belly of the earth. • Yet, he would rise from the tomb to judge those who claimed that he performed miracles by the power of Beelzebub (Matt. 12:24).	• Jonah brought a sermon of condemnation, not expecting any repentance. Yet, the Ninevites repented. • Jesus brings a message of salvation. However, for those who reject his teachings, his message is one of condemnation. Unlike the Ninevites' repentance, Jesus' accusers remained unrepentant.

Both texts remind believers that the message of the gospel is one of compassion and grace. Even for those people we might think are beyond God's grace, God reaches to them with mercy and salvation. As Jonah learned, the role of judge to give salvation or condemnation belongs to God alone. Those who have experienced God's tender mercies must be willing to extend those mercies to all people.

BIBLE FAVORITES: NEW TESTAMENT

THE GOSPELS SIDE BY SIDE

Why Do We Need Four Gospels?

Because the four Gospels contain different accounts of the same or similar events in the life of Jesus, readers of the Gospels have often sought to compare and contrast these accounts by placing them next to each other. These side-by-side comparisons attempt to harmonize the work of the four Evangelists and so are often called "Gospel Harmonies."

FOUR POINTS OF VIEW

Gospel	Symbol	Viewpoint	Audience	Jesus the Son of God
Matthew	Man	Palestinian Jewish	Jewish world	Is the Messiah King of Israel
Mark	Lion	Hellenistic Jewish	Greek-speaking world	Is the Power of God in the world
Luke	Bull	Greco-Roman	Gentile world	Is the Ideal Man of God
John	Eagle	Heavenly	Whole world	Is the Word of God

Why are there four Gospels instead of just one? One answer is that it takes four points of view to get the whole story about Jesus. Some might argue that one authoritative story should be enough. However, God chose to reveal himself using four Gospels. The Gospel of John begins with these words: "In the beginning was the Word … (vs. 1) and the Word became flesh … (vs. 14). In other words, God chooses as his preferred method of communication to speak to humans by means of the human. This is true of the Bible and it is supremely true of Christ whom we are told is God in the flesh (John 1:14–18). So then, the Gospels are, like Jesus, both a Divine work as well as a human work. They have real human authors and one divine Author. They give details that might be difficult to understand, but they are never truly contradictory. They have four different points of view on the history of Jesus but only one Divine conclusion as to his identity as the Son of God.

Harmony of the Gospels

EVENT	MATTHEW	MARK	LUKE	JOHN
The genealogy of Jesus	1:1–17		3:23–38	
Jesus' birth and childhood	1:18–2:23		1:5–2:52	
John the Baptist's ministry	3:1–12	1:1–8	3:1–18	1:19–34
Christ's public ministry and first Passover	3:13–4:12	1:9–14	3:21–4:13	1:35–4:42
Christ's ministry in Galilee	4:12	1:14–15	4:14–15	4:43–54
His rejection at Nazareth and move to Capernaum	4:13–22; 8:14–17	1:16–34	4:16–41	
His first ministry tour and second Passover	4:23–12:14	1:35–3:6	4:42–7:50	5:1–47
His second ministry tour	12:15–13:58	3:7–6:6	8:1–56	
His third ministry tour	9:35–11:1; 14:1–12	6:6–29	9:1–9	
Ministry to his disciples and third Passover	14:13–18:35	6:30–9:50	9:10–56	6:1–71
Ministry in Judea			10:1–13:21	7:1–10:39

EVENT	MATTHEW	MARK	LUKE	JOHN
Ministry beyond Jordan	19:1–20:34	10:1–52	13:22–19:27	10:40–11:54
The last week (Passover/Easter)	21:12–28:20	11:1–16:20	19:28–24:53	11:55–21:25
Arrival in Bethany and Mary anoints Jesus' feet	26:6–13	14:3–9	19:28	11:55–12:11
Triumphal entry	21:1–11	11:1–11	19:29–44	12:12–19
Second cleansing of the temple; barren fig tree cursed	21:12–13; 18–22	11:12–18	19:45–48	
Greeks seek Jesus; fig tree withered	21:19–22	11:19–25	21:37–38	12:20–50
Jesus' authority challenged	21:23–22:46	11:27–12:37	20:1–44	
Denouncing the scribes and Pharisees	23:1–39	12:38–40	20:45–47	
Widow's offering		12:41–44	21:1–4	
The Olivet discourse	24:1–25:46	13:1–37	21:5–36	
Crucifixion predicted	26:1–5	14:1–2	22:1–2	
Judas's bargain	26:14–16	14:10–11	22:3–6	
Preparation and the Passover	26:17–30	14:12–26	22:7–20	13:1–14:31
Discourse and high priestly prayer				15:1–17:26
Gethsemane	26:36–46	14:32–42	22:39–46	18:1
Betrayal, arrest, and trial	26:47–56	14:43–52	22:47–53	18:2–14
Jesus condemned to death and Peter's denial	26:57–75	14:53–72	22:54–65	18:15–27
Formal condemnation after dawn	27:1–2	15:1	22:66–71	
Judas' suicide	27:3–10			
Jesus' first time before Pilate	27:11–14	15:1–5	23:1–5	18:28–38
Jesus before Herod the Tetrarch			23:6–12	18:39–19:16
Jesus' second time before Pilate	27:15–26	15:6–15	23:13–25	
Soldiers mock Jesus	27:27–31	15:16–23	23:26–33	19:16–17
The crucifixion	27:32–49	15:21–36	23:26–43	19:18–29
Jesus' death	27:50–56	15:37–41	23:44–49	19:30–37
Jesus' burial	27:57–66	15:42–47	23:50–56	19:38–42
Earthquake and tomb opened	28:1–4			
Visit of women at dawn	28:5–8	16:1–3	24:1–8	20:1
Women report to the apostles; Peter and John visit the tomb			24:9–12	20:2–10
Jesus appears first to Mary Magdalene		16:9–11		20:11–18
Jesus appears to other women; the guards report to the rulers	28:9–15			
Jesus appears to two on the road to Emmaus		16:12–13	24:13–32	
Jesus appears to Peter			24:33–35	
Jesus appears to ten, Thomas absent		16:14	24:36–43	20:19–25
Jesus appears to the eleven, Thomas present				20:26–31
Jesus appears to seven on the sea of Galilee				21:1–25
Jesus appears to about five hundred at an appointed mountain in Galilee	28:16–20	16:15–18		
Jesus appears to his brother James—1 Corinthians 15:7				
Jesus appears to his apostles again, his ascension		16:19–20	24:44–53	
Jesus appears to Paul—1 Corinthians 15:8				

Miracles of Jesus

The Gospel of John records the least number of miracles. Most of John's miracle accounts are not in the other Gospels. John seems to have intentionally included new material that had not previously been written down. At the same time John's focus is more on Jesus' words, his teaching, rather than on the miraculous signs Jesus did. Perhaps conscious of his readers' desire for miracle stories, John adds to his Gospel the words, "I suppose that even the world would not have room for the books that would be written" about Jesus' many other deeds (John 21:25).

MIRACLE	MATTHEW	MARK	LUKE	JOHN
Water into wine				2:1–11
Official's son healed				4:46–54
Healing of demoniac in the synagogue		1:21–28	4:33–37	
Healing of Peter's mother-in-law	8:14–17	1:29–31	4:38–39	
Many healed at sunset		1:32–34	4:40–41	
Miraculous catch of fish			5:4–11	
Healing of a leper	8:2–4	1:40–45	5:12–16	
Healing of a paralytic	9:2–8	2:1–12	5:17–26	
Healing at Bethesda				5:2–15
Withered hand healed in a synagogue	12:9–14	3:1–6	6:6–11	
Many healed	12:15–21	3:7–12	6:17–19	
Centurion's servant healed	8:5–13		7:1–10	
Widow's son raised at Nain			7:11–17	
Demon-possessed man healed	12:22–23	3:20–21		
Calming of the storm	8:23–27	4:36–41	8:23–25	
Demonic legion cast out	8:28–34	5:1–20	8:26–39	
Healing of the woman with the flow of blood	9:20–22	5:24–34	8:42–48	
Raising of Jairus' daughter	9:23–26	5:35–43	8:49–56	
Healing of two blind men	9:27–31			
Healing of a mute demoniac	9:32–34			
Many healed, feeding of five thousand	14:13–21	6:30–44	9:10–17	6:1–14
Walking on water and calming of the storm	14:22–33	6:45–52		6:16–21
Syro-Phoenician woman's daughter healed	15:21–28	7:24–30		
Deaf mute healed		7:31–37		
Many healed, feeding of four thousand	15:29–39	8:1–10		
Blind man of Bethsaida healed		8:22–26		
Healing of demoniac boy	17:14–19	9:14–29	9:37–43	
Healing of the man born blind				9:1–7
Crippled woman healed on Sabbath			13:10–13	
Healing of a man with dropsy on the Sabbath			14:2–6	
Jesus raised Lazarus				11:38–44
Ten lepers cleansed			17:11–14	
Healing of two blind men near Jericho	20:29–34	10:46–52	18:35–43	
Many healed in the temple	21:14			
Healing of the severed ear			22:51	
Resurrection	28:1–20	16:1–19	24:1–53	20:1–31
Miraculous catch of fish				21:1–8

The Parables of Jesus

PARABLE	MATTHEW	MARK	LUKE	JOHN
The Bridegroom, Cloth and Wineskins	9:10–17	2:15–22	5:29–39	
The Sower	13:3–23	4:3–20	8:5–15	
The Lamp	5:15–16	4:21–25	8:16–18; 11:33	
The Seed Growing		4:26–29		
The Weeds	13:24–30; 36–43			
The Mustard Seed	13:31–32	4:30–32	13:18–19	
The Leaven	13:33–35		13:20–21	
The Hidden Treasure	13:44			
The Pearl of Great Price	13:45–46			
The Net	13:47–50			
The Householder	13:51–53			
On Defilement	15:1–20	7:1–23		
The Narrow Door	7:13–14		13:22–30	
The Unmerciful Servant	18:23–35			
The Good Samaritan			10:29–37	
The Friend at Midnight			11:5–10	
The Rich Fool			12:16–21	
The Waiting Servants			12:35–38	
The Watchful Householder	24:42–44		12:39–40	
The Wise Steward and the Wicked Steward	24:45–51		12:41–48	
The Fig Tree 1			13:6–9	
The Guests			14:7–11	
The Banquet			14:12–24	
The Lost Sheep	18:10–14		15:1–7	
The Lost Coin			15:8–10	
The Lost Son			15:11–32	
The Unrighteous Steward			16:1–13	
The Rich Man and Lazarus			16:19–31	
The Returning Servant			17:7–10	
The Unjust Judge and the Widow			18:1–8	
The Pharisee and Publican			18:9–14	
The Laborers in the Vineyard	20:1–16			
The Fig Tree 2	21:18–22	11:12–24		
The Ten Minas			19:11–27	
The Two Sons	21:28–32			
The Tenants	21:33–46	12:1–12	20:9–18	
The Wedding Banquet	22:1–14			
The Fig Tree 3	24:32–35	13:28–31	21:29–33	
The Ten Virgins	25:1–13			
The Talents	25:14–30			
The Sheep and the Goats	25:31–46			

Tracking Jesus' Moves

The use of this kind of harmony is also helpful to get a picture of Jesus' movements.

PLACE	EVENT OR TEACHING	SCRIPTURE
Bethlehem	Birth of Jesus	Mt. 1:24–25; Lk. 2:1–7
Egypt	Flight from Herod	Mt. 2:13–15
Nazareth	Early childhood	Mt. 2:19–23; Lk. 2:39
Jerusalem	Passover celebration	Lk. 2:41–52
Jordan River	Baptism of Jesus	Mt. 3:13–17; Mk. 1:9–11; Lk. 3:21–23; Jn. 1:29–34
Wilderness	Temptation of Jesus	Mt. 4:1–11; Mk. 1:12–13; Lk. 4:1–13
Going to Galilee	Calling of Philip and Nathaniel	Jn. 1:43–51
Cana in Galilee	First miracle	Jn. 2:1–11
Capernaum	Family stay	Jn. 2:12
Jerusalem	First Passover	Jn. 2:13–25
Judea	Baptizing new disciples	Jn. 3:22
Returning to Galilee	Jesus goes through Samaria	Jn. 4:1–4
Samaria	Jesus talks to the women at the well	Jn. 4:5–42
Cana in Galilee	Healing of official's son and the beginning of Jesus' Galilean ministry	Jn. 4:43–54; Mt. 4:12; Mk. 1:14–15; Lk. 4:14–15
Nazareth	Rejection at Nazareth	Lk. 4:16–30
Capernaum	Move of ministry base	Mt. 4:13; Mk. 1:21; Lk. 4:31
Galilee	Preaching tour	Mt. 4:23–25; Mk. 1:32–39; Lk. 4:42–44
Jerusalem	Second Passover	Jn. 5:1–47
Galilee	The parable of the Sower and Seed	Mt. 13:1; Mk. 4:1; Lk. 8:1–4
Gennesaret	Healing of multitudes	Mt. 14:34–36; Mk. 6:53–56
Tyre and Sidon	Faith of the Canaanite woman	Mt. 15:21–28; Mk. 7:24–30
The Region of the Decapolis	Healing of deaf and dumb man, feeding of the 4000	Mt. 15:29–38; Mk. 7:31–8:9
Galilee	Teaching and healing	Mt. 15:39–16:5; Mk. 8:10–26
Caesarea Philippi	The question of Jesus' identity	Mt. 16:13–20; Mk. 8:27–30; Lk. 9:18–21
Galilee and Capernaum	Jesus tells of his death a second time, the half-shekel tax	Mk. 17:22–27; Mk. 9:30–50
Jerusalem	Feast of Tabernacles	Lk. 9:51; Jn. 7:2–10
Various places in Judea	Preaching tour	Lk. 10:1–24
Jerusalem	Feast of Dedication (Hanukkah)	Jn. 10:22–23
Across the Jordan	Preaching tour	Mt. 19:1; Mk. 10:1; Lk. 13:22; Jn. 10:40–42
Between Galilee and Samaria	Ten lepers healed	Lk. 17:11–19
Jericho	Jesus heals blind men	Mt. 20:29–34; Mk. 10:46–52
Bethany	The raising of Lazarus	Jn. 11:1–53
Ephraim	Jesus stays with his disciples	Jn. 11:54
Bethany, Jerusalem and places in the vicinity	Jesus' last week (Passover/Easter)	Mt. 26:6–28:15; Mk. 14:3–16:11; Lk. 19:28–24:49; Jn. 11:55–20:31
Galilee	Appears to his disciples	Mt. 28:16–20; Mk. 16:15–18; Jn. 21:1–23
Mount of Olives	Jesus' ascension	Mk. 16:19–20; Lk. 24:50–53

Israel During Jesus' Time

Jesus' three-year ministry occurred all over the ancient cities. From Syria to Judea, Jesus brought the gospel's powerful words and actions.

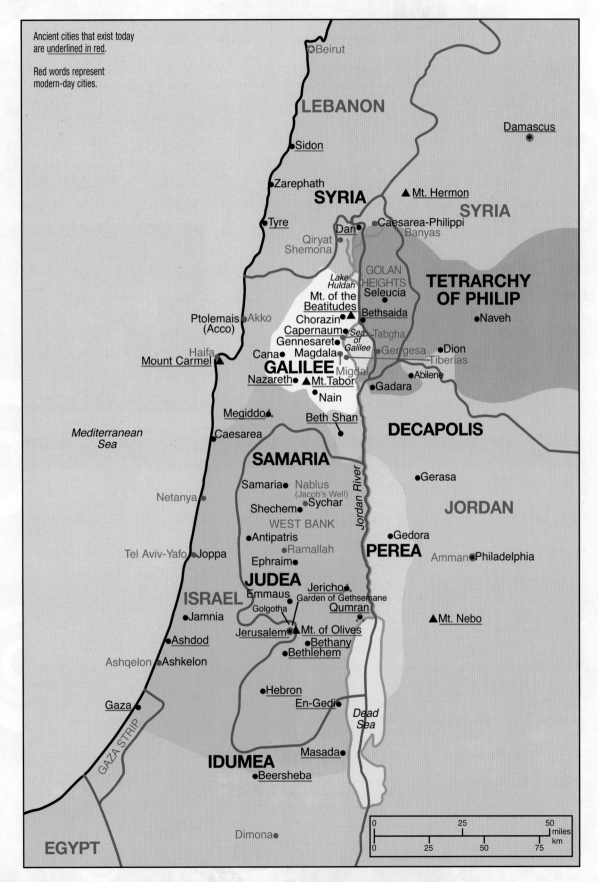

Ancient cities that exist today are underlined in red.

Red words represent modern-day cities.

Beirut

LEBANON

Sidon

Zarephath

SYRIA

Damascus

Mt. Hermon

SYRIA

Tyre

Dan

Caesarea-Philippi
Banyas

Qiryat Shemona

Lake Huldah

GOLAN HEIGHTS

TETRARCHY OF PHILIP

Seleucia

Mt. of the Beatitudes

Bethsaida

Naveh

Ptolemais (Acco)

Akko

Chorazin

Capernaum

Tabgha

Gennesaret

Sea of Galilee

Gergesa

Dion
Tiberias

Mount Carmel

Haifa

Cana

Magdala

GALILEE

Migdal

Abilene

Nazareth

Mt. Tabor

Gadara

Nain

Megiddo

Beth Shan

DECAPOLIS

Mediterranean Sea

Caesarea

SAMARIA

Gerasa

Samaria

Nablus (Jacob's Well)

JORDAN

Netanya

Sychar

Shechem

WEST BANK

Antipatris

Gedora

Tel Aviv-Yafo

Joppa

Ramallah

PEREA

Amman

Philadelphia

Ephraim

JUDEA

Jericho

ISRAEL

Emmaus

Garden of Gethsemane

Golgotha

Qumran

Jamnia

Jerusalem

Mt. of Olives

Ashdod

Bethany

Bethlehem

Ashqelon

Ashkelon

Hebron

Gaza

GAZA STRIP

En-Gedi

Dead Sea

Mt. Nebo

IDUMEA

Masada

Beersheba

EGYPT

Dimona

0		25		50	
miles

| 0 | 25 | 50 | 75 | |
km

Galilee and Judea

Jesus began his public ministry in Galilee, in the northern region. He spent much, if not most of his time there. Jesus frequented Judea and Jerusalem for the required religious festivals, but it seems he only spent significant time there late in his ministry (Luke 9:51). John affirms that his safety was compromised in Judea, and that it was only under cover that Jesus made his way to Jerusalem (John 7:1–10).

Yet, even this seeming insignificant fact about Christ's life was foretold in Scripture. Matthew 4:12–17 shows us that Isaiah had prophesied hundreds of years in advance that Christ's brilliant light would shine forth in Galilee (Isaiah 9:1–2).

Jesus' Last Week

The Gospel writers center much of their attention on the last week of Jesus' ministry. About a fourth to a half of the Gospel's material has to do with the incidents surrounding Christ's death and resurrection. This should tell us of the importance of this week in their minds. It holds the key to the central issue of the church and of all history, for in that last week, the life and death of the whole world and the whole of human history were at stake. Without the death and resurrection of Jesus there is no hope, nor can there be any salvation.

Jesus' Passovers

One way to measure the length of Jesus' public ministry is by counting the number of Passovers the Gospels record. Since the Passover festival only happened once a year, counting the Passovers gives a rough idea of how long Jesus' ministry lasted. The Gospels suggest that Jesus' public ministry continued for at least three years. Notice, John is the writer most concerned to give us the details about the festivals in Jesus' life.

FEAST	EVENT OR TEACHING	SCRIPTURE
First Passover	Jesus went to the Passover. He cleansed the temple, talked with Nicodemus and ministered in Judea for a while.	John 2:13–25
Second Passover	Jesus went to the "feast" (probably Passover) and healed the man at the pool of Bethesda.	John 5:1–47
Third Passover	Jesus delivered his "Bread of Life" teaching. However, he did not go to Passover because of a threat to his life in Judea.	John 6:4–7:1
Tabernacles (Booths)	Jesus went secretly for reasons of security. Teaching in the temple, he encountered opposition from the religious leaders. Jesus claimed to be the "Light of the World." He healed the man born blind near the pool of Siloam.	John 7:2–9:41
Hanukkah (Dedication)	Jesus attended the feast. He spoke of his "sheep." Again he escaped stoning.	John 10:22–42
Last Passover/ Last Supper	Jesus went to the Passover and the last week of his life took place.	Matthew 26:17; Mark 14:12; Luke 22:7; John 12:1

The Synoptic Gospels and John

The word "synoptic" means "seen together." It refers to the first three Gospels: Matthew, Mark and Luke. When seen together, these Gospels often reveal related accounts in very similar language. Scholars agree there is some relationship between these three books. The exact nature of this relationship has been the subject of much debate. It seems that these three authors either read one another or some common source, which explains why so much of their substance and language are the same.

Papyrus 1, also known as P[1], shows a fragment of the Gospel of Matthew. The fragment, housed in the University of Pennsylvania Museum, dates to around AD 250.

The Gospel of John, however, is different than the first three Gospels. John uses material that the other writers do not have. The wording of some of the stories is different. John often added details that the others do not include. For example, the name of the woman who washed Jesus' feet with her hair (John 12:3) or that he beat Peter in a foot race to the empty tomb on Easter Sunday (John 20:4). Many of these details have a personal tone.

The Synoptic Gospels Compared to John
Three Examples

THE GOSPEL TEXT	EVENT	DESCRIPTION
Matthew 3:11–12; Mark 1:7–8; Luke 3:15–18	John the Baptist's introduction of Jesus	General and generic language is used about the crowds.
John 1:24–44		John names specific individuals who become disciples of Jesus through John the Baptist.
Matthew 14:13–21; Mark 6:30–44; Luke 9:10–17	Feeding of the 5000	Dialogue with Jesus is attributed to the disciples as a group.
John 6:1–14		John names specific individuals who speak.
Matthew 28:1–10; Mark 16:1–11; Luke 24:1–12; John 20:1–18	The Resurrection	Individuals are named in all accounts to a greater or lesser extent.
		John is specific about the actions of Mary Magdalene, Peter and himself (the unnamed disciple).

The First Gospel

Because the first three Gospels so closely resemble each other, the question has long been asked, "Who wrote first?" Many modern scholars are inclined in favor of Mark as being the first Gospel in print. This is due in part to the brevity of the work and the fact that most of Mark's material can also be found in Matthew and Luke. The idea is that if Mark wrote first, Luke and Matthew might have read his work and added their own material in their writing. Early tradition holds that Mark became associated with Peter and that his Gospel might be a kind of "Memoirs of Peter." Its rapid-fire style seems like Peter's way of recounting Jesus' life.

Others are convinced, however, that none of the Gospels that exists today was the first to be in print. These scholars believe that there was an earlier writing that the authors of the present Gospels (Matthew, Mark and Luke) drew upon as a reference work. Papias, an early Christian and disciple of the Apostle John, wrote, "Matthew put together the sayings in the Hebrew language, and each one interpreted them as best he could" (in Eusebius, Ecclesiastical History 3.39.16). Since Matthew was a tax collector (Matthew 9:9), he was a good pick to be the scribe among the disciples. So this tradition may bear some weight. It may be that Matthew recorded much of what happened in Jesus' ministry in the native tongue of Palestine. This document may later have been translated into Greek and used by him and the other synoptic writers to produce our present Gospels.

Medieval manuscript known as *Aachen Gospels*, folio 13r, made around AD 820.

The Gospels as we now have them were first written in Greek, which was the popular common language of the Roman world. It is entirely possible that Matthew made the first record in Aramaic, but that Mark drafted the first Gospel in Greek drawing on Matthew's record and adding what he had heard from Peter. Luke and Matthew (in present form) would then have been written. John wrote his account after the others had been in circulation for some time.

Harmonies Through History

Over the years, people have created different types of "Gospel Harmonies." These are some of the main types of harmonies:

- **Synthetic Harmonization:** One approach is to cut out any variation in similar accounts and replace it with preferred wording to create a kind of "official version."

- **Sequential Harmonization:** This type attempts to bring together two or more versions of an event by keeping both. The separate details are seen as separate incidents within the same story.

- **Parallel Harmonization:** A final approach may be to show two or more versions next to each other for comparison and contrast.

Gospel harmonies began to be produced early in the history of the church. Concern for accuracy and a full account of the gospel message became important for the church as it strove to remain faithful. These early harmonies bear witness to the church's use of the four canonical Gospels. Already by the post-apostolic age, the authority of the four to the exclusion of other texts is recognized.

AUTHOR	TITLE	DATE
Justin Martyr	Evident in his writings	Second Century
Tatian	Diatesseron	Second Century
Unknown	Dura-Europas Harmony	Second Century
Eusebius of Caesarea	Sections and Canons	Third Century
Augustine	Consensus of the Gospels	Fourth Century
Andreas Osiander	Gospel Harmony	Sixteenth Century

The Gospels as Biography

The four Gospels are best understood as biographies about the life and times of Jesus. However, there are important differences between modern and ancient biographies. The main difference is the notion of historical sequencing.

MODERN BIOGRAPHIES	ANCIENT BIOGRAPHIES
Biographies written today place a premium on sequencing. The events of the subject's life are typically narrated in the order in which they happened. Beginning with the birth of the individual, relevant events and information are viewed in sequential order up to the death of the subject. While chapters may present different phases in the subject's life, these phases are arranged in the order in which they are supposed to have happened.	Ancient biographers had a general commitment to an historical sequence. They did not feel the need to place every detail in their writings in the exact order in which it happened. Much more emphasis is given to developing an accurate picture of the character of the subject. Deeds and happenings are seen as illustrative of that character no matter when they occurred.

THE GOSPELS AS BIOGRAPHIES
Luke 7:36–50 is an example of the non-sequential nature of ancient biographies. This passage is Luke's account of the woman who anoints Jesus' feet. Matthew, Mark and John tell this event as part of Jesus' arrival at Bethany just before the events of Easter week (see Harmony Chart). Despite Luke's care as an accurate historian (Luke 1:1–4), he places this event much earlier in Jesus' ministry—that is, if we read Luke like we would read a modern biography. Some have tried to resolve the difficulty by suggesting that there were two such events, two times when various women anointed Jesus' feet. But the details of Luke's account too closely resemble the other Gospel accounts to make it a separate incident. It is much more likely that Luke (and so the Holy Spirit) was simply using this event out of historical sequence to illustrate the Pharisees and their lack of faith in contrast to the faith of the centurion (Luke 7:2–10).

Parables of Jesus

Stories Jesus Told

Jesus' parables are among the most read and loved sections of the Bible. Just as in the times of Jesus, the parables are filled with vivid images and touch the readers in powerful ways. In short, the parables have been an important source of wisdom, instruction, and solace for Christians everywhere.

In the following pages, we will understand what parables are, what they do in the Gospels, and why they matter so much to us today. We will also learn some general suggestions for reading the parables fruitfully.

What Are Parables?

Parables are stories that fulfill a specific function in a specific way. Parables are extended analogies. In other words, parables are extended comparisons between two objects. This comparison seeks to identify similarities or highlight differences to explain or clarify something about one of the objects. Some parables are extended similes or extended metaphors, others are brief allegories. This means that in our reading of the parables, we must be careful to not interpret the metaphors, similes, and allegories beyond what the Bible itself allows.

Characteristics of Jesus' Parables

Jesus' creative stories were:

- Brief
- Simple and repetitive
- Composed of items, examples, or experiences from his audience's daily experience
- Meant to have major and minor points
- Engaging for listeners at different levels
- Shocking, surprising, challenging, appealing, and relevant
- Often connected to the Old Testament and the kingdom of God

Function of Parables in Jesus' Ministry

Jesus' chief message was the arrival of God's kingdom to the world. Jesus' life, ministry, death, and resurrection bear witness to the reality and power of the kingdom. The parables also bear witness to this coming kingdom.

Although the parables were an important teaching tool for Jesus' ministry, their importance goes beyond instruction. Like the prophets of the Old Testament, Jesus used the parables as a way to confront people with God's word.

Parables are stories that demand a response. More than simply instructing, Jesus seeks from his audience a response to the coming of the kingdom. To do that, the parables are designed to provoke emotions, reactions, repentance, and recognition of who Jesus is and what the coming of the kingdom means.

The parables are an invitation to those who belong to God to strengthen their faith and knowledge. For those who have rejected God, the parables become confirmation of their unbelief. Like Isaiah before him, Jesus knew his message would present opposition, skepticism, and hostility. Because the parables appeal to our emotions and will, their message often produces a strong reaction in us.

Word Pictures

Metaphor: Comparison of two objects, emphasizing a specific similarity or similarities. When the psalmist affirms that "God is my rock" (Ps. 18:2, 31; 42:9), we should not understand that God is literally a rock. Rather, the psalmist is comparing a specific characteristic of rocks with a specific characteristic of God. That is, just as rocks are solid and strong, so is God.

Simile: Like a metaphor, a simile is a comparison between two objects. However, the comparison is more evident, which makes the comparison more emphatic and vivid. Similes use the words *as* and *like* to make the comparison between the two objects obvious. When the psalmist writes, "man is like a breath," (Ps. 144:4) the comparison is direct and clear. The parables of the kingdom of God that begin with "the kingdom of God (or heaven)" are examples of similes.

Allegory: An allegory is an extended metaphor. It refers to stories, poems, images, and words that convey meanings beyond the literal one. An example of an intended allegory in the New Testament is found in Gal. 4:21–31, in which Sarah and Hagar stand for two covenants.

Parables in the Gospels

	Parable	Matthew	Mark	Luke
1	A Lamp on a Stand	Matt. 5:14–16	Mark 4:21–22	Luke 8:16–17; 11:33–36
2	The Wise and Foolish Builders	Matt. 7:24–27		Luke 6:47–49
3	New Cloth on an Old Garment	Matt. 9:16	Mark 2:21	Luke 5:36
4	New Wine in Old Wineskins	Matt. 9:17	Mark 2:22	Luke 5:37–38
5	The Sower	Matt. 13:3–9	Mark 4:2–9	Luke 8:4–8
6	The Weeds	Matt. 13:24–30		
7	The Mustard Seed	Matt. 13:31–32	Mark 4:30–32	Luke 13:18–19
8	The Yeast	Matt. 13:33		Luke 13:20–21
9	The Hidden Treasure	Matt. 13:44		
10	The Pearl	Matt. 13:45–46		
11	The Net	Matt. 13:47–50		
12	The Lost Sheep	Matt. 18:12–14		Luke 15:3–7
13	The Unmerciful Servant	Matt. 18:23–35		
14	The Workers in the Vineyard	Matt. 20:1–16		
15	The Two Sons	Matt. 21:28–32		
16	The Tenants	Matt. 21:33–45	Mark 12:1–12	Luke 20:9–19
17	The Wedding Banquet	Matt. 22:2–14		
18	The Ten Virgins	Matt. 25:1–13		
19	The Talents	Matt. 25:14–30		
20	The Growing Seed		Mark 4:26–29	
21	The Absent Householder		Mark 13:34–37	
22	The Creditor and the Two Debtors			Luke 7:41–43
23	The Good Samaritan			Luke 10:30–37
24	A Friend in Need			Luke 11:5–13
25	The Rich Fool			Luke 12:16–21
26	The Watchful Servants			Luke 12:35–40
27	The Faithful Servant	Matt. 24:45–51		Luke 12:42–48
28	The Barren Fig Tree			Luke 13:6–9
29	The Place of Honor			Luke 14:7–11
30	The Great Banquet			Luke 14:16–24
31	The Cost of Being a Disciple			Luke 14:25–35
32	The Lost Coin			Luke 15:8–10
33	The Prodigal Son			Luke 15:11–32
34	The Shrewd Steward			Luke 16:1–13
35	The Rich Man and Lazarus			Luke 16:19–31
36	The Obedient Servant			Luke 17:7–10
37	The Persistent Widow			Luke 18:1–8
38	The Pharisee and the Tax Collector			Luke 18:9–14
39	The Ten Minas			Luke 19:11–27
	Total Parables in each Gospel	20	8	27
	Unique Parables in each Gospel	10	2	17

TITLE	SUMMARY	COMMENTS
1 *A Lamp on a Stand* Matt. 5:14–16 Mark 4:21–22 Luke 8:16–17; 11:33–36	Jesus declared that his followers are the light of the world. He then asks them not to hide their light, but rather put it on a stand to be effective.	Christians are called to be light in a darkened world. This involves living according to Christ's commandments and allowing our lives to reflect Jesus' love, obedience, humility, and forgiveness.
2 *The Wise and Foolish Builders* Matt. 7:24–27 Luke 6:47–49	At the conclusion of the Sermon on the Mount (Matt. 5:1–7:29), Jesus contrasts those that understand and do his words with those who do not. A wise person builds upon a rock and endures the storms; a foolish person builds upon sand and suffers loss.	Jesus stresses the importance of having a sure and steady foundation. Scripture tells us that Jesus alone is that worthy foundation (1 Cor. 3:11).
3 *New Cloth on an Old Garment* Matt. 9:16 Mark 2:21 Luke 5:36	Jesus explains the danger of patching a garment with new cloth. Once washed, the new cloth would shrink and make the tear worse.	The parable challenges its audience to understand the newness of Jesus' message. Jesus did not come to get rid of the law but to fulfill it. By fulfilling it, Jesus extends the meaning of the law (love your enemies, for example). The ritual-and-sacrifice faith of the Old Testament would not make room for this type of change. What Jesus offers, then, is a whole "new cloth."
4 *New Wine in Old Wineskins* Matt. 9:17 Mark 2:22 Luke 5:37–38	Jesus refers to the fact that wineskins stretch as the wine they contain ferments. If a wineskin is used again, it is unable to stretch any further and breaks.	As in the parable of the new cloth on the old garment, this parable also challenges its audience to understand the newness of Jesus' message. Jesus did not come to get rid of the law but to fulfill it. By fulfilling it, Jesus extends the meaning of the law (love your enemies, for example). The ritual-and-sacrifice faith of the Old Testament would not make room for this type of change. What Jesus offers, then, is a whole "new wineskin."
5 *The Sower* Matt. 13:3–9 Mark 4:2–9 Luke 8:4–8	A farmer spreads seed that falls into four types of soil. Seed that falls on hard soil is eaten by the birds. Seed that falls on rocks springs up quickly, but withers due to lack of root. Seed that falls in weeds is overtaken. Seed that falls in good soil produces much fruit.	This parable includes an explanation of the four soils as symbolic of the responses of people who hear the proclamation of the kingdom of God. The parable challenges its audience to receive the word about the kingdom of heaven, be focused on that message, and grow. A true hearing of the message of the kingdom of God becomes a productive hearing and productive living.
6 *The Weeds* Matt. 13:24–30	A farmer sows good seed but his enemy comes in the night and plants weeds also. The farmer decides to allow them both to grow, planning to separate them at harvest time.	This parable explains the co-existence of believers and unbelievers until the Lord's return (Matt. 13:36–43).

	TITLE	SUMMARY	COMMENTS
7	*The Mustard Seed* Matt. 13:31–32 Mark 4:30–32 Luke 13:18–19	The kingdom of heaven is compared to the mustard seed. This seed, the smallest known to Jesus' audience, becomes so great a bush that birds build their nests in it.	The kingdom does not come as a powerful mustard tree; rather, it arrives as a small seed that grows and provides shade and refuge. The kingdom of God is already present in the ministry of Jesus, but its fullness will only happen when Jesus comes back.
8	*The Yeast* Matt. 13:33 Luke 13:20–21	The kingdom of heaven is compared to yeast which, when put in dough, spreads throughout the entire mixture, causing it to expand.	The yeast is symbolic of the growing influence of the kingdom of God on the world (Matt. 28:19–20).
9	*The Hidden Treasure* Matt. 13:44	The kingdom of heaven is compared to a found treasure that is so desirable that a man sells all he has to acquire it.	Jesus announces the presence of the kingdom of heaven and invites his audience to rejoice in finding it.
10	*The Pearl* Matt. 13:45–46	The kingdom of heaven is compared to a pearl buyer who finds such a desirable pearl that he sells all he has to purchase it.	In this parable, Jesus urges his audience to recognize the value of the kingdom of heaven in their midst.
11	*The Net* Matt. 13:47–50	The kingdom of heaven is compared to a net that draws in both good (which is kept) and bad (which is burned).	This parable illustrates the separation of believers from unbelievers when Jesus returns (Matt. 25:32–46).
12	*The Lost Sheep* Matt. 18:12–14 Luke 15:3–7	When a sheep gets lost, the shepherd searches for the missing sheep and rejoices when he finds it.	The parable invites readers to participate in seeking and to join in celebrating the finding of the lost.
13	*The Unmerciful Servant* Matt. 18:23–35	A king, at his servant's pleading, forgives him of a great debt, which he could never repay. This same servant then imprisons a fellow servant who could not repay a much smaller debt. In response, the king has the first servant imprisoned.	We should be forgiving of others, realizing the great debt we have been forgiven by Christ (Ephesians 2:13).
14	*The Workers in the Vineyard* Matt. 20:1–16	A vineyard owner hires workers at 6 am for a day's wages to work in his vineyard. At 9 am, noon, 3 pm and 5 pm he hires additional workers. At 6 pm, he pays them all a full day's wages. The first workers feel cheated, but the owner reminds them that he paid them exactly what they agreed to.	The parable challenges the audience to understand that the way God treats people is not based on human standards of justice. The parable emphasizes God's mercy as the basis for salvation as it forces listeners to confront issues of envy, a sense of superiority, and jealousy.
15	*The Two Sons* Matt. 21:28–32	A man has two sons, whom he asks to work in his vineyard. The first says he will not, but later regrets it and goes to work. The second says he will work, but does not. The first son is the one that did the father's will.	A contrast of sinners who repent and are saved versus hypocrites who say the right things but do not do them (Ezek. 33:31–32).

Title	Summary	Comments
16 *The Tenants* Matt. 21:33–45 Mark 12:1–12 Luke 20:9–19	A landowner prepares a vineyard and rents it out to farmers while he goes far away. At harvest time, he sends servants to collect the "rent" (first fruits) but the farmers treat the servants shamefully. He finally sends his son, whom they kill. He will therefore destroy the wicked farmers and rent the vineyard to others.	This is one of the most difficult parables to interpret. The parable does not say that God has rejected the Jewish people as a group. It is an indictment against the Jewish leaders who rejected John the Baptist and Jesus. The parable demands from its audience that they reject, in turn, those leaders and follow Jesus.
17 *The Wedding Banquet* Matt. 22:2–14	A king prepares a wedding feast for his son and sends for the guests, who all give poor excuses for not attending and even murder his servants. The king destroys those people and invites others to the feast.	An indictment of the Jewish leaders' treatment and rejection of the prophets and Jesus. The offer of salvation is now open to all that will trust in Christ (Acts 28:28).
18 *The Ten Virgins* Matt. 25:1–13	Ten bridesmaids await the arrival of the bridegroom, but only the five that were wise enough to prepare with extra oil for their lamps were ready when he arrived and went with him.	The parable urges people to be ready and prepared for Christ's imminent return.
19 *The Talents* Matt. 25:14–30	Before going on a long trip, a man gives each of his three servants a different sum of his money to invest. Two double the money they were given and are rewarded; the third buries his for no profit and loses his reward.	At his return, Christ expects Christians to have used the gifts and opportunities he has given them (Col. 1:10). The central issue of the parable is faithfulness. The parable exhorts its audience to remain faithful disciples of Jesus in the time before his return.
20 *The Growing Seed* Mark 4:26–29	The kingdom of God is compared to seeds that grow to maturity. We do not understand the process of growth the seed experiences. However, when the fruit is ripe, it is harvested.	The parable conveys confidence and comfort to its audience by assuring that the kingdom of God will find fulfillment in God's time. It also reminds us that this fulfillment is inevitable and does not depend on human efforts.
21 *The Absent Householder* Mark 13:34–37	Christ is compared to a homeowner who goes on a trip and leaves his servants in charge. The servants must not be caught idle upon his return.	This brief comparison calls all believers to be ready for the return of Jesus. Being ready means that Christians are occupied with the matters and issues of the kingdom of heaven. Christ has left Christians to do his work in the world as salt and light. Our joy is to be found faithful upon his return (Matt. 5:13).
22 *The Creditor and the Two Debtors* Luke 7:41–43	A creditor forgives two debtors. One is forgiven an amount ten times greater than the other is. Christ confirms that the one that was forgiven the larger amount will love the creditor more.	As we come to understand more and more how great a debt we have been forgiven, we will love Christ more (Mark 12:30).

TITLE	SUMMARY	COMMENTS
23 **The Good Samaritan** Luke 10:30–37	A Jew traveling to Jericho was beaten, robbed, and left for dead. Both a priest and a Levite passed him by, but a Samaritan (hated by the Jews) rescued the man and ensured his recovery.	As a response to, "Who is my neighbor?" Jesus shows that life in the kingdom of God requires us to love our neighbors, even our enemies. The parable is a call to action; love is not only a matter of feelings or thoughts but of actions.
24 **A Friend in Need** Luke 11:5–13	A man goes to his neighbor late at night to ask for bread for a friend who has arrived from a long journey. Although the neighbor initially refuses, he eventually gives in to end the knocking at his door.	This is an encouragement to Christians to continue in prayer with perseverance and hope because God hears prayers and responds.
25 **The Rich Fool** Luke 12:16–21	A rich man has a harvest that will last him many years so he decides to "eat, drink, and be merry." God calls him a fool because that same night he will die and not enjoy his riches.	This brief parable reminds us that wisdom attends to the things of God, while foolishness concerns itself only with this life. We have very little control over life and our own success. God is the source of life, all that we need for that life, and satisfaction with our life.
26 **The Watchful Servants** Luke 12:35–40	A homeowner is pleased when he returns unexpectedly and finds his servants are ready to receive him at any time. Whether it is the master or a thief, the servants ought to be ready for each.	Jesus did not reveal the time of his second coming. Yet, he expects his servants, all Christians, to be ready to receive him when he comes back. The church is ready by doing the work of the kingdom of God and by remaining holy and faithful to Christ.
27 **The Faithful Servant** Luke 12:42–48 Matt. 24:45-51	A master will reward the servant that cares for his duties in the master's absence. Conversely, a master will punish the servant who willfully disregards his duties during his master's absence.	The parable urges its audience to right and wise living. Wisdom, in this parable, is living with the end in mind.
28 **The Barren Fig Tree** Luke 13:6–9	A vineyard owner becomes frustrated because a fig tree has not produced in three years. He commands that it be cut down, but his servant asks for one more year to nurture it.	The parable demands a response to the privilege of being God's people: Christians must "bear fruit." Bearing fruit in Luke means to live in obedience to God's will. This includes being witnesses, loving our neighbor, doing justice and loving mercy.
29 **The Place of Honor** Luke 14:7–11	When someone is invited to a feast, that person is wise to choose a humble place.	The parable confronts its audience with our natural desire to be noticed, loved, and exalted. Yet, Jesus reminded his audience that a wise person understands his own value and place in the kingdom of God (Phil. 2:3).

TITLE	SUMMARY	COMMENTS
30 *The Great Banquet* Luke 14:16–24	A man prepares a great feast for many people, but when he summons them they have a number of poor excuses for not attending. The man instead invites all the poor and disadvantaged in the city.	Salvation and the blessings of God are received by those who gladly accept and appreciate his good gifts (James 1:17).
31 *The Cost of Being a Disciple* Luke 14:25–35	It is wise to consider the cost before undertaking an important task. A person ensures sufficient funding for a building project. A leader ensures his military might is sufficient before engaging in war.	The parable urges its audience to carefully consider the cost of following Christ: surrendering our all to him and choosing his will over our own (Mark 8:34–35).
32 *The Lost Coin* Luke 15:8–10	A woman loses one of ten coins and looks diligently until she finds it. When it is found, she rejoices greatly.	Christ seeks those that are lost, and the inhabitants of heaven rejoice every time a person is saved (John 3:16).
33 *The Prodigal Son* Luke 15:11–32	A man with two sons is asked by the younger for his share of the family money. The son goes off and lives a riotous life until his money is exhausted. While working feeding pigs, he decides to go back and ask to be one his father's servants, since they were well cared for. His father sees him coming home while he is still far away and runs to him, kisses him, and treats him as an honored guest and son.	This parable challenges its audience to identify with the three main characters of the parable: The father, whose love allows him to move beyond his anger and disappointment and welcomes back his son; the older brother who, despite being a good son, is unable to move beyond his anger and welcome his once lost brother; and the younger son, who is able to move beyond his rebellion and pride and return to his father with humility and repentance. God, our Father, is compassionate and greatly rejoices when we return to him. God accepts all people, regardless of their past and actions, when they humbly come back to him with repentance.
34 *The Shrewd Steward* Luke 16:1–13	A steward is accused by his master of mishandling goods. The steward makes deals to reduce the amount owed by each of his master's debtors so that they will take care of him if he is dismissed.	This parable looks to what is wise living in light of the second coming. A wise person handles worldly wealth for the kingdom of God. No one can serve two masters: "God and Money" (Luke 16:13). The parable challenges us to use all of our resources to the service of the kingdom of God.
35 *The Rich Man and Lazarus* Luke 16:19–31	A rich man and a beggar (Lazarus) from his gates both die; Lazarus goes into Abraham's bosom (Paradise) and the rich man to torment in hell. The rich man asks Lazarus to bring him water (but he cannot pass) and to warn his brothers (but they would not believe).	This parable challenges its audience's notion of who has God's favor. Although the rich man felt confident that God was with him, God favored Lazarus. The problem with the rich man in the parable is not his wealth. Rather, the problem is wealth that ignores poverty and suffering.

TITLE	SUMMARY	COMMENTS
36 *The Obedient Servant* Luke 17:7–10	A master expects a servant to perform his assigned duties. No additional reward is necessary.	Christians should not seek to be rewarded for their obedience. Rather, we should serve him out of love.
37 *The Persistent Widow* Luke 18:1–8	A widow continuously pleads for justice from an uncaring judge. He grants her desire simply to spare himself her persistent requests.	The parable emphasizes God's patience toward his people, the assurance that God will act on their behalf, and the need to live with faithfulness and readiness for Jesus' return. The parable also shows the importance of persistence and perseverance. It is an invitation to ask God for what we need. It promises that a loving God is far more likely to respond positively to the perseverance of his people's requests than would an uncaring judge.
38 *The Pharisee and the Tax Collector* Luke 18:9–14	A Pharisee goes to the temple and prays boastfully about his works, how good he is, and how much better he is than the publican (tax collector). The tax collector humbly bows his head and asks God to forgive him of his sins.	This powerful, short parable makes an important implied conclusion: "righteous acts without compassion and love are not considered righteous by God."[1] It forces its audience to recognize that when we exclude anyone from God's grace, we run the risk of excluding ourselves from God. God honors and uplifts the humble but rejects the arrogant.
39 *The Ten Minas* Luke 19:11–27	Before traveling afar, a master gave each of his three servants ten minas (about three month's wages) to invest. One servant profited ten minas and another servant five. As a reward, the first was made ruler of ten cities, the second ruler over five. A third servant refused to invest the money because he feared his master; his mina was given to the servant who gained ten minas.	At his return, Christ expects Christians to have used the gifts and opportunities he has given them (Col. 1:10). The central issue of the parable is faithfulness in the way we use the gifts God has given to us. The parable exhorts its audience to remain faithful disciples of Jesus in the time before his return.

Interpretation of Parables

Parables can be difficult to understand.

- One problem is the chronological and cultural gap between Jesus and us. The parables are expressed with objects and experiences of daily life: parenthood, seeds and grains, trees and animals. However, these are things not always accessible for people today.

- A great deal of the effectiveness of the parables lies in their evocative power. The parables remind people of their lives and important things in their lives. Parables in the Bible are effective because the original audiences "get them." Interpreting parables is like *getting* jokes; explaining a joke kills the joke. As modern readers, we may be too far removed from the original context to "get" the parables. Thus, we need to explain parables in such a way that we do not kill their effectiveness on today's audience.

- When we take the meaning of the Bible beyond what the Bible means, we often *allegorize*. Allegorization is the practice of turning into allegory what was *not* intended to be an allegory. An often-quoted example is Augustine's interpretation of the parable of the Good Samaritan. For Augustine, the man traveling represents Adam, Jerusalem is the heavenly city, Jericho stands for our mortality, the robbers are the devil and his angels, the priest and Levite are the priesthood and ministry of the Old Testament, the good Samaritan is Christ, the inn is the church, and so on. We can know whether a parable is an allegory if the Bible itself interprets it as an allegory. For example, in the parable of the Tenants in Matthew 21:33–45, the gospel writer suggests an allegorical parable. The audience of the parable understand that Jesus is referring to the prophets, which Jesus supports with his quote from Psalm 118. Although the landowner (God), the servants (the prophets), and the son (Jesus himself) do have an allegorical meaning, we should not extend the allegory to other elements of the story. The watchtower, for example, should not be allegorized, nor the journey. They are only support elements for the parable.

Following are general suggestions for interpreting parables. These suggestions are useful for understanding how parables work and what they mean. As an example, we read the parable of the lost sheep in Matt. 18:12–14 and Luke 15:4–7.

1. *Read the parable carefully and more than once. Read it in more than one translation.*
2. *Notice the structure of the parable.*
   - The structure of the text helps us discern what is important to the gospel writer. It helps us know where the main point is.
   - In the parable of the lost sheep, because Matthew emphasizes the action of seeking, the main point—the lost sheep—is right in the middle of the parable. Since Luke focuses on the joy that the finding causes, the main point of the parable is at the end.
   - Often, the main point of parables tends to be at the end of the story, but every parable must be interpreted on its own.
3. *Pay attention to the context of the parable.*
   - The evangelists present the parable to different audiences. In Matthew, Jesus tells the parable of the lost sheep to the disciples, whereas in Luke, Jesus speaks to the Pharisees.
   - Because the parables challenge listeners to do or change something, identifying the parable's audience is important in order to understand its meaning.

4. *Interpret what is given and not what is omitted.*
   - The fact that the shepherd leaves behind ninety-nine sheep should not prompt us to ask any "what ifs." Any dangers that the ninety-nine sheep may face are imaginary and not part of the parable. We must interpret only what is present in the parable.
   - The parable should not be used to define the salvation Jesus offers. The parable itself does not teach that God is a shepherd, though that is an image the Bible uses elsewhere.
   - Jesus' own interpretation of the parable makes it clear that the shepherd stands as a metaphor of God. However, we should not extend the metaphors and seek meaning for the hills or the one hundred sheep.

5. *Identify the main points and any secondary ones.*
   - The parable challenges its hearers to understand the value of all people, especially those who are lost.
   - It shows that just as a shepherd goes out of his way to find one lost animal and rejoices when he rescues his sheep, so does God rejoice when lost people are found by him.
   - Seeking the lost sheep and the joy of finding it are the main points of the parable.

6. *Detect the important cultural details in the parable that need explaining.*
   - The image of the shepherd was common in Jesus' times and instantly connected listeners with the Old Testament and the patriarchs.

   - But there's a twist: Shepherds were practical, and people assumed that a shepherd would not risk ninety-nine to save one. It is precisely this reversal of expectation that makes the parable so compelling. Sheep were valuable assets. Risking ninety-nine sheep for one is not a practical choice.
   - So Jesus used the expected to show something about God's character to bring his audience up short: God loves us so much he will risk everything for just one.

Studying the Parables

Choose a parable to study. (You might want to start with The Pharisee and Tax Collector, The Good Samaritan, or The Rich Fool.) Study the parable by yourself or with a group.

Step one: Read the parable three times.

Step two: Examine the structure. How many parts does the parable have? Draw a simple outline of the parable.

Step three: Note the context. To whom is Jesus telling this parable? What is the setting? Did some event or question prompt Jesus to tell this parable?

Step four: Look up cultural and historical questions. When you read the parable, what questions about biblical culture or historical setting came to mind? (For example: What is a Pharisee? Who were the Samaritans? What did it mean for someone in Jesus' time to own large barns?) Write down your questions and look for answers using Bible dictionaries and commentaries.

Step five: Find the main point. What is the lesson to be learned for Jesus' audience? If a question or challenge prompted Jesus to tell the parable, how does this parable address that?

Step six: Consider how the parable can strengthen your faith and knowledge of God. Do you see similarities between the events or characters described in the parable and today's society or your own life? What does this parable teach you about God? What does it motivate you to do?

Endnote
1 Snodgrass, 473

Suggested Books

The Parables of Jesus. J. M. Boice. Moody Press, 1983.

How to Read the Bible for All Its Worth. G. D. Fee and D. Stuart. Zondervan, 1981, 2003.

The Hermeneutical Spiral. G. R. Osborne. IVP, 1991.

Stories with Intent. K. R. Snodgrass. Eerdmans, 2008.

ACTS

THE BEGINNING OF CHRISTIANITY

Jesus' disciples were riding a roller coaster of emotions and insights. First there was the hope and expectation raised by Jesus' life and ministry. Then it all seemed to go so wrong with his horrible death, only to turn right side up once and for all with the resurrection! But their new joy lasted only a few days when they gathered to see their Lord ascend to heaven and leave them behind. Yet the Lord had promised a Comforter, one who would come to the disciples, and to all believers, who would guide them "into all the truth" (John 16:13).

This small and confused group of disciples gathered to pray and seek the Lord's guidance. But when the Holy Spirit overpowered that room with the sound like a roaring windstorm and what seemed like tongues of fire, history changed forever! People from many nations were beside themselves with wonder at hearing of God's amazing acts in their own languages. The Spirit set Jerusalem ablaze, and the good news spread like wildfire.

Back to the Beginning

When Adam and Eve rebelled in the garden of Eden, God began a rescue mission. God wanted to restore his world and creatures so they would fulfill his original intentions for them: to enjoy him and praise him forever.

Throughout history, God has shaped events to bring about his plans of renewal. While God is the force, mind, and will behind the mission, he has chosen humans to work alongside him. The stories in the book of Acts show us how God is moving his mission forward.

The book of Acts shows God's actions in fulfilling his plan. This is picked up from the ending of the Gospel of Luke, where the apostles are commissioned to be part of that fulfillment: "You are witnesses of these things" (Luke 24:48). Empowered by the Holy Spirit, Jesus' disciples become an extension of God's plans to reach the whole world. The story of the church becomes the story of the fulfillment of God's mission to make all things new.

Outline

1. The Work of Jesus Continues with the Apostles (1:1–11)
2. The Mission in Jerusalem (1:12–8:3)
   a. The ministry of Peter (1:12–5:42)
   b. The ministry of Stephen (6:1–8:3)
3. The Mission in Samaria and Judea (8:4–11:18)
   a. The ministry of Philip (8:4–40)
   b. The conversion of Saul (Paul) (9:1–31)
   c. The ministry of Peter continues (9:32–11:18)
4. The Mission to the Ends of the Earth (11:19–28:31)
   a. The ministry of Barnabas (11:19–30)
   b. The conclusion of Peter's ministry (12:1–19a)
   c. The death of Herod Agrippa I (12:19b–25)
   d. The ministry of Paul and Barnabas: First missionary journey (13:1–14:28)
   e. The Jerusalem Council (15:1–35)
   f. The ministry of Paul and Silas: Second missionary journey (15:36–18:22)
   g. The ministry of Paul: Third missionary journey (18:23–21:14)
   h. Paul in Jerusalem (21:15–23:10)
   i. Paul in Caesarea (23:11–26:32)
   j. Paul taken to Rome (27:1–28:29)
   k. Conclusion: The gospel preached throughout the world (28:30–31)

PENTECOST

Pentecost, also known as the Feast of Weeks or *Shavuot* in Hebrew, marked the high point of events that began with the Passover. This Old Testament feast commemorates the giving of the Law at Mount Sinai. In the wilderness, the Law (*Torah*) gave God's people guidance, identity, strength, instruction, comfort, and light. On that same feast day (50 days after Jesus' death and 10 days after his ascension) the disciples received the Holy Spirit who would teach, guide, comfort, strengthen, and give light to God's people, the church.

The Gospel in the Book of Acts

This basic outline was helpful for Christians then and is helpful for Christians today.

1. God's promises to Israel are now fulfilled with the coming of Jesus, the Messiah (2:30; 3:19, 24; 10:43; 26:6–7, 22).
2. God anointed Jesus as the Messiah during his baptism (10:38).
3. Jesus began his ministry in Galilee after his baptism (10:37). His ministry showed God's power with words and actions.
4. Jesus, the Messiah, suffered and died on the cross according to God's own plan (2:23; 3:13–15, 18; 4:11; 10:39; 26:23).
5. God raised Jesus from the dead. Jesus appeared to his disciples (2:24, 31–32; 3:15, 26; 10:40–41; 17:31; 26:23).
6. God exalted Jesus and gave him the name of "Lord" (2:25–29, 33–36; 3:13; 10:36).
7. God sent the Holy Spirit to create a new community, the church (1:8; 2:14–18, 38–39; 10:44–47).
8. Jesus will come back one day to judge all people and to make all things new (3:20–21; 10:42; 17:31).
9. The good news of Jesus is for all people. The gospel urges all people to hear the message, repent, and be baptized (2:21, 38; 3:19; 10:43, 47–48; 17:30; 26:20).

THE AUTHOR

An early and reliable church tradition names Luke as the author of Acts and the Gospel of Luke. Because of the historical sequence found in the Gospel of Luke and Acts, it is likely that Acts was written after the Gospel. If Luke wrote the Gospel around the years AD 60–62, it is likely that Acts was written shortly after that period. Luke was one of the apostle Paul's companions during his last three journeys.

The Good News

We learn about the good news the apostles were to share from their own speeches.

- There are 24 speeches in the book of Acts.
- However, only eight of them help us with learning about the content of the gospel message:
  – Six of them are speeches addressed to a Jewish audience (2:14–39; 3:12–26; 4:8–12; 5:29–32; 10:34–43; 13:16–41)
  – Two of them to a Gentile audience (14:15–17; 17:22–34).

Examples:

SPEECH	AUDIENCE	REFERENCE	FOCUS OF THE CONTENT
Peter's speech to the other disciples in the upper room	Christians	1:16–26	• Fulfillment of God's purpose in Scripture (16, 20) • Activity of the Holy Spirit (16) • Decision to replace Judas (24)
Peter's speech to the crowd in Jerusalem on Pentecost	Jewish not-yet believers	2:14–39	• God's actions as fulfilling his promises in Joel (16–21) • God's actions and acceptance of Jesus' life, death and resurrection (22–24) • Conclusion: God made Jesus Lord and Messiah (36)
Peter's speech to Cornelius's household in Caesarea	Gentile not-yet believers	10:34–43	• God shows no partiality (34) • Jesus' preaching came from God (35) • God anointed Jesus with the Holy Spirit (38) • God raised Jesus from the dead (40) • The apostles as witnesses to these events (41) • God appointed Jesus as judge (42)
Paul's speech at the Areopagus in Athens	Pagans	17:22–34	• God has revealed himself (23) • God is creator and sustainer of the world (24–25) • God is the Lord of all nations (26) • God wants people to seek and find him (27–28) • Idolatry misses the mark (29) • God calls all to repentance (30) • God appointed Jesus as judge by raising him from the dead (31–32)

These presentations to different audiences show us the importance of allowing our message today to be adapted to different audiences. Although every person needs to hear and accept the message of the gospel, we must allow our presentation of the gospel to take different forms for different people. However, the message of the gospel is the same.

THE MAIN CHARACTERS

The book of Acts is a story. The focus of this story is God. In the book, we learn what God did in the early life of the church.

God: The Center of the Christian Story

The central character in the book is God. The book of Acts tells us the story of God in relation to the community of followers of Christ, the early church. We learn about God from the different relationships within the book. From the book we learn that:

- God is Creator and greater than the temple (7:48–50).
- He enables people to be his followers (2; 4:24–29).
- He is the God of Israel's ancestors (3:13; 22:14; 24:14).
- He is the God of the Gentiles (10:45; 11:18; 15:7–9, 14; 21:19–20).
- He is the God of history and will accomplish his purposes.

In the book of Acts, we encounter the same God of grace and mercy we find in the Old Testament. He has taken the initiative to rescue his people, as he had promised he would, and extends the invitation to all the nations.

Jesus: The Kingdom of God and the Mission

We learn about God by knowing Jesus Christ. As the epistle to the Hebrews teaches us, " ... in these last days he has spoken to us by his Son ... " (Heb. 1:1). If the Old Testament reveals God, the New Testament perfects that revelation in the person of Jesus. We learn much about Jesus from the speeches in the book of Acts. We learn that Jesus is:

- The Promised Messiah (2:36; 3:20; 5:42; 8:5; 17:3; 18:5)
- Son of David (2:30; 13:23)
- Lord (2:36; 10:36)
- Son of God (9:20; 13:33)
- Prophet like Moses (3:22–23; 7:37)
- Servant of the Lord (3:13, 26; 4:30; 8:32–33)
- Son of Man (7:56)
- The righteous one (3:14; 7:52; 22:14)
- The author of life (3:15)
- Leader and Savior (5:31)
- One destined to suffer (3:18; 17:3; 26:23)
- Rejected (2:23–24; 3:13–15; 8:32–33; 13:28)

WHO WAS THEOPHILUS?

Both Luke and Acts address a man named Theophilus (Luke 1:3; Acts 1:1). He is addressed as "most excellent," a common way of addressing socially important people.

Books were expensive, and only a few people and groups were able to afford them. It was common to write books for a wealthy patron who would keep them and grant access to others to read. If Theophilus was wealthy, then it is possible that he financed Luke's writing, paid for copies of the books, and granted churches access to the books.

Acts was meant for several audiences: first, the book is addressed to an individual—Theophilus; second, it was for other people like him—perhaps Romans who were intrigued by Christianity; and third, it's for all Christian believers—Jews and Gentiles alike.

At the center of the apostolic message we find Jesus. Jesus is presented as God's ultimate solution for all humanity, Jews and Gentiles alike. In all of it, Jesus is presented as representing God and carrying on God's plans for humanity. Jesus makes it possible for God's mission to save his creation to be fulfilled. Consistently throughout the book, Jesus is presented as Lord. As Lord, he sent his followers as ambassadors to carry on his will, to spread the good news that the kingdom of God had arrived.

The Church

As the number of believers grew, the book of Acts summarizes the life of this new community: "They devoted themselves to the apostles' teaching and to fellowship, to the breaking of bread and to prayer. Everyone was filled with awe at the many wonders and signs performed by the apostles" (2:42–43).

This emphasis on the mission can be best seen in the movement of God in Luke and Acts:

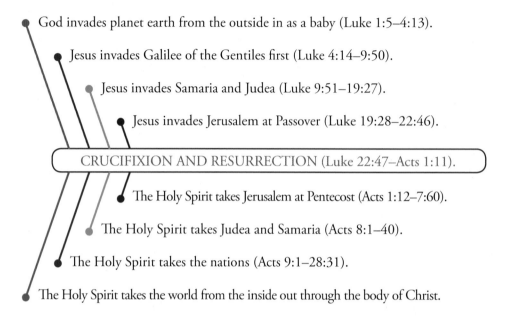

God invades planet earth from the outside in as a baby (Luke 1:5–4:13).

Jesus invades Galilee of the Gentiles first (Luke 4:14–9:50).

Jesus invades Samaria and Judea (Luke 9:51–19:27).

Jesus invades Jerusalem at Passover (Luke 19:28–22:46).

CRUCIFIXION AND RESURRECTION (Luke 22:47–Acts 1:11).

The Holy Spirit takes Jerusalem at Pentecost (Acts 1:12–7:60).

The Holy Spirit takes Judea and Samaria (Acts 8:1–40).

The Holy Spirit takes the nations (Acts 9:1–28:31).

The Holy Spirit takes the world from the inside out through the body of Christ.

GOD'S COMMUNITY IS CHARACTERIZED BY:

Baptism. The powerful symbolism of baptism shapes the character and identity of the church. People in this new community are those who die and are born again, empowered and sealed by the Spirit. This is a new identity; there is no longer Gentile or Jew, or any other social or biological characteristic that separates them. They are all united as one body.

Worship. Worship is a visual declaration of our deepest beliefs. In worship, we express with our whole beings what is most important to us. Worship is also a humbling experience where we recognize our ultimate dependence on God. Worship shapes this new community.

Fellowship. The life of the new community was central to their message. This community is characterized by an intimate fellowship with other believers and with the Lord. Fellowship with other believers flows from our fellowship with God. In the breaking of bread, which most likely included the Lord's Supper, fellowship became a central part of that community.

Instruction. The church is apostolic because it is founded on the teachings of the apostles. They taught all that Jesus had taught them and what the Spirit revealed to them. The church is God's initiative. The church is an extension of her Lord.

Mission. The main reason for the existence of the church is God's mission. Through her life and spoken testimony, God would spread the kingdom of God. A kingdom that was already active but not yet completely here. The church is God's active representative on earth.

Stephen: The First Christian Martyr

Stephen, one of the seven men the church chose and the apostles ordained to serve alongside them. Stephen became a leader of the early church, "a man full of God's grace and power, performed great wonders and signs among the people" (Acts 6:8). His speech before the religious leaders of the Jews caused an angry response that led to Stephen's death. Jesus had warned the disciples, "If they persecuted me, they will persecute you also" (John 15:20). However, Jesus promised that when persecution occurred, the Holy Spirit would be present encouraging and strengthening believers (John 14:16; 15:26). The story of Stephen shows the strength, conviction, and faithfulness that is possible through the power of the Spirit.

The Leaders of the Mission

Most of the book deals with how Jesus' followers carry on God's mission. The challenges that the apostles faced teach us that Jesus is faithful and his presence and protection is with his people.

Rather than a detailed account of the ministry of all the disciples, the text concentrates on two strong leaders: the apostles Peter and Paul. Their stories illustrate well the task and challenges of the mission. They also illustrate the ways the Holy Spirit has equipped us to fulfill our calling.

ACTION	PETER	PAUL
Healed a lame man	3:2–8	14:8–10
Performed a miracle at a distance	5:15	19:12
Exorcised evil spirits	5:16	19:12
Defeated sorcerers	8:18–24	13:6–11
Raised the dead	9:36–43	20:9–12
Defended themselves against Jewish authorities	4:8–12; 5:27–32	23:3–21; 23:1–6; 28:25–28
Received heavenly visions	10:9–16	16:9
Present when the Spirit came upon new believers	8:14–17	19:1–7
Miraculously released from prison	5:19; 12:7–11	16:25–27
Proclaimed the same message	2:27	13:35

THE MISSION TO THE WORLD

The starting point of the mission was Jerusalem. Slowly, the Holy Spirit pushed the apostles away from Jerusalem to Judea, Samaria and to all the nations. This outward movement shows God's desire to reach all peoples on earth. The stories of the mission work of the apostolic church are powerful and inspirational. They not only show the faithfulness and determination of the apostles, but, more importantly, they show God's guiding and protecting hand. It is God's mission, as the early refrain in the book reminds us: "And the Lord added to their number day by day those who were being saved" (Acts 2:47).

The Apostle Peter and the Mission

The apostle Peter had an exceptional spiritual journey. He became one of the first disciples Jesus called (Matt. 4:18). He was a leader among the disciples during and after Jesus' ministry on earth. After Pentecost, Peter was the first to bring testimony of the resurrected Jesus (Acts 2:14–41). Peter's spiritual story led him to recognize many times his personal struggles and his surrender to God's will.

In the book of Acts, the encounter of Peter and the Roman centurion Cornelius confronted the apostle with God's broad plan for humanity. But this event also became a hinging moment in the history of the church. The renewal of all creation started on Pentecost, but the world had continued turning apparently unperturbed. The world was still divided. Jews and Gentiles were separate. But Peter's vision in Acts 10 changed everything.

A Roman Centurion—it would be equivalent to the rank of captain in today's armies—Cornelius was "devout and God-fearing" (10:2). God revealed himself in a vision to Cornelius (10:3–8). God also gave Peter a vision of the "unclean" animals. These were ritually unclean animals not fit for consumption according to the law (Lev. 11). The point of this vision is clear: "Do not call anything impure that God has made clean" (10:15). For many Jews at that time, the impurity of those animals was equivalent to the impurity of the Gentiles. God was preparing Peter for the next phase of the mission: the gospel for the Gentiles.

The conclusion of the story is remarkable: after hearing Peter's presentation of the gospel (10:34–43), "the Holy Spirit came on all who heard the message" (10:44). God was putting his seal of approval and welcoming on the Gentiles. Peter understood what God was doing. He said, "Surely no one can stand in the way of their being baptized with water" (10:47). As he explained his actions in Jerusalem, Peter concludes, "So then, even to Gentiles God has granted repentance that leads to life" (11:18).

But you will receive power when the Holy Spirit comes on you; and you will be my witnesses in Jerusalem, and in all Judea and Samaria, and to the ends of the earth.

— ACTS 1:8

The Apostle Paul and the Mission

Before becoming Paul, Saul was a deadly enemy of Christianity. After a personal encounter with the resurrected Christ (9:1–19), Paul became God's special representative to the Gentiles. His ministry, as recorded in the book of Acts, changed the history of the church and of the world. In four recorded trips, Paul preached the gospel from Jerusalem to Philippi, Athens, Corinth, Ephesus, Rome, and back to Jerusalem. He planted new churches and trained new leaders. His letters, which form the bulk of the New Testament and are aimed at instructing and guiding those new groups and leaders, continue to shape, inform, and nurture the faith of millions of believers today all over the world.

THE MISSION IN JERUSALEM

- After Jesus ascended to heaven (1:8), the disciples received the Holy Spirit on Pentecost (2:1–4).

- Peter preached and 3,000 people received the gospel (2:5–41).

- The apostles Peter and John performed miracles (3:1–10) and preached the gospel in the temple in Jerusalem and 5,000 people believed (3:11–4:4).

- Despite the persecution against the disciples, many people believed in the gospel. The apostles chose seven believers "full of the Spirit and wisdom" (6:3) to help them with the life of the growing group of believers.

THE MISSION IN JUDEA AND SAMARIA

- In the midst of persecution, Christ's disciples continued to proclaim the good news. Stephen, one of the seven chosen by the apostles, provided an example of perseverance, faith, and obedience when he faced an angry crowd. He preached a powerful message, the longest speech in the book, and argued for the gospel using the Old Testament as his basis. Stephen became the first recorded martyr (6:8–7:60). Saul, a Jewish leader who would later become the apostle Paul, was present at that moment.

- After Stephen's death, the persecution against believers increased dramatically and "all except the apostles were scattered throughout Judea and Samaria" (8:1). As they moved away from Jerusalem, they brought the gospel with them. Philip preached in Samaria and to the Ethiopian eunuch, who had been to Jerusalem to worship God. After his baptism, the Ethiopian official returned home, bringing along with him the transformative power of the gospel (8:26–40).

- Jesus confronted Saul on the road to Damascus (9:1–22) and called him to become his instrument "to carry my name before the Gentiles and their kings and before the people of Israel" (9:15). The church found peace throughout Judea, Galilee and Samaria and "grew in numbers" (9:31).

THE MISSION TO THE GENTILES

- Jesus' disciples continued to preach the gospel outside of Jerusalem, reaching places like Joppa (9:42), Caesarea (10), Phoenicia, Cyprus, and Antioch (11:19). Antioch became the base for Paul's missionary journeys.

- Despite persecution, Jesus' followers continued to preach the gospel in and around Jerusalem so that "the word of God continued to spread and flourish" (12:24).

- Along with Barnabas, Paul began an adventure that would take him to Asia Minor, the Greek Islands, and beyond. He rarely traveled alone. Barnabas was his first companion (15:39–40). Silas would be his next companion (15:40). Along the way, other companions joined the apostle in his journeys.

THE HOLY SPIRIT

- The Spirit is involved in the works of God:
  - Creation (Ps. 104:30)
  - Incarnation (Matt. 1:18; Luke 1:35)
  - Resurrection (Rom. 1:4; 8:11)
  - Salvation (John 15:26; 16:8; Rom. 8:14–17)
  - Christian Life (John 16:13; Rom. 8:26–27; 15:18–19; 1 Cor. 2:10; Gal. 5:22–23)

- The Spirit is a person:
  - He can be lied to (Acts 5:3–4)
  - He can be grieved (Eph. 4:30)
  - He has a name (Matt. 28:19).

- The Spirit is God (Acts 5:3; 1 Cor. 3:16; 12:4–6; 2 Peter 1:21)

Paul's Missionary Journeys

JOURNEY	ACTS	BASIC INFORMATION	HIGHLIGHTS
First Journey AD 47–49	13:1–14:28	**Travelers:** Paul, Barnabas, John Mark **Main Route:** (Modern names) Cyprus and Turkey **Distance:** 1,400 miles	After being set apart for this journey, Paul and Barnabas faced a sorcerer, opposition from Jewish leaders, sick people who were healed, persecutions, and the crucial Jerusalem Council at the end of the journey (15:1–35).
Second Journey AD 49–51	15:36–18:22	**Travelers:** Paul, Silas, Timothy, Priscilla and Aquilla, Luke **Main Route:** (Modern names) Syria, Turkey, Greece, Jerusalem **Distance:** 2,800 miles	Paul and Barnabas went separate ways. With Silas, Paul visited churches, and received visions from God. They were thrown in jail and met people who eagerly received their message. At Athens, Paul preached to the Greeks.
Third Journey AD 52–57	18:23–21:16	**Travelers:** Paul, Timothy, Luke, others **Main Route:** (Modern names) Turkey, Greece, Lebanon, Israel **Distance:** 2,700 miles	Paul visited the churches of the area. He remained for two years at Ephesus. Paul wrote several of his letters during this journey. He revived a young man who had an accident. He also experienced persecution and suffering. At the end, he went to Jerusalem.
Journey to Rome AD 57–62	21:17–28:31	**Travelers:** Paul, Roman guards, Luke, others **Main Route:** (Modern names) Israel, Lebanon, Turkey, Crete, Malta, Sicily, Italy **Distance:** 2,250 miles	Paul was arrested in Jerusalem. In Caesarea, Paul was tried before two governors: Felix and Festus. After two years, Paul appealed to Caesar and appeared before King Agrippa. Paul was sent to Rome. After a shipwrecked trip, Paul arrived in Rome. He remained there under house arrest for two years.

TIME LINE OF THE BOOK OF ACTS

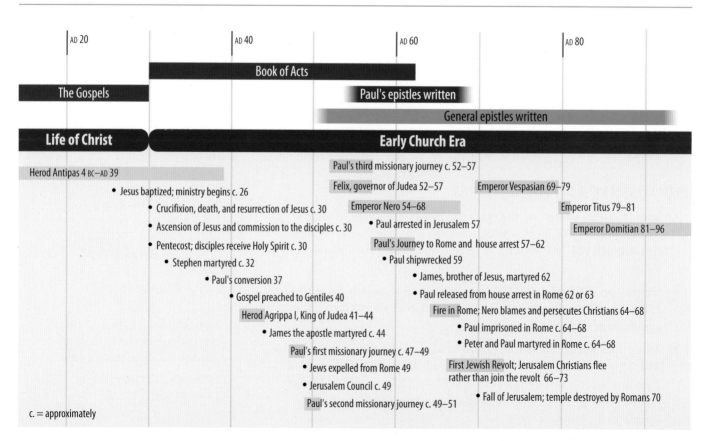

c. = approximately

©2014 Bristol Works, Inc.   www.rose-publishing.com

OUR HISTORY AND HERITAGE

The book of Acts is not simply ancient history. It is our story, the story that informs who we are. We are God's people, called to be witnesses of what God did and continues to do in Jesus. By studying and understanding the way God acted in history, we become more attuned to the ways God is active among us today. God is active, as the book of Acts shows. We must be sensitive to the way the Spirit moves in our midst and in the world to join in the mission.

The Scriptures do not promise that the mission is easy and painless. To the contrary, being Jesus' disciples implies danger and opposition. But the stories in the book of Acts show that Jesus is faithful to his promise to be with us always. The stories inspire us to be brave and obedient. The end of the book of Acts represents only the beginning of the church's life and mission: "[Paul] proclaimed the kingdom of God and taught about the Lord Jesus Christ—with all boldness and without hindrance!" (Acts 28:31).

THE SPREAD OF CHRISTIANITY IN THE FIRST CENTURY AD

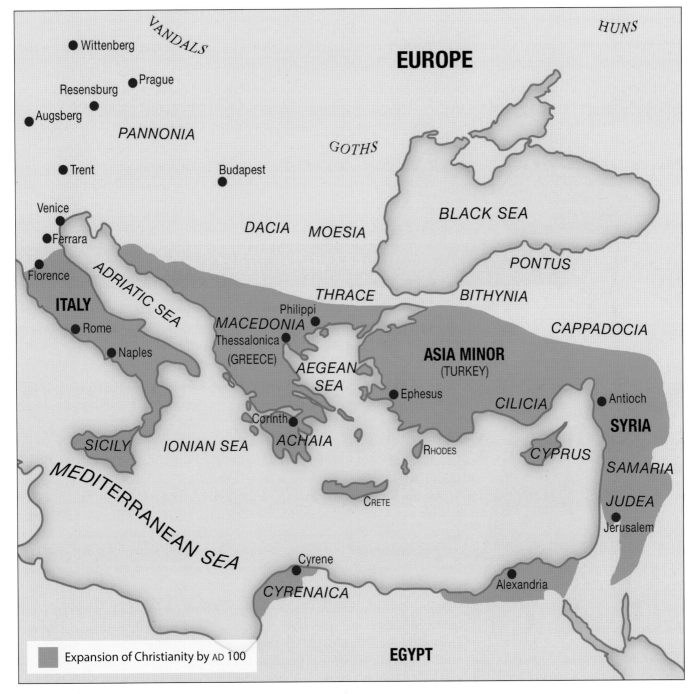

Expansion of Christianity by AD 100

Romans

PAUL'S EPISTLE TO THE ROMANS

Many years ago, a very successful young man sat on a bench. He was disgusted with his life. His success could not hide his terrible failings. Lust and greed ruled his life. In despair, he picked up a book and read:

Let us behave decently, as in the daytime, not in carousing and drunkenness, not in sexual immorality and debauchery, not in dissension and jealousy. Rather, clothe yourselves with the Lord Jesus Christ, and do not think about how to gratify the desires of the flesh (Rom. 13:13–14).

He awoke from his "slumber" (Rom. 13:11): "No further would I read, nor had I any need," he said. "Instantly, at the end of this sentence, a clear light flooded my heart and all the darkness of doubt vanished away."

The young man was Augustine. In the fourth century AD he became bishop of Hippo and one of the most influential Christian thinkers in the history of the church. Through the message of Romans, God transformed the life of that anguished young man and then used him in powerful ways. It is the same message we read today, and it has the same power to transform us.

Studying the letter to the Romans will help us understand what God has done in and through Christ, and letting the Word of God and the Holy Spirit shape our minds and hearts will transform our lives. Open your mind, your heart, and your will to the powerful words of this letter.

WHO WROTE THE LETTER?

Paul, the author of Romans, was a one-time enemy of Christianity who God transformed into the greatest Christian missionary of all time! Paul came from a well-respected Jewish family in Asia Minor (Turkey today) where his father was an official. As a young man, Paul—whose Jewish name was Saul—was sent to Jerusalem to study under the great teacher Gamaliel.

Paul belonged to a group of people who thought the followers of Christ were dangerous. He hated Christians and participated in the first execution of a Christian leader, a man named Stephen. Paul was determined to destroy Christianity everywhere (Acts 7:54–8:3).

Paul hated Christians so much that he asked the chief priest in Jerusalem to give him authorization to arrest any follower of Jesus in Damascus (about 100 miles away). On his way from Judea to Damascus, a light from heaven blinded him. He fell to the ground and a voice said, "Saul, Saul, why do you persecute me?" Paul answered, "Who are you?" The voice said, "I am Jesus, the one you are persecuting. Get up! Go into the city, and you will be told what to do." Paul went to a house and waited for a Christian man named Ananias to come restore his sight (Acts 9:1–12).

During the early years of Christianity, Jesus' disciples preached only to Jews, so most converts at that time were Jewish. As Jews scattered throughout the Roman Empire, they told their neighbors about Jesus. Many of these Gentiles (non-Jews) then became followers of Jesus too (Acts 11:19–21). While traveling throughout the Roman Empire, the apostle Paul preached and ministered to Gentile Christians. Paul became one of God's powerful tools to spread the good news of Jesus.

Paul's Journey to Rome, AD 57–62 (Acts 21:17–28:31)

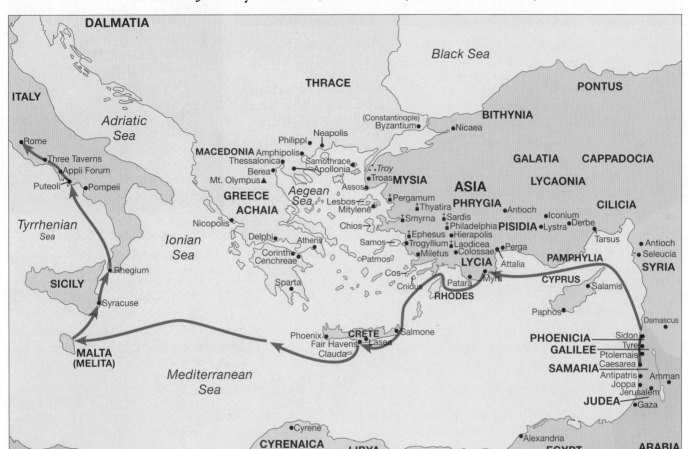

TO WHOM WAS THE LETTER WRITTEN?

Paul wrote this letter to the church in Rome. In the first century, Rome was the center of nearly all that happened in the Mediterranean world. The church at Rome during this time was a mix of both Jewish and Gentile believers. There was a large Jewish presence in Rome, as we learn from the expulsion order given under Emperor Claudius (Acts 18:2–3). Many Christian believers were already there before Paul made his first journey to Rome around AD 57.

Though there is no mention of who first brought the gospel to Rome, Christianity had spread quickly to the capital city of the Roman Empire, probably through travelers engaged in business, political, and religious activities. By the time of the great persecution under Emperor Nero (AD 64), the historian Tacitus could say a "great multitude" of Christians lived in Rome.

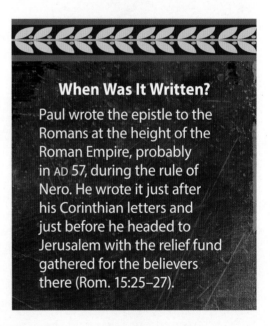

When Was It Written?

Paul wrote the epistle to the Romans at the height of the Roman Empire, probably in AD 57, during the rule of Nero. He wrote it just after his Corinthian letters and just before he headed to Jerusalem with the relief fund gathered for the believers there (Rom. 15:25–27).

But God demonstrates his own love for us in this: While we were still sinners, Christ died for us.— Romans 5:8

Purposes of the Letter

Inspired by the Holy Spirit, and borne from his desire to visit the church in Rome, Paul wrote the letter with very specific purposes in mind:

- **Missionary.** Paul's ministry was, at its core, missionary—spreading the gospel throughout the world. Paul's travels describe an apostle profoundly involved with Jesus' commission to spread the gospel. The Epistle to the Romans reveals Paul's heart for missions. The apostle had not visited the church in Rome, yet he wanted to make it his church base for launching a missionary effort that would reach the end of the known world: Spain. Paul also might have wanted Roman believers to know the content of his missionary preaching—in other words, the message of the gospel.

- **Teaching.** Paul explained in detail many crucial topics of the Christian faith. The letter to the Romans is not a complete handbook of Christian beliefs. Rather, this book reveals an interest in themes like the human need for salvation, the relationship between Jewish and Gentile Christians, the death and resurrection of Jesus as the way of salvation, justification by faith alone, and the role of faith in people's lives.

- **Pastoral.** Paul's letter is not just a doctrinal letter; it is a personal letter. The apostle Paul sends personal greetings to many people, and he is aware of the different house churches in Rome. He is also aware of potential divisions and troubles. Gentile Christians might have lost view of the importance of their fellow Jewish Christians. With pastoral love, he writes to encourage and exhort Roman believers to unity and wisdom.

These three purposes develop a central concern in the letter, which is found in Romans 1:16–17:

For I am not ashamed of the gospel, because it is the power of God that brings salvation to everyone who believes: first to the Jew, then to the Gentile. For in the gospel the righteousness of God is revealed—a righteousness that is by faith from first to last, just as it is written: "The righteous will live by faith."

For all have sinned and fall short of the glory of God.—Romans 3:23

Three Important Themes

- **Redemption/Ransom.** Many of the people Paul addressed in Rome were or had been slaves. At this time in history, slavery was a reality most people experienced on a daily basis. Most domestic workers, teachers, low government functionaries, and manual laborers were slaves. In New Testament times, slaves had many protections and freedoms. In fact, slaves could become free people and, in some cases, even Roman citizens. One way to acquire freedom was simply to buy it, though the price for one's freedom was very high. A ransom—often money—was the payment for a slave's freedom. Redemption occurred when someone else, a master or another slave, paid the ransom for a slave. The freed person was redeemed. Paul knew that his audience would readily understand this image, and so he used it to speak of what God had done in Christ. Christ's sacrifice on the cross and resurrection from the grave redeems us from our bondage to sin and death. God makes us free!

- **Atonement.** The origin of the English word *atonement* has been attributed to William Tyndale, the sixteenth-century English Bible translator, to express what Jesus accomplished on the cross: the cancellation of sins and reconciliation of God with humanity. The word has two parts: "at" and "onement." Atonement, then, is God's way to bring reconciliation and restoration to the problem of human sin and its effects.

- **Justification.** In Christ, God has justified us and opened the way to serve him and love him. Justification is a word that comes from the courts of law. Paul uses this word to explain to the Romans—well acquainted with the court system—the effects of Jesus' death for believers. In Christ, God has declared us just, or acceptable, before God.

1 INTRODUCTION: AN APOSTLE TO THE GENTILES (1:1–17)

Paul started the churches in Corinth, Galatia, and Philippi, but he did not start the church in Rome. The apostle Paul had to introduce himself to the Christians at Rome because they did not personally know him. Notice the descriptions he used:

1. **A servant of Christ Jesus**—Here, Paul drew from the Old Testament concept of servanthood—Moses was the Lord's servant, the kings of Israel and Judah were God's servants, the prophets and priests were God's servants.

2. **Called to be an apostle**—Paul was "called to be an apostle" (v. 1) and the Roman Christians were "called to be his [God's] holy people" (v. 7). Each one called for a purpose, and Paul's purpose was a special one. An apostle is a messenger, one who brings his master's will to others. Moreover, Paul was an apostle to the Gentiles (v. 5), such as to the Roman Christians who received his letter.

3. **Set apart for the gospel of God**—Paul was "set apart" (v. 1) and the Christian Romans were "called to be his holy people" (to be "holy" is to be "set apart"). Paul's main calling as servant of Christ Jesus and as an apostle was to be a witness to the gospel. Paul's missionary heart comes through from the beginning of the letter.

And we know that in all things God works for the good of those who love him, who have been called according to his purpose. —Romans 8:28

Paul offers an explanation of "the gospel of God." Notice the terms he used:

1. **Promised**—Paul declared that the life and ministry of Jesus were anticipated in the Old Testament. Jesus was the fulfillment of God's promises in the Old Testament. The good news began in Genesis!

2. **About Jesus**—Paul stated that Jesus is the heart of the gospel. All of salvation history centers on Christ: his divinity and humanity, his ministry on earth, death and resurrection. All of it testifies to Jesus' lordship.

   a. Jesus is God's Son.
   b. Jesus was a human, descendant of David.
   c. Jesus was ministered by the Spirit of holiness.

3. **Effects**—Paul explained that through the gospel we receive God's grace. God's grace makes all the difference in the world! The effects of the gospel are central to Paul's letter. We, as Christians, also receive a calling: Paul was called to apostleship, but all Christians are called to belong to Jesus Christ.

2 GOD IS RIGHT TO JUDGE AND SAVE (1:18–3:20)

The message of the gospel brings salvation to the Jew first, then to the Gentile. This is an important point that Paul makes throughout the letter. The first step in his argument is to show that both Jews and Gentiles are in need of salvation.

Paul deals with the sinfulness and perversions found in the Gentile world in the first section, 1:18–32. The apostle Paul did not list all possible sins, or even the worst of them, that one could find in the Gentile world. If the Roman Christians had any feeling of ethnic superiority over the Jewish Christians, Paul's reasoning erased it. Paul's evidence is conclusive: the Gentile world is in need of salvation.

However, the apostle wasn't finished with unveiling the ugliness of human sin. He turned to the Jewish world: "You, therefore, have no excuse, you who pass judgment on someone else, for at whatever point you judge another, you are condemning yourself, because you who pass judgment do the same things" (Rom. 2:1). Paul leveled the playing field for Jews and Gentiles! The main point of this section is this: humans, Jew and Gentile alike, with or without the law, share the same problem—sin—and equally need God's solution—the gospel. The apostle Paul arrives to a powerful conclusion: "Therefore no one will be declared righteous in God's sight by the works of the law" (3:20).

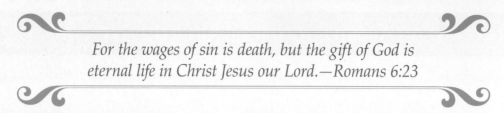

*For the wages of sin is death, but the gift of God is
eternal life in Christ Jesus our Lord.—Romans 6:23*

God's Righteousness Is Revealed in His Wrath

God's anger is neither irrational nor capricious. Rather, human rebellion and willful rejection of the light God has given to both Gentiles and Jews are good reasons for his anger. God's wrath, however, is not revealed in what God *does* but in what he does *not* do. God allows humanity, Gentiles and Jews alike, to suffer the disastrous consequences of their own evil.

However, Paul's ultimate goal is to show that:

1. There is no difference between Jew and Gentile,

2. for all have sinned and fall short of the glory of God,

3. and all are justified freely by his grace through the redemption that came by Christ Jesus (Rom. 3:22–24)

Paul wants to present the power of the gospel to his readers. Just as we can better understand the light when we contrast it with the darkness, so also the ugliness of human sin makes us long for God's gracious help.

3 THE POWER OF THE GOSPEL (3:21–8:39)

The apostle Paul has shown that God is right in being angry. Human sin is destructive and offends God. As Paul explains God's solution to the horror of human sin, he focuses on a different side of God's righteousness.

God's Righteousness Is Revealed in His Plan of Salvation

In Romans 3:21–8:39, the apostle Paul explains what the power of the gospel achieves:

1. **Forgiveness** (3:21–4:25)—Forgiveness of sin through the ministry of Jesus is a revelation of God's righteousness and of the power of the gospel. All the images the apostle used before—commercial, religious, and legal—point to this essential benefit. The benefits of the gospel, the apostle insists, are not something people earn or deserve. Rather, they come from God's grace, as a gift, and are appropriated by faith. Sin offends God's holiness and justice, breaks any possibility of a relationship with humanity, and brings death and destruction. The first step in God's amazing grace is to forgive people who do not deserve forgiveness.

2. **Peace** (5:1–21)—Because of God's gracious forgiveness, humanity can start a new relationship with God. The enmity that sin causes between God and humans is now overcome. The Roman audience understood the concept well because of the *Pax Romana*, the peace within the Roman Empire that allowed for consistent commerce, growth of cities, and peaceful travel. The peace that Christ brings, however, is just the beginning of a new life. It also includes perseverance, character, and hope. This peace also brings a new freedom that believers must learn to experience.

One of Paul's main arguments throughout his ministry in general, which is expressed in his letter to the Romans, is that God's offer of salvation to all people is free. In other words, there is nothing people can do to earn or merit or influence God's decision to save us. Salvation is an undeserved gift from God. However, this

The Good News

As Paul did in his letter, our presentation of the gospel has to move beyond noting what is wrong with our society, our neighbors, or young people. We must proclaim the good news: we believe in a God who has done something about the human problem, the solution is free and available to all, and it makes all the difference in the world.

important teaching raises the serious problem of so-called cheap grace—also known as *antinomianism*. Paul gives an answer to that problem in Romans, chapters 6 and 7. In the apostle's answer, it is clear that cheap grace and legalism—the teaching that we must obey the Law to be saved—are two sides of the same coin: both represent the inability to understand or accept the wondrous grace of God.

3. **Freedom from the power of sin** (6:1–23)—Believers are free from the power of sin. This does not mean that Christians do not sin at all. Rather, because of Christ's death, sin no longer controls us; we can choose not to sin. Returning to his image of slavery, the apostle Paul affirms that we are no longer slaves to sin. We "have become slaves to righteousness" (6:18). We are free to do what is right in a world where wickedness and injustice abounds. The following table[1] shows important contrasts the apostle makes in this chapter of Romans.

Rom. 6:	Dead to Sin	Alive in Christ
13	Instruments of unrighteousness to sin	Instruments of righteousness to God
14–15	Not under the law	But under grace
16	Sin unto death	Obedience unto righteousness
18	Free from sin	Enslaved to righteousness
19	Slave to impurity unto wickedness	Slave to righteousness unto holiness
20	Slaves to sin	Slaves to God
21-22	End is death	End is eternal life
22	Free from sin	Slaves to God
23	Wages of sin is death	Gift of God is eternal life

4. **Freedom from the condemnation of the law** (7:1–25). The law condemns us because of our sin. The law cannot remove the stain of sin nor transform our hearts so we can become free from the slavery to sin. But God has delivered us "through Jesus Christ our Lord!" (7:25).

5. **New Life in the Spirit** (8:1–39). Rather than condemnation, "the law of the Spirit who gives life has set you free from the law of sin and death" (8:2). In chapter 8 of Romans, Paul neatly brings the arguments from the previous chapters to a closing; and a glorious closing it is. The apostle has concluded that God's solution to the greatest human problem is found in Christ's death and resurrection (chapter 5 and verse 6:4). How do we see the benefits of Christ's death and resurrection in the life of believers? The answer is found in chapter 8: God gives us a new life in the Spirit. "For those who are led by the Spirit of God are the children of God" (Rom. 8:14). This salvation that the Spirit makes active in the believers has consequences beyond the individual. It has cosmic consequences.

The entire universe groans for God's deliverance, just as believers groan for God's deliverance and the Spirit groans as he intercedes for us (8:22, 23, 26). However, even in this context of suffering in life, Paul offers encouragement and comfort by reminding us that we, as believers, are safe in God's loving hands. Therefore, because of what Christ did on the cross and the presence of the Spirit in our lives, we can proclaim along with the apostle Paul, "in all these things [trouble, hardship, persecution, famine, nakedness, danger, sword (8:35)] we are more than conquerors through him who loved us" (8:37).

Therefore, I urge you, brothers and sisters, in view of God's mercy, to offer your bodies as a living sacrifice, holy and pleasing to God—this is your true and proper worship.
—*Romans 12:1*

©2014 Bristol Works, Inc.   www.rose-publishing.com   May be reproduced for classroom use only, not for sale.

4 GOD'S RIGHTEOUS PLAN FOR ISRAEL AND GENTILES (9:1–11:36)

After teaching about the revelation of God's righteousness in judgment and in salvation, which is the heart of the gospel, the apostle Paul now deals with a vital and practical problem in the church: divisions between the Roman Gentiles and Jewish Christians.

Divisions within the body oppose the very gospel that Paul describes. For this reason, Paul refutes questions about Israel's place in God's plans. Did God's plans fail? Is God still faithful to his promises to Israel? Are Gentile Christians above the Jews now? If God's faithfulness to Israel changed, could his faithfulness to believers, as expressed in 8:31–39, also change? Are we truly safe in his hands?

Division Among Gentiles and Jews

For most of his ministry Paul dealt with the problem of Jewish Christians wanting Gentiles to follow Jewish Laws. In this letter, Paul deals with the opposite problem: Gentile Christians who seem to regard Jews as inferior. Paul's appeal to the Roman Christians, and to all believers, is a personal one: as an apostle of the Lord and as a Jew. In the previous section, Paul used examples from the life of Abraham and Adam to connect more directly with the Gentile experience. In chapters 9–11, Paul argues using many Old Testament quotations and allusions. Paul begins his argument alluding to Moses' own appeal on behalf of God's people in the aftermath of the golden calf catastrophe (Ex. 32:32): "For I could wish that I myself were cursed and cut off from Christ for the sake of my people, those of my own race" (Rom. 9:3).

To explain the place of Israel in God's plans, the apostle presents a three-part salvation plan: God rejects Israel for the sake of the Gentiles (11:11–12), the Gentiles will be saved "until the full number of the Gentiles has come in" (11:25), and, then, "all Israel will be saved" (11:26).

Paul's conclusions:

1. First, rejection of Israel is temporary and has a vital purpose. Paul's teaching is clear: "But if their transgression means riches for the world, and their loss means riches for the Gentiles, how much greater riches will their full inclusion bring!" (11:12).

2. Second, Gentiles should not feel superior to the Jews. Salvation is not by works, so no one can boast about it. Gentiles' attitude toward Jews should be one of humility and hope. The beautiful doxology at the end of the section (11:33–36) suggests this attitude of humility before "the depth of the riches of the wisdom and knowledge of God! How unsearchable his judgments, and his paths beyond tracing out!" (11:33).

5 THE POWER OF THE GOSPEL IN THE LIFE OF BELIEVERS (12:1–15:13))

So far, the apostle Paul has covered much doctrinal ground in this most impressive letter. But having explained the basis for his gospel, and the role of Israel in the history of salvation, he now turns to the consequences of all he has taught. The power of the gospel, Paul says, has concrete and decisive effects in the lives of believers.

- The basis for Christian living apart from the Mosaic law (12:1-2)
  - The body of Christ as the social expression of God's people (12:3-8)
    - Love as the fundamental moral rule in human relationships (12:9-21)
      - ### Christians and the powers that be (Romans 13:1-7)
    - Love of neighbor as the fulfillment of the law in human relationships (13:8-10)
  - Christ as the pattern of Christian living (13:11-14)
- The basis for social interaction apart from the Mosaic law (14:1-15:13)

The power of the gospel is creative and transformative. The consequences are equally radical. In light of all he has written, the apostle Paul now appeals to his readers to become living sacrifices. The concept captures what he has hinted at before: If we are not bound to the law, which requires daily sacrifices, we are now bound to the law of love (see Rom. 13:8–10), which requires that we offer our whole selves to God. Our entire lives should be an act of worship to God.

But love is not all that the gospel demands. The apostle uses another radical concept: Our minds must be transformed and renewed. Paul means that we need a radical change in worldview. If we were once slaves of sin, we are now slaves of righteousness. This transformation begins with being made into a new creation, with the surrender of our bodies and our minds. The apostle teaches us a wonderful and hopeful idea: Transformation is possible, and it can occur in this life. This is good news indeed!

The following table shows the connections between this section and the beginning of the letter and it reveals the way God is solving the problem of human sin and its effects.[2]

1:24	degrading of their bodies	12:1	offer your bodies
1:25	worshiped created things	12:1	proper worship
1:28	a depraved mind	12:2	renewing of your mind
2:18	know his will and approve	12:2	test and approve what God's will is

The apostle provides several examples of how a renewed mind deals with difficult ethical and moral issues. He does not give us a comprehensive list. Rather, the apostle expects his readers to understand his examples and apply his insights to all areas of life. He expects us to exercise our moral muscles to develop renewed discernment. We can do that because now "we can test and approve what God's will is" (12:2).

6 CONCLUSION (15:14–16:27)

After sending extended greetings to many people in Rome, the apostle offers a final exhortation: "I urge you, brothers and sisters, to watch out for those who cause divisions and put obstacles in your way that are contrary to the teaching you have learned" (16:17).

Application Questions:

- Reread Romans 1:16-17. What is power of the gospel? How does it accomplish God's purposes in the lives of people?

- How have you seen that power at work in your own life?

- What are the dangers of valuing God's creation more than the Creator himself (see especially Romans 1:21-29)? In what ways have you struggled with this?

- How should our inability to "be declared righteous in God's sight by the works of the law" (Romans 3:20) affect our attitudes toward God? Toward others?

- How should Paul's arguments regarding the Jews throughout this section give us reassurance about our own salvation?

- Reread Romans 10:9–15. What is our role in spreading the gospel, and why? What are some different ways we can fulfill that?

- Reread Romans 12:1–8. Practically speaking, what does it mean to be "a living sacrifice" (verse 1)? How does it enable us to know God's "good and pleasing and perfect" will—and actually do it?

- How does a sacrificial attitude help us relate better to those who are built differently from us (see also Romans 14)?

- What's your reaction to Paul's statement in Romans 15:14, that your "brothers and sisters… are full of goodness"?

- How would (or does) believing Paul's statement change the way you approach and work together with your "brothers and sisters"?

Notes:

1.   Adapted from Dunn, James D. G. WBC Vol. 38A, *Romans 1–8*.

2.   Adapted from Dunn, James D. G. WBC Vol. 38A, *Romans 1–8*.

JAMES

A Letter for Our Daily Walk...

Remember that strict middle school teacher who made your life difficult but now you may remember with great fondness? At the time, it seemed like unnecessary harshness; today, in hindsight, you might remember that teacher as one who cared about you; a teacher who wanted you and your classmates to succeed in life. At that moment, we might have resented strictness; looking back, however, we realize that it was for our benefit and learn to appreciate it. That's the case with the book of James. It's a wonderful book, with great lessons for our life. But it's a stern letter; it expects much, but it promises much as well. As you plunge into the letter, keep in mind that strict teacher who's made such a difference in your life.

The Letter of James deals with a question that many Christians still ask: *how do I know that I'm growing as a Christian?* In the following pages, we'll see that James addresses this important question in a clear and practical way.

It gives us good news: God has given us his wisdom and every good and perfect gift so that we can grow and become mature Christians!

OUTLINE OF THE LETTER

- Greetings (1:1)
- Test of a living faith (1:2–18)
- Faith tested by its response to the Word of God (1:19–27)
- Faith tested by its reaction to favoritism (2:1–13)
- Faith tested by its doing of good works (2:14–26)
- Faith tested by its production of self-control in speech and humility (3:1–18)
- Faith tested by its reaction to quarreling, judgmentalism, arrogance, selfishness, and suffering (4:1–5:12)
- Faith tested by its resort to prayer (5:13–18)
- Conclusion (5:19–20)

WHO WAS JAMES?

- He was one of Jesus' half-brothers (Matt. 13:55).
- He was an unbeliever during Jesus' ministry (John 7:5).
- After Jesus' ascension, he was among the believers in the Jerusalem prayer meeting (Acts 1:14; 1 Cor. 15:7).
- After Peter left Jerusalem, James became the leader of the church there (Acts 12:17).
- James was one of the pillars of the church (Gal. 2:9; Acts 15:13–29).
- His final appearance in the New Testament is in Acts 21:18 when he meets with Paul.
- According to tradition, James was martyred in Jerusalem in AD 62.
- Eusebius, the third century church historian, called him "James the Just." Eusebius also referred to James as "camel knees" because he constantly prayed on his knees.

This is what the LORD says:
"Let not the wise boast of their wisdom or the strong boast of their strength or the rich boast of their riches, but let the one who boasts boast about this: that they have the understanding to know me, that I am the LORD, who exercises kindness, justice and righteousness on earth, for in these I delight," declares the LORD. —Jeremiah 9:23–24

Blessed is the one who perseveres under trial because, having stood the test, that person will receive the crown of life that the Lord has promised to those who love him —James 1:12

THEMES OF THE LETTER

- **Temptation and maturity** (1:2–8; 12–18): Christians are faced with many temptations in this world. However, for James, temptations are tests that strengthen our faith and make us mature.

- **Wealth and poverty** (1:9–11; 2:1–13; 4:8–10, 13–16; 5:1–6): James does not condemn wealth. Rather, just as in other biblical texts about riches, James condemns the abusive use of wealth. That is, James condemns two attitudes toward money: (1) an attitude that abuses or ignores the poor, (2) allowing riches to substitute for God and become an idol.

- **Sins of speech** (1:26–27; 3:1–12; 4:11–12; 5:12): Self-control is an important feature of true faith. Our speech can be a source of great goodness or great evil.

- **Patience and prayer** (5:7–11, 13–20): Prayer becomes a test of faith when it requires patience. The patience James writes about is born from a great dependence on God, which is born from wisdom.

- **Faith and actions** (1:19–25; 2:14–26; 3:13–18; 4:1–7, 17): James writes about faith in action. He does not address faith leading to salvation; the Apostle Paul wrote about this faith in his letters. Rather, James writes about the lived-out faith of those who have already been saved. It is a visible faith, a faith shown in deeds rather than words.

Choose one theme to pray about for a week.

WISDOM

It is often defined as "the ability to make godly choices." In the Bible, wisdom is tightly connected to creation. The way God created the universe has a direct effect on the way nature and society behave. In an important sense, wisdom is the ability to see life and the world the way God sees them. Wisdom is practical knowledge that allows people to live fully.

The Letter of James and the Sermon on the Mount

Although James does not directly quote Jesus, there are many important parallels with one of Jesus' most important speeches in the Gospels: The Sermon on the Mount from the Gospel of Matthew.

- Joy in the midst of trials (James 1:2; Matthew 5:10–12)
- Exhortation to be perfect (James 1:4; Matthew 5:48)
- Asking God for good things (James 1:5; Matthew 7:7–11)
- God the giver of all good things (James 1:17; Matthew 7:11)
- Warnings against anger (James 1:20; Matthew 5:22)
- Becoming hearers and doers of the word (James 1:22; Matthew 7:24–27)
- The poor inherit the kingdom (James 2:5; Matthew 5:3, 5)
- Keeping the whole law (James 2:10; Matthew 5:19)
- Being merciful to receive mercy (James 2:13; Matthew 5:7)
- To be known by our fruits (James 3:12; Matthew 7:16)
- The blessings of peacemakers (James 3:18; Matthew 5:9)
- Ask and you will receive (James 4:2–3; Matthew 7:7–8)
- Serving God vs. friendship with the world (James 4:4; Matthew 6:24)
- Comfort for mourners (James 4:9–10; Matthew 5:4)
- Warnings against judging others (James 4:11–12; Matthew 7:1–5)
- Living for today (James 4:13–14; Matthew 6:34)
- Moth and rust spoiling earthly treasures (James 5:2–5; Matthew 6:19)
- Prophets as examples (James 5:10; Matthew 5:12)
- Warnings against making oaths (James 5:12; Matthew 5:33–37)

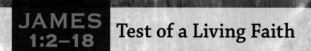

JAMES 1:2–18 — Test of a Living Faith

Topic	Danger to believers	Response that leads to maturity	Benefit
Trials/ troubles	Falling into the temptation to blame God or others when troubles happen	Rejoice!	Maturing and strengthening of our faith
Wisdom	Failing to ask God for wisdom—wisdom comes from above!	Ask for wisdom. God will give exactly what we need for life.	Having wisdom from God allows us to overcome temptation and grow from trials.
Wealth	Taking pride in wealth tempts us to forget that all we have comes from and belongs to God.	Remember that wealth is temporal and that we should only take pride in knowing the Lord (Jer. 9:23–24; 2 Cor. 10:17).	When we humble ourselves, God lifts us up. For God "crowns the humble with victory" (Ps. 149:4).
Perfection, Maturity	Failing to surrender to God's will. Double-mindedness is the opposite of perfection. It is a half-hearted surrender. It refers to people unwilling to fully commit their whole beings to God—similar to those in Laodicea, who are described as being "lukewarm—neither hot nor cold" (Rev. 3:16).	Wise and single-minded people realize that trials are opportunities to grow in our dependence on and love for God.	As we become more mature believers, we grow "until we all reach unity in the faith and in the knowledge of the Son of God and become mature, attaining to the whole measure of the fullness of Christ" (Eph. 4:13).
Evil Desires	Because of our own struggles with sin, our own weaknesses and desires transform a test from an opportunity to become more mature to an opportunity to fall into sin.	Sin leads to death (1:15). But grasping hold of God's grace, through the word of truth, leads us to a new life (1:18).	The word of truth here is the gospel. Just as God created the universe through his Word (Gen. 1), so now God creates us anew through the gospel.

Share about a difficult time and how trusting in the Lord made you stronger. How might your experience in growing maturity help another person this week?

MATURITY

The idea of maturity is crucial for James (the Greek word *teleios*, translated as the idea of perfect completeness or maturity, occurs five times in the letter). What does James have in mind? Can we really become mature—or perfect, holy?

- The call to holiness occurs all over the Bible: "Be perfect, therefore, as your heavenly Father is perfect" (Matt. 5:48; see Lev. 19:2).

- To be completely mature as a Christian means to live an upright, righteous, truthful, trustworthy, honest, and pure life in faithfulness and loyalty to God and his will, seeking him with sincerity of heart and singleness of mind.

- God shows all of these characteristics in the way he relates to humans. We are called to be imitators of God (Eph. 5:1). Our life must show those characteristics as well.

- Empowered by the Spirit, the call to Christian maturity is not an unattainable dream. Rather, it is a call to be exactly what God intended us to be from the beginning: people who reflect God's glory because we are made in God's image.

- Our spiritual maturation is a process. Reaching maturity requires hard work from us. But here's the good news: God is doing the most difficult parts of that work in us. Be comforted knowing that "he who began a good work in you will carry it on to completion until the day of Christ Jesus" (Phil. 1:6). We will be fully matured only when Jesus returns.

- In the meantime, growing maturity and holiness are exercised by the ways we respond to God's Word, relate to other people, especially the poor and weak, show self-control and restraint, and react to trials and temptations.

JAMES 1:19–27 — Faith Tested by its Response to the Word of God

TOPIC	DANGER TO BELIEVERS	RESPONSE THAT LEADS TO MATURITY	BENEFIT
LISTENING AND DOING	Defensiveness and anger when confronted with the truth	Patient listening and application of truth that leads to obedience	God has planted the word of the Gospel in our hearts. This word is powerful and transformative. The word transforms us when we not only listen but also "do what it says" (1:22).
TRUE RELIGION	A religious appearance can make us feel safe and righteous. But it's a dangerous deceit. The appearance of being religious without obedience is useless. James considers this religiosity "worthless" (1:26).	Take care of those in need and keep God as our focus (1:27).	Shallow religiosity might feel good for awhile, but it's a destructive lie. Only when we submit to God by obeying his Word can our faith mature and become complete.

How has the word of God changed your life? Think and, if you feel comfortable, share how God is "re-programming" your mind.

THE POWER OF THE WORD
Therefore, get rid of all moral filth and the evil that is so prevalent and humbly accept the word planted in you, which can save you. —James 1:21

Sin is pervasive and insidious; before we know it, we are slaves to our sin. Sin becomes second nature. However, the word of God, through the power of the Holy Spirit, transforms us and frees us from the slavery of sin. Like any "spring-cleaning project," the transformation is a process that can be challenging. But the word of God can re-program our minds so we can "be made new" in the attitude of our minds, and "put on the new self, created to be like God in true righteousness and holiness" (Eph. 4:23–24).

JAMES 2:1–13 — Faith Tested by its Reaction to Favoritism

TOPIC	DANGER TO BELIEVERS	RESPONSE THAT LEADS TO MATURITY	BENEFIT
FAVORITISM	Considering those with external wealth as more important	Keep the royal law: "Love your neighbor as yourself" (2:8) without bias.	By remaining obedient to God's will, we will receive mercy from God's judgment.

Many societies measure people's worth based on their material wealth. However, the Scriptures make it clear that *caring for the poor and powerless is a crucial characteristic of God's covenant* (Ex. 22:22; Deut. 24:17–21; Ps. 146:9; Isa. 1:17; Jer. 5:28). James also makes it clear that caring for the poor and the powerless is not optional for Christians. Rather, it represents the fulfillment of the *royal law*.

Think of a time when mercy triumphed over justice in your life. What were some of the results?

GENERAL EPISTLES

The book of James is one of the General Epistles (letters) in the New Testament. Unlike Paul's letters, which are addressed to specific churches (such as Romans, Corinthians, Galatians, Ephesians, Philippians, Colossians, and Thessalonians) or individuals (Timothy, Titus, and Philemon), the General Epistles (James, 1 and 2 Peter, 1, 2 and 3 John, and Jude) do not have a clear addressee. Rather, most scholars think that they were circular letters, meant to be shared with many churches.

THE ROYAL LAW

When James wrote about the law (the perfect law, the royal law, the law of liberty—James 2:8), he surely had in mind the **law of love**: Jesus replied: "Love the Lord your God with all your heart and with all your soul and with all your mind." This is the first and greatest commandment. And the second is like it: "Love your neighbor as yourself." All the Law and the Prophets hang on these two commandments (Matt. 22:37–40).

As citizens of God's kingdom (Phil. 3:20), we are subject to the law of the King. James reminds us that breaking even one part of the law, such as showing favoritism to those with wealth, makes us lawbreakers (see Matt. 5:19).

Obedience to the royal law, with the power of the Spirit, gives us freedom.

JAMES 2:14–26 — Faith Tested by Doing Good Works

TOPIC	DANGER TO BELIEVERS	RESPONSE THAT LEADS TO MATURITY	BENEFIT
FAITH WITH DEEDS	Having a faith with all the right beliefs but that lacks good works	A living faith is demonstrated with good deeds. Knowledge and feelings are not enough: right actions are a crucial test of our faith.	In our desire to imitate God, compassion and action in favor of those in disadvantaged positions is the clearest indication of our journey toward perfection.

James makes his point of the importance of a living faith that produces good works in three ways:

- An example of a believer's hypocrisy (2:15–17).

  A faith that fails to act on known need is a failed faith. Words and good intentions are not enough. True faith shines forth as good works.

- Knowledge by itself is not enough (2:19).

  Often, we can fall in the trap of thinking that believing the right doctrines is enough for our Christian life. Right belief is crucial, but so are right actions. Belief alone affects demons' feelings (they "shudder") but makes no difference in their conduct. Right belief must produce good fruit.

- The illustration of Abraham's and Rahab's works (2:20–26).

  James uses the example of Abraham to show that faith is perfected ("made complete") by works. The goal of the whole letter is precisely to show the need, possibility, and way for all Christians to perfect their faith, to become mature believers. One cannot become a mature Christian without good works. Instead of quoting Rahab's surprising confession of faith (Josh. 2:9–11), James focuses on Rahab's hospitality. Her faith, while expressed in words, is validated by her deed of hospitality toward the spies. Again, James concludes that valid faith is expressed through right actions. This is the faith that pleases God. Note, however, that James is not saying that salvation depends on works. Rather, that "faith without deeds is dead" (2:26).

FAITH AND WORKS

The Apostle Paul dealt with one of the problems new Christians face, the need to add something to "help" God's grace for salvation. His conclusion is clear: "For it is by grace you have been saved, through faith—and this is not from yourselves, it is the gift of God— not by works, so that no one can boast" (Eph. 2:8–9).

James deals with the other side of that problem: a misunderstanding about grace that results in an inactive faith: "In the same way, faith by itself, if it is not accompanied by action, is dead" (James 2:17).

"As the body without spirit is dead, so faith without deeds is dead."—James 2:26

JAMES 3:1–18 — Faith Tested Through Self-Control in Speech and in Humility

TOPIC	DANGER TO BELIEVERS	RESPONSE THAT LEADS TO MATURITY	BENEFIT
CONTROLLED TONGUE	Failure to control one's speech is likened to a spark that starts a forest fire. Just one unwise or unkind comment can have damaging effects we regret.	A living faith is not controlled by the tongue. Rather, a mature person is controlled by "wisdom that comes from above" (3:17).	A controlled tongue creates unity among believers. A controlled tongue is a sure path toward Christian maturity and perfection (3:2).
TRUE RELIGION	A natural tendency to envy and selfish ambition causes "disorder and every evil practice" (3:16).	Submitting to God's wisdom promotes peace and unity among believers and roots out selfishness.	A life characterized by wisdom produces people who are: Pure Peace-loving Considerate Submissive Merciful Impartial Sincere

James illustrates these two principles with an important example: a teacher. Teachers have a great deal of responsibility in their work. Their influence can build up or destroy people. Teachers depend on their words to do their jobs.

An uncontrolled tongue can cause much damage to an individual or to a whole group, such as the church. James describes the damage as a raging fire: it spreads quickly and destroys all in its path. This illustration is true of each of us, but it's highlighted in the work of a teacher.

Examine the words of the Proverbs about human speech. How can they help you with controlling your tongue? Pray that the Holy Spirit will help you discern what needs changing and empower you to do it.

PROVERBS ABOUT SPEECH

THE DESTRUCTIVE POWER OF HUMAN SPEECH

The words of evil men (1:11–19; 10:6; 11:9, 11; 12:5–6)

The words of the adulteress (5:2–5; 6:24–35; 7:5; 9:13–18; 22:14)

The words of the liar (6:12–15, 17, 19; 10:18; 12:17–19, 22; 14:5, 25; 17:4; 19:5, 9, 28; 21:28; 24:28; 25:18; 26:23–28)

The words of the fool (10:10, 14; 14:3; 15:14; 18:6–8)

The words of false witnesses (6:19; 12:17; 19:5, 9, 28; 21:8; 24:28; 25:18)

The words of a gossip (6:14, 19; 11:13; 16:27–28; 20:19; 25:23; 26:20)

The words too quickly spoken (6:1–5; 12:18; 20:25; 29:20)

The words of flattery (29:5)

Too many words (10:14, 19, 23; 11:13; 13:3, 16; 14:23; 15:2; 17:27–28; 18:2; 21:23; 29:20)

Perverted words (17:20; 19:1)

THE POSITIVE, HEALING AND EDIFYING POWER OF HUMAN SPEECH

The words of the righteous (10:11, 20–21, 31–32; 12:14; 13:2; 15:23; 16:13; 18:20)

The words of the discerning (10:13; 11:12)

The words of knowledge (15:1, 7, 8; 20:15)

The words of healing (15:4)

The words of a gentle answer (15:1, 4, 18, 23; 16:1; 25:15)

The words of a pleasant answer (12:25; 15:26, 30; 16:24)

The words of the law (22:17–21)

JAMES 4:1–5:12 — Faith tested by its reaction to quarreling, judgmentalism, arrogance, greed and suffering

TOPIC	DANGER TO BELIEVERS	RESPONSE THAT LEADS TO MATURITY	BENEFIT
QUARRELS	Envy and covetousness lead to quarrels. These two traits come from a life controlled by sinful passions. This life makes us enemies of God.	James calls us to submit ourselves to God (4:7). Faith, at its most basic, is dependence on God. True dependence begins with submission of our whole lives to God. Just as we need reconciliation with God, we need to be in peace with our fellow believers.	Submission to God means that we become God's friends (4:4). God gives us more grace (4:6). Peace with believers promotes unity.
SLANDER	Speaking evil of other believers causes disputes and fights. Judging others places us in a position of judge that does not belong to us.	Humility allows us to understand our proper place: We are subject to the law, not its judges. It is again a call to control our tongue when dealing with our neighbors.	A mature faith allows us to have good relationships with God and our neighbors. Finding our proper place in our submission to God helps us promote unity and love.
ARROGANCE	Planning for the future while ignoring God's will is arrogant and foolish. Allowing our activities and plans to dominate our lives instead of God is sinful.	God is in charge of the universe, so we must allow him to be in charge of our plans and dreams. A mature faith rests on the knowledge that God allows and blesses our plans and our activities.	Realizing we don't have control over the future is a stamp of a mature faith. Resting in God's grace when making plans shows our dependence on his provision.
GREED	Greed is born from an uncontrolled desire for something. Greed leads us to unjust treatment of others—for instance, to building wealth on the backs of those oppressed.	Just as with gaining control of the tongue, centering one's desires on God leads to a mature faith.	Centering our desires on God and his will brings our treatment of others in line with the law of love (Matt. 22:37–40).
SUFFERING	Impatience with suffering and injustice that leads to sin or despair	Believers who suffer injustice can find comfort in the promise of Christ's return. At that time, Jesus will render judgment against those who made believers suffer.	The promise of Jesus' return fills us with hope despite suffering and injustice and helps us endure patiently.
OATHS	Relying on oaths to guarantee the truthfulness of our words. Making oaths can become a misuse of God's name or his world. (It does not refer to oaths made, for example, in court.)	Our speech must always be truthful so that oath making is not necessary. A mature faith controls the tongue. This control includes the truthfulness of our words.	Refraining from making oaths preserves believers from condemnation.

JAMES 5:13–18 — Faith Tested by its Resort to Prayer

James has dealt with the maturing and perfection of the Christian faith. If the Christian faith is demonstrated with good fruit, it reaches its conclusion with prayer. Prayer needs submission. To pray in times of need or joy requires complete surrender to God's will. In James, prayers for healing and prayers of praise are two sides of the same coin: They show that a mature faith relies on God in all areas of life. This trust is most clearly demonstrated in our prayers. Believing that "the prayer of the righteous person is powerful and effective" requires a mature faith.

TOPIC	DANGER TO BELIEVERS	RESPONSE THAT LEADS TO MATURITY	BENEFIT
PRAYER	When illness, happiness, or suffering occur, we should not forget God. We should not ignore the role of the Christian community during our times of trials or joys. We should not ignore the effects of sin in our lives.	Just as we remember God in times of suffering, God must be present in our minds in times of joy. In addition to one's personal activity, prayer and confession need to remain active in our churches. Confession is a powerful tool for the mature believer.	Prayer is the ultimate test of one's faith. In prayer, one's faith is built up and refined. Prayer for healing and prayers of praise are two tools for the believer. An active life with the body of believers is another tool for perfecting one's faith. The example of Elijah's prayer encourages us in our faith. Just like God answered Elijah's prayer, God answers our prayers when they are in agreement with God's will.

When you're overwhelmed with problems, or guilt, have you ever turned to another believer to share that problem or sin that needs confession? Have you prayed together about it? What were the results of that experience?

JAMES 5:19–20 Conclusion

This important letter, as small as it is, provides us with important lessons for our faith. James reminds us why he wrote the letter: "if one of you should wander from the truth" there can be repentance. The whole letter tells us how to return to the life of truth—that is, to a life of continuous spiritual growth, a life of a matured faith.

Reading the Letter of James

A few pointers about reading biblical text:

1. The very letter you're about to study is a reminder: we read and study the Scriptures not for intellectual stimulation or curiosity, but for spiritual nurturing, character building, and to increase our dependence on God. The goal of Bible study is to help us move forward in our faith "until we all reach unity in the faith and in the knowledge of the Son of God and become mature, attaining to the whole measure of the fullness of Christ" (Eph. 4:13).

2. While knowledge of the historical context, the genre, the audience, and other details are important and helpful, at the end the text is what matters. So, without forgetting some of those important details, spend time in the text of James. Read the whole letter in one sitting. This is probably how the original audience read the letter. Read it more than once. Read it in more than one translation (sometimes reading an unfamiliar translation helps us notice things that we might have skipped).

3. Read each section again. This time, focus on the details of the letter. Take notes as you read. If something strikes you as interesting, write a brief note expressing why you found it interesting. Write questions that arise as you read; you don't need to have answers to your questions, at least not yet.

4. Share your questions, insights, and ideas with others. But, most importantly, make plans to obey and mature in your faith. Like all growth, there will be some "growing pains" in this process. Make good use of the tools found in the letter: submission to God, a controlled tongue and transparent speech, wisdom from above, patience and perseverance, and prayer and confession

REVELATION

HOPE AND ENCOURAGEMENT

The book of Revelation is an exciting yet often misunderstood book of the Bible. It was probably penned between 35 and 65 years after Jesus' resurrection. This text became a source of hope and encouragement for Christians facing persecution.

POINTS OF UNITY

Although the book of Revelation allows for many interpretations, all Christians seem to agree that:

1. The message of the book is relevant for Christians today, as it was for Christians in the times of the apostles;

2. The main purpose of the book is to provide *hope* and *encouragement* for believers of all times, especially in times of persecution or suffering;

3. The message of the book is clear on at least three points:
   - Christ is coming back and will judge humanity;
   - The powers of evil are doomed before Christ;
   - God promises a wonderful future for all who believe in Christ.

GOD ACTING IN HISTORY

Both the Old and New Testaments reveal God as Lord over history. Christians of all eras have believed that Jesus will return a second time, but not all Christians have agreed that Revelation is all about the second coming. Whether the visions in Revelation have been, are being, or have yet to be fulfilled is a matter of debate, but the spirit of the last chapter calling on Jesus to come quickly is something all Christians can agree upon—"Come, Lord Jesus!" (Revelation 22:20)

Following is a comparison of four different approaches to the book of Revelation.

Four Views	How Revelation Is Viewed	More About This View
Historicist	The book of Revelation is prophecy about church history from the time of John to the end of the world.	Historicists view the events in Revelation as symbolic descriptions of historical events throughout church history. (Some futurists also understand the Seven Churches [Revelation 1–3] in a historic manner, treating each church as descriptive of a particular era of church history.)
Preterist	The book of Revelation is prophecy that was fulfilled primarily in the first century AD.	"Partial Preterism" views most of Revelation as prophecy fulfilled in the first century AD, though final chapters of Revelation describe future events to occur at the end of time. "Full Preterists" contend that the return of Jesus described in Revelation 19 was spiritual and occurred in AD 70. Preterists are typically amillennialists or postmillennialists, though some historic premillennialists might fit in this category.
Futurist	Revelation is prophecy primarily about the future end of the world.	In the futurist view, all or nearly all of Revelation is yet to occur. Revelation is a prophecy that describes the end of time and the years leading immediately to the end. Dispensational premillennialists as well as some historic premillennialists interpret Revelation in this way.
Idealist	Revelation is a non-historical and non-prophetic drama about spiritual realities.	This perspective seems to have originated among ancient Alexandrian theologians, who frequently spiritualized and allegorized biblical texts, but this view also has contemporary followers.

Revelation	Revelation 1:1 "soon" 1:3 "near" 1:19 "what is" (Compare, 22:6,7, 12, 20)	Revelation 2:1–3:22 The Seven Churches of Asia Minor	Revelation 4:1–3 God on His Throne	Revelation 5:1–4 The Scroll	Revelation 6:1–17 The Seals
Historicist View	The prophecy began to be fulfilled close to the author's lifetime.	The prophecy begins with the seven actual churches in John's day and proceeds through history from there.	God is about to outline his rule over history: the first part of that history is revealed under the vision of the seven seals.	The scroll is the coming history of the church as God reveals it and is Lord over it.	The seals are the stages of church history, perhaps describing the church from the late first century AD to the late fourth century.
Preterist View	Near, soon, and quickly are taken literally.	The prophecy begins with the seven actual churches of Asia Minor. It then focuses on the land of Israel before AD 70.	God's courtroom in the heavenly temple is the scene. The Judge on his throne is about to hold court.	The scroll is God's bill of divorce against unfaithful Israel.	The seals describe the Roman war with the Jews which led to the destruction of Jerusalem (AD 70).
Futurist View	These words refer to the whole of the "last days" or to the quickness with which Jesus will return.	The prophecy begins with the seven churches, which were actual churches in John's day and may also symbolize the types of churches present in the last days.	God gives John a vision from his throne of the events which are to take place "after these things."	The scroll is either the title deed to the earth or God's prophetic message in Revelation.	The seals begin to describe the great tribulation, with each opened seal leading to a greater tragedy upon the earth.
Idealist View	Christ is always at hand, near and quick to save his people.	The book begins with the seven churches, which symbolize tendencies in the church that can occur in every age.	God gives John the heavenly viewpoint of the important truths about his power over all things and his care for the church.	The scroll is God's last will and testament, revealing his salvation plan for all time.	The seals are about recurring evils throughout history and God's authority over them.

	Revelation 7:1–8 The 144,000	Revelation 8:1–13 The Trumpets	Revelation 9:13–19 The Four Angels at the Euphrates	Revelation 10:8–11 The Little Scroll
Historicist View	The 144,000 is a symbolic number that represents the entire church.	The trumpets are the stages of church history, perhaps from about AD 400 until the fifteenth century (or to the present).	The four angels represent the four principalities of the Turkish empire. The Turks destroyed the last of the Roman empire in AD 1453.	The little scroll is the Bible at the time of the Reformation. It was sweet to those starved for God's Word, but bitter to those who wanted to control its information and keep it from common people.
Preterist View	The 144,000 may be the Jewish Christians who escaped the destruction of Jerusalem.	The trumpets are a vision of the Roman war with the Jews in the first century AD and extend the seals' description in further detail.	The four angels may represent the four legions of Roman soldiers stationed in Syria that Vespasian led against the Jews (around AD 70). The colors mentioned are Roman military colors.	The little scroll is the same divorce bill as in Revelation 5:1–4 but now unsealed and empty of contents, indicating that the judgments against Israel are now occurring.
Futurist View	The 144,000 are Jewish Christians in the last days.	The trumpets describe the events of the tribulation in the last days.	The four angels represent the armies of the Orient that will march against Israel in the last days. They will cross the Euphrates as a signal of war.	The little scroll represents the divine plan for the end of the ages, showing that the Word of God is both sweet and bitter to God's prophets and messengers.
Idealist View	The 144,000 are the true spiritual Israel: the church on earth.	The trumpets are about the cycles of human sin, consequences, and God's salvation.	The four angels represent the judgment of God that comes on evil when there is no more restraint, which is represented by the river Euphrates.	The little scroll is the gospel, which must and will be preached to all "peoples, nations, tongues, and kings."

Revelation	Revelation 11:1–2 The Temple	Revelation 12:13–17 The Persecuted Woman	Revelation 13:18 666	Revelation 14:14–16 The Son of Man with the Sharp Sickle
Historicist View	The measuring of the temple, the altar, and those who worship there points to God's evaluation of the church, the doctrine of justification by faith, and what constitutes true membership in the church, all of which were issues at the Reformation.	The woman is the true church under persecution. The "third of the stars" may refer to the division of the Roman Empire under three emperors in AD 313, or it may refer to post-Reformation divisions in Europe.	It may be the number of the word Lateinos and so refers to the Latin or Roman Catholic pope/papacy.	It is a vision of the end of the age when Christ will come and gather his own to himself.
Preterist View	The measuring of the temple and its rooms, like the eating of the scroll in chapter 10, mirror what happens in Ezekiel 40–47. Both indicate the destruction of the temple and the separation of the faithful (symbolized by the sanctuary) from the unfaithful (symbolized by the court).	The woman is faithful Israel that gave birth to Christ (the Child). The Dragon, Satan, persecuted the Messianic church, but she escaped the destruction of Jerusalem by heeding Jesus' words (Luke 21:20–22) and fleeing to the desert hills (the prepared place).	It is the number that the letters in the name "Nero Caesar" add up to. **666**	It is a vision of the coming of Christ to gather and preserve his church from the judgment that was to befall Jerusalem.
Futurist View	The measuring of the temple refers to the nation of Israel and the temple that will be rebuilt in the last days. Israel has been restored but still awaits the rebuilding of her faith. This faith will center on the new temple and will eventually lead some Jews to faith in Christ.	The woman is Israel (sun, moon and stars, Genesis 37:9). The Child is Christ (rod of iron, Psalm 2:9). The Dragon is Satan behind the coming Antichrist. As the head of the revived "Roman Empire," the Antichrist will attack Israel.	It is the number of the future Antichrist—someone who will be like Nero back from the dead.	It is a vision of the coming harvest at the end of the age when Christ will separate the wicked for judgment.
Idealist View	The measuring of the temple and the leaving of the outer court indicates the division that has always been present between true believers and those who are Christians only in name. The trampling of the court signifies the way the unbelieving world corrupts the church, but this will only be for a short while.	The woman is Israel as the ideal symbol of all the faithful. The Child is Christ and the Dragon is Satan, the great persecutor of the Church in every age. The stars are the angels that fell with Satan at his rebellion. The seven heads and crowns speak of Satan's full political power and authority. The ten horns are military might.	It is the number of imperfection and human evil that leads to idol worship.	It is a vision of the last judgment and the coming of Christ at the end of the age.

Revelation	Revelation 15:1–4 The Song of Moses and of the Lamb	Revelation 16:10–11 The Fifth Bowl	Revelation 17:1–12 The Great Prostitute	Revelation 18:9–24 The Fall of Babylon
Historicist View	The song of final salvation from the slavery of the Roman Catholic religious and political power known as the papacy.	The bowl is the judgment upon the Roman Pope Pius VI that occurred when the French revolutionary forces stripped the Vatican and took the Pope captive in 1798. The Pope was forced to flee Rome again in 1848. This event was actually predicted using 1260 days as years (12:6).	The prostitute is the corrupt Roman Catholic Church, including false "Protestant" churches that have come out of her. Her political and religious influence is carried by the beastly Roman papacy and Western European culture.	The destruction of Papal Rome (Babylon) will be complete and utterly devastating. The consequences of preaching a false gospel, persecuting true believers and dabbling in power politics will bring her to this end. Many will mourn her loss but it will be final.
Preterist View	The song of salvation from and victory over the ungodly religious and political persecution that Christians suffered in Israel and the Roman world.	The bowl is the judgment that fell upon Rome in AD 69. In that single year, Nero committed suicide, three emperors were deposed, civil war set Roman against Roman, and the Temple of Jupiter Capitoline was burned to the ground, causing darkness during the day.	The prostitute is Jerusalem. Her political and false religious influence is carried by the Roman Empire (Beast). The seven heads are Rome and the first seven emperors, Nero (the sixth of the emperors) ruling at that time. The ten horns are the ten imperial provinces.	The destruction of Jerusalem (Babylon) is sudden and complete. The misery and the economic disaster is nearly indescribable and a source of great despair. To this day, the temple has never been rebuilt.
Futurist View	The song of salvation from the last-days persecution of the Antichrist and resulting judgment of God. Believers may experience some persecution but they will not have to endure God's wrath.	The bowl is the coming judgment upon the revived Roman Empire that will happen in the last days.	The prostitute is the symbol of a false religious system, a new world religious order. The religious coalition will have political influence tied to the power of the Beast (Antichrist) who is the head of the alliance (ten horns) of ten nations in Europe in the last days.	The destruction of the coming world religious, political and economic system—under the control of the Antichrist and the False Prophet—will be a crash of unparalleled dimension.
Idealist View	The song of salvation that all the redeemed have sung throughout history and will sing anew when Christ comes again.	The bowl shows what will happen and does happen to those who steadfastly oppose God. The judgments of darkness and sores recall the plagues of Egypt.	The prostitute is all false and corrupt religion that has allied itself with political power in order to dominate. God warns that such religion shall come to an awful end when true faith triumphs.	The destruction of Babylon reveals that God's judgment is complete and final. Whether it is Nineveh, Babylon, Rome or any other economic power that opposes God, it is destined to fail.

Revelation	Revelation 19:1–10 The Marriage of the Lamb and His Bride	Revelation 20:1–15 The Millennium	Revelation 21:1–27 The New Creation	Revelation 22:1–21 The Salvation and Healing of the Nations
Historicist View	The entire removal of false religion represented by Rome/Babylon will leave the faithful to accomplish the purpose for which Christ came—the evangelization of the rest of the world. All people will be invited to come into relationship (the marriage feast with God).	The millennium is viewed as Christ's present, spiritual reign in the lives of his people (amillennialism).	The new creation will come with Christ at his second coming, yet there is a real sense in which it has already arrived in the believer's heart. Christians live now as citizens of the New Jerusalem.	It is happening now and will finally be completed when Christ returns.
Preterist View	The entire book has been about faithfulness using the image of marriage: the divorce bill in chapter 5, the imagery of the persecuted woman and the prostitute. The book builds toward the marriage feast of Christ and his church.	In partial preterism, the millennium may be Christ's literal reign on earth (premillennialism) or a spiritual reign (postmillennialism and amillennialism). In full preterism, the millennium refers to Christ's spiritual return and reign, beginning in the first century (amillennialism).	The new creation is now and future. Since the destruction of the old Jerusalem, Christians are building the New Jerusalem here and now, wherever the gospel is believed, as well as expecting it in full when Christ returns.	It will continue as the gospel grows and spreads throughout the world. Jesus will finalize and renew all things when he comes.
Futurist View	The entire church is the bride of Christ whose marriage is announced and celebrated. This scene refers to events near the end of the world and history.	The millennium is the future, physical reign of Jesus Christ on earth (premillennialism).	The new creation will come when Christ comes again and ushers in the age to come.	It will continue until the great tribulation when the Antichrist will temporarily prevail. Christ in his second coming will triumph and usher in the final salvation and healing of all the faithful.
Idealist View	The entire sweep of sacred history may be seen through the lens of the ancient Jewish wedding tradition. The prophets announced the wedding. Jesus comes and betroths his bride (church), paying the dowry on the cross. When Jesus comes again, he will offer his bride a wedding feast.	The millennium is viewed as Christ's present, spiritual reign in the lives of his people (amillennialism).	The new creation is something God continually does with each new day. Yet there will come a day when Christ will personally return and make all things new.	It is what God has always been doing in the world—seeking and saving the lost. Christ will bring all things right when he returns.

1 Seven Messages to Churches
(Revelation 1:1–3:22)

INTRODUCTION (1:1–8)
Blessing 1
Vision of Christ

MESSAGES TO THE CHURCHES

1. EPHESUS
Praise: Hard work, perseverance
Criticism: Forgot first love
Exhortation: Repent
Reward: Right to eat from the tree of life

2. SMYRNA
Praise: You are rich!
Criticism: None
Exhortation: Be faithful
Reward: Not hurt by second death

3. PERGAMUM
Praise: Remain faithful
Criticism: Idolatry and sexual immorality
Exhortation: Repent
Reward: A white stone with a new name

4. THYATIRA
Praise: Deeds, love and faith, and perseverance
Criticism: Idolatry and sexual immorality
Exhortation: "Hold on to what you have until I come"
Reward: The morning star

5. SARDIS
Praise: None
Criticism: "You are dead"
Exhortation: Wake up
Reward: Be dressed in white, never blotted out from the book of life

6. PHILADELPHIA
Praise: Deeds and faithfulness
Criticism: None
Exhortation: Hold on to what you have
Reward: Become a pillar of the temple

7. LAODICEA
Praise: None
Criticism: You are lukewarm
Exhortation: Be earnest and repent
Reward: Will be seated with Christ

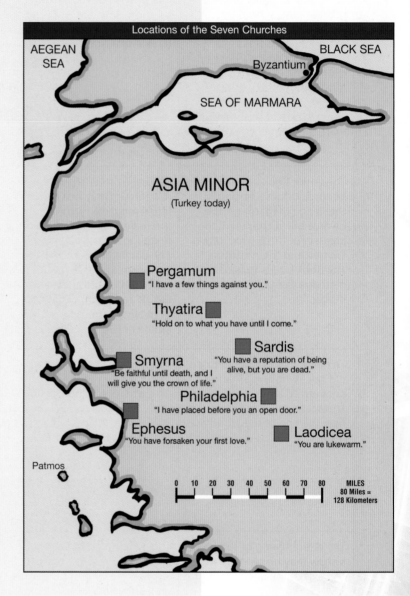

Locations of the Seven Churches

AEGEAN SEA

BLACK SEA

Byzantium

SEA OF MARMARA

ASIA MINOR
(Turkey today)

Pergamum
"I have a few things against you."

Thyatira
"Hold on to what you have until I come."

Sardis
"You have a reputation of being alive, but you are dead."

Smyrna
"Be faithful until death, and I will give you the crown of life."

Philadelphia
"I have placed before you an open door."

Ephesus
"You have forsaken your first love."

Laodicea
"You are lukewarm."

Patmos

0 10 20 30 40 50 60 70 80
MILES
80 Miles = 128 Kilometers

Seven Trumpets
(Revelation 8:2–11:19)

1. First Trumpet—Hail, fire, blood

2. Second Trumpet—Fiery mountain in sea, 1/3 of sea becomes blood

3. Third Trumpet—star falls on 1/3 of rivers

4. Fourth Trumpet—1/3 of Sun, 1/3 Moon, 1/3 Stars

Interlude: Woe! Woe! Woe! (8:13)

5. Fifth Trumpet—Demon locust from the Abyss

6. Sixth Trumpet—Two-hundred-million demonic riders from the Euphrates

Interlude (10:1–11:14)
The Little Scroll: Promise for the church

7. Seventh Trumpet—"The kingdom of the world has become the kingdom of our Lord…" (11:15)

Seven Symbolic Histories
(Revelation 12:1–14:20)

The Woman and the Dragon

SYMBOLIC HISTORIES

1. HISTORY OF THE DRAGON (12:7–12)
Defeated
The "ancient serpent"

2. HISTORY OF THE WOMAN (12:13–17)
Persecuted by the dragon
Defended by God

3. THE SEA BEAST (13:1–10)
Ten horns and seven heads
Blasphemer
Has power to make war

4. THE EARTH BEAST (13:11–18)
Two horns
Deceiver
666—The number of the beast

5. THE 144,000 (14:1–5)
Marked with God's name
Worshippers

6. THE ANGELIC ANNOUNCERS (14:6–11)
First angel: "Fear God"
Second angel: "Fallen! Fallen is Babylon the Great"
Third angel: Warning against the mark of the beast

7. THE HARVEST (14:14–20)

Seven Seals
(Revelation 4:1–8:5)

Interlude:
Vision of Heaven (4:1–11)
Scroll with Seven Seals and the Lamb (5:1–14)

Opening of Seals (6:1–8:5)
1. First Seal: White Horse—*Conqueror*
2. Second Seal: Red Horse—*No peace*
3. Third Seal: Black Horse—*Famine*
4. Fourth Seal: Pale Horse—*Pestilence*
5. Fifth Seal: Martyrs under the altar
6. Sixth Seal: Earthquake, sun black

Interlude:
144,000 sealed (7:1–8)
The Great Multitude (7:9–17)

7. The Seventh Seal:
It contains seven angels with trumpets (8:1–2)
The angel with golden censer (8:3–5)

Seven Bowls
(Revelation 15:1–16:21)

Commissioning of the Seven Angels with the Last Seven Plagues (15:1–8)

The Seven Bowls

1. **First Bowl**—Painful sores

2. **Second Bowl**—Turns sea into blood

3. **Third Bowl**—Turns rivers and springs of water into blood

4. **Fourth Bowl**—Sun burns people with fire

5. **Fifth Bowl**—Plunges kingdom of the beast into darkness

6. **Sixth Bowl**—Dries up the Euphrates; Armageddon

7. **Seventh Bowl**—Judgment against Babylon. "It is done!"

Seven Messages of Judgment
(Revelation 17:1–19:10)

Judgment against Babylon

Description of symbolic characters

1. **First angelic message** (17:7–18)
   Explanation of the vision

2. **Second angelic message** (18:1–3)
   Announcement of the fall of Babylon

3. **Third angelic message** (18:4–8)
   Call to God's people; God's judgment on Babylon

4. **The kings of the earth** (18:9–10)
   Lament for the fall of Babylon

5. **The merchants of the earth** (18:11–17)
   Lament for the fall of Babylon

6. **The seafaring people** (18:18–19)
   Lament for the fall of Babylon
   Rejoice for God's judgment (18:20)

7. **Seventh angelic message** (18:21–24)
   Announcement of the final destruction of Babylon

Seven Visions
(Revelation 19:11–22:5)

1. **First Vision** (19:11–16)
   Heaven opens and the white horse rider appears

2. **Second Vision** (19:17–18)
   Angel invites birds to "the great supper of God"

3. **Third Vision** (19:19–21)
   The beast and kings ready for war

4. **Fourth Vision** (20:1–3)
   The thousand years (millennium)

5. **Fifth Vision** (20:4–10)
   Thrones with judges and Satan's doom

6. **Sixth Vision** (20:11–15)
   Judgment of the dead

7. **Seventh Vision** (21:1–22:5)
   A vision of "a new heaven and a new earth."

Epilogue (22:6–21)

Jesus is coming back: "Amen. Come, Lord Jesus."

TERMS IN THE BOOK OF REVELATION

666—Number of the beast, spelled out in Rev. 13:18 as *six hundred sixty-six*. Greek and Hebrew did not have written numbers. Instead, either they spelled out the number, or they wrote out the number using the letters in the alphabet. For example, the first letter of the alphabet might represent the number one, and so on. Many scholars point out that, in Hebrew, the number of Nero's name can be 666 if written using *Neron*, the Latin spelling of the name. (Nero reigned AD 54–68. He was the first emperor to engage in specific persecution of Christians.) A good approach to this issue is to remember that six is a symbol of incompletion; 666 indicated total imperfection.

144,000—Group of believers who endure the great tribulation (Rev. 7:14). Some believe that these persons are literally 144,000 Jews—12,000 from each tribe—who embrace Jesus Christ as their Lord (see Rev. 7:4–9). Others suggest that the terms "Israel" and "twelve tribes" often refer to Christians (Romans 9:6–8; Galatians 6:16; James 1:1). Therefore, the number would point to God's people (symbolized by twelve tribes, twelve apostles, or both) multiplied by 1,000 (a number that symbolizes an extreme multitude or length of time)—in other words, the full number of those who belong to God.

Abomination of desolation—An event that desecrates the temple in Jerusalem and is a signal to Jesus' followers that soon Jerusalem will be ruined. Mentioned in Matthew 24:15, it may refer to the destruction of the temple in AD 70 by the Romans, or Roman plans to set up a statue of the Emperor in the temple in AD 40, or some future event.

Antichrist—(from Greek, *antichristos*, in place of Christ) Anyone who denies what the apostles taught about Jesus Christ (1 John 2:18–22; 4:3; 2 John 1:7). Specifically, the antichrist is a Satanic counterfeit of Jesus Christ, described as "lawless" and as a "beast" (2 Thessalonians 2:3–8; Revelation 13:1–18; 17:3–17). The antichrist could be a specific person who rises to power during a time of tribulation or a symbol of false teachers and leaders who will arise when the end of the age draws near.

Armageddon—(from Hebrew, *Har-Megiddon*, Mount Megiddo) The city of Megiddo was located between the Plain of Jezreel and Israel's western coast. Deborah, Gideon, Saul, Ahaziah, and Josiah fought decisive battles near Megiddo—largely because the area around Megiddo is broad and flat. So the valley of Megiddo became the symbol of a point of decisive conflict. Some believe that a literal battle will occur near Megiddo near the end of time. Others view the reference to Armageddon as a symbol of an ultimate conflict between spiritual forces of good and evil.

Babylon—Revelation 17 presents the figure of a prostitute called Babylon riding upon a scarlet beast. The name is symbolic, yet interpretations vary:

1. Jerusalem: Jewish people assisted the Romans in their persecution of Christians after AD 64. The fall of Babylon could be a symbolic reference to the fall of Jerusalem in AD 70.

2. Rome: After AD 70, Jewish writers often referred to Rome as "Babylon."[1] The name may symbolize the political and religious powers in every age that attempt to defy God and to persecute His people.

3. One-world government and religion: Babylon may be a reference to a one-world government and one-world religion that will emerge near the end of time.

Beasts, two—Symbolic creatures described in Revelation 11:7 and 13:1–18.

The first beast: This creature rises from the sea and has ten horns and seven heads. The seven heads seem to point to Rome, the city known for its seven hills. Some interpreters understand this reference to Rome as a literal reference to a power that will arise from Rome near the end of time; others view it as a symbolic reference to the powers in every age that defy God's dominion and persecute God's people. The beast claims blasphemous names for itself—much like Domitian, emperor from AD 81 until 96, who demanded that he be addressed as "Lord and God." One of the horns seemed to have died but then returned to life—much like the false rumor that emerged after the death of Nero that he had come back to life.[2]

The second beast: This creature rises from the earth with horns like a lamb and a voice like a dragon—in other words, a satanic parody of Jesus Christ, the Lamb of God. Some interpreters understand this creature as a literal leader who will encourage people to worship the first beast. Others view the second beast as a symbol of any religion in any time period that focuses worshipers on anything other than Jesus Christ.

Final judgment—The event described in Rev. 20:11-15, when God resurrects all people, judges them from the great white throne, and delivers them to their eternal destinies.

Letters to the Seven Churches—After the opening vision (Chapter 1), John begins to write to the messengers (angels) of seven churches, Ephesus, Smyrna, Pergamum, Thyatira, Sardis, Philadelphia, and Laodicea. The messages review the churches' histories, give warnings and commands, and tells them to prepare for what is about to unfold. Scholars agree that these were actual messages to real churches in existence in John's day, though some see in the seven churches patterns that apply to the church in specific past, present, or future eras.

Mark of the beast—Indication of a person's allegiance to the teachings of the antichrist (Revelation 13:16–17). The people of God receive a similar mark, indicating their loyalty to Jesus (Revelation 7:3; 9:4; 14:1; 22:4). Some biblical students believe that the mark of the beast will be an actual mark, required by the antichrist. (Between the Old and New Testaments, some Jews were forced to be branded with the symbol of the god Dionysius.[3]) Other interpreters of Revelation understand the mark as a reference to someone's actions ("hand") and beliefs ("forehead"). "Hand" and "forehead" seem to carry this symbolic meaning in Exodus 13:9, 16.

Views of the Millennium—Chapter 20, the only direct reference in the Bible to a reign of Christ that lasts 1,000 years, is one of the most controversial sections of the Bible.

There are three basic views—Premillennialism, Amillennialism and Postmillennialism—that help to categorize the different interpretations.

- **Premillennialism** holds that Christ will return before the millennium. Jesus will rule the world and begin an age of peace and security. There are two varieties within this view: Historic Premillennialism and Dispensational Premillennialism.

  - *Historic Premillennialism* sees Christ's return at the end of the great tribulation. This time of tribulation may last seven years, or "seven" may symbolically refer to the completeness of this tribulation. The church will go through this time of trouble but endure to greet Christ when he comes.

  - *Dispensational Premillennialism* holds that the church will not endure the great tribulation. Christ will remove the church before that time or, alternatively, at some point before the worst experiences of the tribulation.

- **Amillennialism** is the view that the millennium is not a literal one thousand years. It refers to the period now in progress in which the gospel is spreading throughout the world and Christ is ruling at the right hand of God the Father.

- **Postmillennialism** asserts that there will be a period of great peace and security when the gospel has spread throughout the world and Christ reigns spiritually, through His people. After this time of one thousand years or so, Christ will return to end history.

Witnesses, two—Two beings described in Rev. 11:1–14 who speak the truth about God before being killed and then resurrected. (1) Some believe that these two witnesses are two people who will appear during the tribulation, near the end of time. (2) Others view them as two biblical prophets—perhaps Moses and Elijah—that have been resurrected to proclaim God's truth during the tribulation. (3) Others see the two witnesses as symbols of the Law and the Prophets—both of these testified about Jesus and yet, this testimony was rejected, even to the point of killing those that appealed to this testimony (for example, Stephen in Acts 7). If so, the "resurrection" of the two witnesses would point to a time of final vindication, a point at which God demonstrates that the Law and Prophets did indeed testify about Jesus Christ.

[1] G. K. Beale, *The Book of Revelation* (Grand Rapids, MI: Eerdmans, 1999), 19.

[2] G. E. Ladd, *A Commentary on the Revelation of John* (Grand Rapids, MI: Eerdmans, 1972), 178–179.

[3] 3 Maccabees 2:29.

IMPORTANT TOPICS
FOR
CHRISTIANS

Baptism

Why Be Baptized?

Baptism is one of the most important practices in the life of the church. The need for baptism is something that most Christians recognize. Jesus emphasized the importance of baptism when he commanded his disciples to "Go and make disciples of all nations, baptizing them in the name of the Father and of the Son and of the Holy Spirit" (Matthew 28:19). Baptism reminds us of

- Jesus' death and resurrection
- Our relationship to God and one another through the Holy Spirit (Ephesians 4:4-6).

Committed Christians interpret baptism in different ways, but most Christians agree that baptism

- is central to the Christian faith;
- is not optional but a commandment;
- is often a way for people to show in public their commitment to God;
- unifies Christians as members of the same body;
- has no ultimate significance apart from faith in Jesus Christ.

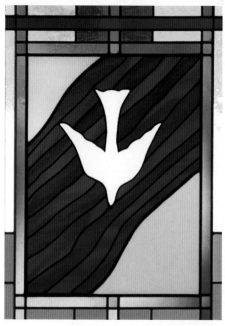

Method of Baptism

Different methods are used in baptism—some groups sprinkle water on the forehead, others pour water from a pitcher over the whole head, and others dip or immerse a person's whole body in water.

- Those who practice believers' baptism believe that the practice of immersion (being completely covered with water) more fully displays the symbolic burial of the believer's old life. As believers go under and emerge from the water, they identify themselves with Jesus' sacrificial death, burial, and resurrection (Romans 6:3–4).
- Other modes of baptism developed in the early church—such as pouring (affusion) and sprinkling (aspersion)—are more practical during times of persecution, and also with infants. As a result, pouring and sprinkling are usually connected with churches that practice infant baptism and with places where Christianity is illegal.

What Happens During Baptism?

Although baptism ceremonies may look quite different from group to group, there are more similarities than differences.

1. Water is always present, whether it is in the form of a natural body of water, a baptismal font, a baptistery, a pool, or simply a bowl of water.
2. A church leader asks a few questions to give opportunity for persons involved in the baptism to profess their faith outwardly, then asks the support of those present. In the case of infant baptism, those questions are for the parents and others present to make certain that the child will have Christian examples, support, and instruction to guide the child toward an eventual profession (public expression) of faith.
3. The leader sprinkles, pours, or immerses the person being baptized and says, "I baptize you in the name of the Father and of the Son and of the Holy Spirit."

Baptize

The term *baptism* comes from a Greek word. The verb *baptizo* means "to cover in water, wash, dip, baptize."

Believer's Baptism vs. Infant Baptism

One of the main points on which Christian groups differ is about who can be baptized. The following table clarifies the emphasis in perspective that each tradition places on its understanding of baptism.

Note the difference in emphasis. Both traditions agree that the act of baptism itself does not save a person. Salvation comes through Christ alone by faith (Galatians 3:26–28; Ephesians 2:8–9). Christians disagree about whether a person must be able to communicate a desire for baptism and an understanding of its meaning (sometimes referred to as the "age of accountability").

Believer's Baptism	Infant Baptism
Emphasis on faith as a human response to God's grace	Emphasis on faith as a gift from God
Believer who trusts	God who acts
Obedience and faith of believer	Command and promise of God
Believer's witness to the world	Covenant and covenant community
Old Testament model of sacrifice	Old Testament model of circumcision

Those who advocate believer's baptism refer to Bible passages that reveal recognition and repentance as a sign of readiness for baptism, such as:

Peter replied, **Repent and be baptized,** *every one of you, in the name of Jesus Christ for the forgiveness of your sins. And you will receive the gift of the Holy Spirit.* (Acts 2:38)

Those who accepted his message *were baptized, and about three thousand were added to their number that day.* (Acts 2:41)

But **when they believed** *Philip as he preached the good news of the kingdom of God and the name of Jesus Christ, they were baptized, both men and women.* (Acts 8:12)

Those who advocate *infant baptism* point to covenantal promises that include children (Genesis 17:7) as well as instances in Scripture where entire households—including children and slaves—were baptized based on the faith of the head of the household, such as:

Then they spoke the word of the Lord to him and to all the others in his house. At that hour of the night the jailer took them and washed their wounds; then **immediately he and all his family were baptized.** (Acts 16:32–33. See also Acts 18:8; 1 Cor. 1:16.)

Peter replied, Repent and be baptized, every one of you, in the name of Jesus Christ for the forgiveness of your sins. And you will receive the gift of the Holy Spirit. **The promise is for you and your children and for all who are far off**—*for all whom the Lord our God will call.* (Acts 2:38–39)

Underlying the issue of believers' vs. infant baptism is the question of whether baptism is *primarily* about the believer personally identifying with the sacrificial death and resurrection of Christ, or whether it is *primarily* about God initiating the believer into the covenant community. (Note: Both traditions include the other view; the distinction is made to show emphasis only.) Below are descriptions of the Old Testament models upon which each tradition is based.

Early Debate

Some of the earliest writings from the church fathers show that a debate over baptism for believers vs. infants was underway within the first hundred years of Christianity's beginnings.

Tertullian (AD 145–220), early church leader, contended that baptism was for believers, arguing that a conscious choice should precede baptism. On the other hand, Cyprian (AD 200–258), bishop of Carthage in North Africa, supported infant baptism, which was becoming a dominant practice in some areas.

The Old Testament Models

Sacrifice	Circumcision
Sacrifice was a conscious act of repentance for sin	Circumcision was the sign and seal of being initiated into God's covenant people
• Identification with the sacrifice for sin • Individual's conscious response to God is crucial. • The faith of the believer connects one to God, not the symbolic act alone	• Sign and seal of initiation • Included entire community • Individual's faith not crucial, as symbol points to God who gives faith • Individual, personal faith will follow God's action in covenant

Sacrifice was a conscious act of repentance for sin and thus, only believers in the God of Israel could bring a sacrifice to the altar of God. In sacrifice, the believer was to be identified with the death of the animal given on behalf of sins. Understood in this way, baptism is seen as identification with the death of Christ (Romans 6:3–4). In both the Old Testament act of sacrifice and the New Testament act of baptism, it is faith that connects the believer to God.

"Wade in the Water." Postcard of a river baptism in New Bern, North Carolina, around 1900.

Since **circumcision** was about God's command and promise in covenant relationship, it involved entire families and nations and included not only adults but also infants. The covenant ceremony included sacrifices and thus pointed to the need for cleansing and faith in God's actions on behalf of believers (Exodus 13:1–16; Leviticus 12:1–8). It also brought the individual into a covenantal relationship that made the need for sacrifice clear.

In circumcision, the immediate faith of an infant was not crucial since the effect of the symbol was to point to God who commands, promises, and gives faith in covenant relationship. Paul connected circumcision with baptism in Colossians 2:10–12: "You were circumcised with a circumcision not made with hands, … having been buried with him in baptism." (Circumcision took place eight days after birth.)

By looking at how the church has practiced baptism over the centuries, it is possible to understand the current variety of views about baptism.

Where Do the Differences Come From?

Growth of the Church

As the early church took root in different places in the Roman Empire, different traditions developed about baptism. The church grew somewhat like a plant (Matthew 13:31–32). The phases of growth may be outlined in three stages:

The Early Church (around AD 1–500)	The Middle Church (around AD 500–1500)	The Modern Church (around AD 1500 to today)
Marked by • Rapid expansion similar to the rapid growth from seed to shoot seen in plants. • Time of great danger when persecutions by Roman rulers and religious authorities threatened to destroy the tender plant (Matthew 13:1–23).	• Despite early threats, the church consolidated and grew into a mature tree. • Many different peoples and cultures found a place in the church's various branches.	• The church grew, broke open, and scattered its seeds throughout the world. • The first split took place between the Roman Catholic and Eastern Orthodox branches (AD 1054), but an even greater scattering occurred at the Reformation (c. AD 1500).

Methods of Baptism Throughout History

Historically, the method of baptism is related to the meaning and symbolism of the ordinance.

Tradition	Meaning	Mode
Initiation	• Meaning centered on the water as a sacramental symbol of God's cleansing.	• Mode of baptism is not critical; any method can be used. • The symbolic application of water is crucial. • Methods needed to be flexible during times of persecution.
Identification	• The act of immersion symbolizes identifying with Christ's death and burial, while rising out of the water symbolizes resurrection and eternal life.	• Emphasis is on outward expression of inward faith through immersion. • One of the main meanings of the Greek word *baptizo* is "to cover with water."
Infusion	• Infusion of the Spirit's power is highlighted.	• The activity of the Spirit is more important than the specific mode of baptism.

Scriptural Roots

During the growth of the church, baptism's various Scriptural roots were emphasized at different times.

Initiation: The word comes from a root meaning "to enter in." Those who are initiated into the church enter into the life of Christ's body.

> *"Therefore go and make disciples of all nations, baptizing them in the name of the Father and of the Son and of the Holy Spirit, and teaching them to obey everything I have commanded you. And surely I am with you always, to the very end of the age."* —Matt. 28:19–20

See also: Acts 2:41; 8:12, 36–38; 1 Cor. 12:13

Identification: The word comes from a root meaning "to treat as the same." Those who are identified with Christ inherit God's riches through Christ (Ephesians 2:6–7), as children of God, because Christ identified with us by being treated as sinful.

> *"Or don't you know that all of us who were baptized into Christ Jesus were baptized into his death? We were therefore buried with him through baptism into death in order that, just as Christ was raised from the dead through the glory of the Father, we too may live a new life."* —Romans 6:3–4

See also: Gal. 3:26–27; Col. 2:9–14; 1 Peter 3:21

Infusion: The word comes from a root meaning "to pour into." Those who have been infused have had the Holy Spirit and his power poured into them. Many biblical passages mention the Spirit's involvement in the lives of believers.

> *"When they arrived, they prayed for them that they might receive the Holy Spirit, because the Holy Spirit had not yet come upon any of them; they had simply been baptized into the name of the Lord Jesus. Then Peter and John placed their hands on them, and they received the Holy Spirit."* —Acts 8:15–17

See also: Matt. 3:11; Lk. 24:49; Acts 1:5; 2:1–4; 8:15–17; 10:44–47; 11:15–16; 19:1–6; 1 Cor. 12:1–31

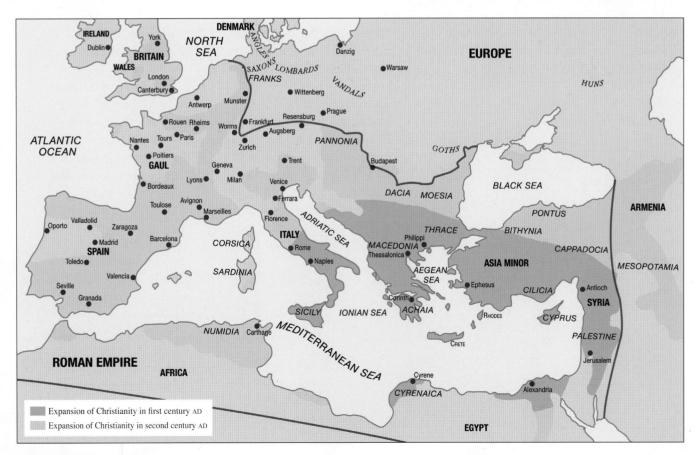

Expansion of Christianity in first century AD
Expansion of Christianity in second century AD

Perspectives Throughout History

	INITIATION	IDENTIFICATION	INFUSION
The Early Church (before AD 500)	• Baptism is a corporate act of **initiation** into the community of God. • Baptism is seen as the act and sign that the Holy Spirit is planting faith and working in the life of the newly baptized. God initiates the person (1 Corinthians 12:13). • Baptism is a group act and may include clans, tribes and families, infants through adults on the model of circumcision.	• Baptism is an individual act of faith and personal **identification** with Christ. • Baptism is seen as a personal act of faith that expresses the repentance and conversion of believers as they identify with Christ (Colossians 2:12). • Baptism is an individual act of faith and is therefore to be restricted to believers who have professed their faith.	• Baptism is God's act of **infusion** of power for ministry. • Baptism is seen as the act of receiving the Holy Spirit sent by the Father and the Son to infuse the believer with power for ministry (Acts 1:8). • Baptism is an act of both God who gives his Spirit and the believer who receives the gift of the Spirit. Only those who can make use of the gift show the evidence of the Spirit's baptism.
The Middle Church (around AD 500–1500)	• Baptism as a corporate act of initiation becomes the dominant view. • The expansion of the church and the end of persecution pushes this majority view to the forefront as the church pursues a group identity.	• Identification through baptism is minimized as churches pursue unity and consistency of teaching. • At this time, the emphasis on group identity rather than individual identity makes this view secondary.	• The infusion tradition is minimized early, becoming associated with heretical groups. • Montanism, a heresy that emphasized ecstatic prophecy, may have understood baptism in terms of infusion.
The Modern Church (around AD 1500 to today)	• Baptism in this tradition is retained by the Reformed, Anglican, and Roman Catholic denominations. **Note:** The act of baptism itself does not save a person. Salvation comes through Christ alone by faith (Galatians 3:26–28; Ephesians 2:8–9).	• Identification becomes the focus among Anabaptists and other Protestant bodies in the free church tradition, and the Greek Orthodox Church. • The fragmenting of the tradition of initiation in the Reformation allows for the re-emergence of the tradition of identification. • With the rise of individualism and personal choice, this view flourishes among independent church groups.	• The tradition of infusion is downplayed at the time of the Reformation, but appears intermittently. • The scattering of the church results in the tradition of infusion resurfacing slowly and sporadically. • The rise of Pentecostal and Charismatic churches (late 1800s to present) brings this view to the church. Many such groups, however, identify infusion with the "second blessing"—usually demonstrated through speaking in tongues—rather than with water baptism (Acts 8:14-17). • Other churches today believe that the Holy Spirit's power is given upon conversion or water baptism, and that believers simply need to be aware of this power from God and use it.

Baptism, Ritual and Ceremonial Cleansing in the Bible

- Baptism is connected to Old Testament practices of cleansing and purification.
- Besides meaning "to cover with water," the Greek word *baptizo* also means "to wash or dip in water."
- Old Testament people saw little distinction between physical washing and ceremonial cleanliness—physical acts were spiritual acts as well.
- Old Testament purity laws pointed toward the spiritual cleansing that was to happen through Christ.
- Thus, baptism came to symbolize the washing away of sin.

Old Testament	New Testament
Aaron—Leviticus 16:4, 24; and other priests—Leviticus 8:6; 16:26, 28; Exodus 29:4; 30:18–21; 40:12, 31, 32; Numbers 19:7–10, 19; 2 Chronicles 4:6; elders, Deuteronomy 21:6; the people, Exodus 19:10, 14.	John the Baptist—Matthew 3:5–11; 21:25; Mark 1:4–5; 11:30; Luke 3:2–3, 12; 7:29; John 1:25–33; 3:23; 10:40; Acts 1:5, 22; 10:37; 11:16; 18:25; 19:3–4
Washing with water used—For clothes, Exodus 19:10, 14; burnt offerings, Leviticus 1:9, 13; 9:14; 2 Chronicles 4:6; infants, Ezekiel 16:4; hands, Deuteronomy 21:6; Psalm 26:6; feet, Genesis 18:4.	Jesus—Matthew 3:13–16; Mark 1:8–10; Luke 3:7–8; John 3:5, 25–26; 4:1
Conditions cleansed—Leprosy, Leviticus 14:8–9; discharge of blood, Leviticus 15:1–13; defilement by dead, Leviticus 17:15–16; Numbers 19:11–13.	Disciples—John 4:2; Matthew 28:19
Common purification for normal body functions —Leviticus 12:6–8; 15:16–30.	Paul—Acts 9:18; 1 Corinthians 1:13–17
Fire and water together as symbols of purification after battle—Numbers 31:19–24.	Church—Matthew 28:19; Acts 2:38, 41; 8:12–13, 36–38; 10:46–48; 16:14–15; 18:8; 19:5; 22:16
<ul><li>People in the Old Testament did not baptize. However, some practices provide the background for the New Testament baptism. Purification rites and sacrifices in the Old Testament point to the need for cleansing of impurity, evil, and sin.</li><li>In Christ, the functions of both water and blood came together.<ul><li>The blood of Christ cleans us from all sin and evil (1 John 1:7).</li><li>The blood of Christ atones for our sins (Romans 5:9).</li></ul></li><li>Baptism symbolizes this cleansing in Jesus' blood (1 Peter 3:21)</li></ul>	Moses, a type—1 Corinthians 10:1–2
	Initiation—1 Corinthians 12:13
	Identification—Romans 6:3–4; Galatians 3:27; Colossians 2:12
	Infusion—Matthew 3:11,16; Mark 1:8; Luke 3:22; 24:49; John 1:32–33; 3:5; Acts 1:5; 2:1–38; 8:15–17; 10:38–47; 11:15–16; 19:2–6
	Water a symbol for the cleansing by the Word and Spirit —Ephesians 5:26; Titus 3:5–6; 1 Peter 3:21

Purification with Water in the Old Testament

- The high priest ritually washed himself before his service on the Day of Atonement, as did the priest who released the scapegoat (Leviticus 16:3, 4, 26–28).
- John the Baptist, from the priestly line of Aaron (Luke 1:5–80), may have transformed the priestly rites of purification into baptism.
- At the time of John the Baptist's preaching, some groups were practicing baptism as a ritual of purification for all believers.
- The Qumran community that produced the Dead Sea scrolls appears to have been one such community.

Baptism and Water Cleansing in the Bible

What Was John the Baptist Doing?

Is the baptism of repentance that John the Baptist practiced the same baptism that is now practiced in the church? No. However, there are several similarities:

- Water is used as a symbol of purification and cleansing. (Matthew 3:5, 6, 11; 1 Peter 3:21)
- Repentance, turning away from the self-centered life to a God-centered one, is central. (Mark 1:4–5; Acts 2:38)
- The practice includes all manner of people, both genders, all levels of society. (Luke 3:7–14; Acts 16:25–33)

There are also important differences between John's baptism and Christian baptism:

John's Baptism	Christian Baptism
John the Baptist and his ministry were the last of the Old Testament order.	With the coming of Christ, a new order begins (Matthew 11:7–15; John 5:33–36).
The old order is not destroyed, but becomes the basis for the new.	The new order fulfills the old but is not identical to it.
John the Baptist pointed to the coming Messianic King.	Jesus the Messiah announces the coming of the Kingdom of God.

One Lord, One Faith, One Baptism (Ephesians 4:4-6)

There is one body and one Spirit—just as you were called to one hope when you were called—one Lord, one faith, one baptism; one God and Father of all, who is over all and through all and in all.

The Spirit of God has an end and goal for believers—to transform us into the image of Christ (Romans 12:1–2). We may be works in progress, but we are God's work (Ephesians 2:10).

The words of the Apostle Paul in Ephesians are a humbling reminder that baptism is an external symbol of our unity as believers. Our baptism, our faith, and our Lord unite us into one body: the church.

Jesus' desire for his church is revealed in his prayer for all believers in John 17:23, "May they be brought to complete unity to let the world know that you sent me and have loved them even as you have loved me." —John 17:23b

The Lord's Supper

What is the Lord's Supper?

In a simple way, the Lord's Supper is a meal that Jesus had with his disciples the night before he was crucified. Jesus commanded them to continue celebrating the supper. Years later, as an explanation of this practice, the Apostle Paul wrote to Christians in Corinth:

I received from the Lord what I also passed on to you: The Lord Jesus, on the night he was betrayed, took bread, and when he had given thanks, he broke it and said, 'This is my body, which is for you; do this in remembrance of me.' In the same way, after supper he took the cup, saying, 'This cup is the new covenant in my blood; do this, whenever you drink it, in remembrance of me.' For whenever you eat this bread and drink this cup, you proclaim the Lord's death until he comes (1 Cor. 11:23–26).

The Lord's Supper is not a common meal. It is a time of fellowship, reflection, remembering, and spirituality. The Lord's Supper is related to how Christians understand who Jesus is and what he did in his earthly ministry. Understanding the meaning and importance of the Lord's Supper in the life of the church will help us to better understand Jesus' life and ministry.

Why do Christians celebrate the Lord's Supper?

We participate in the Lord's Supper because:

- Jesus commanded his followers to do it (1 Cor. 11:24–26).

- Just as a physical meal feeds and strengthens the body, celebrating the Lord's Supper feeds and strengthens the body of Christ, as a community and individually.

- It is a way to proclaim our hope in Christ's return and our forgiveness through his blood (1 Cor. 11:26). Every time we celebrate the Lord's Supper, we proclaim the Gospel and Jesus' return.

- It creates a strong bond of spiritual fellowship among believers (1 Cor. 10:17).

- The Lord's Supper is another form of worship (for many Christians, a special form of worship).

- It is a necessary time for reflection and introspection (1 Cor. 11:28).

- It teaches new believers about who Jesus is and what he did for us (1 Cor. 11:24–26) and refreshes seasoned believers.

- It fosters unity with Christ and among believers. Unity is one of the central messages of the celebration. This unity is symbolized in the one loaf of bread all share (1 Cor. 10:17).

Lord's Supper in History

In the first century, early Christians were persecuted by the Roman authorities. Some influential people in Rome even accused Christians of practicing cannibalism—eating human flesh! This accusation was related to the practice of the Lord's Supper. Christians talked about eating the body and drinking the blood of Christ as part of their rituals. Some uninformed Romans assumed that it was literally people eating people.

The Romans found the Christian celebration of the Lord's Supper strange and worrisome. Non-believers today are often similarly puzzled by the celebration. Imagine a person coming for the first time to a traditional Christian Sunday service, in which the Lord's Supper is served at the end after the sermon. What's the point of this practice? Why do we eat a little piece of bread and a tiny sip of juice? New believers may still have questions about the Lord's Supper after going through a beginner's class in church. Even lifelong Christians may be surprised to learn views of other groups of Christians.

What does it mean?

The Lord's Supper is important to our understanding of being Christ's church. It is meaningful in the following four areas:

- ***Worship.*** It is a way to worship Christ for his work, grace, love, and salvation. We participate with gratitude for Jesus' sacrifice for us.

- ***Witness.*** Participating in the Lord's Supper gives a testimony that Jesus died for our sins and resurrected in victory to give us eternal life, and that Jesus will return as a victorious king (Matt. 26:29; 1 Cor. 11:26).

- **Edification.** In the Lord's Supper, the Holy Spirit ministers to us individually and as Christ's body (1 Cor. 10:16). It is a time for mutual instruction, restoring broken relationships, forgiving past grievances, and repenting for offenses against others (1 Cor. 11:28–29).

- **Service.** The Lord's Supper is an occasion for Christians to serve each other, at the moment of the celebration itself as well as beyond the Lord's Supper. Remembering the sacrificial gift of Christ on the cross (the gifts of the bread and the wine) is a powerful motivation for us to "offer your bodies as living sacrifices, holy and pleasing to God" (Rom. 12:1). Just as we receive abundant gifts from the Lord, so do we extend this generosity unto others around us, starting with those closest to us (1 Tim. 5:8).

Names for the celebration

1. Breaking of the Bread (Acts 2:42; 1 Cor. 10:16)

- In the times of the Apostles, the expression was used for a meal in a family or a larger group.
- Jesus instituted the Lord's Supper at the end of a Passover celebration meal (Luke 22:13–16).
- Sharing a meal with others creates a sense of belonging and unity.

2. Holy Communion (1 Cor. 10:16)

- The Apostle Paul writes about "the communion of the blood" and "the communion of the body" of Christ. The Greek word he used in this verse is *koinonia*, which is a word that speaks of a two-sided relationship. It is variously translated as *communion, fellowship, participation or sharing.*
- Communion with whom? *First*, it refers to communion among believers, with each other, as Paul suggests in verse 17: "Because there is one loaf, we, who are many, are one body, for we all partake of the one loaf." *Second*, it refers to the believers' union with Christ.

3. Table of the Lord (1 Cor. 10:21)

- The Apostle Paul uses this expression to contrast the celebration of the Lord's Supper with the pagan sacrifices common in his time. The pagan celebrations included food sacrificed to their gods and abundant wine. Often these celebrations ended in drunkenness and debauchery.
- The Apostle Paul makes it clear that drunkenness does not have any place at the Lord's Table (1 Cor. 11:34). "You cannot drink the cup of the Lord and the cup of demons too; you cannot have a part in both the Lord's table and the table of demons" (1 Cor. 10:21).

4. Lord's Supper (1 Cor. 11:20)

- It refers to the historical event in which Jesus instituted this practice for his followers (Matt. 26:26–28).
- During this last meal, Jesus instructed his disciples about the Holy Spirit and their task after Jesus left them (John 13–16). At the end of the meal, Jesus established and commanded the celebration of the Supper.

5. Eucharist (1 Cor. 11:24)

- The word *eucharist* is a Greek word meaning "thanksgiving." It is a reference to the Apostle's teaching that Jesus gave *thanks* before giving the Apostles bread and wine (1 Cor. 11:24).
- The Corinthian Christians celebrated the Lord's Supper in the context of a group meal (also called "love feast," see 2 Peter 2:13; Jude 12). After the meal, the Christians from Corinth would celebrate the Eucharist by giving God thanks for the gifts of the Lord's Supper.

The Lord's Supper: Practice among Christians

Christian Unity in the Lord's Supper

One of the central purposes of the Lord's Supper is unity. The Apostle Paul wrote in 1 Corinthians 10:17: "Because there is one loaf, we, who are many, are one body, for we all partake of the one loaf." One of the main themes in First Corinthians is the unity of the church. Here, the Apostle suggests that the unity of all believers is expressed symbolically when we share together the Table of the Lord. In Christ, believers are one, like a loaf of bread.

Paul's conclusion about the oneness of all Christians agrees with Jesus' own prayer for the unity of the church: "Holy Father, protect them by the power of your name, the name you gave me, so that they may be one as we are one" (John 17:11; see, also, 17:20–23). The New Testament makes it clear that Christian unity is not an option but part of God's plan for his people.

Important Themes Christians Agree on

- *Jesus instituted the Lord's Supper* (Matt. 26:26–30; Mark 14:22–25; Luke 22:19–20; 1 Cor. 11:23–26). Jesus wants his disciples to celebrate the Lord's Supper.

- *The new covenant* (1 Cor. 11:25, Matt. 26:27–28, Mark 14:23–24). In the new covenant, God promised to write his law in our hearts (Jer. 31:32–34). It is based on Jesus' sacrifice on the cross, and it includes forgiveness and removal of sin and cleansing of our consciences (Heb. 10:2, 22).

- *Remembrance* (1 Cor. 11:24, Luke 22:19). The Lord's Supper allows Christians to remember and celebrate Jesus' birth, life and ministry, death and resurrection.

- *Thanksgiving, fellowship and unity* (1 Cor. 10:16 See also Matt. 26:26–27, Mark 14:22–23). It is gratitude for what God has done through Jesus, the new fellowship we now have with God and each other through Christ's sacrifice, and the unity of Christ's body.

- *The Lord's return* (1 Cor. 11:26 See also Matt. 26:29, Luke 22:16; 1 Cor. 16:22; Rev. 22:20). The Lord's Supper anticipates the celebration of the wedding supper of the Lamb (Rev. 19:9). Every time we participate in the Lord's Supper, we announce that Christ is coming back and has invited us to a glorious supper with him.

- *Separation from sin* (1 Cor. 10:21). Remembering Jesus' sacrifice gives us the opportunity to re-commit ourselves to God. Participating in the Supper requires us to examine our lives, confess our sins and ask God for forgiveness (1 Cor. 11:27–32).

- *A foretaste of heaven* (Matt. 26:29, Mark 14:25). The unity Christians can experience in the Lord's Supper as a special moment of celebration anticipates what life will be like with God in the new heavens and the new earth (Rev. 21:1–5).

Is Christ Present in the Wine and Bread?

One of the most controversial questions about the Lord's Supper is whether Jesus is present or not. For many Christians, Jesus is truly present at the moment of the consecration and celebration of the Lord's Supper. Because of this special presence of Christ, the Lord's Supper is a special tool and channel for God's grace.

Many other Christians believe that Jesus is neither *more* nor *especially* present in the Lord's Supper. Rather, Jesus is present always and in all moments of a worship service, including the Lord's Supper.

Christians have tried to explain in different ways how it is that Christ is present, or absent, in the elements of the Lord's Supper. The first three views attempt to explain how Christ is present in the Lord's Supper. The fourth view attempts to explain the main function of the Lord's Supper without appealing to Christ's presence.

Transubstantiation

If the participants really eat the body and drink the blood of Christ, how does it happen? Scholars used the idea of transubstantiation to avoid a crass materialism (that is, affirming that people eat actual flesh and blood) or pure intellectualism (the idea that the elements are merely a sign). These scholars made a distinction between *accident* and *substance*. The *substance* of a thing is that which makes the thing be what it is, and it is invisible to the eyes. The *accidents* of a thing are the visible characteristics of the thing: color, shape, weight, and so on. According to the theory of transubstantiation, the *accidents* of the bread and wine remain unchanged, but their *substance* changes into the body and blood of Christ. Thus, Catholic scholars speak of the substantial presence of Christ in the Eucharist. That means that Christ is present in the underlying reality of the elements. The bread and wine continue to be bread and wine (their *accidents*) while Christ's body and blood are present (their *substance*).

Consubstantiation

Martin Luther, the German Reformer, agreed that Jesus is really present in the elements of the Eucharist. However, he disagreed with the idea that the elements change in *substance*, as Catholics explained through transubstantiation. He argued that the full bread and wine are present alongside the body and blood of Christ. He called this *sacramental union*, and he refrained from giving any further explanations. Later Lutheran scholars used the concept of *consubstantiation* to explain Luther's understanding of *sacramental union*. They explained that the *substance* of Jesus' body and blood is present alongside the *substance* of the bread and wine.

Instrumental View

John Calvin disagreed with Catholic and Lutheran scholars about Christ's real presence in the Lord's Supper. For Calvin, Christ's presence in the Supper is real, but no change of the elements occurs. He also disagreed with Zwingli that Christ's presence is merely symbolic.

In his view, the biblical sacraments are instruments of the Holy Spirit to confer grace to believers. In addition, Calvin considered the doctrine of the union with Christ to be central in understanding faith in Christ. While our union with Christ is initiated in baptism, it is confirmed and sustained in the Lord's Supper. Through the elements of the Lord's Supper, the Holy Spirit unites us with the ascended Christ's body and blood, but not because Jesus descends into the bread and wine. Rather, the miracle of the Supper is that we are spiritually taken to heaven to commune with Christ.

Symbolic or Memorial View

Ulrich Zwingli was a pastor of the church in Zurich during the Reformation. Zwingli disagreed with the Catholic understanding of the Eucharist as well as with that of Martin Luther and John Calvin. Whereas they argued for the real presence of Christ in the communion—while explaining how that happens in different ways—Zwingli disagreed that there was a "real presence." His view, later known as a symbolic or memorial approach, says that the elements of the Lord's Supper are signs that point to the risen Christ. They function to make us observe, remember, proclaim, and worship this risen Christ.

Two Main Views

Sacrament

The Latin word *sacramentum*, which means "sacred oath," was the normal word used for translating the Greek word *musterion*, which means "mystery." In liturgical churches, such as the Catholic, Lutheran, Anglican, Reformed, it refers to the practices the Bible prescribes through which God's grace is specially received by the participants of the ceremonies. Protestant churches affirm only two sacraments: Baptism and the Lord's Supper. A sacrament is a witness to God's grace through Christ. In the sacramental view, the Lord's Supper is a divine instrument to bless and nurture believers with God's grace. The sacraments are tied to the Word of God in that the Word of God validates the sacraments. The sacraments, on the other hand, make the Word of God visible. Faith in the people participating is necessary so the sacraments can effectively communicate God's grace.

Ordinance

Ordinances are ceremonies that allow believers to express their faith. Many Christians believe that Baptism and the Lord's Supper are ordinances or external symbols of internal truths. Jesus commanded or ordered his followers to baptize and to celebrate the Lord's Supper. For this reason alone, the ordinances are very important. In this view, the main point of the Lord's Supper is commemorative. That is, in the Lord's Supper, the church commemorates—remembers, celebrates, and honors—Christ's work of salvation for us.

Main Views of the Lord's Supper

Sacramental View

	Presence of Christ	Benefits of the ceremony	Administration of the ceremony
Real Presence *Catholic* *Orthodox* *Some Anglicans*	• The bread and the wine change when priests consecrate them. • Catholics believe in *the real presence of Christ* in the elements; it is not just a symbolic or spiritual presence. • This change is considered a mystery—*sacramentum*, a miracle. • This change is explained with the philosophical concept of *transubstantiation*.	• The Eucharist re-presents (makes present) Christ's sacrifice on the cross. • It does not mean that Jesus is sacrificed again; rather, that Christ's sacrifice on the cross is made present in the Eucharist. • In the Eucharist, Christ's sacrifice on the cross is celebrated in a bloodless sacrifice. • Because Christ is present in the Eucharist, which also re-presents his sacrifice on the cross, the Eucharist becomes a channel of God's grace apart from the faith of the celebrant.	• Roman Catholics practice a closed communion. • Only ordained priests can consecrate the elements of the Eucharist. • Priests celebrate the Eucharist in the Mass daily. They encourage all Catholics to partake of the Eucharist at least once weekly. • Catholics in the state of mortal sin can participate in the Eucharist only after they have confessed and received forgiveness of their sin.
Sacramental Union *Lutheran* *Some Anglicans*	• Christ is present in the Eucharist. This presence is called *sacramental union*. • The body and blood of Christ are sacramentally (supernaturally) present alongside the bread and wine. • Rather than using the concept of transubstantiation to explain this union, many Lutherans use a similar concept: *consubstantiation*.	• Lutherans do not believe that the participant of the Eucharist offers a sacrifice to God that causes forgiveness of sin in itself. • Martin Luther affirmed that the sacrament offers a special benefit to the participants: forgiveness of sins, to the extent that it is connected to the participant's own faith, and confirmation of faith.	• Most Lutherans practice open communion. • Only ordained clergy can consecrate the elements of the Lord's Supper. • The Eucharist is offered weekly.
Real Spiritual Presence *Reformed* *Presbyterians* *Some Anglicans* *Some Baptists*	• Most Reformed people—or Calvinists—believe in *the real spiritual presence* of Christ in the Lord's Supper. • Although the elements do not experience any transformation, the presence of Jesus in the Lord's Supper is not simply spiritual or symbolic. It is real. • In the Lord's Supper, the Holy Spirit unites the believer with the risen Christ who is in heaven.	• The Lord's Supper is a sacrament and a means of grace. • Through the ministry of the Holy Spirit, believers are spiritually nourished and restored in a special way. • This view affirms the importance of faith in receiving the benefits of the sacrament. • The Lord's Supper is an expression and continuation of God's covenant with his people.	• Churches in the Reformed tradition practice open communion. • Only committed Christians can participate in the Lord's Supper. • The Lord's Supper has been traditionally celebrated either four times a year or the first Sunday of the month. Some churches celebrate it weekly. • Only ordained ministers can administer the Lord's Supper.

Ordinance View

	Presence of Christ	Benefits of the ceremony	Administration of the ceremony
Many Baptists *Pentecostals* *Most Contemporary Evangelicals* *Many non-denominational Churches* *Some Anglicans*	• These churches hold a view called the memorial view. • In this view, Christ is said to be either spiritually present or only symbolically present. • This view rejects the idea of a "real presence" of Christ in the Lord's Supper.	• The Lord's Supper commemorates Christ's sacrifice on the cross. • It benefits participants' spiritual growth in a similar way that renewing wedding vows may strengthen and nurture a marriage. • In this way, the Lord's Supper is another form of proclamation, like preaching or worshiping.	• Most practice open communion. • Only committed Christians can participate in the Lord's Supper. • Churches vary in how often they celebrate the Lord's Supper, such as weekly, monthly, or quarterly. • Some churches allow only ordained people to administer the Lord's Supper. Other churches allow lay leaders to administer the Lord's Supper.

The Orthodox Church holds a very similar view to that of the Catholic Church. The main difference is that the Orthodox view does not appeal to the idea of *transubstantiation* to explain the change in the elements. They are content to call it a mystery.

The Anglican Church is divided in their understanding of the Lord's Supper. High Church Anglicans prefer a view similar to that of the Catholic Church, while not appealing to transubstantiation as an explanation for Christ's real presence. Low Church Anglicans prefer either a more Reformed or Zwinglian view of the Lord's Supper.

Pentecostal churches also have a variety of understandings about the Lord's Supper. However, most of them prefer a Zwinglian understanding of the ordinance. In addition, they emphasize the role of the Holy Spirit in the Supper. For many Pentecostals, the celebration of the Lord's Supper can be a healing experience for the participants.

Quakers understand all of life as sacramental. Most Quakers do not practice the Lord's Supper because they consider that every meal is equally holy

Practical Questions

Why is it important?

• The simple fact that Jesus commanded us to observe it makes it important.

• Participating in this celebration allows us to deepen our relationship with Jesus and with other believers. The better and more deeply we understand Jesus' death on the cross on our behalf, the more we know Jesus' heart, the more we are willing to follow and obey him. Sharing in the meal together as one also promotes unity and love among believers.

• Participation also requires personal reflection and confession of one's sins. The Lord's Supper is an incomparable time for self-evaluation, confession, and repentance.

• The Lord's Supper is a crucial moment for Christian fellowship. It is a moment in which we proclaim we are one in Christ and bear witness as a body that our Lord and Savior has risen and will come back one day.

Open Communion

Many churches allow all Christians—that is, baptized believers from any background—to participate in the celebration of the Lord's Supper.

Closed Communion

Other churches limit who can take the Lord's Supper to members of a specific denomination. They believe that participants should share the same beliefs about the sacraments and the church.

How often should we celebrate the Lord's Supper?

- The Bible does not clearly indicate how often.
- The early church seems to have celebrated the Lord's Supper every time they met to share meals together. It is not clear if that occurred daily, weekly, or on a different schedule.
- The frequency of the celebration depends on our understanding of the Lord's Supper. The central issue is that all believers participate in the celebration, understand its importance, and grow in their relationship with Christ and other believers.

Is there one right way to do it?

No. But there are some elements included in all valid celebrations of the Lord's Supper. Below are some biblical guidelines for meaningful worship:

Before the Lord's Supper

- The Apostle Paul encourages us to examine ourselves before partaking in the Lord's Supper (1 Cor. 11:28). He encourages us to identify sin, bitterness, anger, hatred, or any other feeling or attitude and bringing it before God. Repentance is necessary before participating in the Lord's Supper. He gives warnings that all Christians ought to pay attention to before partaking in the Lord's Supper:

So then, whoever eats the bread or drinks the cup of the Lord in an unworthy manner will be guilty of sinning against the body and blood of the Lord. Everyone ought to examine themselves before they eat of the bread and drink from the cup. For those who eat and drink without discerning the body of Christ eat and drink judgment on themselves. That is why many among you are weak and sick, and a number of you have fallen asleep (1 Cor. 11:27–30).

- Once we have confessed our sins and asked God for his forgiveness, we must come in faith to the Table of the Lord believing that because of Jesus' sacrifice, God offers us his forgiveness. We must end our prayer with the certainty of God's forgiveness. Our eating and drinking of the bread and wine is our witness that we are forgiven.
- Although the Lord's Supper is a solemn moment, it is also a moment of thanksgiving, celebration, and great joy. We are remembering and celebrating Christ's wonderful work of redemption! We are also celebrating our unity with Christ through the Holy Spirit and with each other.

During the Lord's Supper

- We do not have specific instruction in Scripture for how we are to celebrate the Lord's Supper. We only have the words of Jesus and Paul, which often the ministering person will repeat right from the Bible.
- Different churches celebrate the actual Supper differently. Traditionally, many churches use individual cups of grape juice and small pieces of bread, which are distributed among the celebrants. Once all the bread and wine are distributed, the celebrants eat the bread and drink the juice together as a way to emphasize the unity of the church. Other churches prefer to use a chalice with juice or wine and a whole loaf of bread.

After the Lord's Supper

- The celebration of the Lord's Supper reminds us who we are in Christ (the church is Christ's body). With this conviction in mind, we should go out into our lives to live out this reality. We should seek to reflect Christ in our daily lives, pursue reconciliation where relationships are broken and bring peace where unrest exists.
- The Lord's Supper reminds us that Jesus will come back as a victorious King. Our lives are shaped by this knowledge: despite trials and sufferings, we can live in hope that our Lord and Savior is coming back. For this reason, all believers can boldly proclaim, Maranatha! "Come, Lord Jesus" (Rev. 22:20).

> ### Passover & the Lord's Supper
>
> The Passover began when God freed the Hebrew people from slavery in Egypt (Exodus 12). Unleavened bread and the Passover lamb were eaten to commemorate this event.
>
> Jesus transformed the Hebrew Passover meal into what is known as the Lord's Supper. It was during Passover that Jesus celebrated the first Communion with his disciples, using the imagery of bread and wine to point to himself as the real Passover Lamb of God.

How did the early church celebrate the Lord's Supper?

The early church left some instructions about what was important. The chart below lists instructions and suggestions for how to apply those words today.

The Didache: The word *didache* is a Greek word meaning "teaching." Here it is used to refer to an ancient Christian document known as *The Teaching of the Twelve Apostles*. Written some time soon after the time of the apostles, this book gives instruction on the Christian way of life. It contains a short section on the Eucharist.

Early Church: The Didache	Suggestions
"Do not let anyone eat or drink of your Eucharist except those who have been baptized in the name of the Lord. For the statement of the Lord applies here also: *Do not give to dogs what is holy.*"	• Think about your baptism. • Remember the words of Scripture that talk about how you were baptized into Jesus' death (Rom. 6:3–4). • Know that when you became a believer, you died to the old life and were born into a new and holy one.
"On the Lord's day, when you have been gathered together, break bread and celebrate the Eucharist. But first confess your sins so that your offering may be pure. If anyone has a quarrel with his neighbor, that person should not join you until he has been reconciled."	• Think about where you have gotten off track from God's plan for your life. • Have you hurt or argued with someone recently? (Matt. 5:23–24).
"Celebrate the Eucharist as follows: Say over the cup: 'we give you thanks, Father, for the holy vine of David, your servant, which you made known to us through Jesus your servant. To you be glory for ever.'"	• Think about the cup of wine and how it stands for the blood of Jesus. • Think how God will keep all his promises to you because of Jesus!
"Over the broken bread say: 'we give you thanks, Father, for the life and the knowledge which you have revealed to us through Jesus your servant. To you be glory for ever. As this broken bread scattered on the mountains was gathered and became one, so too, may your Church be gathered together from the ends of the earth into your kingdom. For glory and power are yours through Jesus Christ for ever.'"	• Think about how Jesus' body was broken like the bread. Now think how you are a part of Jesus' body, you are like an individual piece of bread. • Think now how someday God will gather all those fragments together from all around the world just like the fragments were gathered up from Jesus' miracles (Matt. 16:8–12). • Think about how your new life is kept alive by Jesus, the Bread of Life. • Ask yourself if you are hungry. Remember Jesus promised to satisfy those who hunger for God (Matt. 5:6).

Meals and the Bible

Is it a coincidence that two of the main celebrations in the Bible, the Passover in the Old Testament and the Lord's Supper in the New Testament, are centered on meals? Many of our fondest memories and relationships tend to be formed around the sharing of food. Meals allow us to develop relationships with others; God invites us into a special relationship with him, our deepest relationship. We get to know God during these special meals in a special way. When we share a meal with others with gratitude to God, we humbly recognize our dependence on God's goodness. Meals address basic human needs: food for hunger and water for thirst. In our daily meals, we remember and are thankful for God's goodness and provision for our lives. Because food and drink are so close to our most basic needs, they become exceptional images for our most basic spiritual needs: forgiveness of sin, reconciliation with God and with other people, and spiritual nourishment.

Heaven

Why is Heaven Important?

Heaven is more than just hope for a better future. It is at the heart of God's plan for all creation. It is also at the center of the human heart.

The common experience of losing loved ones, and the eventual loss of our own lives, make the issue of heaven one with which everyone must wrestle. We wonder what happens when we die, when our loved ones die. Have we lost them forever? Are they in a better place? Will we see them again someday? What is life after death like? What is heaven like? Can we even know something about heaven?

Heaven is a source of hope, guidance, and meaning for every believer.

Heaven gives:

- Hope for our future destination and strength for life in the present
- Guidance for living as God's people today
- Meaning by giving us the certainty that there is more to life than this world

In the following pages, we will answer some of the most common questions about heaven. We will also broaden our perspective about heaven. We will realize that heaven is not only about hope but also about faith and love.

What do we mean by *heaven*?

In popular culture, and for many believers, heaven evokes images of cloudy, ghost-like existence, or angelic beings floating about among the clouds. This image comes directly from the radical separation of the physical and spiritual worlds. Some of the misconceptions are:

Popular View of Heaven
- A place for disembodied, ghost-like beings
- A place where people sing all the time
- A place up by the clouds
- A place everyone goes after death
- A place where all beings live as angels

Biblical View of Heaven
However, the final destination of believers is not an ethereal place like that. The final destination of all believers is *the renewed heavens and earth* anticipated in Revelation 21. A very physical, concrete future awaits us when Christ comes back.

What happens when people die?

When one experiences the loss of a loved one, the pain of the loss makes it difficult to focus on the ultimate destination. The immediate concern is *what has happened to my loved one? Is my loved one in heaven?*

What will happen to me when I die?
Although some of the details remain hidden, we know that:

- Our life and future are secure in God's hands (Ps. 34:6; 91:4; Is. 25:4; Rom. 8:37–39).
- We go to a place of waiting in the presence of God (1 John 3:2–3). Many theologians call this period between our deaths and Jesus' return the *intermediate state.*
- It is not a permanent place; the whole creation waits for the final redemption at the end of time.
- It is not a place up by the clouds; we do not know where it is, but it is where Jesus is present.

Can we be sure what happens after we die? Yes!
- Believers will enjoy the blessing of God's presence (1 John 3:2–3; Rev. 21:22).
- Believers from all of history wait in joy and peace, but with longing, for the return of Christ (Rev. 6:9–10).
- As believers, we will join them at some point.
- When God renews all things, we will all dwell together in the new heavens and the new earth (Rev. 21–22).

What can we know about heaven?

The answer is not as much as we would like; however, we can know just enough to be confident that:

- We can trust in God's promises.
- We will be with God and our loved ones.
- God will do something awesome with his creation.

How do we know anything about heaven?

- The only completely valid source of knowledge about heaven is the Bible. The Bible has direct and indirect information about heaven—over 600 verses in the Bible mention *heaven*.
- The Bible is the rule with which we can decide if other information is valid.
- However, for the most part, people's ideas about heaven come mainly from literature, movies, and television. Media has shaped much of our imagination and knowledge about heaven. Not all of this knowledge is accurate.
- A non-biblical understanding of the world has informed much of what popular culture knows about heaven.
- It mainly portrays heaven as boring and unappealing.

Although sin has profoundly affected creation, God never called creation evil. It is under a curse. However, Jesus came to lift that curse and turn it into blessing. God is redeeming all of creation. At the end of time, God will renew all things to their original intention.

Understanding God's original plan for his creation helps us understand our final destination as well.

A non-biblical understanding of the universe

Behind the cloudy, ethereal idea of heaven lies the old Gnostic belief that the physical world is evil and the spiritual is good. Thus, one must focus on the spiritual to escape this evil world. This is not a biblical idea. It ignores some basic biblical facts:

A biblical understanding of the universe

1. God made the whole universe and called it *very good* (Gen. 1:31).

2. Satan is a spiritual being and is evil—thus, not all *spiritual* is good and not all *physical* is evil.

3. God promises a renewed heaven and earth at the end of time (Rev. 21).

What Was God's Original Intent for Creation?

God created the whole universe for his own glory and relationships. He intended all his creatures to relate to each other, to nature, and to himself in harmony. Humanity's main and great goal in life is to glorify God (Isa. 60:21; 1 Cor. 6:20; 10:31) and enjoy him forever (Phil. 4:4; Rev. 21:3–4).

Human sin twisted God's original intentions. However, because of God's grace and faithfulness, his plans would not be frustrated. He planned to rescue his creation from the effects of sin (Rom. 8:18–27). Through the saving work of Jesus on the cross, people can find peace with God and each other. Through the same process, believers can begin the reconciliation with one another and nature.

Neos and Kainos

Greek has two different words for the idea of *new*. *Neos* is a newness of time; *kainos* is a newness of quality. A *neos* object would mean that the object did not exist and now is there. A *kainos* object means that the object was there but its quality has changed: it is better, it is made different. In this sense, the *new heavens and earth* in Revelation 21:1 are not *neos* but *kainos*. That is, God will renew, transform, improve, and refresh his creation. It will be a *kainos* heaven and earth.

What is the renewed heaven and earth?

This process will have a glorious ending when Christ returns. He will renew all things (Rev. 21:1). It will not be a different creation or a non-creation. It will be *this* creation renewed; God will restore his creation to its original glory and purpose. As if to close the circle, what God began at Eden he will fulfill in Revelation. Not everything will be the same. Some things from the biblical idea of Eden will continue in the renewed creation; others will end.

We do have glimpses of heaven, even if many things are not clear. We can see it in the love we experience for and from people, in the majesty of nature's beauty and power, in the generosity and kindness of people in times of need, in the smile of a happy baby, in the loyalty and warmth of our pets, in the tenderness and wisdom of old age, and in moments of deep emotional and spiritual connections with our loved ones and God.

What is our hope for the future?

Our hope for the future is firmly rooted in God's faithfulness. We can trust that God will do what he has promised us because he has been faithful in the past. We can safely conclude that many features and characteristics of this world will continue in the renewed creation. Of course, there will be things that will end as well. Based on biblical testimony, we can identify many things that will continue and some that will not.

What Will Continue	What Will End

• Physical bodies
• Emotions (relationships)
• Nature
    Daily cycles
    Weather
    Animals—including pets
• Many activities, such as:
    Work (Gen. 2:15)
    Learning (1 Cor. 13:12)
    Science
    Art (Rev. 14:2–3)
    Entertainment
	• No evil
	• No curse
	• No brokenness, emotional or physical
	• No more sin
	• No death
	• No marriage
	• No more suffering or sadness
	• No war
	• No famine
	• No need for temples

"This is the will of Him who sent Me, that of all that He has given Me I lose nothing, but raise it up on the last day."
—John 6:39 (*NASB*)

Besides referring to people, this text also refers to God's creation. The neuter pronoun *it* (Greek *auto*) would seem to extend Jesus' mission from people to all of creation (see Romans 8:19–22 and Colossians 1:20). Jesus' words in John 6:39 are a guarantee that no good thing shall be lost, but rather shall have some new and fulfilled form in the renewed creation. Everything good belongs to Christ, who is the life of the whole world as well as the life of every believer (John 6:33, 40). All things good in this world will continue to exist in the next, but they will be transformed and improved in the renewed creation.

Why does Jesus' resurrection matter?

Jesus' resurrection gives us a good idea of what heaven may look like. The Apostle Paul makes it clear that our future is tied to Jesus' own resurrection (1 Cor. 15:12–34). He concludes, "And if Christ has not been raised, your faith is futile…" (15:17).

- Because Christ has been raised from the dead, our hope is true and secured.
- Christ is the firstfruits or first example of all who will be raised into new life (15:20).
- Our future includes a *resurrected body*; that is, it will be a physical reality. Our future resurrected bodies will be like Jesus' own resurrected body (1 Cor. 15:42–49).
- The women and the disciples recognized Jesus after his resurrection (Matt. 28:9, 17).
- Jesus' body was physical (Lk. 24:39). Jesus ate with his disciples (Lk. 24:41–43). Yet, it was not a body like ours. The Apostle Paul uses two ways to explain this difference:
  1. Just as different animals have bodies suited for their environment (for the sea, the air, and the ground), so our resurrected bodies will be suited for the renewed creation (1 Cor. 15:39).
  2. There are also "natural bodies" and "spiritual bodies." Both Jesus' pre- and post-Resurrection bodies were physical; the difference is about perishability. That is, natural bodies die; spiritual bodies do not. Sin has polluted and damaged our natural bodies; our bodies die, decay, and are unfit for a future in God's presence. Just as God will renew this creation, also marred by sin, God will give us renewed bodies that will not be polluted by sin, will not decay, and will be fit to be in the presence of God.

Natural Bodies	Spiritual Bodies
Psychikos	*Pneumatikos*
Derived from *psyche*, meaning "soul"	Derived from *pneuma*, meaning "spirit"
The ending *ikos* is used in Greek to make an adjective, and it means "in reference to." It does not describe the material out of which something is made. Rather, it refers to the force that animates an object. In this case, *psychikos* refers to the human soul that animates our bodies. In the case of *pneumatikos*, it refers to the Spirit, God's Spirit, as the animating force (see, for example, Rom. 1:11 and Gal. 6:1). Thus, both kinds of bodies are physical. The difference is that a "natural body" dies and a "spiritual body" does not die.	

Will we be able to recognize our loved ones in heaven?

Yes! When Jesus rose from the dead and appeared to his friends and disciples, they recognized him (Luke 24:39; John 20:27). There will be continuity between our bodies today and our resurrected bodies in the renewed creation.

> *I know that my Redeemer lives, and that in the end he will stand upon the earth. And after my skin has been destroyed, yet in my flesh I will see God; I myself will see him with my own eyes—I, and not another. How my heart yearns within me!*—Job 19:25–27

What kinds of relationships will exist in heaven?

Emotions and relationships are a very important part of what it means to be human. There will be emotions and relationships in heaven, though they may not be exactly the same. They will be renewed emotions, emotions as they were meant to be from the beginning: joyful, satisfying, enriching, intimate, and refreshing.

There will be no sorrow, or regrets, or guilt. Rather, love, compassion, gentleness, tenderness, and other emotions will find new heights and depths in heaven. Relationships will be all we can imagine and more.

Will there be disabilities, injuries or deformities in heaven?

No. There will be no brokenness at all, either emotional or physical. God will renew our bodies; they will be beautiful and work as God intended them to. Because Jesus' injuries were present after his resurrection (Luke 24:39; John 20:27), many people think that martyrs, those who died for the name of Jesus, will wear their healed scars as badges of honor. Although it is possible, it remains, like so many other things about heaven, just speculation.

Will our bodies need food, clothing, and language in heaven?

Because we do not understand the nature of the future bodies, it is difficult to know whether they will need food, clothing, and languages. However, since our bodies will preserve much of their characteristics, we could imagine that language, food, and clothing will have very similar functions. The beautiful diversity of characters and gifts makes life more interesting. Each person reflects God's image in a way that none other can. Together, with our differences and similarities, with our talents and strengths, we reflect God's image as no individual human could.

Yet, there will certainly be differences as well. Now, differences in language, culture, and expression can be causes of deep, fierce divisions (Gen. 11:1–9). However, in the renewed creation, communication will be transparent. We will say what we mean, and people will fully understand us. This side of heaven, clothing can be used as a status symbol that can serve our pride. It is also used to cover our shame. There will be no shame in the renewed creation, nor will we have the need to boost our ego at the expense of others. Rather, clothing will not conceal but could reveal our inner being.

Will heaven be boring?

Definitely not! People may get the idea that heaven will be boring because we will worship God all day long in heaven. It is true—we will worship God non-stop! But let's revisit what we mean by *worship*.

Worship is not just the singing and praying part of Christian church services. Everything we do can be worship: from the moment we wake up, take our meals, relate to others, do our work, play games, and live life. Worship is not just an activity; it is primarily an attitude. Worship is the attitude that arises when we recognize who God is and who we are:

God	Human
He is the creator	We are the creatures
He is in control of our lives	We depend completely on God's grace and mercy
He is all powerful	We are limited and weak
He knows all things	We know imperfectly
He loves us unconditionally	We are just learning to love in the same way

Worship is the attitude that acknowledges God's presence at every moment in our daily lives, sometimes moving us to tears, sometimes to great joy, to repentance, to humility, to gratitude, to hard work, to commitment, to compassion, to love.

In the busyness of our lives, we often miss this reality: God is interested and active in our lives! We may go days or weeks without realizing that our words, actions, and thoughts have brought glory or sadness to God. This forgetfulness will find no place in the renewed creation; we will not miss God in our lives because he will dwell in our midst.

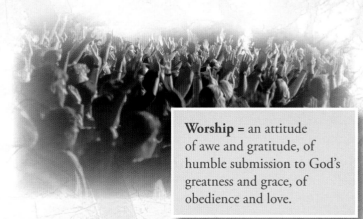

Worship = an attitude of awe and gratitude, of humble submission to God's greatness and grace, of obedience and love.

What will we do in heaven?

The Bible does not give many details about activities in heaven. But we can be sure that:

- God loves his creation. He proclaimed it good (Gen. 1:31).
- Nature itself reflects God's greatness and glory (Ps. 19).
- Nature will be renewed so it may fulfill God's purposes.

So it is at least possible that much of the new creation will be similar to what we experience now. The best things about this world will just become better in the renewed creation.

Will we have pets?

Our relationships with our pets are also important and meaningful. These relationships reflect the way God intended us to relate to animals in general: with love, respect, and companionship. Will God, then, resurrect our beloved pets? Yes, it is perfectly possible. We cannot be sure, since the Bible does not address this issue, but based on God's love for animals, their role as our companions, it is at least possible.

The wolf and the lamb will feed together, and the lion will eat straw like the ox, but dust will be the serpent's food. They will neither harm nor destroy on all my holy mountain.—Isaiah 65:25

Whatever you do, work at it with all your heart, as working for the Lord, not for men, since you know that you will receive an inheritance from the Lord as a reward. It is the Lord Christ you are serving.
—Colossians 3:23–24

Will there be work?

Because work can become an almost painful toil, we often wonder if rest means no more working. But remember that

- Work is also a form of worship;
- God meant for humans to help take care of his creation (Gen. 2:15).

Each person will develop and thrive with his or her own talents. We will no longer work in places that do not allow us to grow as individuals, or where our work might be unappreciated, or where we cannot possibly be happy.

God intended work to be a joyful activity. Rather than just making a living, work should be a way to fellowship with God by caring for his world. For this reason, we can be sure we will have plenty of interesting things to do in the renewed creation!

Will there be learning, science, sports, and arts?

As with work, we could imagine the same for learning, science, arts, and sports. The gifts and talents of painters, poets, athletes and scientists will be used simply to worship God.

So, what's so great about heaven?

Everything! Heaven is all we ever dreamt and more. In this life, we grow, reach our peak, and begin a slow descent until our life ends. Life in the intermediate heaven will be much better because we will be in God's presence. However, life in the renewed creation will be beyond our imagination.

It is true that we do not know many facts about the renewed creation, heaven, and even less about the intermediate state, intermediate heaven. However, what we read in the Bible and what we know about God give us great hope and joy.

Dear friends, now we are children of God, and what we will be has not yet been made known. But we know that when he appears, we shall be like him, for we shall see him as he is. Everyone who has this hope in him purifies himself, just as he is pure.
—1 John 3:2–3

The Ultimate Great Escape?

- Heaven is not an escapist idea.
- We do not think about heaven to escape this world's troubles—we think about heaven as a guide to live better in this world, to serve God with greater joy, and to show others God's great love.
- For many believers who suffer persecution for their faithfulness, and others who suffer in this life in indescribable ways, heaven is a great source of comfort.
- Knowing that God will make all things right one day gives us strength to continue life in faithfulness and obedience.

Who will be in heaven and how do we get there?

- In popular culture, it's common to believe that all people go to heaven, and, in some cases, they become angels. However, biblical testimony does not support either of these ideas.
- Just as we acknowledge the reality of heaven, we must recognize the reality of hell. We don't know very much about hell either, except that it exists, it is a place of punishment, and there is only one way to escape it. The other details are hidden from us.
- The Bible is clear, however, to specify who will go to heaven. Only those who have surrendered their lives to Jesus and who experience the renewal of their hearts will be allowed in God's presence.

For God so loved the world that he gave his one and only Son, that whoever believes in him shall not perish but have eternal life. For God did not send his Son into the world to condemn the world, but to save the world through him.—John 3:16–17

What is the New Jerusalem?

The book of Revelation provides another image of the renewed creation: the city of Jerusalem (Rev. 21:2). The city is described as a bride and its dimensions are detailed. Believers understand this text in different ways. Some understand the city to be a literal city, and the dimension an accurate representation of what the city will be like. The resulting picture is an enormous cube of about 1,400 miles per side.

Others take this image as a symbolic representation of God's people. Since the image of the bride ready to marry the Lamb occurs before, and it seems applied to God's people (Rev. 19:7), it is possible that the Holy City stands for God's holy people. It is perfectly possible that there will be no seas (21:1), or sun and moon (21:23). It is also possible that the language is symbolic— it says the "city does not need the sun or the moon…" not that they will not exist. If there is continuity between this creation and the renewed creation, as we have suggested, then the beauty of the sun and the moon will be present, even if not needed.

In any case, it is clear that:

- The renewed creation is God's work, since it comes from above.
- It is large enough to fit all of God's people and more.
- It points at the beauty and splendor of the renewed creation.
- God dwells in its midst.
- It closes the circle from Paradise in the Garden of Eden to the Holy City in the new heavens and new earth.

Original Creation (Genesis)	Renewed Creation (Revelation)
Heaven and earth created, 1:1	Heavens and earth renewed, 21:1
Sun created, 1:16	No need of sun, 21:23
The night established, 1:5	No night there, 22:5
The seas created, 1:10	No more seas, 21:1
The curse enters the world, 3:14–17	No more curse, 22:3
Death enters the world, 2:19	Death is no more, 21:4
Humanity is cast out of paradise, 3:24	Humanity is restored to paradise, 22:14
Sorrow and pain begin, 3:17	Sorrow, tears, and pain end, 21:4

Regarding knowledge of heaven, we must humbly recognize our limits.

The secret things belong to the Lord our God, but the things revealed belong to us and to our children forever.
—Deuteronomy 29:29

- Mystery requires faith to know that God is in control.
- We do not need to know everything.
- We know all that we need to be faithful and obedient.

ATTRIBUTES OF GOD

A RELATIONSHIP WITH GOD

God created humanity for relationships: relationships with each other, with nature, and with God. However, human sin separated us from God, turning what should have been a loving relationship into one filled with hate and disobedience (Rom. 5:10). Yet, God has reached down to us to deliver us from sin and death because he wants to have a relationship with us. In Christ, God has built a bridge that allows us to relate to him.

Deep, meaningful relationships require knowledge of the other person. The more we know God, the more our love can grow and mature. Also, our obedience and service will spring forth from this knowledge and love of God.

Then, how do we get to know God? Our relationship with God begins and ends with Jesus. We get to know God as we know Jesus. His death and resurrection have given us direct access to God. We now know Jesus and God in two ways:

1. Through the work of the Holy Spirit in each believer

2. Through the revealed Word of God

> "This is what the LORD says: 'Let not the wise boast of their wisdom or the strong boast of their strength or the rich boast of their riches, but let the one who boasts boast about this: that they have the understanding to know me, that I am the LORD, who exercises kindness, justice and righteousness on earth, for in these I delight,' declares the LORD." —Jeremiah 9:23–24
>
> "Now this is eternal life: that they know you, the only true God, and Jesus Christ, whom you have sent." —John 17:3

It is good for us to be near unto God. It is eternity to know him intimately in our daily lives... That's the mark of believers. They know what joy there is in being near unto God, and they want nothing else.
——Abraham Kuyper, *Near Unto God*

JESUS: A MODEL OF GOD'S ATTRIBUTES

God is spirit. We can discern some of his attributes in nature—for example, his power in the storms, his goodness in the bounty of the earth, his love in the loving actions of people around us. We also know about God's attributes through the Scriptures.

The book of Hebrews teaches us that "In the past God spoke to our ancestors through the prophets at many times and in various ways, but in these last days he has spoken to us by his Son, whom he appointed heir of all things, and through whom also he made the universe. The Son is the radiance of God's glory and the exact representation of his being, sustaining all things by his powerful word" (Heb. 1:1–3). Jesus models the attributes of God, especially the communicable attributes.

• Jesus showed his *love* for all people (Luke 7:47; Mark 10:21). His love is especially clear in his sacrifice: "This is how we know what love is: Jesus Christ laid down his life for us. And we ought to lay down our lives for our brothers and sisters" (1 John 3:16).

• Jesus demonstrated a life without sin (Heb. 4:15)—he was *holy*. His sacrifice on our behalf was perfect and sufficient because: "Such a high priest truly meets our need—one who is holy, blameless, pure, set apart from sinners, exalted above the heavens" (Heb. 7:26).

• Throughout his ministry, Jesus showed compassion and *mercy*: for the multitude (Matt. 9:36), for the unfortunate (Matt. 20:34), for Jerusalem (Matt. 23:37), for the leper (Mark 1:41).

• Jesus is *faithful*. He promised to be with us always (Matt. 28:20), and we can rest knowing that "the Lord is faithful, and he will strengthen you and protect you from the evil one" (2 Thess. 3:3). For this reason, we can be "confident of this, that he who began a good work in you will carry it on to completion until the day of Christ Jesus" (Phil. 1:6).

GOD'S ATTRIBUTES AS A WINDOW

Knowing who God is, his character and his nature, can be discovered through learning about his attributes. One way to think about God's attributes is by distinguishing between the attributes that belong only to God and the attributes that we also share with him—we share these attributes with God because he made us in his image. The first kind of attributes is called *incommunicable*, while the second kind is called *communicable*. In God, no attribute is more important than the others are. All of them, in conjunction, make God who he is.

INCOMMUNICABLE (THE ATTRIBUTES THAT ONLY GOD HAS)	COMMUNICABLE (THE ATTRIBUTES WE SHARE WITH GOD)
1. TRIUNE	1. LOVING
2. ONE	2. HOLY
3. TRANSCENDENT	3. GOOD
4. INFINITE	4. JUST
5. ETERNAL	5. JEALOUS
6. CREATOR	6. MERCIFUL
7. OMNIPRESENT	7. SOVEREIGN (AUTHORITY)
8. IMMUTABLE	8. OMNIPOTENT (POWERFUL)
	9. KNOWLEDGEABLE (OMNISCIENT)
	10. PATIENT
	11. FAITHFUL
	12. SPIRIT

The attributes of God provide us with a window through which we can contemplate who God is. As we contemplate and learn about God's character, we begin to grasp the glorious, loving, awe-inspiring, and holy person that is the only one worthy of our allegiance. Jesus modeled these characteristics in his life and ministry. By learning what they mean and how they apply to our lives, we can grow in our faith by being imitators of God.

But the plans of the LORD stand firm forever, the purposes of his heart through all generations. —Psalm 33:11

God is perpetually the same: subject to no change in His being, attributes, or determinations. Therefore God is compared to a Rock (Deut. 32:4, etc.) which remains immovable, when the entire ocean surrounding it is continually in a fluctuating state; even so, though all creatures are subject to change, God is immutable. Because God has no beginning and no ending, He can know no change. He is everlastingly 'the Father of lights, with whom is no variableness, neither shadow of turning' (James 1:17). —A. W. Pink, *The Attributes of God*

Attributes that Only God Has

1-2 TRIUNE AND ONE

While being one, God is triune. It's easy to see that these two attributes exist in tension with each other. We know both are correct, but it's not easy to understand how they exist together.

- God is *one*: "Hear, O Israel: The Lord our God, the Lord is one" (Deut. 6:4). God is one in two ways: There is no other being like God. And God is the only real God. Because God is one, he is the only being worthy of praise.

- God is *triune*. God is one being who exists in three persons. God the Father, God the Son, and God the Holy Spirit are three separate persons, but they all share the same divine being. This unity of persons is called the "Godhead." God is a person who desires to relate to his creation (Matt. 28:19; 2 Cor. 13:14; Eph. 4:4–6; Titus 3:4–6): "As soon as Jesus was baptized, he went up out of the water. At that moment heaven was opened, and he saw the Spirit of God descending like a dove and alighting on him. And a voice from heaven said, 'This is my Son, whom I love; with him I am well pleased'" (Matt. 3:16–17). We have a model for healthy personal relationships in the way the persons of the Trinity relate to each other.

REFLECTION

- How does knowing that God is in a relationship with the Godhead help you have a personal relationship with him?

- God is one. Does he have any competition for your love and loyalties? Are there other things or beings that are more important to you than God? Should that be the case?

3-4 TRANSCENDENT AND INFINITE

When trying to understand God, we must humbly keep in mind two other attributes of God: he's *transcendent* and *infinite*.

Transcendent means that he's beyond the universe and beyond our intelligence and imagination. This attribute means that we naturally have limits to how far our understanding of God can go. It also means that God is not united, or somehow connected, with the created universe. He is outside the universe. When God's face is hidden from his people (Ps. 13:1; 22:24; Isa. 8:17), we are reminded that God is beyond us and only accessible to us because he reaches first.

God is also beyond our understanding because he is *infinite*. This means that God is above our standards. He's not only wise or gracious; no one is wiser or more gracious than he is. It also means that God has no limits because he is beyond limits. This is an encouraging thought when we face troubles and trials: "I know that you can do all things; no purpose of yours can be thwarted" (Job 42:2; see 1 Kings 8:27; Job 5:9; Ps. 145:3).

REFLECTION

- God is so much greater than we are. He knows the future, he laid out the universe, and he planned our lives. Through Scripture, God has given us hints about what he is like, but it also says God's ways are mysterious and they are good beyond our imagination. How does this affect the way we worship God?

An infinite God can give all of Himself to each of His children. He does not distribute Himself that each may have a part, but to each one He gives all of Himself as fully as if there were no others. —A. W. Tozer

Attributes that Only God Has

5–6 ETERNAL AND CREATOR

While being *infinite* refers to limits—and God has no limits—being *eternal* refers to time. God does not have a beginning or an end. Before all things were, God already existed: "'I am the Alpha and the Omega,' says the Lord God, 'who is, and who was, and who is to come, the Almighty'" (Rev. 1:8; Deut. 33:27; Ps. 90:1–2; Isa. 40:28; Jer. 10:10; Jude 25).

If God is eternal—he existed before anything else—it also means that God is *creator*. No one created God, but he created all things. God's existence doesn't depend on anything; he is free from obligation. God doesn't owe anything to anyone. We can trust that God always wants what is best for us because—unlike human authorities—God's loyalties are not compromised.

REFLECTION

- We all have experienced betrayal of one kind or another. Often, it happens when other people's commitments prevent them from keeping their word to us. However, God doesn't experience those conflicts of interest. Nothing will stop him from loving us. What keeps us from trusting God fully? What would our lives be like if we did?

7 OMNIPRESENT

As an *eternal* and *infinite* God, God is also not limited by space. God is *omnipresent*—God is present everywhere. God is present at all moments of our life. God is always accessible because he is always present. We can be strong and courageous because God will never leave our side. We can't hide from God or escape his rule over our lives. There is nowhere to run away from God. His love finds us everywhere: "No one will be able to stand against you all the days of your life. As I was with Moses, so I will be with you; I will never leave you nor forsake you" (Josh. 1:5; Ps. 33:13; Ps. 139:7–12; Jer. 23:24).

REFLECTION

- God often calls us to do things we'd rather not do—forgive, love, speak up, care for others. What happens when we try to ignore God and run from him?

8 IMMUTABLE

Finally, since God is *eternal, infinite,* and *omnipresent*, we can be sure that he's always the same; he's *immutable*— God doesn't change. He will never become evil, or weak, or hateful, or cruel. No matter what happens to us or to our surroundings, we can depend on God, our firm foundation, to always remain the same. We can learn God's attributes, essence, nature, and we can trust that it will always be consistent and unchanged. God's nature is reliable and trustworthy.

These incommunicable attributes remind us what an awesome and glorious God we worship. Also, they show that although God is so far away from any of our common experience, he still reaches out to us, he still desires to relate to us in personal, intimate ways.

REFLECTION

- Find a rock and hold it in your hand. Squeeze it, knock on it, and try to bend it. The rock is pretty hard to move or change, but with enough pressure or heat it would probably change. God, however, doesn't change no matter what you do.

- How is God's changelessness a comfort to you?

Attributes that We Share With God

9 LOVING	10 HOLY	11 GOOD
The first communicable attribute—this means that we share that characteristic with God—is that God is *love*: "Whoever does not love does not know God, because God is love" (1 John 4:8; Jer. 31:3; John 3:16; 13:34). Because of human rebellion and sin, God could justly destroy us. Yet, because of his love, God has extended his grace and forgiveness to us. His love for us—and the love we see in the Godhead, among the persons of the Trinity—is an example of how to love: "We love because he first loved us" (1 John 4:19). God's love is best seen in Jesus: "But God demonstrates his own love for us in this: While we were sinners, Christ died for us" (Rom. 5:8).	While *love* drives God's grace, his *holiness* sets natural limits to how we can relate to him. It's not that God's love and holiness are in a struggle; rather, they complement each other. God is separated from sin and evil. Therefore, in our sinful state, we cannot approach God or even be near his holiness. Because of Jesus' sacrifice for us, we can now be in a relationship with God. The cross of Jesus bridged the chasm between us (a sinful people) and God (The Holy One). God expects us to be holy—"Be holy because I, the LORD your God, am holy" (Lev. 19:2; Ps. 99:9; Isa. 6:3; 1 Peter 1:15).	In God, we learn that love is more than a feeling: it's active and dynamic. The engine that moves love to action is God's *goodness*. We experience God's goodness in his love, patience, provision, and compassion. All good things in our lives come from God's goodness: "The LORD is good to all; he has compassion on all he has made" (Ps. 145:9; Ps. 25:8; Nahum 1:7; Rom. 2:4).
REFLECTION • Bring to mind the name of one person you love or have been in love with at some point in your life. • What are some things you expect or expected from that person? • What are some things that person expects or expected from you? • How does this type of love differ from the love of God? How is it the same?	**REFLECTION** • Pour a tablespoon of oil in a glass of water. Watch to see if the oil mixes with the water. The water and the oil will always remain separate; the oil will not corrupt the pure water. • "Holiness" means separate from sin. Why is God's holiness so important?	**REFLECTION** • Write down five things you're grateful for and then thank God for his goodness and for blessing you with those five things.

Attributes that We Share With God

12 JUST	13 JEALOUS	14 MERCIFUL

As *holiness* balances *love*, God's *justice* balances his *goodness*. God is *just* because he judges with fairness and always does the right thing. God will judge the whole world (Rev. 20:13), and the wrongs will be righted: "The LORD within her is righteous; he does no wrong. Morning by morning he dispenses his justice, and every new day he does not fail, yet the unrighteous know no shame" (Zeph. 3:5; Ps. 33:5; Ps. 97:1–3; Isa. 42:1).

Because of our sin, we reject God. Yet, he's the only being worthy of praise—as seen in the incommunicable attributes. In our rebellion, we offer our allegiance to idols and make God secondary. God is *jealous*. God does not share his glory with anyone or anything. God wants first place in our lives. He wants our loyalty over any other thing—even good things such as family, friends, church group, and country: "Do not worship any other god, for the Lord, whose name is Jealous, is a jealous God" (Ex. 34:14; Deut. 4:24; Zech. 8:2; James 4:5).

Although *justice* demands that "the wages of sin is death," God's *mercy* paves the way for "the gift of God [which] is eternal life in Christ Jesus our Lord"(Rom. 6:23). God is *merciful*. Out of his love and goodness, God's mercy holds rightful judgment against sin and evil to allow the salvation of those who come to him in faith: "But in your great mercy you did not put an end to them or abandon them, for you are a gracious and merciful God" (Deut. 4:31; Neh. 9:31; Dan. 9:9; Rom. 9:14–18).

REFLECTION

JUST
- When Christ comes again, he will right the wrongs: He will judge those who have cheated us and been cruel to us, but he will also look at our lives and judge our selfish and self-righteous behavior toward others. All of our hidden deeds will be made known. All of our worst thoughts will be revealed. When you go to the Lord in prayer, what do you need to be forgiven for?

JEALOUS
- It's easy to allow family, friends, hobbies, and recreation to take first place in our lives. Even good things, such as career, church activities, and loyalty to country, can get in the way of following God. Make a list of the 10 things you spend the most time and money on and rank them in order of importance. What would be the most difficult ones to give up?

MERCIFUL
- Read Matthew 18:21–35.
- Reflect on a time you withheld mercy from someone or someone didn't show you mercy. How did this lack of mercy affect your life?
- How does God's mercy affect whether or not you show mercy to someone else?

Attributes that We Share With God

15 SOVEREIGN (AUTHORITY)	16 OMNIPOTENT (POWERFUL)	17 KNOWLEDGEABLE
God is *sovereign*. This means that God rules the universe and that he is not ruled by anything or anyone. Also, it means that nothing is beyond God's control: evil, death, blessings, relationships, all things happen within his authority. God has absolute *authority*, while humans have a limited authority in different areas of life. As a *sovereign God*, he provides faithfully for his creatures, in general, and for his people, in particular: "How great you are, Sovereign LORD! There is no one like you, and there is no God but you, as we have heard with our own ears" (2 Sam. 7:22; Ps. 33:8–11; Isa. 46:9–11; Dan. 4:32–35).	Being the creator of all things gives God the authority to be king. God is *all-powerful— omnipotent*. God has the power to do whatever he pleases, but he never contradicts his nature. He can meet our needs and can help us through any trial, no matter how overwhelming or impossible to overcome it may be. Unlike God who can do all things, humans have power limited by our condition as creatures. With the same power that raised Jesus from the dead, God will also raise us from the dead and give us victory (2 Cor. 4:13–14; Phil. 3:10; 1 Peter 1:5; Gen. 18:13–14; Isa. 40:25–26; Jer. 32:17).	As you pray to God, know that he already knows what you need. God knows all things— he is *omniscient*. God knows the past, the present, and the future. God knows our hearts. He knows what we think, say, and do. Nothing is a surprise to God. Nothing catches him off guard. Whereas God knows all things, humans have a limited knowledge. Our knowledge is limited by our condition as creatures. "Nothing in all creation is hidden from God's sight. Everything is uncovered and laid bare before the eyes of him to whom we must give account" (Heb. 4:13; 1 Sam. 2:3; Ps. 139:1–6; 147:5; 1 John 3:20).

REFLECTION

15 Sovereign
- When the storms of life seem to overwhelm you and all seems lost, what do you think Jesus would want to tell you?

16 Omnipotent
- Make a list of all the obstacles in your life that seem impossible to overcome.
- Pray that our omnipotent God will take care of each of the items in your list.

17 Knowledgeable
- In what way does God's knowledge of every person and every situation comfort you?
- How does knowing that God knows everything about you—that you can't hide from God— help you grow closer to him?

Attributes that We Share With God

18 PATIENT	19 FAITHFUL	20 SPIRIT
God is *just* and *holy*, and he will judge all people; however, God is *patient* and slow to carry out his righteous judgment. God waits patiently for his people to repent and come back to him. God sent his only Son, Jesus, to atone for our sins and appease that judgment and condemnation. Now, God waits patiently for people to turn to Christ in faith: "And he passed in front of Moses, proclaiming, 'The Lord, the Lord, the compassionate and gracious God, slow to anger, abounding in love and faithfulness'" (Ex. 34:6; Ps. 86:15; Jonah 4:2; 2 Peter 3:8–9).	God is *faithful*. In our relationships, we're afraid to become vulnerable and allow someone to take advantage of us. However, God is faithful to his word. He'll do just as he said. He'll never take advantage of us. We can trust that God will be faithfully good to us, show mercy and forgiveness to us, and do justice in the world. When we are in trouble, we can completely rely on God's promises, because God is faithful: "Praise be to the Lord, who has given rest to his people Israel just as he promised. Not one word has failed of all the good promises he gave through his servant Moses" (1 Kings 8:56; Deut. 7:9; Ps. 57:10; 1 Thess. 5:24).	Finally, it is important to remember that God is spirit. It means, first, that God does not have a body. When the Bible speaks of God's face, hands, or any "body language," it is using comparison with our bodies that we can understand and relate to. It also means that God is the source of all life. Whereas God is spirit, humans have both a spirit and a body. "God is spirit, and his worshipers must worship in the Spirit and truth" (John 4:24; 1:18; Acts 17:24; 2 Cor. 3:17; 1 Tim. 1:17; 6:16).
REFLECTION • Read the Parable of the Lost Son (Luke 15:11–31). This parable illustrates God's love and patience for the lost. • Which son do you most identify with and why? • What are some ways you can exercise the attribute of patience?	**REFLECTION** • How has God shown his faithfulness in your life despite your failures? • How have you responded to God's faithfulness?	**REFLECTION** • How does creation point you toward the invisible God? • How has the physical human being, Jesus Christ, helped you develop your relationship with God, who is spirit?

CREEDS and HERESIES

WHERE DID THE CREEDS COME FROM?

As the gospel spread in the first centuries after Jesus' death and resurrection, people wondered about the beliefs of this new religion. Like today, believers then needed quick, accessible answers to questions. Early Christians formulated simple creeds that expressed essential Christian beliefs. These creeds served at least three purposes:

1. *Explanation of the faith.* Creeds are basic, memorable statements of belief.

2. *Training of believers.* Creeds help believers understand who they are, what they believe, and how they should act as Christians. They are like posts that delimit the boundaries of what it means to be, to believe, and live as Christians.

3. *Identification and correction of false teachings:* Even in the first century AD, false teachers abounded—teachers who claimed to follow Jesus but who promoted a message about Jesus that differed radically from the historical accounts proclaimed by apostolic eyewitnesses. Early Christian creeds helped believers to distinguish the truth about Jesus from the alternative perspectives presented by false teachers.

WHAT DOES A CHRISTIAN BELIEVE?

Early Christians struggled to keep their faith rooted in the historical truth about Jesus Christ—a truth first proclaimed by apostolic eyewitnesses, then passed on through oral traditions, and recorded in the New Testament writings. By providing brief summaries of the truth about Jesus, creeds promoted unity and identity among believers in Jesus Christ.

RELIGIOUS PERSECUTION

Jesus Christ is the fulfillment of God's promises to the people of Israel. For this reason, Christianity was not simply another Jewish sect like the Pharisees and Sadducees. Early Christian writings, including the earliest of the creeds, clearly reflect efforts to demonstrate that Christian faith consummated and fulfilled the Old Testament promises of a Messiah. Eventually, this radical claim led to a separation between the church and mainstream Judaism. Some Jewish religious leaders persecuted believers in Jesus. One of these religious leaders—Saul, later known as Paul—eventually trusted Jesus as his Lord and Messiah.

POLITICAL PERSECUTION

The early church also experienced persecution from the Roman Empire. The Romans were tolerant of other people's religions to a point; because of their respect for ancient and venerable traditions, the Romans even tolerated the Jewish religion. As persecution drove believers away from Jerusalem, it became clear that Christianity was not simply another Jewish sect, and the Romans began to demand that Christians worship the Roman emperor. Christians refused to worship the Emperor and declared that Jesus alone is Lord. Christians' refusal to worship the Emperor was one reason for the vicious Roman persecution in the latter half of the first century. The powerful influences of pagan culture—both in the state religion of emperor worship and in the growing presence of Gnosticism—made it all the more important to articulate clearly what Christians ought to believe. Identifying God as the sole Creator of all things and declaring Jesus as the only Lord became an important confession for the early church.

CONFESSING THE GOOD NEWS

Jesus' life and ministry challenged Jewish expectations and hopes. The radical call to be transformed by the power of the Holy Spirit and live a different life is not easy to digest. New Testament writers had to stretch their knowledge and understanding. These Spirit-inspired authors presented the truth about Jesus in ways that could be understood not only by Jewish people but also in the broader Greco-Roman world and beyond. The New Testament writings and the creeds of early Christianity answered some of the challenges of the Greco-Roman world.

Today, the creeds still give us identity as Christians. They tell us the following and much more:

- What does it mean to be a Christian?
- Why is it important to believe in the Trinity?
- Why is it important that Jesus is fully God and fully human?
- What unites us as believers?

The Apostle Paul emphasizes "one Lord, one faith, one baptism" (Eph. 4:2). When we recite the creeds, we agree with them; and this agreement joins us in one Lord—the God of the Bible, revealed to humanity as one God in three persons—and one faith: the confession of our common belief. The creeds identify us as the church, the called-out people of God.

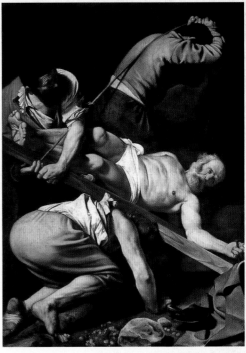

Caravaggio: Crucifixion of St. Peter, Santa Maria del Popolo, Rome

KEY WORDS

KEY WORD	MEANING	EXPLANATION
DOCTRINE	From the Latin word *doctrina*, meaning "teaching, learning."	A doctrine is a belief that a group holds as true. Christian doctrines organize and explain the beliefs the church learns from the Bible.
CREED	From the Latin word *credo*, meaning "I believe."	Creeds are simple summaries of beliefs. They are easy to memorize and flexible to teach.
CONFESSION	From the Latin word *confiteri*, meaning "acknowledge."	Like creeds, confessions are an active acknowledgement of the church's faith and teachings. Often, "confessions of faith" include not only creedal declarations but also statements that summarize the unique teachings of a particular denomination or group of believers.
HERESY	From the Greek word *hairesis*, meaning "choice."	It refers to teachings that contradict another teaching that has been accepted as the norm. Many heretics in the early church began as believers trying to understand difficult teachings about the Trinity (three persons in one perfect divine unity) and the Incarnation (the embodiment of God the Son in human flesh).
ORTHODOX	From the Greek words *ortho*, "straight," and *doxa*, "belief, opinion."	Irenaeus coined the word *orthodox* to characterize his own teachings, which most other Church Fathers agreed with, and the word *heresy* to define those of his adversaries.

Note: The text of the Apostles' Creed and the Nicene Creed are modified from *Creeds of Christendom, Vol. 1* by Philip Schaff.

CREEDS IN THE BIBLE

The Bible is a confessional document. It is God's revelation of God's plans for humanity. It also includes human responses to God's revelation: praises (psalms), confessions (for example, Naaman's and Peter's in 2 Kings 5:15 and Matthew 16:16), petitions, and creeds. To treat the Bible as a confessional document means that Christians affirm (confess) its teachings as truthful. These confessions identify Christians as God's people.

BIBLE	SUMMARY	IMPORTANCE TODAY
Deuteronomy 6:4–5 (Shema) Hear, O Israel: The Lord our God, the Lord is one.	In the midst of peoples with many gods, the Shema sets the Israelites apart. It expresses the basic belief about the uniqueness of God.	We live in a world in which many different gods claim people's allegiance. The confession of the Shema sets Christians apart by their belief in the one true God.
Romans 10:9 If you confess with your mouth, "Jesus is Lord," and believe in your heart that God raised him from the dead, you will be saved.	This passage is a brief summary of a basic Christian belief: the confession that Jesus is Lord as a public testimony of faith.	This text declares the Lordship of Jesus. Jesus is both our one God and our Master. He has proven his divinity and power through his resurrection.
1 Corinthians 15:3–4 For what I received I passed on to you as of first importance: that Christ died for our sins according to the Scriptures….	This confession about Jesus' resurrection captures the centrality of the resurrection for the believer.	As the Apostle Paul wrote, if Jesus was not raised from the dead, our faith is in vain (15:17).

WHAT DOES A CHRISTIAN NOT BELIEVE?

Creeds are constant reminders of what is central to our faith. Creeds are also boundary markers that set the rules for intelligent, creative conversation about God and his creation. Like fences, creeds protect us from "heresy"—choosing to wander away from the historical testimony about the nature and workings of God found in Holy Scripture.

The creeds of the early church—the Apostolic, Nicene, Athanasian, and Chalcedonian creeds—were responses to heretical teachings. The heresies in the early church were, for the most part, related to our understanding of God and Jesus. Studying the creeds helps us understand the heresies of the past. By understanding those heresies, it is easier to avoid repeating them today.

THE APOSTLES' CREED

The Apostles did not write the Apostles' Creed. No one knows for certain when this creed was written. References to and quotation of similar statements—known as the "Rule of Faith"—can be found in writings as early as the second century AD. The name "Apostles' Creed" means that the creed contains the Apostolic tradition. The Apostles' Creed is the most universal of all the creeds. Most Christian denominations continue to recite and teach it.

Early creedal statements were very helpful for new Christians in understanding their faith. These early creedal statements were used in baptism. New believers memorized and studied them before being baptized. It is quite possible that from these baptismal "formulas," the ancient church developed what we now call the Apostles' Creed.

APOSTLES' CREED	SUMMARY OF MEANING
I believe in… (Isa. 44:6)	The basic meaning of creed. It expresses the beliefs that unite all Christians. The words that follow preserve the teaching of the Apostles.
God, the Father Almighty (Isa. 44:6)	Not just belief in an impersonal force or in many gods, but rather, a deep trust in a personal, caring, loving God.
Maker of heaven and earth. (Gen. 1:1; John 1:1)	God is powerful. Just as God created the universe, God can heal, save, guard, comfort, and guide us. The whole universe is his.
And in Jesus Christ, his only Son, (John 9:38; 20:28)	We believe Jesus is the promised Messiah. Believing in God is also believing in Jesus.
Our Lord; (Phil. 2:9–11)	No nation, no king, no Caesar comes first: only Jesus is Lord. He has all authority and power; only he deserves praise and worship.
Who was conceived by the Holy Spirit, and born of the Virgin Mary; (Luke 1:35)	Jesus' birth and life were a miracle. By being fully human, Jesus has given us an example of life, taken upon himself the penalty of sin, and given us a new life and a new future.
Suffered under Pontius Pilate, (Luke 23:23–25)	Many have blamed Jews for Jesus' death. The Creed makes it clear that Pilate decided Jesus' death. Jesus died an innocent man. Pilate's injustice contrasts with God's justice; Pilate's arrogance contrasts with Jesus' humility.
Was crucified, died, and buried (1 Cor. 15:3–4)	These events really happened. Jesus' crucifixion and death were not merely staged; Jesus' death was real and a sad necessity for our sake.
He descended into hell; (1 Peter 3:18–19)	The meaning of this line is not clear; some think it refers to 1 Peter 3:19: "He went and preached to the spirits in prison." It is also possible to translate this line as "he descended to the dead," emphasizing the reality of Jesus' death. The phrase was not in the oldest available copy of the creed.
On the third day he rose from the dead; (1 Cor. 15:4)	Jesus' resurrection is fundamental. His resurrection points to the fulfillment of all justice and the hope for all believers. Jesus is the "firstborn from among the dead" (Col. 1:18).
He ascended into heaven and is seated at the right hand of the Father; (Luke 24:51)	Ascending to heaven and sitting at the right hand of the Father demonstrate Jesus' authority over the whole creation.
From thence he will come to judge the living and the dead. (2 Tim. 4:1; John 5:22)	Jesus' second coming will not be like a humble lamb. He will return like a triumphant king and judge. With his authority, he will judge all of creation. Christians rest assured that there is "no condemnation for those who are in Christ Jesus" (Rom. 8:1).
I believe in the Holy Spirit, (John 15:26; 16:7–14)	Jesus promised to send us a comforter, guide, equipper, and advocate. The Holy Spirit is God's presence in our midst.
The holy catholic church, (Gal. 3:26–29)	God has called his people out of sin and death; it is a group separated (holy) and from the whole world and throughout all time (catholic, or universal). The church is a people bought with the precious blood of Jesus on the cross.
The communion of saints, (Heb. 10:25)	In Jesus, all believers from all places and all times are brothers and sisters; we all share the same fellowship, the same Spirit, and the same Lord. We, who were many, are now one people in Jesus.
The forgiveness of sins, (Heb. 8:12; Luke 7:48)	Sin had broken our relationship with God, with creation, and with one another. Jesus has reconciled us with God, freeing us from our sin and death.
The resurrection of the body, and the life everlasting. (1 Thess. 4:16; John 10:28)	Unlike the Gnostics who viewed every physical reality as evil, Christians believe that they will receive new bodies and a new creation. Jesus' resurrected body was real (he could eat and could be touched); our resurrection bodies will also have a physical nature. And we will live with Jesus forever in a new creation.

HERESIES IN THE EARLY CHURCH

HERESY	SUMMARY	COMMENTS
DOCETISM First Century	This heresy denies the reality of Jesus' human nature. Jesus only *appeared* to be human. (The word *docetism* is derived from a Greek word meaning "appearance.") Docetism was imported directly from Gnosticism into Christianity.	Today many people deny Jesus' divinity and consider him just a human. But Christians who focus only on Jesus' divinity and ignore the physical reality of Jesus' resurrection fall into a mild form of docetism.
EBIONITISM First Century	Ebionites denied Jesus' divinity and proposed the full continuity of the Old Testament Law. In other words, Christians should still submit to the Old Testament Law. Ebionites rejected Paul's teachings.	This heresy is significant because it prompted the church to define itself as distinct from Judaism, though still connected to the Old Testament.
ADOPTIONISM Second Century	Adoptionism claims that Jesus was born as (only) a human. Later, he became divine when God adopted him. This common position among Gnostics is a form of *Monarchianism*.	The Bible clearly shows that Jesus is God. Adoptionism arises from a misplaced respect for God's uniqueness. The idea that God became human is very difficult to understand. Today, some scholars still teach adoptionism as a way to understand Jesus as a human being who became divine in a *metaphorical* way.
MANICHEANISM Second Century	A heresy fusing Christian, Zoroastrian and Buddhist beliefs in a religion that was very popular and widespread until around the AD 600's. Mani called himself the Paraclete who would complete the work of people like Zoroaster, Plato, Buddha, and Jesus.	Manicheanism is important because it spread Gnosticism in the West and in Christianity (Augustine was a Manichean before becoming a Christian). Mani did not believe in a personal God; good and evil were equal but opposing forces.
MARCIONISM Second Century	Marcion made a radical break between Christianity and the Old Testament. Marcion proclaimed himself a follower of Jesus but rejected Paul's writings and anything that sounded like the Old Testament.	Today, many Christians who ignore the Old Testament are functional Marcionites. Whatever our doctrinal differences may be, the church confesses that the whole Bible, both Old and New Testaments, is the Word of God.
MODALISM Second Century	Modalism teaches that God takes on different modes of being at different times. In the Old testament God manifested himself as the Father. In the New Testament, God manifested himself as the Son. In the Church age, God manifests himself as the Holy Spirit.	Modalism attempts to make sense of the difficult doctrine of the Trinity. However, it is inconsistent with biblical testimony. Some people today continue to hold to a form of modalism. Though they identify themselves as Christians, they understand God in modalist terms.
MONTANISM Second/Third Century	Montanists emphasized the spiritual gift of prophecy. Montanus, the founder, believed he received direct revelation from God through the Holy Spirit. Church fathers were divided concerning his teachings. However, Montanus's followers were more radical, claiming their prophecies were superior to the Bible. They also identified their three leaders with the Father, the Son, and the Holy Spirit. The church condemned their teachings and their legalistic way of life.	This heresy reminds us of the importance of the Holy Spirit. It also warns us of the excesses of some prophetic claims. Some Christians believe the Holy Spirit continues to give the gift of prophecy in our times. However, such prophecy must depend on biblical revelation to be valid.

HERESY	SUMMARY	COMMENTS
APOLLINARIANISM Fourth Century	The idea that Jesus had a full human body and soul, but no human reason. Instead, the divine *logos* was Jesus' rationality. Apollinaris, Bishop of Laodicea, could not understand the union of two very different natures, human and divine. He attempted to preserve the divine glory by separating the human and the divine.	This view is based on a semi-Gnostic understanding of reality: the "soul" is good; the "material world" is bad. A rejection of the world as God's good creation can lead one to this position.
ARIANISM Fourth Century	Arianism argues that Jesus does not share the same essence with God, and thus does not share in the same divine nature with eternity and authority. The Nicene, Chalcedonian, and Athanasian Creeds are primarily responses to this heresy.	This heresy prompted the church to define its understanding of Christ. The question of Jesus' nature, divine or not, is directly related to his work of salvation.
MACEDONIANISM Fourth Century	A heresy similar to Arianism, also denying that Jesus is the same *essence* of God the Father, although affirming Jesus as eternal. In addition, believers denied the divinity of the Holy Spirit.	Despite the strong condemnation from the Nicaea Council, the rise of this heresy shows the extension and powerful effect of the Arian heresy in Christianity. It extended the doubts from the nature of Jesus to the nature of the Holy Spirit.
PELAGIANISM Fourth Century	Pelagius taught that sin had not affected human nature at all. Adam's sin set a "bad example," which people choose to follow or not. Christ came to offer a "good example" of life. Salvation means choosing to follow Jesus' example.	Pelagianism represents a conscious rejection of God's grace-filled action to save humans and reconcile people with himself. A milder form, called semi-Pelagianism, suggests that we cooperate with God for our justification.
NESTORIANISM Fifth Century	Nestorius attempted to explain Jesus' incarnation by suggesting that Jesus has two separate natures: a human and a divine nature. However, the separation is so extreme that it would appear that Jesus had both two natures and two persons: a divine nature for one "person" and a human one for another "person."	Nestorianism was a reaction to the teaching that Jesus had only one nature (Apollinarianism is an example of this teaching). This teaching caused a great split in Christianity.

TRADITION When contemporary Christians speak of *tradition*, they may mean a human teaching that is not found in the Bible; in this sense, traditions cannot have the same authority as the Bible.

The early church did not use the word *tradition* in this way. The Apostle Paul wrote, "Stand firm and hold to the teachings [or *traditions*] we passed on to you, whether by word of mouth or by letter" (2 Thess. 2:15). *Tradition* meant the handing down of the Apostles' teachings. For the earliest church, the Scriptures were the Old Testament books—the New Testament did not yet have a final form.

Around one hundred years after the death of Jesus, Gnostics produced many writings similar to those in our New Testament; some of those writings claimed to have apostolic authorship—these writings are called the "Gnostic Gospels." The church realized the need to identify and make official the writings that faithfully contained the Apostles' teachings. This became urgent when the influential heretic Marcion questioned the authority of most writings that church fathers accepted.

MARCIONISM Marcion was born around AD 85 and was condemned around AD 144. Marcion rejected the Old Testament. He taught that the God of the Old Testament was angry and vengeful. He taught that the Old Testament God had nothing to do with the God of the New Testament, who is loving and forgiving. Marcion even threw out all writings that agreed, quoted, or referenced the Old Testament! Marcion rejected the Epistle of James and all the other books except Luke and the Pauline epistles. Marcion had rejected the full Apostolic teaching, so the church rejected Marcion's teachings.

GNOSTICISM

One ancient and important heresy that still thrives today is Gnosticism. The word *Gnosticism* is derived from the Greek word *gnosis*, meaning "knowledge." Gnosticism emphasized secret knowledge and secret rituals. Salvation consisted of experiencing the secret knowledge and rituals.

Ancient Gnosticism incorporated many beliefs from different religions. As Christianity spread throughout the Roman Empire, Gnostics quickly adopted some Christian practices and terminology. However, Gnosticism completely contradicts Christianity and opposes the biblical understanding of creation and God himself.

In the first two centuries AD, Justin Martyr, Irenaeus, Tertullian, Eusebius, and many others challenged specific forms of Gnosticism and wrote powerful critiques to demonstrate how Gnosticism contradicted biblical Christianity. Partly due to the Gnostic heresy, these three areas became critical for the early church to define:

- The books of the New Testament
- Salvation
- The nature and work of Jesus

TOPIC	GNOSTIC BELIEF	BIBLICAL BELIEF
Cosmogony (Origin of the universe)	A form of pantheism—a belief that identifies God with the universe. God and creation are one. The material world flows out of the divine essence. However, this god is not the God of the Bible, but a fallen god.	God created all things. The Creator and the creation are separate.
Cosmology (Nature, order, and function of the universe)	God is real, but the material world is an illusion. The material world is evil. The human soul, a remnant of the divine, is imprisoned in the body, which is part of the evil world. Humans have forgotten about their divine inner being.	The material world is as real as God. The world is not evil—God called it *good* and *blessed* it.
Origin of Evil	One dominant form of Gnosticism was based on the myth of Sophia, who lusted after the "First Father." Matter is the fruit of her sin. The physical world is evil.	Human sin originates with pride and disobedience. Creation is not evil, although it has been corrupted as a result of human sin.
Salvation	Salvation comes through experiential knowledge—a secret knowledge that teaches one how to escape the evil of a physical world. Its ultimate goal is a return to the original condition of being one with the First Father. In Christian-influenced Gnosticism, Jesus is the one teaching this secret knowledge. The knowledge of people's divine inner being is the main secret knowledge.	God is rescuing humanity through the work of Jesus, not through any special, hidden knowledge.
Jesus	Jesus is not really a human at all; he just appeared to be one. He was an *aeon*, an intermediary between the real world (the world of the spirit) and this evil reality, the material world.	He is the second person of the Trinity. He was incarnated as a real, full human, who atoned for the sins of humanity on the cross.

Gnosticism became such an influential belief system that it has continued to appear over the centuries in people's ideas about God and the world. Much of today's popular spirituality is Gnostic in its orientation.

THE NICENE CREED

The greatest doctrinal challenge to the church arose internally. Arius, a priest in Alexandria, suggested that if God begat Jesus, then Jesus had an origin. As such, Jesus did not share in the same divine essence with the Father. Therefore, Jesus was a lesser god.

In AD 325, Constantine called the leaders of the church to participate in a council—that is, an assembly of bishops. They met in the city of Nicaea, in present-day Turkey. The Council of Nicaea, made up of about 300 participants, overwhelmingly voted against the Arian teachings—ancient documents suggest that only three bishops refused to sign their agreement. The council expressed its views about God, Jesus, and the church in the Nicene Creed.

A CHRISTIAN EMPIRE

In AD 313, Constantine became the sole ruler of the Roman Empire. His Edict of Milan, put into effect in 313, granted full tolerance to all religions of the Empire. Constantine fought hard to gain stability for the Empire. Scholars have debated much whether Constantine really converted to Christianity—and if so, at what age he did. Whatever the case, Constantine became the protector and, in time, promoter of Christianity throughout the Empire.

During Constantine's reign, the Arian controversy threatened to divide Christianity and bring chaos to the Empire. Constantine understood that a divided Christianity would also divide the Empire. To keep his Empire together, he needed to keep Christianity together. From a political standpoint, the Nicaea Council solved and prevented a schism in Christianity and the Roman Empire.

ATHANASIUS AND THE TRINITY

Athanasius was one of the most active opponents of Arius' teachings. His persistence and clear mind helped the church to clarify its positions and write it in a creed, the Nicene Creed.

Athanasius' teachings are summarized in the Athanasian Creed. While it is likely that Athanasius did not write it, the creed contains his teachings and main ideas. The Athanasian Creed begins by affirming, "This is what the catholic [or universal] faith teaches: we worship one God in the Trinity and the Trinity in unity. We distinguish among the persons, but we do not divide the substance [or essence]." After unpacking these ideas, the creed concludes, "So that in all things, as aforesaid, the Unity in Trinity and the Trinity in Unity is to be worshipped."

NICENE CREED	MEANING	COMMENTS
We believe in one God, the Father Almighty, Maker *of heaven and earth, and* **of all things visible and invisible.**	As in the Apostles' Creed, the foundation of the Christian faith is the uniqueness of God. He alone is God. The Father is a distinct person, or individual reality, within the Godhead. In addition, God created *all* things. He is not created, but the Creator.	In Gnosticism, the God of the Bible is just the *demiurge*, an evil god who brought about the material world. This god is himself created.
And in one Lord Jesus Christ, *the only-begotten* **Son of God, begotten of the Father** *before all worlds,* **Light of Light, very God of very God, begotten, not made, being of one substance with the Father; by whom all things were made;**	The creed affirms Jesus' • Lordship: The same title applied to God the Father in the Old Testament. • Equality: Jesus is as much God as the Father. They share the same divine *essence*. Thus, Jesus is eternal. • Distinctness: Although they share the same essence, Jesus is a *person* distinct from the Father.	In the New Testament, Jesus' Lordship is directly connected to his divinity. He is not Lord simply because he earned it; rather, he is Lord because he is God. Arius tried to understand the Incarnation, but his approach ignores the broad context of the Scriptures.
Who for us, and for our salvation, came down *from heaven,* **and was incarnate** *by the Holy Ghost of the Virgin Mary,* **and was made man;** *he was crucified for us under Pontius Pilate,* **and suffered,** *and was buried,* **and the third day he rose again,** *according to the Scriptures,* **and ascended into heaven,** *and sits on the right hand of the Father;* **from thence he shall come** *again, with glory,* **to judge the living and the dead;** *whose kingdom shall have no end.*	The creed emphasizes both Jesus' divinity and humanity. • The image of coming down from heaven shows his divinity. • His miraculous virgin birth shows his humanity. • His suffering and death on the cross, again, show his full humanity. • His resurrection and ascension show his perfect work of salvation on behalf of humanity. • His final judgment shows his authority over the whole creation.	Heresies about Jesus denied either his full divinity or his full humanity. • Denying Jesus' divinity removes his ability to save humanity from sin and death. Jesus is reduced to being a *model* of perfection. • Denying Jesus' humanity removes his ability to intercede and represent humanity in his death.
And in the Holy Spirit, *the Lord and Giver of life, who proceeds from the Father, who with the Father and the Son together is worshiped and glorified, who spoke by the prophets.*	The creed confirms the Bible's doctrine of the Trinity: The Holy Spirit is fully divine, of the same *essence* as the Father and the Son, and is a distinct person within the Godhead. In the sixth century, Western churches added "who proceeds from the Father *and the Son*." It is this last addition, known as the *filioque* (Latin for "and the Son") that has caused division and conflict between the Eastern Orthodox and Western churches.	The natural consequence of denying Jesus' divinity is that the Holy Spirit is not divine either. After the creed of AD 325, the heresy about the Holy Spirit arose as a follow-up to Arianism.
In one holy catholic and apostolic church; we acknowledge one baptism for the remission of sins; we look for the resurrection of the dead, and the life of the world to come. Amen. [NOTE: The words in italics were added after the First Council of Nicaea in AD 325. The Council of Constantinople made these additions in AD 381.]	One of the main purposes of the creed was to promote the unity of all believers in one universal church within the Apostolic tradition. Baptism represents this unity, as does the forgiveness of sins, the resurrection, and the world to come. These are all promises and hopes that link all Christians everywhere and at every time.	The Arian controversy threatened to split the young and growing church. The creed allows the possibility of unity of belief and practice. The word *catholic* means "universal," in the sense of the whole world. It refers, then, to the worldwide fellowship of all believers.

THE CHALCEDONIAN CREED

Understanding the incarnation of Jesus—the embodiment of God the Son in human flesh—was one of the greatest challenges for the early church. In AD 451 the Council of Chalcedon (located in today's Turkey) provided a clear statement of the Apostolic teachings concerning Jesus. The Chalcedonian Creed made it clear that Jesus is fully God and fully human, two natures existing in perfect harmony in one person.

HERESIES ABOUT CHRIST CORRECTED IN THE CHALCEDONIAN CREED

SUBJECT	HERETICAL POSITION	APOSTOLIC TEACHING
Nature of Christ	Arianism: Jesus was the first created being, similar to God, but not fully divine like the Father. Docetism: Jesus was only a divine being. He merely *appeared* human.	Christ is *fully* God and *fully* human.
Relationship of Christ's Two Natures	Nestorianism: No connection between Jesus' two natures. Practically, Jesus had two natures and was two persons. Eutychianism: The divine and human natures are fused into one nature.	Two natures, divine and human, and one person.

WHY DO THE CREEDS MATTER?

1. Creeds help Christians to distinguish between essential and nonessential beliefs. Not everyone who disagrees with you is a heretic! There are some beliefs on which Christians cannot compromise. On others, we can agree to disagree. The creeds—which focus on the essential beliefs that cannot be compromised—help us to distinguish between essential and nonessential beliefs.

2. Creeds help Christians to focus their faith and worship on the issues that matter most. The issues that the creeds emphasize—such as the Trinity, the character of God, the nature of Jesus, and the resurrection, for example—are the ones that the earliest Christians understood to matter most. These same beliefs can provide a unifying focus for contemporary Christians' teaching and worship.

3. Creeds help Christians to articulate clearly how their beliefs differ from other teachings. The apostle Peter commanded his readers always "to be ready to provide to anyone who asks a defense for the hope that is in you" (1 Peter 3:15-16). When it comes to giving a defense for our faith, the creeds are crucial! When someone asks what Christians believe about the resurrection of Jesus, the Apostles' and Nicene Creeds provide concise summaries of this core doctrine. When a child in Sunday school asks why Jesus came to earth, a teacher who remembers the Nicene Creed can tell the child immediately, "It was for us and for our salvation." If someone asks whether the virgin conception of Jesus really matters, the Christian who knows the creeds can immediately recall that, even for the earliest believers in Jesus, this was an essential doctrine.

HERESIES TODAY

Many heresies—wrong beliefs—relate to two central biblical teachings: the Trinity and the Incarnation. Misunderstanding who God is will lead to misunderstanding what God has done and will do. Knowing the basic teachings of the church will help us identify and respond to heresies still existing today.

ANCIENT HERESY	WHAT IT LOOKS LIKE TODAY	CORRECT APOSTOLIC TEACHING	COMMENTS
GNOSTICISM	• Confusing God with his creation. Taking things and people as part of the divine. • Rejecting the physical world as evil. • Belief that salvation is inside every person. • Speaking about Jesus as a guru or only as a great teacher. • "Pop spirituality" based on Gnostic ideas. *The Secret, The Power of Now*, and many self-help teachings fall into this category.	• God is the Creator of all things. • The world is good, though corrupted through human sin. • Salvation is possible only through Jesus.	• Christians need to be careful not to reject this material world. Radical separation of the body and soul is not a biblical teaching. God loves the world he made. He blessed it. We should do likewise.
MARCIONISM	• Rejecting the Old Testament. • Rejecting anything that sounds too Jewish from the New Testament. • Completely divorcing the Old Testament from the New Testament.	• The Old and New Testaments together are the Word of God. • Some ideas and concepts in the Old Testament continued in the New. Others Jesus fulfilled and are no longer binding in the New Testament. • God reveals himself in both Testaments. But Jesus is the fullness of God's revelation to humanity.	• Sometimes Christians make too strong a distinction between the Law and the Gospel. • The New Testament revelation is more complete than the Old Testament revelation because of Jesus (Heb. 1:1–3). • The revelation of the New Testament depends on God's works and words in the Old Testament.
MONARCHIANISM	• Denying the Trinity. • Claiming one god with three functions: First appearing as Father, then as Son, and now as Holy Spirit. • Both forms are active: Adoptionism and Modalism.	• There is one God in three distinct Persons: God the Father, the Son, and the Holy Spirit. • All three persons participate in the divine nature but have distinct personalities. • All three are involved in God's work of Creation, redemption, and restoration.	• Some groups believe that only Jesus (of the three members of the Trinity) is God. This is a form of modalism. • Other groups, like the Jehovah's Witnesses, confess a form of adoptionism. They deny that Jesus is fully God. Rather, they may believe Jesus is an angel, a special divine being, but not God.
ARIANISM APOLLINARIANISM DOCETISM MACEDONIANISM NESTORIANISM	• Claims that Jesus was human only and became divine. • Claims that Jesus was only divine and merely appeared human. • Claims that Jesus was two persons with two natures in one being.	• Jesus is the second Person of the Trinity. • He is fully God and fully human. • He is one person with two natures, divine and human. The natures are joined, but not mixed.	• Jehovah's Witnesses and Mormons show clear examples of such errors. • It is possible to emphasize Jesus' divine character to the point of forgetting that he is fully human as well. Jesus suffered, was hungry, and was tempted like any other human.
MONTANISM	• Offering prophecy beyond what the Bible reveals. • Claiming greater authority than the Bible. • Making the Holy Spirit more important than Jesus. • Using prophetic gifts to abuse other Christians' trust and faith. • Misleading people through unverifiable prophecies.	• God has revealed his will in the Scriptures and in Jesus. • The Holy Spirit only testifies about Jesus. • Although there are gifts of prophecy, prophecies are still subject to the authority of the Bible. • Prophecies from God are for building up the church, not for personal gain.	• Most founders of current cults—like Jehovah's Witnesses, Mormonism, and Christian Science—have claimed to receive new revelations from God. • These revelations contradict the Bible. • The prophetic claims of groups like Heaven's Gate, Peoples Temple, and many others have had tragic consequences.

INDEX

(i-ii = Jerusalem Time Line foldout)

Bestselling Bible Reference Books

Rose Book of Bible Charts, Maps & Time Lines, Volume 1

Dozens of popular Rose Publishing Bible charts, maps, and time lines in one spiral-bound book. Topics include • Christianity, Cults & Religions • Jesus' Genealogy • Islam and Christianity • Denominations Comparison • Bible Time Line • Bible Maps • Christian History Time Line • Bible Bookcase • Trinity • How We Got the Bible • Bible Overview • Temple and High Priest • Tabernacle • Ark of the Covenant. Hardcover. 192 pages. ISBN: 9781596360228

Rose Book of Bible Charts, Volume 2

Topics include • Bible Translations comparison chart • Why Trust the Bible • Heroes of the Old Testament • Women of the Bible • Life of Paul • Christ in the Old Testament • Christ in the Passover • Names of Jesus • Beatitudes • Lord's Prayer • Where to Find Favorite Bible Verses • Christianity and Eastern Religions • Worldviews Comparison • 10 Q & A on Mormonism/Jehovah's Witnesses/Magic/ Atheism and many others! Hardcover. 240 pages. ISBN: 9781596362758

Rose Book of Bible Charts, Volume 3

Topics include • Who I Am in Christ (Assurance of Salvation) • What the Bible Says about Forgiveness • What the Bible Says about Money • What the Bible Says about Prayer • Spiritual Disciplines • Heaven • Attributes of God • How to Explain the Gospel • Parables of Jesus • Bible Character Studies and many more! Hardcover. 240 pages. ISBN: 9781596368699

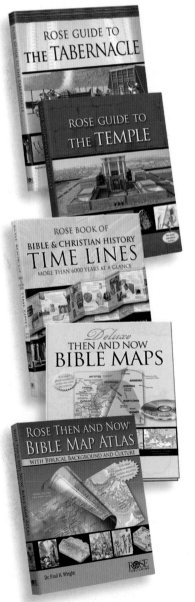

Rose Guide to the Tabernacle

Full color with clear overlays and reproducible pages. The Tabernacle was the place where the Israelites worshiped God after the Exodus. Learn how the sacrifices, utensils, and even the structure of the tabernacle were designed to show us something about God. See the parallels between the Old Testament sacrifices and priests' duties, and Jesus' service as the perfect sacrifice and perfect high priest. See how • The Tabernacle was built • The sacrifices pointed Jesus Christ • The design of the tent revealed God's holiness and humanity's need for God • The Ark of the Covenant was at the center of worship. Hardcover. 128 pages. ISBN: 9781596362765

Rose Guide to the Temple

Simply the best book on the Temple in Jerusalem. It is the only full-color book from a Christian viewpoint that has clear plastic overlays showing the interior and exterior of Solomon's Temple, Herod's Temple, and the Tabernacle. Contains more than 100 color diagrams, photos, illustrations, maps, and time lines of more than 100 key events from the time of King David to modern day. It also includes two full-color posters: the Temple of Jesus' time and the stunning National Geographic poster on the Temple Mount through time. You will understand how the Temple looked, its history, and its biblical importance. Hardcover. 144 pages. ISBN: 9781596364684

Rose Book of Bible & Christian History Time Lines

Six thousand years and 20 feet of time lines in one hard-bound cover! These gorgeous time lines printed on heavy chart paper, can also be slipped out of their binding and posted in a hallway or large room for full effect. The Bible Time Line compares Scriptural events with world history and Middle East history. Shows hundreds of facts; includes dates of kings, prophets, battles, and key events. The Christian History Time Line begins with the life of Jesus and continues to the present day. Includes key people and events that all Christians should know. Hardcover. ISBN: 9781596360846

Deluxe Then and Now® Bible Maps Book with CD-ROM!

See where Bible places are today with Then and Now® Bible maps with clear plastic overlays of modern cities and countries. This deluxe edition comes with a CD-ROM that gives you a JPG of each map to use in your own Bible material as well as PDFs of each map and overlay to create your own handouts or overhead transparencies. PowerPoint® fans can create their own presentations with these digitized maps. Hardcover. ISBN: 9781596361638

Rose Then and Now® Bible Map Atlas with Biblical Background and Culture

Your 30 favorite Bible characters come alive with this new Bible atlas. Find out how the geography of Bible Lands affected the culture and decisions of people such as David, Abraham, Moses, Esther, Deborah, Jonah, Jesus, and the disciples. Hardcover. 272 pages. ISBN: 9781596365346